What's
God
Have
To Do
With It?

Contributors

Tim Beals
Dave Branon
John Carvalho
Kurt De Haan
Mart De Haan
Dave Egner
Tom Felten
Darrow Parker

Cartoonist

Rob Wheeler

Discovery House
PUBLISHERS
BOX 3566 · GRAND RAPIDS, MI 49501

*PUBLISHING BOOKS THAT FEED
THE SOUL WITH THE WORD OF GOD.*

What's God Have To Do With It?

365 DAILY DEVOTIONS FOR STUDENTS FROM *CAMPUS JOURNAL*

What's God Have To Do With It:
365 Daily Devotions for Students from
Campus Journal

Copyright © 1993 Discovery House
Publishers

Discovery House Publishers is affiliated
with Radio Bible Class, Grand Rapids,
Michigan

Discovery House books are distributed to
the trade by Thomas Nelson Publishers,
Nashville, Tennesse 37214

Developed and edited by Blue Water Ink,
Grand Rapids, Michigan

Cartoons by Rob Wheeler

Scripture quotations are from the New
International Version. Copyright © 1973,
1978, 1984 International Bible Society.
Used by permission of Zondervan Bible
Publishers.

ISBN 0-929239-76-8

Printed in the United States of America

93 94 95 96 / CHG / 10 9 8 7 6 5 4 3 2 1

What's God Have To Do With It when . . .

➡ Your roommate files an official complaint with the dorm council because your lifestyle is a threat to public health?

➡ Your girlfriend flirts with your roommate to get even with you for not taking her out over the weekend?

➡ Your boyfriend threatens to break up with you if you won't . . . ?

➡ Your boss demands that you work more hours or lose your job?

➡ Your professors load you down with guilt as well as homework by telling you what marvelous things you could accomplish if your life just had more focus?

➡ Your parents threaten to cut off your finances if you don't cut down your social life and bring up your grades?

With so many people to please, who has time to please God? Surely He understands the pressure you're under and won't make any additional demands until you get your life under control.

But that's just it. You'll never get your life under control until you let God control it. Sounds contradictory, but it's not. Having successful relationships with other people without having a healthy relationship with God just won't happen.

What will happen, however, is that when you give more time to God you'll have more time for others (and even for yourself). Jesus summed it up like this: "Seek first his kingdom and his righteousness, and all these things will be given to you as well" (Matthew 6:30).

"But how can I seek God's kingdom?" you ask. "And how can I ever know God's will for my life?"

You're not alone. Questions about God's will are the most common ones asked by Christians.

If you're one of the many who has been going around in circles trying to figure out what God wants you to do with your life, you can give up your dizzying routine. The mystery has been solved. You can now know exactly what God's will is every moment of every day.

Jesus Himself revealed it. And He made it so obvious that it's kind of surprising people spend so much time looking for it. It's found in Mark 12:30: "Love the Lord your God with all your **heart** and with all your **soul** and with all your **mind** and with all your **strength**."

It's as simple, and as difficult, as that.

What's God Have To Do With It will take you on a one-year devotional excursion in search of God's kingdom. Using Scripture, true stories, and pertinent thoughts, it explores the four areas of our lives Jesus emphasized in what He called the greatest commandment.

Contributors to *Campus Journal,* the popular daily devotional for students published by Radio Bible Class, use problems and experiences common to young adults to illustrate what it means to follow this awesome command. With wit and candor, and without condescension, the devotions not only help clarify God's will, they also generate enthusiasm for following it.

Young adults who get into the habit of going to God with their questions won't be falling for the world's answers. And those whose love for God determines every decision don't have to worry about making the wrong ones. Stop going in circles; start going to God.

What's God Have To Do With It?

Everything. That's all.

Fighting like dogs

READ
Matthew 18:15–20

MEDITATE
Proverbs 3:3
Let love and faithfulness never leave you.

REFLECT
➡ What should I do about the instructor or boss who has offended me? Should I go to him or her and express my feelings?

➡ What happens when I talk about a friend behind his or her back? What happens when I address that person one-to-one? Which is more Christlike?

CONSIDER
When you throw mud, you always lose ground.

Talk about stupid pet tricks! A woman in San Diego thought she had found the all-time champion. Every night between 2 and 3 A.M. her phone would ring. When she picked up the receiver, all she heard was barking. She asked the phone company to find out who was yipping in her ear, but they couldn't trace the call. Finally, she figured out that her mysterious midnight caller was a neighbor. He had decided that every time he was awakened by her barking dog, he would do a little barking at her. He was not content to let this sleeping dogowner lie.

So what do you think about his idea? Would you sometimes like to take care of a problem that way? After all, it got the point across.

But is that the way God would have us solve our people problems? Take a look at Matthew 18. In this passage, Jesus told us to solve our interpersonal problems face to face, not through some irritating trick.

Here's the principle in simple terms: When people bug you, instead of bugging them back, talk to them about it.

Sound revolutionary?

Instead of talking critically to our friends about the offender, we're supposed to talk lovingly to the offender about the offense. Instead of burying our anger and watching a grudge sprout, we need to bury the hatchet and watch godliness sprout after we've confronted a person in gentleness of spirit.

The next time someone upsets you so much that you think something must be done, don't do what the barking neighbor did and let your reputation go to the dogs. Respond instead with "love and faithfulness"— trusting God to take care of the details. —M.D.

Through preaching, teaching, and the Bible, God is telling me . . . _____

_____

Through nature and the lives of other believers, God is showing me . . . _____

_____

I will respond by . . . _____

_____

Mud puddle drowning

READ
2 Chronicles
26:16–21

MEDITATE
Psalm 119:165
Great peace have they
who love your law,
and nothing can make
them stumble.

REFLECT
➡ What little things
bother me?
➡ How can I keep
these pet peeves
from turning into
major problems?
➡ How does God
want me to deal
with them?

CONSIDER
*People are
measured by
what it takes to
stop them.*

If you're going to drown, don't do it in a mud puddle." Applied to Christians, this old saying means don't let something unimportant destroy your faith. It's one thing to struggle to stay afloat in the deep water of some major issue, such as serious illness or having your tuition money stolen. But it's quite another to get in a flap over something minor.

Here's how it happens. A Christian files a lawsuit against a neighbor over a bush along their property line. As a result, the Christian gets a bad reputation. Or a Bible study group dissolves because two of the members can't get along.

King Uzziah is a Bible person who "drowned in a mud puddle." For fifty years he was one of Judah's best kings. But then he stumbled into a muddy quagmire. Was it a lost battle that caused him to doubt God? The untimely death of a child?

Neither one.

Uzziah's problem was simple pride. He couldn't understand why he should be denied the privilege of performing worship tasks God had assigned to the high priest. So he went busting into the temple sanctuary to burn incense, totally disregarding God's command. The result: instant leprosy. The decay of Uzziah's skin symbolized the decay that had occurred in his soul.

You can probably list ways you could become mired in minor issues: a friend who ignored you, a teacher who was unfair, or kids who just bug you. You have a choice. You can either deal with it properly, or you can let the mud puddle become a drowning pool.

Ask for God's help. Don't let the tombstone of your Christian witness be engraved with the epitaph: "Drowned in a mud puddle."

—J.C.

Through preaching, teaching, and the Bible, God is telling me . . . _____

Through nature and the lives of other believers, God is showing me . . . _____

I will respond by . . . _____

Ya gotta have

Caught in the loop

READ
Proverbs 3:1–7

MEDITATE
Proverbs 3:7
Do not be wise in your own eyes.

REFLECT
➡ Am I more likely to be independent from God or dependent on God?
➡ What warning signs have I been ignoring from the Bible or from my family and friends?
➡ Is God my primary or secondary concern when it comes to making important decisions?

CONSIDER
Using your Bible as a roadmap keeps you off the detours of sin.

How do you spell nightmare? I spell it L-O-O-P. Let me explain. You've heard the old saying, "If at first you don't succeed, try following directions." Well, with the help of the city of Chicago, I slowly and painfully learned this lesson.

For part of our family vacation, we decided to go to Great America. Unfortunately, I failed to get directions before we left. Fortunately, there were signs along the way. Unfortunately, I didn't follow them As a result, we ended up right in the middle of Chicago's *Loop*—in five o'clock traffic!

If you are familiar with Chicago, you know that the one thing to avoid, besides walking alone while counting your money at two in the morning, is the *Loop* at rush hour. I, however, could not count myself among the enlightened. As a result, my "quick trip" through

Chicago turned out to be two hours of bumper-to-bumper stress in the Twilight Zone. And to think that I could have avoided it if I had first gotten directions and then followed them.

Proverbs 3 tells us to trust in the Lord and receive direction from Him rather than to depend on ourselves. Failing to follow God's instructions for living can result in more than just a messed-up vacation. It can produce a ruined life, a damaged reputation, broken relationships, and blown opportunities.

How much better to follow the instructions God has clearly given in His Word! Trusting God's wisdom and not our own will leave us right in the middle of His will and help us avoid life's *Loop* experiences. —D.P.

Through preaching, teaching, and the Bible, God is telling me . . . _____

Through nature and the lives of other believers, God is showing me . . . _____

I will respond by . . . _____

It's not my fault!

READ
Luke 18:9–14

MEDITATE
Luke 18:13
"God, have mercy on me, a sinner."

REFLECT

➡ Whom do I blame for my problems? My parents? Teachers? Friends? Society? Myself?

➡ Why is repentance the first step toward forgiveness?

➡ How should I change my attitude?

CONSIDER
Sin is easy to point out— except when it's our own!

People just don't want to take responsibility for their own actions anymore.

For example, our country is struggling through some rough problems, but no one seems willing to step forward and say, "Hey, we're all at fault. Let's work on fixing things together!"

The flood of lawsuits also shows how people avoid accepting responsibility. A woman drinks excessively during her pregnancy and her baby is born with defects. So she sues the liquor company. A man is dying from lung cancer from years of smoking, so he sues the cigarette company.

To God, accepting responsibility is a strength, not a weakness. Admitting our sinfulness to Him is the first step toward being forgiven. When we blame others and refuse to acknowledge our shortcomings, we only find self-righteousness.

While Frederick, King of Prussia, toured a prison, inmate after inmate tried to win him over with their woeful tales of innocence, misunderstood motives, and exploitation. Finally, however, one prisoner admitted, "Sir, I'm guilty, and I deserve my punishment."

To everyone's surprise, Frederick turned to the warden and said, "Release this man before he corrupts all these innocent people!"

Take an honest look at yourself. Don't try to "snow" God with proud declarations of how good you are compared to others. Acknowledge your sins.

"If we confess our sins, he is faithful and just and will forgive us our sins and purify us from all unrighteousness" (1 John 1:9).

Being justified by God— rather than trying to justify ourselves—is the way to find freedom from sin and guilt.

—J.C.

Through preaching, teaching, and the Bible, God is telling me . . . _____

Through nature and the lives of other believers, God is showing me . . . _____

I will respond by . . . _____

Angry at God?

"Life stinks!" If your friends aren't actually saying this, many of them are feeling it. Maybe you even feel that way. Consider the growing suicide rate, especially among young people. But it's not just the suicidal who are unhappy with life. Almost everyone feels the darkness of despair at one time or another.

A brief look at what life sends our way reveals why people get down.

• The person you love decides to end the relationship.

• A lack of money threatens to end your dreams of a college education.

• A life-threatening illness strikes someone close to you.

These are downers that can defeat us. When we become bitter about life because of things like this, we often direct our anger toward God.

In a letter I read recently, a young person blamed God for everything that was wrong in his life. When I read it, my first thought was "What has happened to cause him to be so angry? How did he get to the point of giving up on God?"

I may never know, but I do know that the One he has cast aside is the only One who can provide lasting solutions to his problems.

James 5:17 tells us that Elijah was a man just like us. In 1 Kings 19, Elijah was so worn out by his struggles that he wanted to die. But the significant difference between Elijah and the person I spoke of earlier is that Elijah turned to God, while this young person turned from God.

Are you downcast? Psalm 43 says to look up. Put your hope in God, and put your trust in His love for you. He alone can heal your broken heart. —D.P.

Through preaching, teaching, and the Bible, God is telling me . . .
_____

_____

Through nature and the lives of other believers, God is showing me . . .
_____

_____

I will respond by . . .
_____

_____

Riding the ox

If I just had a little more money. Or a new car to replace that old embarrassment sitting out in the parking lot. Or a few more clothes, a nicer place to live, a better complexion, more brains, or Mr. or Ms. Right at my side.

Ever noticed that there's always "just one more thing" necessary to make life complete?

According to a story credited to Thomas Aquinas, a man heard about a very special ox, and he wanted it badly. (T.A. lived in Italy in the thirteenth century; that's why the man in his story wanted an ox and not a Corvette.) Anyway, the man traveled all over the world, spending all his money and his whole life, looking for this beast. Just before he died, he made a depressing discovery. He had been riding that ox all along.

The writer of Ecclesiastes would have been able to identify. He too spent much of his life looking for that missing "something." He tried partying, studying, and working. But he never found what he was looking for. Toward the end of his life, he finally realized that "he had been riding the ox" all his life.

When we read Ecclesiastes 5 in the context of the entire book, we realize that we can find fulfillment in life only in knowing and serving God. When we do that, God makes us content with what we have and where we are.

Maybe it's time now, before you spend your whole life "chasing the ox you are riding," to thank God for what He has given you. Then promise Him that you'll use what He has given you to help you know Him more and serve Him better.

—K.D.

Through preaching, teaching, and the Bible, God is telling me . . . _____
_____
_____

Through nature and the lives of other believers, God is showing me . . . _____
_____
_____

I will respond by . . . _____
_____
_____

Take heart!

MEDITATE
John 16:33
"But take heart! I have overcome the world."

REFLECT
➡ What is it about my life as a Christian that discourages me most?

➡ How might Bible study, fellowship with believers, church attendance, and prayer help me overcome feelings of defeat?

➡ When I realize I'm down, what can I do about it?

CONSIDER
Christ overcame the world so it wouldn't overcome us.

Lisa was discouraged. She was trying to live for the Lord, but everything she did seemed to end in failure.

She tried to keep a positive relationship with her mom, but they kept getting into arguments. She had been witnessing to her friend Beth, but another friend kept discrediting her and mocking Christians. A couple of times at her job she had disappointed the Lord by saying things she knew He didn't like. Her father had suffered a mild heart attack, and she was worried that God was using it to punish her. And more and more she wanted to be like her nonChristian friends in the kind of clothes she wore, the music she listened to, and the things she did.

So, Lisa was ready to quit. The world was just too strong to fight.

Ever feel like that? So have I. That's why John 16:33 is so important. Jesus knew that His disciples were going to feel discouraged. In fact, within a very few hours, He would leave the upper room for Gethsemane, where He would be arrested. Then He would be given a mock trial, pronounced guilty by the mob, and publicly executed. His followers would be scattered and defeated. It would look as though the enemy had won.

So Jesus said to them, "Take heart! I have overcome the world." And He had! By living without sin. His death—voluntary, undeserved, and sacrificial— would be a profound and stunning victory over Satan. He would rise from the dead, providing undeniable evidence that He had won.

Discouraged? Struggling to fight off the world? Ready to give up? Don't! Take heart. The world that has you so discouraged is the same one Jesus has overcome! —D.E.

Through preaching, teaching, and the Bible, God is telling me . . . _____

_____

_____

Through nature and the lives of other believers, God is showing me . . . _____

_____

_____

I will respond by . . . _____

_____

_____

Another ring?

READ
Psalm 92

MEDITATE
Psalm 92:12
The righteous will . . .
grow like a cedar of
Lebanon.

REFLECT
➡ Looking back at last
year, how did I do
spiritually? Did I
add a "growth
ring" or was it a lost
year?
➡ What are some
things 2 Peter 3:18
tells me I can do to
make certain I will
grow in my rela-
tionship with Christ
in the coming year?

CONSIDER
*Give your future
to God and you
won't regret
your past.*

Suppose you're playing a word association game and someone says "Lebanon." Cedar trees probably would not be the first word to rush into your mind. Instead, you'd proba- bly think of bombed-out buildings.

Yet, the writer of Psalm 92 says that Lebanon is noted for her stately cedar trees. Author W. Philip Keller did some research on those trees. In his book *As a Tree Grows,* he said, "The cedars of Lebanon . . . are unique trees of breathtaking beauty, massive size, rich fragrance, and high-quality timber. The cedars of Lebanon are used as a symbol of all that is to be desired in Christian char- acter. . . . A tiny cedar seedling, by growing steadily and surely, matures into a mighty monarch of the mountain forest.

"But the tragedy is that some never get much beyond being tiny, stunted seedlings. They are alive; they are true trees; but . . . there is no growth."

For some reason, a year goes by and the tree fails to add a growth ring. If this continues, the tree never becomes the towering, mag- nificent cedar it could have been.

The same thing can hap- pen to us as Christians. We can let a whole year go by without growing spiritually. We might make progress in lots of areas—schoolwork, relationships, job training, athletics, knowledge—but fail to grow in our Christian life.

If you're afraid this might happen to you, spend time with other Christians (more mature ones especially), read the Bible daily, pray often, and obey Christ.

Ask God to help you to be like a flourishing tree of Lebanon rather than one of its bombed-out buildings.
—D.E.

Through preaching, teaching, and the Bible, God is telling me . . . _____
_____

Through nature and the lives of other believers, God is showing me . . . _____
_____

I will respond by . . . _____
_____

Playing second fiddle

READ
Mark 10:35–45

MEDITATE
Mark 10:44
"Whoever wants to be first must be slave of all."

REFLECT
➡ What does Christ's example show us about the kind of servants we're to be (Philippians 2:5–9)?
➡ What are three tasks I often do that require me to serve others?
➡ What does the Bible mean when it challenges us to be "first" by serving others?

CONSIDER
The greatest ability is availability.

If you ever played in the school band, you probably argued with other band members about which instrument is the most difficult to play. When a reporter asked the conductor of a great symphony orchestra that question, he replied, "Second fiddle. I can get plenty of first violinists," he explained, "but to find someone who can play second fiddle with enthusiasm—that's a problem. And if we have no second fiddle we have no harmony."

Let's face it. It's easy to feel unimportant because our place in life seems insignificant. We're always standing in the shadow of the one playing the lead in the school play or starting on the football team. In the great drama of life, we never get to center stage. As part of the supporting cast, we seem incidental to the main plot. Making sub sandwiches in a fast-food restaurant or selling towels at the mall seems far removed from where the real action is. But doing God's will where He alone sees us is just as important as doing it where thousands of people see us.

This doesn't mean that God is pleased when we're lazy or complacent. He wants us to be ambitious and industrious—to set high goals for ourselves and strive to reach them. Yet He calls many of us, in fact most of us, to fill positions in life away from the spotlight. He asks us to assume supportive roles. But He does more. He offers us the potential for true greatness—and that lies in doing each task as a humble service to our relatives, friends, or employers.

Here's one of the secrets of Christian living: Being great does not depend on what we have, but on what we do with what God has given us. —T.B.

Through preaching, teaching, and the Bible, God is telling me . . . _____

_____

_____

Through nature and the lives of other believers, God is showing me . . . _____

_____

_____

I will respond by . . . _____

_____

_____

Unplugging the alarm

When local fire investigators sifted through the remains of the burned-out apartment, they made a sad discovery. The two young women who died when flames swept through their home had deactivated their smoke detector. If it had been hooked up they probably would still be alive.

There had been a party at their place the night before the fire, and the women had disconnected the smoke detector so it wouldn't go off during the get-together. That simple act, which seemed so inconsequential at the time, cost the young women their lives.

Acts 5 tells the story of two other people who died because they deactivated an "early warning system." Ananias and Sapphira sensed that they were doing the wrong thing when they lied about the money they had given to the church. But like partygoers who don't want their fun interrupted by the beeping of a smoke alarm, they apparently "turned off" the Spirit's warning by ignoring it. Or maybe they had rationalized, "The money we bring will benefit others, so who cares if we lie about it?" They had probably rationalized many times before and nothing happened. Why stop now? But the patience of God came to an end, and they both lost their lives.

The Holy Spirit was not given to us to annoy us like a highly sensitive smoke detector at a party. When God activates our conscience by bringing to mind a principle of God's Word, it's serious. It is His love and wisdom in action.

It pays to listen to His warnings. He's there for our protection, and He can keep us from getting burned by sin. —M.D.

Through preaching, teaching, and the Bible, God is telling me . . . _____

Through nature and the lives of other believers, God is showing me . . . _____

I will respond by . . . _____

Give till it helps

READ
Proverbs 11:24–28

MEDITATE
Proverbs 11:25

A generous man will prosper

REFLECT

➡ On a scale of 1 to 10, with 10 being The World's Most Generous Person, what rating would I give myself? What rating would my best friends give me?

➡ Who do I know that personifies the second half of Proverbs 11:25? Why is that person so nice to be around?

CONSIDER
Forget what you give. Remember what you get.

Years ago, a couple of enterprising Stanford University students needed money. Instead of writing a "No mon, no fun, your son" letter (which, by the way, usually gets a response like "Too bad, so sad, your dad"), they got busy and planned a concert. They asked Paderewski, a famous Polish pianist, to perform for two thousand dollars. Whatever money was left they would use for their schooling.

The students worked hard to promote the event but came up four hundred dollars short. Disappointed, they went to Paderewski and gave him all the money they raised and promised to pay the four hundred dollars as soon as they could.

"That won't do," said the pianist. "Take your expenses out of this sixteen hundred dollars. Then each of you keep ten percent of the balance for your work. Let me have the rest."

Years passed, and in 1919 Paderewski became premier of Poland. It was the worst of times. Thousands in his country were starving, and only one man could do anything—the head of the U.S. Food and Relief Bureau. When Premier Paderewski appealed to him for help, thousands of tons of food came pouring into Poland. Later, Paderewski met the American statesman to thank him. "That's all right," replied Herbert Hoover. "You probably don't remember, but you helped me once when I was in college."

Whether these men knew it or not, they were demonstrating a biblical principle: "A generous man will prosper." God, whose heart of love is the source of all generosity, has made giving to others one of life's pleasures.

Are you looking for happiness? Then don't look for handouts. Give them. —D.B.

Through preaching, teaching, and the Bible, God is telling me . . . _____

_____

_____

Through nature and the lives of other believers, God is showing me . . . _____

_____

I will respond by . . . _____

_____

Got any painkiller?

READ
Psalm 32

MEDITATE
Psalm 32:3
When I kept silent, my
bones wasted away.

REFLECT
➡ In what ways have I
been ignoring my
conscience and the
conviction of the
Spirit? What area in
my life needs work?
How can I make
David's words in
Psalm 51 my own?
➡ What happens if I
put off going to the
dentist for too
long? What hap-
pens if I repeatedly
ignore my con-
science?

CONSIDER
*You can't put
your sins behind
you till you face
them.*

Do you enjoy the high-speed whine, the burning smell, and the jarring vibrations of the dentist's drill as he tears into a cavity-ravaged tooth?

Me neither.

My problem is that I have this thing about pain. I don't like it! And when the dentist asks "Would you like something to numb it?" I say, "Yes! A megadose of Novocaine, please!"

Even with the anesthetic, I don't exactly enjoy myself. My stomach muscles are tight and my palms are sweaty. And even when it's over, I walk around for a couple of hours feeling like I have only half a face.

I know. The temporary discomfort is worth it. Unchecked tooth decay would lead to much greater pain and problems. That's what keeps me going back to the dentist.

Dealing with decay in our relationships with others, in our attitudes, and in our actions can be painful too. It hurts to admit that we are wrong. Submitting ourselves to God so He can clean out the dead areas in our lives and fill them with purity is not something we look forward to. But if we fail to deal with problems when they are small, we're headed for greater pain later on.

In Psalm 32, we read about the pain David endured because he put off going to the Lord. But when he finally did confess his sin, he experienced the joy of forgiveness and the freedom of a clear conscience.

There are many times when we have to choose to do things that by nature we do not enjoy doing, and confessing sin is one of them. Then God can do the needed repair work in our lives.
—K.D.

Through preaching, teaching, and the Bible, God is telling me . . . _____

_____

_____

Through nature and the lives of other believers, God is showing me . . . _____

_____

_____

I will respond by . . . _____

_____

_____

Pest-strip Personality

READ
John 13:1–17

MEDITATE
Romans 12:3
Do not think of yourself more highly than you ought.

REFLECT
➡ If I always do my best how should I handle pride when I outperform others?
➡ What five things can I do today to demonstrate humility?
➡ My problem is feeling insignificant. How does knowing Christ as Savior help with that?
➡ What are five reasons why I am significant?

CONSIDER
You can't get anywhere with others if you're stuck on yourself.

Perhaps you've seen this guy before. He glides across campus with an air of self-importance. Crowds are attracted to him like flies to a pest strip. He considers himself a Very Important Person, and he makes sure everybody knows it.

If you're like me, however, most of the time you feel like a Very Insignificant Person—kind of like the fly caught on the pest strip.

But guess what. Neither attitude is the one God wants us to have. He doesn't want us to expect to draw crowds every time we enter a room, but He doesn't want us to consider ourselves insignificant either.

A right view of self falls somewhere in the middle—we are valuable because God loves us, yet we need a good supply of humility.

Not long ago, I heard about an athlete who charged fifteen dollars for his autograph. At one sports memorabilia show he made ten thousand dollars just by signing his name! What an example of overblown self-importance.

In a real sense, there is only one VIP—Jesus Christ. But notice something. Although He was the most important person who ever lived, He was also humble. He said that He "did not come to be served, but to serve" (Mark 10:45). To prove that He meant what He said, Jesus washed His disciples' feet. Imagine that! The Creator of the universe—the holy Son of God—washing the dirty feet of sinful men!

So where does that leave us? It reminds us that if we want to honor the Lord, we will have enough humility to take the spotlight off ourselves and shine it on Him. He alone deserves praise and honor.   —D.P.

Through preaching, teaching, and the Bible, God is telling me . . . _____ _____

_____

_____

Through nature and the lives of other believers, God is showing me . . . _____

_____

_____

I will respond by . . . _____

_____

_____

Christians reject Gandhi!

READ
James 2:1–9

MEDITATE
James 2:9
If you show favoritism, you sin.

REFLECT
➡ What are the qualities of the people God has called (1 Corinthians 1:26–27)? Why did He call them?

➡ Everyone has preferences. We quickly accept people who think and act like we do. What people or groups do I admire least? How can I encourage people in this group or tell them about God's love?

CONSIDER
Do unto others as if the others were you.

Mahatma Gandhi was in the wrong place (church) at the wrong time (Sunday).

Gandhi, who gained world attention for his political views, said in his autobiography that in his student days he was very interested in the Bible. Deeply touched by reading the gospels, he seriously considered becoming a follower of Jesus. Christianity seemed to offer a solution to the caste system which was dividing the people of his native India and breaking his heart.

One Sunday he attended a nearby Christian church to learn more about the doctrines of the church and to ask the minister how he could be saved. But when he entered the sanctuary, the ushers refused to give him a seat. They suggested firmly that he go and worship with his own people. Gandhi left and never returned.

"If Christians have caste differences also," he reasoned, "I might as well remain a Hindu."

It's easy to ask "what if?" about the man who became a Hindu religious leader and one of the key political thinkers of our times. But it's more important to ask, "When was the last time I turned someone off because of something I said or did?"

It's easy to do.

We prefer hanging out with high achievers who get A's in International Marketing and wear only brand-name sportswear. But by doing so we miss out on the opportunities God gives us to show "losers" like Gandhi that the only way to God is through Christ.

—T.B.

Through preaching, teaching, and the Bible, God is telling me . . . _____

Through nature and the lives of other believers, God is showing me . . . _____

I will respond by . . . _____

A perfect error?

READ
Luke 22:14–34

MEDITATE
Galatians 6:2
Carry each other's burdens, and in this way you will fulfill the law of Christ.

REFLECT
➡ How can I help the Christians in my world?
➡ When was the last time a Christian friend overlooked my failures and encouraged me?
➡ God looks beyond our faults to our hearts. How can I do that today with the people I know?

CONSIDER
When you toss out ideas, make sure somebody catches them.

The score was tied 5-5. The Yankees had runners on first and second when the Brewers relief ace took the mound. The next batter laid down a bunt. Quickly the pitcher pounced on the ball, whirled, and fired a perfect strike to third. But there was one big problem—nobody was covering the bag! The man on the mound made a perfect play—or was it a perfect error? His untimely toss allowed two Yankees to score as the ball died in the left-field corner. If only he had checked to see where his fielder was!

Similar situations exist among Christians. We can field tough problems, fire off quick answers, and execute our tasks efficiently. But when we fail to survey the playing field and find out where other Christians are, our wise words end up bouncing uselessly in foul territory.

Christ set the example for the perfect game plan. He knew what had to be accomplished, but He also made allowances for teammates who were out of position. He showed great patience with the doubting one—Thomas. He put up with the impulsive acts of Peter. And He didn't put James and John on waivers when their mother tried to get them front-row seats in God's kingdom. Jesus never approved of their failings, but He understood their limitations and corrected them in love. He didn't make profound statements that went over the head of the person He was aiming at. He hit the mark every time.

What about our daily opportunities? Are we so eager to make the "perfect play" that we never stop to consider whether or not it will help our team? Or are we always looking out for each other, realizing that winning the game is more important than making one impressive play.   —T.F.

Through preaching, teaching, and the Bible, God is telling me . . . _____

_____

Through nature and the lives of other believers, God is showing me . . . _____

_____

I will respond by . . . _____

_____

That's what they say!

READ
Exodus 33:12–13;
34:6–7

MEDITATE
Exodus 33:13
"Teach me your ways so I may know you."

REFLECT
➡ Is Moses' God "too good to be true"? How has my understanding of God become distorted?

➡ How can I find out for myself who God really is? I can:
Pray "God, show me who You are."
Search Scripture, using a concordance, to find references to God.

CONSIDER
Knowing God is more than knowing about Him.

Louis Harris, head of the Harris polling organization, was curious about people's perception of God. So in 1986 he took a poll to find out. Here's what he discovered about the many ways people see God. Those who see him as:

Father	65%
Mother	8%
Master	68%
Spouse	8%
Judge	58%
Lover	17%
Redeemer	49%
Friend	44%
Creator	37%
King	27%
Healer	14%

Moses had some ideas of his own about God. For example, he apparently believed that the Lord was, at the very least, approachable and responsive, because he came right out and asked God to show him who He was. Moses didn't rely on what the polls said. And the Lord told him what he wanted to know.

Moses found out that God is "compassionate and gracious . . . slow to anger, abounding in love and faithfulness, maintaining love to thousands, and forgiving wickedness, rebellion and sin" (Exodus 34:6–7).

Contrary to what people might say, this is who God claims to be—exactly the kind of God I want to get to know better.

Take another look. God says He is patient, full of love, faithful, and forgiving. Does this sound like the God you know? If not, forget what people say about Him. Starting today, get to know Him as He says He is. —T.B.

Through preaching, teaching, and the Bible, God is telling me . . . _____

_____

_____

Through nature and the lives of other believers, God is showing me . . . _____

_____

I will respond by . . . _____

_____

Ya gotta have

A bargain at any price

READ
Acts 8:26–35

MEDITATE
Acts 8:30
"Do you understand what you are reading?"

REFLECT
➡ How much of the New Testament have I read? What keeps me from reading more of it? I will read it by

_____.

➡ What are the important things to look for in choosing a Bible?

➡ Why is it important to understand all of the Bible?

➡ How will knowing the Bible help me to live better?

CONSIDER
Investing in a Bible pays rich dividends!

For my first college philosophy class the professor assigned twenty pages of reading for the next class. The night before it was due, I sat down to do the assignment, allotting the amount of time it usually took me to read twenty pages. I read the first three pages and nothing happened. It went right over my head. I didn't understand a word of it! I must have read those pages a dozen times before class, and I still wasn't sure what they meant. I needed help.

That's how the Ethiopian official must have felt when he tried to read Isaiah's prophecy (see today's Scripture reading). It went right over his head. He must have been glad when Philip climbed aboard his chariot and told him what the prophet was talking about.

You've probably felt the same way when you tried to read Leviticus, Job, Ezekiel, Hebrews, or other difficult books of the Bible.

If so, save up a little money and purchase a good study Bible. Get one with an introduction to each of the Bible books, a cross-reference section, study notes, maps, and a concordance.

It will cost about the same as a good baseball glove or a new sweater. Less than a pair of Reeboks. It's an investment every Christian should make, and it will last a lot longer than a pair of designer jeans. Furthermore, if used properly, it will become more important to you than your tennis racket or favorite jacket.

If you've ever had trouble understanding the Bible, I challenge you to do without some other stuff and buy a good study Bible.

Once you start using it you'll see that it's a bargain at any price.   —D.E.

Through preaching, teaching, and the Bible, God is telling me . . . _____

_____

_____

Through nature and the lives of other believers, God is showing me . . . _____

_____

_____

I will respond by . . . _____

Is it still warm?

READ
Psalm 78:1–8

MEDITATE
Psalm 78:7
Then they would put their trust in God and would not forget his deeds.

REFLECT
➡ Do I think of the Bible as a bunch of stories about people who had no physical or emotional needs? Why?
➡ Was it easier for Bible people to trust God than for me? Why or why not?
➡ Who is the biblical person I identify with the most? Which traits should I emulate?

CONSIDER
The Bible is a real book for real people.

Imagination is powerful. It can transport us to another land via a Tolkien story or pull us through a time warp in a family tale about a colorful ancestor who lived a hundred years ago.

A class of second graders found out about imagination when they watched a video about a volcano. They stared wide-eyed as molten lava poured into the sea and steam shot a mile into the air.

Then the teacher passed around a piece of lava. After two dozen eager hands had examined it, a little boy bounced up to the front of the room. Carefully cradling the material, he exclaimed in awe, "It's still warm!"

Are the biblical accounts of God's mighty acts "still warm" for you? They probably were when you first heard them from your parents or at Sunday school, but do you really feel that the people you read about in the Bible had the same problems that you have? Did you ever think about Moses feeling insecure and unqualified to lead? Or about the heart-pounding fear the Israelites experienced as they fled Pharaoh's army? Or the joyful excitement the disciples felt when Jesus appeared to them after His resurrection?

Abraham, Miriam, Noah, Paul, David, Mary, and other Bible persons cried, became angry, doubted, had headaches, colds, impossible deadlines, and too little money. Their hassles weren't all that different from ours. The Lord used real people with real emotions in real situations to give us His truth.

Biblical characters express reality in a way that can help us deal with our confusing world. Their stories point us to God, who has redeemed us and who lifts us above our circumstances. They were for real.   —M.D.

Through preaching, teaching, and the Bible, God is telling me . . . _____

_____

Through nature and the lives of other believers, God is showing me . . . _____

_____

I will respond by . . . _____

_____

Another way to say it

READ
2 Timothy 2:11–26

MEDITATE
2 Timothy 2:14
Keep reminding them of these things.

REFLECT

➡ In what way do I twist Scripture to make room for my favorite sin?

➡ How do I respond when I hear attacks on the Scripture? Am I a good defender of truth? What else do I need to know to speak wisely to those who detract from the Word?

CONSIDER
Get to know the Living Word if you wish to understand the written Word.

Well-known filmmaker Samuel Goldwyn didn't know the correct plural of the word mongoose, but he needed two of them for a movie. He asked his secretary what word he should use. She didn't know either, so he said, "Okay, take a letter to the San Diego Zoo. Have it read, 'We'd like to rent a mongoose for use in a motion picture. And while you're at it, send us another one.'" (Try that strategy on your next English exam and see how far it gets you.)

As this story points out, we can say the same thing in many different ways. Even the Word of God does it. The guidelines for godliness, for instance, appear in different ways. God gives truth in various settings, styles, and figures of speech. If we can't figure out the meaning of one passage, we'll usually find the same principle clearly explained somewhere else in the Bible.

College classrooms and dorms are a common battleground for heated arguments about Scripture and God. The Bible is divinely designed to help us when we face these questions. Comparing Scripture with Scripture, and not with the arguments people concoct to confuse issues, will always lead us out of controversy and into confidence in His Word.

If you are engaged in arguments that aren't building up your faith, read Scripture, study it, and compare it with other Scriptures until you understand.

Remember, if you correctly handle the Word of truth, you will find God's message. And you'll also gain His approval.   —M.D.

Through preaching, teaching, and the Bible, God is telling me . . . _____

_____

Through nature and the lives of other believers, God is showing me . . . _____

_____

I will respond by . . . _____

_____

How to listen to a sermon

READ
Romans 10:12–15

MEDITATE
Acts 13:7
He wanted to hear the word of God.

REFLECT
➡ What was the theme of last week's sermon? What made it memorable? (Or, Why can't I remember?)

➡ What do I do as I enter the sanctuary? Talk? Look around? Prepare for worship?

CONSIDER
A poor listener seldom hears a good sermon.

SUGGESTION
Make a copy of this page and put it into your Bible to remind you how to get the most out of the next sermon you hear.

Okay, I confess. One of the most difficult things for me to do is to listen to a sermon. My mind wanders. I get distracted. I find other things to think about. I catch up on my worrying.

I'll be even more honest. The problem is not the preacher. It's me. True, he probably could use more colorful words, snappier phrases, and more captivating sentences. But it's still my responsibility to listen.

Here are some things I've learned to do that help me pay closer attention.

1. Want to listen. I'm not there to be entertained but to be taught and challenged. So I ask God to help me want to hear.

2. Listen for the outline. Almost every preacher gives the theme and outline at the beginning of the sermon. I pay careful attention as he identifies his points (that way I also know how far he has to go before he's done).

3. Read the Scripture. The reference is noted in the bulletin, so I take a moment before church starts to read it.

4. Take notes. No, I won't be tested on the sermon at the end of the day, but I will be held accountable by the Lord. Taking notes helps me follow along as well as remember what was said.

5. Test what I hear. Instead of turning off my mind, I ask questions: Is this right? Where did he get that? How does it fit in? So what?

6. Make applications. A sermon isn't complete until it's been applied. James told us not only to hear the Word, but to do what it says (James 1:22–24). So before leaving church I decide what action I should take during the following week.

If you're serious about wanting to get more out of the sermons you hear, try my approach. And do me a favor. Let me know what you learn.   —D.E.

Through preaching, teaching, and the Bible, God is telling me . . . _____

_____

_____

Through nature and the lives of other believers, God is showing me . . . _____

_____

_____

I will respond by . . . _____

_____

Remember when . . .

MEDITATE
1 Chronicles 16:12
Remember the wonders he has done.

REFLECT

➡ What are the top three items on my list of things God has done for me?

➡ How do they motivate me to follow God?

➡ My reasons for obeying God are . . .

CONSIDER
***Blessings from
the past fuel
faith for the
future.***

It's a typical scene: Mom says, "Clean up your room!" You respond, "Why?" Mom's response usually varies between a couple basic themes: Either "Because it's a mess!" or "Because I told you to!"

But let's say Mom tries a different tactic. Suppose she sets you down and lists everything she's done for you that week—driven you to classes, made dinner, washed your clothes, given you money to buy a new tape or CD, and on and on. By the time she finishes, you either (a) feel pretty guilty or (b) have already started cleaning your room.

In the book of Deuteronomy, we find Moses calling on Israel to obey God. The fact that God is God should be reason enough for them to obey Him, but Moses takes the time to list what God has already done for them. (It's so long it takes up the first three chapters of the book.) In today's Scripture reading, for example, he reminded them of how God helped them defeat Og, king of Bashan. (Is that a great name, or what!) Then, after Moses was finished with the reminding, he said, "Hear now, O Israel, the decrees and the laws I am about to teach you" (Deuteronomy 4:1).

That's a good exercise for any Christian. If you're searching for motivation to obey God (and we all need it from time to time), sit down and write out everything God has done for you. (Well, maybe not everything—you would never finish it.)

Think of the prayers God has answered, the freedom from guilt His forgiveness provides, the joy of being His special child. A little reminiscing will go a long way toward making you a stronger Christian!   —J.C.

Through preaching, teaching, and the Bible, God is telling me . . . _____

_____

_____

Through nature and the lives of other believers, God is showing me . . . _____

_____

I will respond by . . . _____

_____

Vegetables? No thanks!

READ
Daniel 1

MEDITATE
Daniel 1:8
Daniel resolved not to defile himself.

REFLECT
➡ What are the dangerous areas of life for me? What hard choices must I make this week to be faithful to God?

➡ How do some TV programs and magazines weaken me? How can certain friendships be harmful?

➡ What kind of insults have I faced for taking a stand for what I know pleases God? Was it worth it?

CONSIDER
Take a stand or you'll take a fall.

I've never been a big fan of lima beans. It took me years to choke down my first bite of tomato. And those canned peas with the pale green tint have never made a big hit with my taste buds. Too many veggies would do me in.

Instead I'll take a good hamburger, pepperoni pizza, or pork chop any day.

Daniel didn't choose his diet in quite the same way. Instead of choosing his menu according to his own likes and dislikes, he based his eating habits on his convictions. He decided to be a vegetarian while in the service of Nebuchadnezzar because it was the only way he could obey God.

The royal food and wine of Babylon were unacceptable fare for a faithful Jew. Apparently, the palace food service had ties with idol worship, and the meat was either prohibited by Jewish law or had not been prepared according to God's instructions.

Daniel's culinary decisions demanded courage (more courage than it takes to tell Mom you're not going to eat your broccoli). He could have been killed.

This was not a spur-of-the-moment decision for Daniel. He had dedicated his life to pleasing God—and he had already decided not to let anything get in his way.

You have to make tough decisions every day. If you want to be different from a world that does not serve God, you have to hang tough. Even though everyone around you pressures you to go against your convictions, you have to choose not to defile yourself. You have to choose to follow the Lord.

I've asked the Lord to help me make choices that will please Him. Why don't you do the same? Like Daniel, we'll both be better off.   —K.D.

Through preaching, teaching, and the Bible, God is telling me . . . _____

_____

Through nature and the lives of other believers, God is showing me . . . _____

_____

I will respond by . . . _____

_____

God in the background

MEDITATE
1 Corinthians 10:13
God . . . will not let you be tempted beyond what you can bear.

REFLECT

➡ What will I be tempted by today? When it occurs, what will I do?

➡ Part of staying away from sin is recognizing the danger of getting close to it. What can I learn from 1 Corinthians 10:6–10 about staying away from things that lead me to sin?

CONSIDER
Fight as if beating temptation depends on you. Pray as if it depends on God.

You've heard about the Hundred Years War, I'm sure. It was that overtime conflict between England and France that lasted from 1338–1453. (Okay, so it was the 115 Years War, but who's counting?) One of the key skirmishes of the war was the 1346 Battle of Crecy, France. The British forces were led by Prince Edward, son of King Edward III. While the prince took his soldiers into battle, the king stood nearby with a strong battalion, ready to help if needed.

Not long after the fighting began, the prince got nervous about how things were going. He sent a courier to his father, asking for help. But none came. So young Edward sent another message, pleading for immediate assistance. Again the king refused. But this time he sent a return message. It said "Go tell my son that I am not so inexperienced a commander as not to know

when help is needed, nor so careless a father as not to send it."

It may have looked to the prince as if his father didn't care what happened to him, but the opposite was true. His dad cared enough to let him fight his own battles without intervening unless he, in his wisdom, saw that it was necessary.

Did you ever feel toward God the way the prince must have felt toward his father? You cry out for help to fight temptation, yet God leaves you on your own. You ask God to rescue you from your battles with sin, but He doesn't swoop in and zap the enemy. You begin to think He's not paying attention.

Not true. He is standing by. "God is faithful," Paul said in 1 Corinthians. He will always make a way for us to escape temptation.

He is there. He knows our needs. We are not alone.

—D.B.

Through preaching, teaching, and the Bible, God is telling me . . . _____

Through nature and the lives of other believers, God is showing me . . . _____

I will respond by . . . _____

The real you

READ
Romans 8:28–39

MEDITATE
Romans 12:2
Do not conform any longer to the pattern of this world.

REFLECT
➡ What are some of the dangers of conforming to the lifestyle of my friends?
➡ What does Proverbs 29:25 mean to me?
➡ Are people pulling my strings, or am I letting God help me stand on my own?

CONSIDER
When you conform to Christ, you confirm your faith.

It's hard to dress cool these days. Fashion is fickle. By the time we achieve "the look," the look is gone. With every new day comes a new (usually recycled) style, yet we continue to wear what is in because we don't want to be left out.

Many times we trick ourselves into believing "I'm my own person." If you feel that way, look around and you'll see yourself in the people you hang out with. Same hair. Same shoes. Same look. You may even wear the same stains from eating the same pizza. Whether your clothes are made by Ralph Lauren or K-Mart, you chose them so you would conform to your crowd.

Stuart Anderson, who was imprisoned for armed robbery, knows all about conformity. He wrote a letter to Radio Bible Class. He said, "I started out on grass, like all others in the sixties. The motto then was 'Do your own thing.' Only everyone was doing the same thing—conforming to non-conformity." Anderson's rejection of traditional values didn't make him unique; it simply made him the same as a different social group.

How can we resist being conformists? Only by realizing that true individuality comes through conformity to Jesus Christ. He alone is unique, for His life on earth was faultless. His kind of holy living is the pattern for our lives. Stuart Anderson says, "Jesus is the answer. I now open the day with prayer instead of a fix. I carry a Bible instead of a gun or knife."

Stuart Anderson is finally becoming a genuine non-conformist—by being conformed and transformed into the unique image of Christ.

Are you? —T.F.

Through preaching, teaching, and the Bible, God is telling me . . . _____

Through nature and the lives of other believers, God is showing me . . . _____

I will respond by . . . _____

OOOO! WOW! LIKE YOU'VE BECOME A REAL
NON-COMFORMIST, MAN.

A STRONG CHARACTER

They're ba-a-a-ck!!

READ
Romans 6:11–14

MEDITATE
Romans 6:14
Sin shall not be your master.

REFLECT

➡ In which areas of my life do I need to experience victory?

➡ What sins have I had victory over in the past? What did I learn in the process that can help me now?

➡ What might be the consequences of giving up and letting just a small sin get the best of me every now and then?

CONSIDER
Satan can control only what you give him.

Just when you thought you had them licked, those pesky little sins have attacked again. No matter what you do, they keep pestering you.

But wait! What's that verse say? "Sin shall not be your master"? Doesn't that mean this shouldn't be happening?

A friend of mine had this problem. Ashley kept losing out to a sin she couldn't conquer. Every time she was under pressure, she would scream and swear at her son and daughter. They were typical two- and five-year-olds. Noisy. Demanding. Messy. (You remember how you used to be.) Ashley was usually in the kitchen when she lost control, often just before her husband came home from work. No matter how much she prayed and asked God for forgiveness and help, she kept losing the battle.

Then one Friday, just before their vacation, she won! The pressure on her was enormous. She had a zillion things to do, and she was way behind. To make things worse, her husband wanted to leave as soon as possible, and the children were wound up with excitement.

Suddenly, while all of them were in the kitchen getting in each other's way, the kids started to fight. Ashley was just about to open her mouth for one of her screaming and swearing sessions when a great calm came over her. "I don't have to swear," she said to herself. And with God's help, she didn't. Finally, she had won the battle over sin. It was a great victory!

Your defeat by sin probably doesn't come in the kitchen. Maybe it's in the gym. Or the car. Or in the dorm. Or places you go with your friends. Wherever it is, with God's help, you can win the victory.   —D.E.

Through preaching, teaching, and the Bible, God is telling me . . . _____

_____

_____

Through nature and the lives of other believers, God is showing me . . . _____

_____

_____

I will respond by . . . _____

_____

_____

The hall of pain

The Hall of Fame in
Cooperstown, New
York—that nearly sacred
shrine of baseball—turned
fifty last year. There you can
see remnants of glory like Ty
Cobb's sliding pads, Mickey
Cochrane's catcher's mask,
and even Babe Ruth's bowl-
ing ball.

George Kell, former
Detroit Tiger and now broad-
caster for the club, talked to
Sports Illustrated about his
own induction in 1983:
"Changes your life, getting
into the Hall of Fame. For the
rest of my life I'll be known
as 'Hall-of-Famer George
Kell.' And a hundred years
from now my great-grand-
children will come here and
they'll think I was as good as
Cobb or Ruth."

Hebrews 11 has been
called Faith's Hall of Fame. In
it we see the results and
rewards of faith in the lives
of such well-known Bible
characters as Abel (v. 4),
Abraham (vv. 8–19), and

Moses (vv. 23–28). But near
the end of the chapter something seems terribly wrong.

Instead of fabulous fin-
ishes—like Enoch who "did
not experience death . . .
because God had taken him
away" (v. 5)—we find some
Hall of Famers who were tor-
tured, flogged, sawed in
two, and sent out in goat-
skins to wander in the desert.
And unlike baseball Hall-of-
Famer George Kell, they
don't even get their names
mentioned. Yet their experiences show that God uses
both the Babe Ruths and the
George Kells of the faith.

If we serve the Lord in
faith, we can say with the
apostle Paul, "We are hard
pressed on every side . . . but
not in despair" (2 Corin-
thians 4:8). If we keep the
faith and keep on going, we
will hear the same words the
Bible's Hall of Famers heard
at the end of their lives:
"Well done, good and faithful servant."   —T.B.

Through preaching, teaching, and the Bible, God is telling me . . . _____
_____
_____

Through nature and the lives of other believers, God is showing me . . . _____
_____
_____

I will respond by . . . _____
_____
_____

Looking for a match

READ
Genesis 24:1–12

MEDITATE
Proverbs 31:10
A wife of noble character who can find?

REFLECT
➡ How do I decide whom to date?
➡ Why are dating choices so vital?
➡ Am I willing to break up a relationship that does not measure up to biblical principles?
➡ What do I need to work on in order to become a "good catch" for someone?

CONSIDER
Looking for someone to marry? Be someone worth finding.

Do you ever have trouble finding a matched pair of socks, earrings, or gloves? For whatever reason (such as aliens who collect one of everything), a matched pair is sometimes hard to find.

Looking around for the right person to marry can be frustrating too—and a lot more important. Marrying a person who is not a good match can lead to a lot of unhappiness. But how can you know whom to marry? If you are a Christian, consider these basic biblical principles:

1. Choose a believer. "What does a believer have in common with an unbeliever?" (2 Corinthians 6:15; see vv. 14–18). Nothing will enhance your spiritual life more than spending your life with one who shares your love for God.

2. Trust God. Ask for His help (James 1:5). If you expect Him to lead you tomorrow, you need to be following Him today.

3. Consider character. Look for someone with godly qualities like humility, purity, love, self-control, honesty, devotion to Christ, and commitment to church. (Are you like that too?)

4. Use wisdom. Marriage is nothing to rush into. With God's help, consider many factors, not just one "sign" or a feeling. Seek advice from wise counselors.

5. Look ahead. Marriage is a lifetime partnership, a giving of oneself for the other (Ephesians 5:21–33). It is both fulfilling and demanding.

6. Examine your love. Compare your idea of love with 1 Corinthians 13:4–7. Each time the word love appears, substitute your name and the name of the person you think may be right for you.

If marriage is part of God's plan for you, He will guide you as you apply these principles.   —K.D.

Through preaching, teaching, and the Bible, God is telling me . . . _____

_____

_____

Through nature and the lives of other believers, God is showing me . . . _____

_____

_____

I will respond by . . . _____

_____

_____

Getting physical

You've heard stories about dating relationships that got too physical. Maybe you've played a starring role.

Take Judy and Steve, for instance. She was looking for romance; he was looking for manhood. Although Steve genuinely cared about Judy, he had a difficult time suppressing the message his hormones were sending. After all, sex is a normal part of romance, he reasoned. So they tried it. But they didn't live happily ever after. They broke up. And when they began to date others, they each had to deal with guilt and lingering memories.

Life often resembles a soap opera with its lust, broken relationships, and unbridled passions. Sex seems to have a mind of its own, and its IQ isn't too high. Sexual desires pull us along until we go too far. Then we forfeit two of our most precious gifts from God—purity and peace of mind.

First Thessalonians 4 gets right at the truth of the matter. Contrary to what you might hear, purity is not just some prude's opinion, it won't ruin your life, and it's not impossible to hang on to. Here's what Paul said:

1. Purity is God's will (vv. 1–5). Sexual standards are not determined by public opinion polls.

2. Purity protects us and others (v. 6). Promiscuity produces victims. God wants to protect us from guilt, haunting memories, damaged emotions, fractured relationships, physical illness, and His discipline.

3. Purity is an attainable goal (vv. 7–8). God not only tells us to be holy, but He also gives us the means to achieve holiness. God's Spirit within us gives us the ability to resist temptation.

Are you striving for purity? Is your body under control? It can be. God wants it to be. Do you?   —K.D.

Through preaching, teaching, and the Bible, God is telling me . . . _____
_____
_____

Through nature and the lives of other believers, God is showing me . . . _____
_____
_____

I will respond by . . . _____
_____
_____

Thoughts about rules

MEDITATE
Deuteronomy 15:8
Be openhanded.

REFLECT
➡ Would I describe myself as a willing servant or a reluctant slave? Why?
➡ How can I change my attitude about obeying God?

CONSIDER
Let the One who rules the universe make your rules.

My brother used to have this great ploy for getting out of washing dishes. Dad would order him into the kitchen to help Mom. (Funny thing, I don't recall Dad ever volunteering to help.) Tom would go to the kitchen and get in Mom's way. Finally, in utter frustration, Mom would order him out of the room.

As Tom plopped down on the couch to watch TV, Dad would ask him why he had left the kitchen. "Mom told me to," he'd say with a shrug. That was only half the story, of course. If Dad had asked for more details, he would have realized that Tom obeyed the "letter of the law" while ignoring the "spirit of the law."

We sometimes have that attitude toward God's law. We grudgingly go along with what we know God wants from us, but all the time we're seeing how much we can get away with. But God is looking for obedient hearts, people who want to do what He says.

Look at today's Scripture reading. It contains guidelines for how the people of Israel were to treat the poor. It seems to be a warning not to ignore the needs of the poor as the year of canceling debts drew near.

But God was looking for more than simple adherence to financial rules. He wanted His people to have love and compassion for those who, for whatever reason, needed to borrow from the wealthy.

So how is it with you? When you read one of God's clear biblical principles, how do you respond? Do you just grudgingly go along with it, never stopping to acknowledge the love behind it? Or do you see it as a great way to please the Lord and honor Him? Don't just follow the rules; follow the Ruler. —J.C.

Through preaching, teaching, and the Bible, God is telling me . . . _____

_____

Through nature and the lives of other believers, God is showing me . . . _____

_____

I will respond by . . . _____

_____

"You coward!"

READ
**Numbers
13:1–2,17–33**

MEDITATE
Proverbs 29:25
Fear of man will prove
to be a snare.

REFLECT
➡ What kind of
people make me
afraid? Authority
figures? Unbeliev-
ers? Friends who
might abandon
me?

➡ What examples do
I find in the book
of Acts of believers
who were more
afraid of displeas-
ing God than dis-
pleasing people.

CONSIDER
*People who
don't fear God
fear each other.*

Mrs. Ima Tarur was chas-
ing her husband
around the zoo, waving her
umbrella, and unleashing
insults. Her perspiring husband, seeing that the lock on
the lion's cage was not quite
closed, yanked open the
door, jumped into the cage,
and hid behind the aston-
ished lion. His frustrated wife
shook her umbrella, stut-
tered in anger, and exploded, "R-R-R-Ralph, you coward, come out of there!"

In a way, Ralph is like the
Israelites we read about in
Numbers 14. Their spies had
seen something that fright-
ened them. Just as Ralph's
wife terrified him, so the
giants in Canaan looked
absolutely terrifying to the
people of God. The Israelites
should have feared the Lord
more than they feared the
giants, but they let fear confuse them. Then, like Ralph,
they put themselves in real
danger by running from the
wrong enemy.

So where does that leave
you? You probably don't
have a fearsome spouse (or
any other kind for that matter), and the only giant you
know about is Manute Bol.
But you certainly know people who frighten you:

A classmate who doesn't
like what you stand for.

An instructor who makes
you feel like a dunce.

A boss who is unreason-
able.

Will you let them intimi-
date you? If you're so afraid
of people that you've stopped
following the Lord, you've
also stopped trusting Him.
Remember that God has the
power to help you and some
promises to guide you. But
He can't do much for you if
you're cowering in the corner, afraid to trust Him.

If there is someone you're
afraid of, you might want to
pray: *Father, forgive me for
fearing what I should not be
afraid of, and for not fearing
and trusting You.*   —M.D.

Through preaching, teaching, and the Bible, God is telling me . . . _____

_____

Through nature and the lives of other believers, God is showing me . . . _____

_____

I will respond by . . . _____

_____

Broken-heart repair

READ
Psalm 43

MEDITATE
2 Corinthians 7:6
God, who comforts
the downcast, com-
forted us.

REFLECT
➡ When was the last
time someone
comforted me?
What did he or she
do to make me feel
better?
➡ When was the last
time I comforted
someone?
➡ How can I use
these tips to help
others who need
first aid for their
broken heart?

CONSIDER
*The Great
Physician is a
heart specialist.*

A fourth-grade class in Edmonds, Washington, was asked to take a first-aid test on medical techniques. Here is how some children said they would treat the following emergencies:

For head colds: "Use an agonizer to spray the nose until it drops in the throat."

For fractures: "To see if the limb is broken, wiggle it gently back and forth."

For asphyxiation: "Apply artificial respiration until the victim's dead."

I don't think I would want those ten-year-olds treating me.

Here's another emergency. A broken heart. How would you treat the problem of prolonged feelings of anxiety, discouragement, hopelessness?

In his book *Broken Things*, Dr. M.R. De Haan discussed David's brokenness in Psalms 42–44 and offered these suggestions:

1. Remember what God has done for you in the past (Psalm 44:1–3). David remembered that God had never failed his fathers in the days of old.

2. Read the Bible. David could only remember what God had done by turning to the record in the Word of the Lord. And as he read of God's faithfulness, his soul was restored.

3. Pray. "God's sufferers have always been the best pray-ers."

4. Have faith and hope (Psalm 43:5). In effect, David declared, "Hope in God, for I will yet praise Him. This trouble may be severe, but it is only for a moment, it will not last."

5. Praise Him at all times (Psalm 43:5). We have a bright tomorrow. Soon the day of Christ's coming will be here.

Is your heart sad? David has the right remedy for spiritual and emotional heart failure. —T.B.

Through preaching, teaching, and the Bible, God is telling me . . . _____

_____

Through nature and the lives of other believers, God is showing me . . . _____

_____

I will respond by . . . _____

_____

Dates become mates

READ
2 Corinthians
6:14–18

MEDITATE
2 Corinthians 6:14
Do not be yoked to-
gether with unbeliev-
ers.

REFLECT
➡ Have I ever said, "I
can date non-
Christians if I try to
win them to the
Lord"? Is that line
of thinking biblical?

➡ If dating unbeliev-
ers is not good pol-
icy, what about
having them as
friends? Does that
constitute being
"yoked together
with unbelievers"?

CONSIDER
*Select only a
date who would
make a good
mate.*

She was a Christian. He was not. Yet she found him so attractive that she dated him anyway. They fell in love. She knew she couldn't live without him, yet she also knew she couldn't marry him.

Then the story takes a twist. He has good news for her. He is now a Christian, he says. Buoyed by this happy change, she agrees to marry him.

All goes well in their marriage at first. Until he drops another bomb. He is not really saved, he tells her. He just said that to get her to marry him. In a few years he's gone. The marriage seems doomed. With two kids, she seems headed for the world of single parenthood.

But not all sad stories have sad endings. He finally does turn to Christ and is saved. And so is the marriage. He returns, they are reconciled, and all appears at last to be well.

True story. With a happy ending. Yet imagine the roller coaster ride this woman has had over the years. Think of the problems she faced of first living with an unsaved mate, then having to live without him.

Are you thinking of dating an unsaved person? First answer the tough questions Paul asked in 2 Corinthians. "What do righteousness and wickedness have in common?" (v. 14). "What fellowship can light have with darkness?" (v. 14). "What does a believer have in common with an unbeliever?" (v. 15). Answer: Not much.

Imagine spending your life with someone whose standards, points of view, and motives are different from yours. Imagine sharing life with one who does not share your love for Jesus.

Don't take a chance. Isn't it better to lose a good date than to end up with a bad mate?   —D.B.

Through preaching, teaching, and the Bible, God is telling me . . . _____

_____

_____

Through nature and the lives of other believers, God is showing me . . . _____

_____

_____

I will respond by . . . _____

_____

_____

The right medicine

READ
Ephesians 3:14–21

MEDITATE
Proverbs 18:14
A man's spirit sustains him.

REFLECT
➡ Choose one: I am most easily affected by: (a) hassles that involve people; (b) hassles that involve situations; (c) hassles that involve my faith.
➡ Consider how the woman in the story dealt with her problems.
➡ Which of her medicines do I need to apply? How will I apply it?

CONSIDER
Until your spirit is right, your life never will be.

If you've played sports at all, you've probably had to rub a little medicine on a sore spot. Maybe you've rubbed Ben-Gay on aching muscles. (That stuff smells awful!) Or used Absorbine Jr. on athlete's foot. (That stuff hurts!) Or put iodine on a cut. (That stuff kills!)

We can rub a little medicine on sore spots in our Christian lives too. One woman who always seemed to have a good attitude no matter what, put it this way: "I have special ointments for all problems. For irritations caused by people I apply affection. For those caused by circumstances I apply prayer. If sickness or unexpected obstructions hinder my well-laid plans, I say to the Lord, 'Your will be done.'"

Life can be pretty irritating. We can't always control our circumstances, but we can control our reactions. A positive attitude will help you deal with problems a lot better than a negative attitude will.

Proverbs has a couple of verses that can help us understand that. "A cheerful heart is good medicine," according to Proverbs 17:22. And today's verse tells us that the right spirit will help us hang in there.

In Ephesians 3, Paul said that we are being renewed by God's Spirit on the inside. If we deal with problems from the inside out, rather than letting them affect us from the outside in, we can face anything with calmness and composure.

The key is applying the right medicine on the inside. Is life getting you down? Then offer this prayer: "God . . . renew a steadfast spirit within me" (Psalm 51:10).   —J.C.

Through preaching, teaching, and the Bible, God is telling me . . . _____

_____

_____

Through nature and the lives of other believers, God is showing me . . . _____

_____

_____

I will respond by . . . _____

_____

_____

Spiders and chickens

READ
Numbers 13:17–33

MEDITATE
1 John 4:4
The one who is in you is greater than the one who is in the world.

REFLECT
➡ What problems seem to get the best of me? Am I depending on God or have I given up?
➡ Am I afraid I won't succeed or am I living in confidence, knowing that God wants to help me?
➡ Do I recognize the importance of receiving Christ so I will have the power of God within me?

CONSIDER
When fears come, God sits down beside you.

You may want to put a sack over your head before you read this article. It's about a nursery rhyme, and the last thing you need is somebody to recognize you while you're reading about Little Miss Muffet.

Remember her? She's the one who was scared out of her lunch by a little ol' spider. It wasn't one of those huge science fiction jobs that devour entire metropolitan areas. It was just your basic, garden-variety spider. She should have just brushed it away. Why run from the problem and give up a good meal?

Christians sometimes have a case of the Miss Muffets. Something enters our life that catches us by surprise. It might even be a bit scary. But instead of confronting the problem and overcoming it through the power of God, we scream and run. This happened to the Old Testament children of Israel. Twelve of them were sent into Canaan to spy out the land God had promised to give them. But when they saw their opposition, ten of them decided that the wise thing to do would be to run. They felt like grasshoppers and acted like chickens.

Don't do as they did. When you face a problem on the job, at school, or within yourself, don't run from it. Rely on God's strength to overcome it.

Instead of being depressed over another battle lost, you'll be rejoicing in your relationship to God and the victory it brings.   —D.P.

Through preaching, teaching, and the Bible, God is telling me . . . _____
_____
_____

Through nature and the lives of other believers, God is showing me . . . _____
_____
_____

I will respond by . . . _____
_____
_____

Bombs away!

Nobody's perfect. Not even the U.S. Navy. They managed to bomb one of their own ships. An article in the *Detroit News* reported, "A U.S. warplane accidentally dropped a 500-pound bomb on the guided missile cruiser USS *Reeves* during maneuvers in the Indian Ocean. The bomb slightly injured five sailors, left a five-foot hole in the deck, and started a small fire, the Navy said. The single-seat F/A-18 Hornet had taken off from the carrier USS *Midway*." The pilot had mistaken the *Reeves* for a target ship.

But that wasn't all. The day before, a rookie pilot had come in "low and slow" and slammed his plane into the deck of the carrier USS *Lexington*, killing several people, including himself. About the same time, another naval ship had some expensive missiles wash overboard and sink to the bottom of the ocean. Finally, the whole Navy shut down for two days to try to find out what was wrong.

True, nobody's perfect. Not the Navy. Not the church. Not me. But that doesn't mean we should lose all confidence in the Armed Forces, forget about the church, or give up on ourselves.

As Christians, we can do something about it when we goof up—we can turn to Christ and ask His forgiveness (1 John 1:9).

But it takes real maturity to admit our mistakes. It's hard to say to the Lord, "I was wrong. I admit it. I won't let it happen again." But that's the only way to get out from under the guilt of our sin.

Mistakes getting you down? Feel like a walking failure? Then take the 1 John 1:9 route to forgiveness.

—D.E.

Through preaching, teaching, and the Bible, God is telling me . . . _____

Through nature and the lives of other believers, God is showing me . . . _____

I will respond by . . . _____

An unpayable debt

READ
Romans 1:8–17

MEDITATE
Romans 1:14
I am obligated both to Greeks and non-Greeks.

REFLECT
➡ Do I feel an obligation to God?
➡ Which is worse—not having enough money to pay a debt or not serving God out of gratitude for what He has done for me?
➡ When I have the opportunity to either show kindness or show disdain, what do I normally do?

CONSIDER
Pay your debt to God by giving out kindness.

It's one of those shopper's nightmares. You plunk down your ten items or less at the checkout counter and watch anxiously as the cashier adds it all up. Then, to your total humiliation, the bill comes to fourteen dollars and all you have in your pocket is a ten.

That's what happened to a young woman at a local supermarket. But someone bailed her out. The man behind her in the checkout lane noticed her dilemma and motioned to the cashier to add the four-dollar overage to his bill. When she asked his name so she could pay him back, he wouldn't tell her. A few days later, a charity organization received a four-dollar check with the following note: "This check is for the man who helped me out of a tight spot. I came up with the idea of giving it to you as a thank-you to him."

This illustrates a principle that should be part of every Christian's life. When someone is kind to us, we should pass some kindness along to others.

Paul took this a step further. Although he could never repay the Lord for his salvation, Paul showed his gratitude to God by passing the gospel message along to others. For the sake of Christ, he regarded himself a debtor to all people, Jews and Gentiles alike. Thankful for what he had received, he showed the highest kind of charity—sharing the gospel with others.

Obviously, we can't repay God for saving us. But that doesn't mean we are not obligated to Him. The least we can do to show our appreciation is to demonstrate to others the incredible difference He has made in our lives. —M.D.

Through preaching, teaching, and the Bible, God is telling me . . . _____

_____

Through nature and the lives of other believers, God is showing me . . . _____

_____

I will respond by . . . _____

_____

Ya gotta have

$6 quadrillion man

READ
Matthew 25:14–30

MEDITATE
Psalm 139:14
Your works are wonderful.

REFLECT
➡ How does knowing that I have a future appointment with God affect my decisions?
➡ What dividends will I receive if I invest God's gifts to me wisely?

CONSIDER
God invested in you. Are you showing any interest?

Yale biophysicist Harold J. Morowitz reached a startling conclusion about just how much our bodies are worth. Taking into account the proteins, enzymes, RNA, DNA, amino acids, and other complex biochemicals that make up the stuff of life, he figures that these raw materials would be very expensive indeed—more than any previous estimate. Says Dr. Morowitz, "Fashioning this chemical shopping list into human cells might cost $6,000,000,000,000,000 (six quadrillion dollars). Assembling the resulting heap of cells into tissue, the tissue into organs, and the organs into a warm body might drain all the treasuries of the world, with no guarantee of success."

Now consider that the physical part of our bodies isn't nearly as important as the spiritual stuff that goes inside, and you're on to something. Bodies are here today and gone tomorrow. Yet God didn't consider His investment in them unimportant. He added to our bodies life, minds, emotions, personality, and gifts that make each one of us distinct.

But what are we doing with His investment. What are we doing to build our bodies, control our emotions, develop our minds, and nourish our souls?

As the parable in Matthew 25 makes clear, the Lord expects us to increase the value of what He has given us. I'm not trying to send you on a guilt trip, but I do want to remind you that someday we'll have to answer for the way we handled God's investment (Romans 14:12).

Until then, we need to increase our return by yielding to Him.   —T.B.

Through preaching, teaching, and the Bible, God is telling me . . . _____
_____
_____

Through nature and the lives of other believers, God is showing me . . . _____
_____

I will respond by . . . _____
_____
_____

No getting away with it!

READ
Galatians 6:1–10

MEDITATE
Isaiah 59:12
Our sins testify against us.

REFLECT

➡ What have I been caught at that I thought I was getting away with? How did I feel?

➡ What are some good things about the fact that God always knows where I am and what I'm doing?

➡ What does the following statement mean to me? God will not let me get away with sin forever.

CONSIDER
There is no right way to do a wrong thing.

Things couldn't have gone worse for a group of students at Renaissance High in Detroit. They cut classes to attend a rock concert at Hart Plaza. They enjoyed their "day off" and were pleased with themselves for not getting caught.

But the next day when the *Detroit News* hit the street, it had bad news for the hooky players. The paper carried a color picture of the concert—on the front page. And who was in the picture? You guessed it—the delinquent students of Renaissance High. Right there in living color, easily recognizable by anyone. According to a follow-up article in the paper, "Eagle-eyed assistant principal Dr. Isaiah Porter spotted the students and had a conversation with them." As for the kids, the story went on, "There was nothing they could say."

It may be that you have something you're trying to get away with, some sin you're hiding. If so, I urge you to confess it to the Lord and stop doing it right now. You can hide what you're doing for a while. You may even seem to be getting away with some things completely, like cheating on exams or sneaking out at night. You may convince yourself that you are succeeding, that no one knows. But the Bible makes it clear that you can't hide it from God. "A man reaps what he sows," Paul wrote in Galatians 6:7.

Your picture may not appear on the front page of the newspaper letting an entire city know what you've done, but according to the Bible, you can't get away with it any more than those school-skipping students did!
—D.E.

Through preaching, teaching, and the Bible, God is telling me . . . _____

_____

Through nature and the lives of other believers, God is showing me . . . _____

_____

_____

I will respond by . . . _____

_____

The worth of integrity

READ
Genesis 43:17–23

MEDITATE
Luke 6:31
Do to others as you would have them do to you.

REFLECT

➡ What matters of integrity have I been fudging on recently? Tests? Research papers? Roommates' stuff?

➡ Why is doing to others as I want them to do to me such a good guideline for helping me establish integrity?

CONSIDER
No person is poor who has integrity.

Sa'ad is quite a man. Oh, he doesn't drive a nice car or wear a power tie. And his job is not something any of us would want to do. But Sa'ad has one thing we could all use more of: Integrity.

Sa'ad is a garbage collector. Not the drive-a-truck-through-the-neighborhood kind, but the rummage-through-the-dump kind.

He lives in Zarayed, one of the garbage dumps of Cairo, Egypt. Every day he sifts through the refuse of Cairo's more affluent citizens, looking for salvageable trash to sell. On most days, he earns about fifty cents, hardly enough to keep his wife and family alive.

Then one day something exciting happened. He found a gold watch. He knew it was valuable, so he had it appraised. It was worth nearly two thousand dollars—more money than he would make in the next ten years. So what did he do with it? He found out who the owner was and returned it.

But why? Just as Jacob's sons could have claimed for their own the silver that was put in their packs in Egypt, so Sa'ad could have said the watch he found in Egypt was his. Who would have known?

But Sa'ad had a special reason to demonstrate integrity. The same reason you have if you are a follower of Jesus. He's a Christian, and he believes it's wrong to keep what doesn't belong to him. He knew that keeping the golden rule is much more important than keeping a gold watch.

We honor God when we act with integrity. It's just one small way to show that we trust Him to take care of us when taking what belongs to someone else might seem an easier way to get ahead. If you had been in Sa'ad's sandals, what would you have done? —D.B.

Through preaching, teaching, and the Bible, God is telling me . . . _____
_____
_____

Through nature and the lives of other believers, God is showing me . . . _____
_____
_____

I will respond by . . . _____
_____
_____

That's that!

READ
Ephesians 1:11–14

MEDITATE
Ephesians 1:13
Having believed, you were marked in him with a seal, the promised Holy Spirit.

REFLECT
➡ Salvation is a once-for-all transaction between God and me. What are some reasons I might begin to wonder if it's really true and if it will last?

➡ How open am I to the presence and work of the Spirit within me?

➡ What can I do to become more aware of the Spirit's presence?

CONSIDER
What God seals, He delivers.

When a young man slips an engagement ring on a young woman's finger he is making a promise.

For Christians, the Holy Spirit is our engagement ring. He is our guarantee of heaven. The Spirit is the seal of the promise of our salvation. In fact, the contemporary Greek word for seal can be translated "engagement ring."

Author Jill Briscoe illustrated this truth by telling what happened when she received her engagement ring. "Well, Jill," Stuart said as he put it on her finger, "that's that!" She thought those words were rather unromantic—until later in the day.

Her mother had promised a family friend that they would purchase the ring from her. They hadn't, and the woman just happened to be on the phone when Jill and Stuart came in with the news. "Here," her embar-

rassed mother said, "you explain." Feeling bad, Jill stammered into the phone, "Sorry, Mrs. Conel, we've already purchased a ring. Maybe next time." Stuart gently took the phone out of her hands, took her in his arms, and said, "Jill, there won't be a next time. When I said 'That's that!' I meant it for the rest of our lives." Jill commented, "Suddenly those two little words sounded like the two most romantic words in the world."

In a sense, God has said "That's that" to us. We are His. He has promised us salvation through our faith in Jesus Christ. The indwelling Holy Spirit is the "engagement ring," the seal, which assures us that the realities of heaven await us.

The next time you start to wonder if God really loves you, think about the Holy Spirit. He is God's guarantee. Then say to yourself, "That's that!"
—D.E.

Through preaching, teaching, and the Bible, God is telling me . . . _____

_____

_____

Through nature and the lives of other believers, God is showing me . . . _____

_____

_____

I will respond by . . . _____

_____

_____

Slow down to catch up!

READ
Psalm 44:1–8

MEDITATE
Psalm 40:4
Blessed is the man who makes the Lord his trust.

REFLECT
➡ How's my schedule? Am I frustrated because I can't get everything done? Do I sometimes panic? Wish I could get out of some commitments?

➡ What am I doing to take care of my soul? How do I attend to my inner needs?

CONSIDER
The Christian race is a marathon, not a sprint.

How are you doing in life's marathon. Are you lagging behind in the race? Speed up! Still behind? Go faster! Get more involved! Push yourself! Run—keep on running until you drop! You've got too much invested to slow down.

This might be the counsel of someone who spent too much time pushing athletes as a football coach, but it is not good advice for Christians. On the contrary, to be more effective for the Lord we must slow down, put our confidence in Him, and take the heat off ourselves.

Astronaut Michael Collins wrote an article describing how two orbiting vehicles link up with each other in space. It's different from two airplanes that rendezvous for in-flight refueling. (The plane behind increases its speed until it overtakes the other aircraft.) In outer space, speeding up would put the trailing craft into a higher orbit and cause it to move away rather than closer. Instead, the commander must go against all natural instincts and slow down, thereby causing the spaceship to drop into a lower orbit, which enables it to catch up, maneuver into position, and make contact.

So it is with busy Christians. Taking on more activities can mean losing ground due to lost time with the Lord. To get ahead, we must slow down and wait on the Lord. When we do, we have time for the things that keep us spiritually strong: prayer, Bible reading, thinking through our priorities.

Are you behind? Then slow down and wait for God! Then you'll get caught up in doing His will.   —M.D.

Through preaching, teaching, and the Bible, God is telling me . . . _____

_____

Through nature and the lives of other believers, God is showing me . . . _____

_____

I will respond by . . . _____

_____

A RESPONSIVE SOUL

Eat a Yugo?

READ
John 6:32–40

MEDITATE
John 6:35
"I am the Bread of Life. He who comes to me will never go hungry."

REFLECT
- What things do I want more than Christ?
- What does it mean to be satisfied with Christ alone?
- What person do I know who seems to be content no matter what happens?

CONSIDER
Only the Bread of Life can satisfy spiritual hunger.

A recent report states that the average American will consume about 1,400 pounds of food this year. That means we will ingest the approximate weight of a loaded Yugo. Open wide! Here's a partial list of this three-quarter-ton diet: 80 hot dogs, 200 hamburgers, 4 pounds of potato chips, 18 pounds of candy, and 50 gallons of soft drinks. Whew! We're talking major junk food here. But not all the edibles on the list are of the low-nutrition variety. You and I will also down close to 300 pounds of fruits and veggies.

Fast food or fresh fruit, it looks like we've got some feast-filled days. And most of us will be chowing down at least three times every twenty-four hours. Even if we scarf down a Whopper and large fries for dinner today, we'll be scrounging around the kitchen looking for breakfast tomorrow. And after eating 1,400 pounds of food this year, we'll still expect to eat next year. No earthly food can stop our ravaging hunger.

It's not that way with spiritual hunger, though. There is one "food" that can completely satisfy us spiritually—the Bread of Life. Jesus Christ used this description of Himself to help us understand what He means to those who receive salvation. When we ask Him to be our Savior, we are filled by Him, and we receive eternal life. He said, "I am the Bread of Life. He who comes to me will never go hungry."

Because of Christ, we no longer have to nibble on the empty crumbs the world offers. Our spiritual hunger has been satisfied forever.

—T.F.

Through preaching, teaching, and the Bible, God is telling me . . . _____

_____

_____

Through nature and the lives of other believers, God is showing me . . . _____

_____

_____

I will respond by . . . _____

_____

_____

A second chance

READ
1 Corinthians
3:1–15

MEDITATE
1 Corinthians 3:13
The fire will test the quality of each man's work.

REFLECT
➡ If I died today would I be happy with my obituary?
➡ What would people remember about me?
➡ What do I want people to remember about me after I die? What can I do to make sure that happens?

CONSIDER
Has your work been worthwhile?

Alfred Nobel (1833–1896) woke up one morning to find his own obituary in the local Stockholm newspaper. The newspaper intended to print the obituary of his brother, but someone in the newsroom got a bit confused and gave Alfred an early dismissal. Reading his own obituary, Alfred was dismayed to learn that the only thing he would be remembered for was his invention of mass destruction: dynamite.

Realizing he had a second chance—so to speak—Alfred decided to do something about it. He initiated an annual award for the outstanding individual or group that promoted the cause of peace. He left more than $9.2 million for the endowment, and the first Nobel Prize was awarded in 1901, five years after he really did die.

Few of us will get to read our own obituaries. But if you were reading your death notice today, what would it say? How would you be remembered by your family and friends? And perhaps more important, how would your life stack up before Jesus the Judge? These questions may strike you as morbid or irrelevant. Yet if you are guided by an eternal perspective, no other question is more important.

Paul compared our lives to a building under construction (1 Corinthians 3). And how we build dictates the result. If we choose the narrow path of righteousness, stand for the truth, and say what's right, the yield is "gold, silver, and costly stones." If we take the easy way out, back down from the truth, and flatter others, we win "wood, hay, and straw."

The choice is yours. You won't get a second chance.

—T.B.

Through preaching, teaching, and the Bible, God is telling me . . . _____

_____

_____

Through nature and the lives of other believers, God is showing me . . . _____

_____

_____

I will respond by . . . _____

_____

_____

There when you need it

READ
Psalm 119:9–16

MEDITATE
Psalm 119:11
I have hidden your word in my heart.

REFLECT
➡ Why is it so easy for me to remember the bad things in life and so hard to remember the good things?

➡ What kind of Bible passages should I be memorizing? How about Psalms 1, 23, 100; Isaiah 53; John 14:1–6; Philippians 2:5–8.

➡ What methods can I use to improve memorization? 3 x 5 cards? Work with a friend?

CONSIDER
Carry your Bible in your heart.

One thing about students: they know how to memorize! Whether it's the symbols of all the elements in chemistry, the names of all the bones in the human body, or the chronological sequence of Shakespeare's twenty-three plays, students can learn huge amounts of information to pass exams.

It's a good thing God gave us such large-capacity brains. We not only store the info we study, but we also keep it all in order and recall it when we need it. A magazine called *THINK* said our brains can store enough information to fill several million books! Think about that the next time you feel like complaining when your science instructor says to memorize the distances of all the planets from the sun.

But classroom work may not be the best use of memory. As good as that is, a better use is to "hide" God's Word in our hearts. Then the Holy Spirit can help us recall it when we need it.

Chet Bitterman, a Wycliffe missionary, was kidnapped by Colombian terrorists and held captive for seven weeks before being killed. Before his capture, Chet had memorized 1 Peter, a book written to first-century believers who were suffering for their faith. During Bitterman's captivity, he wrote a letter to his wife in which he quoted 1 Peter 3:15–16. He said he was using those verses to strengthen and guide him in his response to his captors. Months earlier, when he was memorizing 1 Peter, he had no way of knowing how he would be using it.

So, in addition to memorizing the names of the kings of England and all of the parts of speech, why not memorize some of God's Word. Hide it in your heart. No telling when you'll be needing it.   —D.E.

Through preaching, teaching, and the Bible, God is telling me . . . _____
_____
_____

Through nature and the lives of other believers, God is showing me . . . _____
_____
_____

I will respond by . . . _____
_____
_____

Who knows best?

READ
Proverbs 1:1–9

MEDITATE
Proverbs 1:8
Listen, my son, to your father's instruction.

REFLECT
➡ When was the last time I felt resentment because my parents tried to give me advice? Looking back, can I see how they were trying to help?

➡ How does my response to my parents show my honor for them? (See Ephesians 6:2.)

CONSIDER
He who will not be counseled will not be helped.

Have you ever heard this quote? "When I was 17, my father didn't know anything. But when I was 21, I was surprised how much he'd learned in four years."

Why is it that during high school and college we have a hard time taking advice from dear old Mom and Dad? We say they just don't understand and believe they just want us to fit into their mold. We're convinced we're old enough to make our own decisions.

Proverbs tells us that we need to hear our parents out (1:8). Why? For one thing, wisdom about life doesn't "kick in" automatically at puberty. Nor does it come from a textbook.

For example, I could learn all the facts and statistics about AIDS in a medical course. But knowing those facts won't make me wise about sex. We know that's true by looking at all the foolish advice about sex we hear from well-educated, informed "experts."

Being wise means considering how biblical principles apply to me. It means thinking about how my actions will affect my relationship with God. Being wise means seeing how each choice fits into God's desire for my life.

There's another reason for giving our parents the courtesy of our sincere attention. It's that God expects parents to be learning from Him and passing along that information to their children.

So next time your parents try to talk things over with you, do something radical—listen. If you want them to understand you, show them that you want to understand them. It's a good way to show your love for your Father in heaven.   —K.D.

Through preaching, teaching, and the Bible, God is telling me . . . _____

_____

Through nature and the lives of other believers, God is showing me . . . _____

_____

I will respond by . . . _____

_____

What does God want?

READ
1 Thessalonians
5:16–18

MEDITATE
Psalm 143:10
Teach me to do your will, for you are my God.

REFLECT
➡ Can I expect God to reveal His will to me if I am living out of fellowship with Him?

➡ If I am living in fellowship with Him and have a choice between two good Christian colleges, how can I determine God's will?

CONSIDER
Living God's way is step one in doing God's will.

The head basketball coach from Marquette University had most of his audience hooked as he explained how we could improve our guards' defensive play. He was busy drawing X's and O's, barking instructions to some local JC players who were demonstrating for him, and sprinkling his remarks with stories of major college basketball.

To a young coach like me, it should have been invigorating and challenging. It wasn't. I just couldn't get interested. I almost felt out of place. Just a few days before, I had been offered a job that would take me out of the classroom, and I was in the middle of seeking God's direction. Here, during what was an annual highlight for me, a basketball clinic, I was bored and uninterested. The Lord used that to show me that my days as a teacher and coach were over.

Although we don't always sense God's will for us clearly, we do sometimes get what Philip Yancey calls "quiet nudges" that give us a sense of direction. These nudges may come in the form of circumstances that change or through godly advice from other Christians.

Quiet nudges or not, if we live godly, thankful, joyful, and prayerful lives, we won't go wrong when we limit our choices to things that are moral, good, and God-honoring.

Would you like to know what God wants you to be doing ten years from now? Forget it. God doesn't reveal His will by ten-year plans. You know what He wants you to do today—live for Him. If you are doing that, you can trust Him that He will show you tomorrow and the next day.   —D.B.

Through preaching, teaching, and the Bible, God is telling me . . . _____
_____
_____

Through nature and the lives of other believers, God is showing me . . . _____
_____

I will respond by . . . _____

The staredown

READ
2 Timothy 3:12–17

MEDITATE
2 Timothy 3:16
All Scripture is . . . useful for teaching.

REFLECT

➡ What biblical territory have I left unexplored?

➡ Where should I start to get into the Bible in a new way?

➡ When was the last time I read from Ezra? 1 Kings? Hebrews? 2 Peter?

CONSIDER
Unbalanced Bible study may make you stumble.

Have you ever tried to stare someone down? It's hard, isn't it? And there's a good reason. Researchers exploring the phenomenon of "eye contact" in conversation have found that it is difficult, if not impossible, to sustain it for any length of time.

Special cameras used in their research reveal that what appears to be a steady gaze at someone is actually a series of rapid, repeated scans of the face, centering chiefly on the bridge of the nose, the eyebrows, and the mouth. And studies show that if we look precisely at the same spot continuously, the visual field will go blank. The nerves in our eyes need a constant change if we are to see properly.

Bible study is a lot like that. If we get preoccupied with one biblical truth and "stare at it" while excluding other important doctrines, our spiritual vision begins to blur out. Some people, for instance, have a tendency to look only at the love of God. They concentrate so hard on that single idea that they can't see His justice, His holiness, or His authority. We can blind ourselves with any Bible truth—God's sovereignty, His promises, evangelism, the Holy Spirit—if we spend all our time on one topic.

Perhaps you are just getting started in serious Bible study. Notice 2 Timothy 3:16. It says that "all Scripture" is God-breathed and useful. Try to balance your Bible study so you don't start staring down just one topic. Study the whole Bible.

—T.B.

Through preaching, teaching, and the Bible, God is telling me . . . _____

_____

Through nature and the lives of other believers, God is showing me . . . _____

_____

I will respond by . . . _____

_____

Search for meaning

READ
Ecclesiastes 12

MEDITATE
Ecclesiastes 12:13
Fear God and keep his commandments, for this is the whole duty of man.

REFLECT
➡ What do I want to do with my life? Why?
➡ How does my attitude toward my classes, my friends, or my job show my purpose for living?

CONSIDER
Is what you are living for worth dying for?

You don't have to be suicidal to wonder if life is worth living.

You don't have to be on skid row to feel like a loser.

You don't have to be in jail to be a prisoner of your desires.

You don't have to be a prostitute to sell your body.

You don't have to be a playboy to be preoccupied with sex.

You don't have to be a drug addict to exist on artificial "highs."

You don't have to be a millionaire to be consumed by the love of money.

You don't have to be psychotic to run from the deeper issues of life.

You don't have to be a garbage collector to think that life stinks.

You don't have to drive a BMW to try to find joy in your possessions.

You don't have to be homeless to feel lost and out of place in the world.

You don't have to be stupid to misunderstand what life is all about.

And you don't have to be a genius to discover the real meaning of life.

So what is the secret to discovering the meaning of life? The writer of Ecclesiastes had struggled with trying to find direction for his life. He had tried it all, and he ended up latching on to something he had learned as a young man. He concluded that life's purpose is wrapped up in knowing God and living for Him.

Jesus said, "Now this is eternal life: that they may know you, the only true God, and Jesus Christ, whom you have sent" (John 17:3). That's the secret!

Do you know God? Are you living for Him? If not, you're going to waste a lot of time, energy, and effort in a vain attempt to uncover a secret that is already out.

—K.D.

Through preaching, teaching, and the Bible, God is telling me . . . _____

_____

_____

Through nature and the lives of other believers, God is showing me . . . _____

_____

_____

I will respond by . . . _____

_____

_____

Battle for the body

This article is about sex. Now that I have your attention, I must tell you that I'm not talking about the appealing side of the subject. I'm talking about something that's been described by a very reliable source as "wicked," "detestable," and "indecent." I'm talking about homosexuality.

A vigorous campaign is being waged in our society to change our thinking about homosexuality. Militant, divisive groups are disrupting meetings, threatening law-abiding citizens, demanding legislation, questioning church standards, and trying to control the media to make Americans accept homosexuality.

If you have committed your life to Jesus Christ and have vowed to live according to God's standards in the Bible, you have ample reason to reject this thinking.

The Bible calls homosexuality "this wicked thing" (Genesis 19:6). It says "If a man lies with a man as one lies with a woman, both of them have done what is detestable" (Leviticus 20:13) and "Men committed indecent acts with other men, and received in themselves the due penalty for their perversion" (Romans 1:27).

Also, the Bible forbids sexual activity outside of marriage (Hebrews 13:4) and says that marriage is intended for a man and a woman (Genesis 2:24; 1 Corinthians 7:2). If sex outside of marriage is wrong and if only people of the opposite sex can be married to each other, then all same-sex sexual activity is outside of marriage and therefore wrong.

Don't be tricked by those who want to substitute the beauty of the God-given sexual relationship in marriage for something unnatural. Trust God's standards if you want to win the battle for the body.   —D.B.

Through preaching, teaching, and the Bible, God is telling me . . . _____

_____

Through nature and the lives of other believers, God is showing me . . . _____

_____

I will respond by . . . _____

Tale of the toxic toads

READ
Proverbs 6:20–29

MEDITATE
Proverbs 6:27
Can a man scoop fire into his lap without his clothes being burned?

REFLECT
➡ Are some of my friends experimenting with sex? What damage has it done? What damage will it do?
➡ What do I do when temptation strikes? What should I do? (See Matthew 4:1–11.)
➡ What are the benefits of remaining sexually pure?
➡ Am I committed to staying pure?

CONSIDER
Illicit highs lead to incredible lows.

I have heard of kissing frogs in search of a prince, but licking toads in search of a high? It's true. That's what some people are actually doing! And it works (unlike frog-kissing). But it's also very dangerous.

According to a *Detroit News* article, the hallucinogenic drug that certain toads secrete through their skin is meant as a defense against predators, not as a potion for thrill seekers. Besides, some of these toads are more toxic than others, and the chemicals they release can cause seizures and even death. University of Michigan herpetologist Carl Gans said, "If you pick the wrong toad, you won't only get high, you'll get dead."

Proverbs 6 and 7 warn about seeking a different kind of excitement—the "high" of illicit sex. Going to bed with someone you have not married is as self-destructive as licking a toxic toad.

Sure, some people seem to get away with it. They may not get AIDS, herpes, or some other disease. They may actually seem to be happy. But the warnings in Proverbs are right—we can't scoop fire into our laps without getting burned. Sooner or later we will suffer the emotional, physical, and spiritual consequences.

So the next time you are faced with sexual temptation, remember the tale of the toxic toads. If you give in, you are doing far more than taking a chance on getting hurt. We're talking about a sure thing here. (See Galatians 6:7.)

Instead of scooping fire into your lap, why not demonstrate your love for God and His standards. Reserve the sexual high for the marriage relationship.
—K.D.

Through preaching, teaching, and the Bible, God is telling me . . . _____

_____

Through nature and the lives of other believers, God is showing me . . . _____

_____

I will respond by . . . _____

_____

To marry or not to marry

READ
1 Corinthians 7:1–9

MEDITATE
1 Corinthians 7:2
Each man should have his own wife, and each woman her own husband.

REFLECT
➡ Where do I get my ideas about marriage? From watching television? Listening to friends? Watching my parents? Reading secular fiction?

➡ Is my attitude toward marriage secular or biblical? How do I know?

CONSIDER
Singleness is no less a gift from God than marriage.

When I was a kid, my favorite verse was 1 Corinthians 7:1. In fact, several of us nine-year-old boys thought Paul was pretty wise to say, "it is good for a man not to touch a woman." (We read it in the King James Version.) We couldn't figure out why anyone would want to do that anyway. All we knew was that most girls didn't like to play baseball.

But we didn't stay nine years old. The older we got, the less we liked that verse. We began to see why Paul put verse 2 in there.

What Paul is talking about in 1 Corinthians 7 is the question of marrying or not marrying. Some people were saying it wasn't right for Christians to marry—that it detracted them from the Lord's work. So Paul set the record straight.

Verse 1 is not the commandment we nine-year-olds thought it was. It's probably a restatement of the issue the Corinthian people had written to him about. His answer begins with verse 2: Marriage is the institution provided to keep people sexually pure. It gives a man and woman the only proper relationship for the expression of sexual intimacy.

Should everyone get married though? Not necessarily, as Paul indicated in verse 8. Yet one thing is clear: If a Christian cannot tolerate the life of sexual abstinence as a single, he or she should seek God's guidance in finding a mate. Sexual intimacy outside marriage is always wrong.

Serving God is not reserved exclusively for either the single or the married. Both should do God's will. Paul said that "each man has his own gift from God" (v. 7). Plan now to use your gift in the way that will best bring glory and honor to Him—whether you get married someday or not. —D.B.

Through preaching, teaching, and the Bible, God is telling me . . . _____

Through nature and the lives of other believers, God is showing me . . . _____

I will respond by . . . _____

"Gunned down"

READ
1 Peter 2:1–3

MEDITATE
1 Peter 2:2
Crave pure spiritual milk.

REFLECT
→ What are the five greatest hindrances I face in trying to live for Jesus every day?
→ Why do little sins cause so much trouble? How are they affecting my relationship with God?
→ If I have been struggling with little sins, have I tried confessing them to God?

CONSIDER
To fight "truth decay," read the Bible every day.

Some ducks are giving new meaning to the phrase "bite the bullet." In heavily hunted habitats, webfoots are facing a double danger. If they don't get shot down by the hunters' guns, they get "gunned down" by the hunters' shot. The lead shot from all those 12-gauge shells intrigues the ducks, so when they see it lying on the bottom of the lake, they eat it. As they do, they poison themselves. Conservationists say that many ducks are dying from lead poisoning.

Lead poisoning is not a pretty sight. In humans it causes a loss of strength that shows up first in the fingers, hands, and wrists. A condition known as "wrist drop" soon follows, making the victim unable to work. The palsy eventually extends to the shoulders and then to the legs. Eyesight is often damaged. If it affects humans that way, you can imagine what it does to a mallard with a stomach full of lead B-Bs.

A similar thing could be happening to us in spiritual matters. Even if we are able to resist the big dangers Satan fires our way (you know, the stuff people get kicked out of Christian colleges for) we still aren't out of the woods. We can cause ourselves great harm by nibbling at the wrong things.

Once we've been poisoned by the morsels the enemy puts before us, we begin to show signs of having spiritual palsy. We become listless in our efforts for the Lord. Our eyes start to wander off good things. We become useless for the work God wants us to do for Him.

Be careful about your diet. Make sure your main course is "pure spiritual milk."
—M.D.

Through preaching, teaching, and the Bible, God is telling me . . . _____
_____
_____

Through nature and the lives of other believers, God is showing me . . . _____
_____
_____

I will respond by . . . _____
_____
_____

Don't argue with Bubba!

MEDITATE
Proverbs 20:1
Wine is a mocker and beer a brawler.

REFLECT
→ How can I resist the pressure from my friends to drink with them?

→ And if I resist can I keep their friendship?

→ What additional Bible passages can I find to help me decide whether or not I should use alcohol?

CONSIDER
Only weak people depend on strong drink.

Bubba Smith was a living legend when he played defensive tackle for the Michigan State Spartans. The stadium was always filled when he played, and I can still hear the student body chant, "Kill, Bubba, kill!"

Bubba downed lots of opposing linemen and running backs during his college days, but that's not all he downed. He also downed a lot of beer and wine.

Bubba was drafted by the Baltimore Colts, played on championship teams with Johnny Unitas, and was a perennial Pro Bowl selection. After retiring from football, he went on to a career in Hollywood and is still seen on TV programs.

He has also been seen in the familiar beer commercials chanting "Tastes great"—"Less filling." But not anymore. And he's not going to do any new ones. Why? Because he went back to his alma mater, spent some time with the students, and saw how common alcoholism is on campus. He also got a firsthand look at the harm it is doing. He doesn't want to encourage its use in any way.

Neither does Glenn Davis, outstanding slugger for the Houston Astros. He has refused to be named "Player of the Game" because the honor is bestowed by a brewery. He doesn't want his name associated with beer because it might influence kids to think drinking is okay.

These are not publicity stunts. Bubba Smith and Glenn Davis are responsible men who are concerned about their fellow human beings. They have seen what alcohol abuse can do, and they want no part of it. They are sending the same message the author of Proverbs 20:1 sent from the Lord. When it comes to wine or beer, "whoever is led astray by them is not wise"! —D.E.

Through preaching, teaching, and the Bible, God is telling me . . . _____

_____

_____

Through nature and the lives of other believers, God is showing me . . . _____

_____

_____

I will respond by . . . _____

_____

_____

Give till it feels good

READ
2 Corinthians
9:6–15

MEDITATE
2 Corinthians 9:7
God loves a cheerful
giver.

REFLECT
➡ What do my
spending habits
say about my prior-
ities? (See Matthew
6:21.)
➡ What do I have
that God can use—
for my benefit and
His glory?
➡ How can I begin to
give regularly some
portion of my tal-
ent and income?

CONSIDER
*Give all you can
for the One who
gave all He had.*

"There are three kinds of givers," James Dunn wrote in *Flashes of Truth,* "the flint, the sponge, and the honeycomb. To get anything out of a flint you must hammer it, and then you get only chips and sparks. To get water out of a sponge you must squeeze it, and the more you squeeze it the more you get. But the honeycomb just overflows with its own sweetness."

God wants us to be like the honeycomb—not for His benefit but for ours. Everything we have and are comes from God. And although He doesn't need our acts of service or our money, He has promised to reward those who give cheerfully of themselves and their finances.

The apostle Paul talked about this in 2 Corinthians 9. Paul reminded the believers at Corinth that "whoever sows generously will also reap generously. . . . God loves a cheerful giver" (vv. 6–7).

Notice that nothing is said about the size of the gift or age of the giver or whether the gift should be cash, check, or charge.

The principle, however, is clear: "He who supplies seed to the sower and bread for food will also supply and increase your store of seed and will enlarge the harvest of your righteousness" (v. 10). What a bonus! When we give happily to God, He will provide for every need (v. 8), increase our right-eousness (v. 10), and make it possible for us to give more in the future (v. 11). The result? Thanksgiving to God (v. 11), as it should be.

Decide today to be a honeycomb giver. It will honor God and make you feel good about yourself.

—T.B.

Through preaching, teaching, and the Bible, God is telling me . . . _____

_____

Through nature and the lives of other believers, God is showing me . . . _____

_____

I will respond by . . . _____

_____

Tell them? No way!

READ
Jonah 1:1–3:4

MEDITATE
Jonah 4:11
"Should I not be concerned about that great city?"

REFLECT
➡ What types of people do I avoid? Why? Do they need to hear about Christ?
➡ In Matthew 9:12–13 what did Jesus say about who needs the gospel?
➡ How can my prayers change the way I view other people?

CONSIDER
The best tool in witnessing is contact.

If Jonah were around today and a sophomore at the University of Michigan, the Lord would probably command him to go rescue the students at Ohio State University. In case you're not up on midwest universities, U of M and OSU are arch-rivals in sports, especially football.

In the real situation that Jonah faced, however, the people he was supposed to help were the dreaded and barbaric Ninevites. (I'm not saying that Buckeyes are dreaded and barbaric.) The Ninevites weren't the kind of people Jonah, or any other God-fearing person, would want for friends.

When he finally arrived in Nineveh (after taking a Mediterranean cruise inside a big fish), Jonah was sad instead of glad when the people repented and escaped God's judgment. He pouted because he did something he really didn't

want to do, and he got results he really didn't want to get.

Jonah is not so different from you and me. We too have our own "enemies" we aren't interested in telling about Jesus. We are often more concerned about "our own kind" of people than we are in taking a risk and proclaiming the gospel to someone who isn't like us. And we can get so wrapped up in our hatred of sin that we forget to love the sinner.

Do we dare to tell others? Do we try to see the world as God does? Are we concerned enough to offer the hope of heaven to those on their way to hell? Are we willing to spread the Word to those who act as if they don't want to hear it? Can we say, "Lord, help me tell them"?
—K.D.

Through preaching, teaching, and the Bible, God is telling me . . . _____

_____

Through nature and the lives of other believers, God is showing me . . . _____

_____

I will respond by . . . _____

_____

A chance to sin

READ
Matthew 4:1–11

MEDITATE
James 1:13
No one should say, "God is tempting me."

REFLECT

➡ I know it is best to stay out of places where temptation is natural, but sometimes temptation comes when I least expect it. What can I do to beat temptation then?

➡ What did Jesus do when He was tempted? What are some things I could say to Satan to get him off my back?

CONSIDER
Temptation does not become sin until you yield to it.

We're here in the living room of one of New York's blackout looters," the news reporter says. "When the city's power went out, this man swooped into the neighborhood stores and walked away with as much stuff as he could get. Let's ask him about it." The reporter asks, "Sir, doesn't it bother your conscience to have ripped off all of this property?" Without hesitating, the man looks into the camera and says, "I had an incredible opportunity to get things I never would have been able to get otherwise. I thank God for the blackout! I'm just sorry I didn't have a chance to get a color television."

Sadly, this line of reasoning is not all that uncommon. Not only have people stopped feeling bad about doing wrong, they have begun blaming God for it. They seem to equate opportunity to do evil with God's approval.

By contrast, Christ gave us the right approach when He was tested. He was alone, and His physical resistance was weakened (Matthew 4:2). God seemed to be making it easy for Him to trade off eternal values for a moment of self-gratification (Matthew 4:1). But Christ did not give in. He knew that even though the occasion was within the Father's plan, the temptation came from the enemy.

That's an important distinction. Do you think God would ever put you in a place where you have no choice but to sin? Of course not! Maybe a major test is coming up and you just "happen" to find the answer sheet. God may have allowed the circumstance, but it is Satan who tempts you to sin (James 1:13).

This kind of circumstance is a test—a test Satan turns into a trap. Don't fall into it.
—M.D.

Through preaching, teaching, and the Bible, God is telling me . . . _____

_____

_____

Through nature and the lives of other believers, God is showing me . . . _____

_____

_____

I will respond by . . . _____

_____

Afraid of God?

READ
Hebrews 12:25–29

MEDITATE
Psalm 111:10
The fear of the Lord is the beginning of wisdom.

REFLECT
➡ What are the qualities of God that I should fear?
➡ What does It mean to fear a loving God?

CONSIDER
Fear God and you have nothing to be afraid of.

People don't seem to have any fear of God these days. That means it probably wouldn't increase your popularity If you were to announce in your philosophy class that you're afraid of God. Someone would probably say, "I'd never believe in a God I had to be afraid of."

Let's talk about fear for a minute. I have a healthy fear of water. I know it can kill me. But that doesn't mean I don't love to fish and swim. I do. Yet the whole time I'm enjoying the river, lake, or ocean, I'm aware that it could take my life. In the same way, I fear electricity, gasoline, and high ladders when I'm using them. To assume their benefits without recognizing their dangers would be foolish.

In a more personal way, I fear my dad. I love him and do not for a moment question his good intentions. But I don't kid myself either. As much as I know he loves me and is concerned for me, I have always respected his authority as my father. I fear the corrective measures he would take if I were to embarrass either him or my heavenly family.

So, yes, I fear God. I reverence Him and stand in awe of His holiness. I want to love what He loves and hate what He hates. I want to live my whole life with the realization that He deserves more fear than anyone or anything.

What are your friends—what are you—saying about God? Do they just view Him as a nice old man in the sky? Or do they realize that He will one day be a "consuming fire" to everyone who rejects Him?

I'm convinced that only as I know enough to fear Him do I know enough to love Him.

Be wise. Fear God.

—M.D.

Through preaching, teaching, and the Bible, God is telling me . . . _____

_____

_____

Through nature and the lives of other believers, God is showing me . . . _____

_____

_____

I will respond by . . . _____

_____

_____

An open and shut case

READ
Proverbs 17:7–20

MEDITATE
Proverbs 17:14
Drop the matter before a dispute breaks out.

REFLECT
➡ When was the last time angry words got me in trouble? Did I stop to consider what I was saying?
➡ When it comes to communicating with others, my problem is . . .

CONSIDER
We have two ears and one mouth for a good reason.

John was angry. Yet he was sorry it happened. He thought again about how the argument began.

He had borrowed money from a friend to pay for concert tickets. He and Tracie were celebrating their engagement, so he splurged and got good seats.

Tracie had to work until seven that evening. But they could still make it to the concert if they waited until afterward to eat. But Carol didn't show up for work that night, and Tracie had to fill in for her. She didn't get out until eleven o'clock. By then, John didn't feel like celebrating. The price of the tickets had been out of his reach in the first place—and then they were wasted! When he finally saw Tracie, his angry feelings came tumbling out.

Before the evening was over, John and Tracie had both said things they wished they hadn't. Yet they couldn't take them back. So they parted with a wall between them.

John and Tracie should have heeded the wisdom of Proverbs 17:14, "Starting a quarrel is like breaching a dam; so drop the matter before a dispute breaks out." Just as water rushing from a broken dam fiercely carries away everything in its path, unrestrained words can sweep away all the good feelings you have for someone.

The Lord has given us some clear principles for avoiding the kind of verbal battle John and Tracie fought. He told us to give gentle answers (Proverbs 15:1), to hold our tongue (Proverbs 10:19), and to bring healing with our tongue (Proverbs 15:4).

The next time someone does something you don't like, ask God to help you remember Proverbs 17:14. He will reward you for controlling your tongue. —D.P.

Through preaching, teaching, and the Bible, God is telling me . . . _____
_____
_____

Through nature and the lives of other believers, God is showing me . . . _____
_____
_____

I will respond by . . . _____
_____
_____

What makes you happy?

READ
Ecclesiastes 11:7–10

MEDITATE
Ecclesiastes 11:9
Be happy, young man, while you are young.

REFLECT
➡ What are the five things that make me most happy?
➡ How much of my happiness centers on God?
➡ What do I need to be working on to be happier?

CONSIDER
Happiness is not what you have to live on, but what you have to live for.

Pastor Larry Green asked the young people in his church what made them happy. Here are their top answers:

1. Summer
2. Clothes
3. Going to the mall
4. Going to parties
5. Looking nice
6. Not having a problem in the world
7. Talking on the phone
8. Getting my own way

How does this sound to you? Typical? About the same as your list? Or do you get the feeling that something's missing? That it's pretty shallow? C'mon. Be honest.

Just what makes us happy anyway? What did Solomon have in mind when he told us to be happy while we are young?

The summer sun, a few bucks to buy clothes, and you're happy? No way! If that's all it takes, you're too easy to please!

What about making the basketball team? Getting good grades? Doing well in your recital? Having some really good friends?

Or what about coming home to a happy and secure environment where you are accepted and loved? Being part of a good church? Being able to get along well with all kinds of people? Having a good relationship with Mom? Dad? Being at peace with yourself? With God?

It takes work to be happy. Things can't make you happy because you'll always want more. People alone can't do it, because they're bound to disappoint you. True happiness starts with your relationship with God through Christ. When that's as it should be, real happiness will spread from your heart into all your life. And your friends will be asking you, "What makes you so happy?"   —D.E.

Through preaching, teaching, and the Bible, God is telling me . . . _____

_____

_____

Through nature and the lives of other believers, God is showing me . . . _____

_____

_____

I will respond by . . . _____

_____

_____

I'm in love! (I think)

READ
1 Corinthians 13

MEDITATE
1 Corinthians 13:13
The greatest of these is love.

REFLECT
➡ How do some movies, music, and TV shows wrongly depict love? How can I know if I am buying into that kind of thinking?

➡ What is the difference between love and lust?

➡ What problems do I need to work on to be a better candidate for marriage?

CONSIDER
They do not truly love who do not show their love.
—Shakespeare

How do you know if you're in love? What are the symptoms? A bell ringing in your head? A tingling sensation that runs up and down your backbone? Loss of concentration during classes? Feelings of jealousy? A gnawing emptiness when you're apart?

Although you may experience all those sensations, true love is more. And though you may feel on top of the world when you're with the one you love, feelings can lead you to the top of a mountain one day and take you down into a valley the next.

That's why feelings of infatuation and attraction are not enough.

Before you jump to any conclusions (like making or accepting a marriage proposal), make sure that your love is the highest kind.

Of course, no one on earth (except Jesus) has ever exhibited perfect love. But we can desire the highest human expression of love.

If you think you are in love, take a moment to evaluate it in light of 1 Corinthians 13:4–7. Check the first box if it applies to you, the second box if it applies to the person you think you love.

❑❑ patient with the other
❑❑ kind to the other
❑❑ not jealous of the other
❑❑ not boastful
❑❑ not arrogant
❑❑ not rude to the other
❑❑ not self-seeking
❑❑ not easily angered
❑❑ does not hold grudges
❑❑ does not delight in evil
❑❑ rejoices in the truth
❑❑ protects the other
❑❑ trusts the other
❑❑ hopes in the other
❑❑ never gives up on the other

How did you do? Are you really in love?   —K.D.

Through preaching, teaching, and the Bible, God is telling me . . . _____
_____
_____

Through nature and the lives of other believers, God is showing me . . . _____
_____
_____

I will respond by . . . _____
_____
_____

Me? A missionary?

READ
Colossians 3:22–25

MEDITATE
Colossians 3:23
Whatever you do, work at it with all your heart, as working for the Lord.

REFLECT
➡ Which would I rather be—a teacher, a factory worker, a pastor, or a missionary? Why?
➡ In what ways are all of these full-time Christian work?

CONSIDER
Is this any place for a missionary? Yes!

I wanted to be a teacher, but now I'm in the ministry!" I cringed when the speaker at a college chapel service made that proud pronouncement. The speaker was trying to convince students to abandon worldly pursuits like teaching and go into "the ministry."

I thought about some of the teachers I know. One works in the inner city, providing guidance for kids with few positive adult role models. Another hosts a "lunch bunch" of high schoolers who meet to discuss life, growing up, and God. I have a suspicion that those teachers are "in the ministry."

We sometimes distinguish between "full-time Christian work" and "secular work," but the Bible makes no such distinction. Many Bible characters pursued so-called secular occupations. Luke was a doctor; Gideon was a farmer; Paul was a tentmaker; and Moses had to abandon his work as a successful shepherd to go get the Jews out of Egypt.

Your choice of work is important, but so is your potential as a missionary on the job. True, you have to be careful that your Christian zeal does not jeopardize your integrity. (Witnessing and handing out tracts when you're being paid to work are not examples of good work habits or good Christianity.) But as you develop friendships at work and show by your good attitude that there is something special about you, you create opportunities to witness of your faith in Jesus Christ.

Don't be deceived into thinking that any task is less important than another if God has called you to do it.
—J.C.

Through preaching, teaching, and the Bible, God is telling me . . . _____

_____

Through nature and the lives of other believers, God is showing me . . . _____

_____

I will respond by . . . _____

_____

Up when you're down

READ
Ephesians 2:1–10

MEDITATE
Ephesians 2:10
We are God's workmanship, created in Christ Jesus.

REFLECT
➥ What yardstick do I use to measure my worth? The opinions of others? God's opinion of me?
➥ How does God value me?

CONSIDER
One way to get up is to get down on your knees.

You can find these people anywhere. Slinking across the campus. Putting in time on the job. Sitting on the bench at the athletic field. Holding down the back row at church. Stuck in their rooms at home.

They're the people who always feel rejected, who live with a deep, aching emptiness inside—a desperate need to be loved and accepted by others. Yet they often compensate for feelings of inferiority and inadequacy by pulling away from relationships or by holding on too tightly. When they do that, they just perpetuate the cycle.

The experts have a term for this. It's called low self-esteem—a smothering presence that robs people of their vitality and sense of significance. It's a sad enough situation when it affects somebody else, but what if it describes you? Now we're getting serious.

What can you do about low self-esteem? TV advertisers want you to believe that it's simply a matter of buying the right product. Like if you chew the right kind of gum you'll start "feeling good about yourself, feeling carefree." Or maybe buying a new kind of perfume will do the trick—so the romance inside you can blossom. But let's get real. These products have little chance of fixing low self-esteem.

There is only one way to achieve lasting significance and a healthy view of self: Let God be the most significant person in your life. When He is in control, He can show you who you are, who He made you to be, and what you can become.

As Ephesians 2:10 states, "we are God's workmanship." When you think about it, that can make you feel pretty important.   —D.P.

Through preaching, teaching, and the Bible, God is telling me . . . _____
_____
_____

Through nature and the lives of other believers, God is showing me . . . _____
_____
_____

I will respond by . . . _____
_____
_____

I'M NOT SURE WHO HE IS. I SAID "HI" TO HIM
ONCE AND HE'S BEEN THERE EVER SINCE.

A LOVING HEART 71

How much do I love you?

MEDITATE
Ephesians 5:28
Husbands ought to love their wives as their own bodies.

REFLECT
➡ When was the last time I felt that I was in love? What made me think so?
➡ How is it possible to have the kind of love for someone that Christ has for the church? How can I demonstrate that kind of love?

CONSIDER
Love never suffers from "I"-disease.

Love is one bizarre subject! It brings to mind so many questions: How do I know when I've found the right one? Is it possible to love someone too much? Why do people in love treat each other so badly sometimes? And, of course, the key question: WHY IS IT ALL SO WEIRD?!

The best source for answers to our questions about love is the Bible. Even when it doesn't answer them directly, it gives principles to guide us. Today's passage, for example, offers some helpful (and troubling) teaching on the subject of love.

Before you get too convinced that you've discovered true love, look at today's key verse. It tells husbands to love their wives as much as they love themselves. In today's "me-first" society, that's quite a bit!

One husband thought he loved his wife too much.

Fearing that he was putting her before God, he talked to his pastor about it. The pastor asked him, "Do you think you love your wife as much as Christ loves the church?" "Of course not," the man replied. "Then enjoy it! That's the limit the Bible gives!"

Now, let me ask you a couple of questions about love: First, if every husband in America—or even in the church—loved his wife that much, what do you think would happen to the divorce rate? Second, are you willing to love in that same unselfish way? If not, you don't love enough.

—J.C.

Through preaching, teaching, and the Bible, God is telling me . . . _____

Through nature and the lives of other believers, God is showing me . . . _____

I will respond by . . . _____

Ya gotta have

Faith versus unfaith

READ
John 4:46–54

MEDITATE
James 2:17
Faith . . . if it is not accompanied by action, is dead.

REFLECT
➡ What can I do to put my faith into action?
➡ What is one thing that frightens me about taking this step?
➡ If I run into trouble, how can I know God will be there to catch me?

CONSIDER
If you don't live it, you don't believe it.

Try this with a good friend. (A really good friend.) Ask him or her to stand behind you as you fall backward and to catch you just before you hit the ground. It works best if your friend waits long enough so you feel the sensation of falling for an instant. This is called a trust fall.

Why should you do something this stupid? Because it's a great way to learn about faith.

We all have times in our Christian life when we stumble and fall. And sometimes God doesn't catch us until we feel as if we're about to hit bottom. By showing up at what seems to us to be the last possible minute, God stretches and strengthens our faith.

Jesus Christ showed what kind of faith He is looking for in John 4:46–54. A royal official begged Him to come and heal his son. But rather than go with the man, Jesus commanded him, "You may go. Your son will live" (v. 50).

Jesus wanted the worried father to demonstrate his faith by going home without Him. The Bible tells us that the man "took Jesus at his word" (v. 50) and went home. When he got there, he learned that at the very moment Jesus had spoken the word, his son had been healed.

What separates faith from "unfaith" is action—taking a step to show that you believe God. For example, if you believe that the Bible is God's Word, written to instruct and enlighten you, you will take action. You will set aside time to study it. And if you believe that Christ can truly make a difference in people, you'll tell your friends about Him.

Go ahead, "fall backward." Jesus will catch you!

—J.C.

Through preaching, teaching, and the Bible, God is telling me . . . _____

_____

Through nature and the lives of other believers, God is showing me . . . _____

_____

I will respond by . . . _____

_____

Choose your own God?

READ
Exodus:20:1–6

MEDITATE
Isaiah 45:5
"I am the Lord, and there is no other."

REFLECT
➡ How well do I know God, really? Do I have a relationship with Him like I do with a friend or a parent? Or do I just seem to know about Him, like I know about the President?

➡ Have I ever made myself my own god? How?

CONSIDER
We bear God's image; God does not bear ours.

One of the most unusual religious shrines I have ever seen is "The Temple of the Thousand Buddhas" in Kyoto, Japan. Inside the shrine are more than 1,000 likenesses of Buddha, each just a little different from the others. Worshipers are supposed to examine them and find the one that looks the most like themselves. That image is the god the person then worships. As I looked over that sea of brass Buddhas, I felt sad for people who have such a self-centered concept of God.

Later, I started hearing about the New Age. It reminded me that Japan doesn't have a monopoly on people who fashion gods after themselves. New Age is the ultimate in self-worship.

Listen to the words of New Age spokesperson Shirley MacLaine. Speaking to a group of New Agers at a seminar in Virginia Beach, she said, "As Jesus and Buddha have said, 'Be still and know that you are God.'" That is a horrible misquotation of our Savior, and a blatant misrepresentation of the Lord's call to "be still and know that I am God" (Psalm 46:10). It's the clear blasphemy that marks New Age thinking.

The more you investigate the philosophies of people around you, the more you will run into those who have swallowed this old lie of Satan. It's the same one he used on Eve—that we can be like God. Don't fall for it.

To guard yourself against such thinking study what the Bible says about God's identity. Look up passages such as Isaiah 45:5, John 14:6, Exodus 20, Romans 1. And get better acquainted with God through prayer.

Whether you are in a temple in Japan or a dorm in the United States, choosing your own god is futile.

—D.B.

Through preaching, teaching, and the Bible, God is telling me . . . _____

_____

Through nature and the lives of other believers, God is showing me . . . _____

_____

I will respond by . . . _____

_____

Hey, beautiful!

You don't have to stand in line at the grocery store very long to notice how important beauty is in our society. There before you in the racks are magazine after magazine with covers showing the most dazzling people you'd ever want to see. There's not an ugly person to be seen (except for the "Three-eyed Alien Creature [who] Lands Craft in Cleveland" who is on the front page of a tabloid).

But as important as beauty seems to be, we can't find any biblical basis for emphasizing it so much. You can search the Scriptures from cover to cover and never find that we are to value people primarily on the basis of how they look. Admittedly, the Bible recognizes handsomeness or beauty where it exists. People like Saul and David had a lot going for them socially. But God makes it clear that the real index of a person's worth does not lie in being good-looking, having a good head of hair and a trim body, or being on the best-dressed list.

Don't get me wrong. I'm not campaigning for ugliness. I don't see it as a virtue, nor beauty as a vice. But I am concerned about superficial values, including my own. I'm concerned about how prone I am to write off someone just because his or her face is unattractive. Or how easy it is to show partiality to someone who looks like a million. We all tend to respond to the skin-deep qualities.

But a person's real worth lies far beneath the surface. We don't have to be physically attractive to acknowledge God in all our ways (Proverbs 3:5–6). We don't have to have the face of a model to develop self-control, patience, and courage. And these are the things that make us beautiful in God's eyes.   —M.D.

Through preaching, teaching, and the Bible, God is telling me . . . _____

_____

_____

Through nature and the lives of other believers, God is showing me . . . _____

_____

_____

I will respond by . . . _____

_____

_____

The great salt debate

READ
2 Corinthians
2:14–17

MEDITATE
2 Corinthians 2:16
To the one we are the smell of death; to the other, the fragrance of life.

REFLECT
➡ One good thing about salt is . . .
➡ One bad thing about salt is . . .
➡ Why would some people find me "distasteful" as a Christian?
➡ How does that accurately reflect Christ living in me?

CONSIDER
Salt is always "in season."

Be honest now. Do you put salt on your food before you even taste it? Do you eat fast-food fries without even feeling bad about it?

Your doctor wouldn't be too happy with you. Salt has turned into a dietary enemy. That's why everything from saltine crackers to Alka-Seltzer now has a low-salt version.

NaCl is one of those Catch-22 items in our culture. Spread on slippery roads, it helps keep cars from skidding . . . but then it corrodes a car's paint job. Spread on meat, it keeps it from spoiling when there is no refrigeration . . . but then it causes high blood pressure in people who eat too much.

So when Jesus Christ said, "You are the salt of the earth" (Matthew 5:13), His statement was a two-edged sword. The good qualities of salt—preservation, seasoning—are balanced by some that are not too pleasing.

As Paul pointed out in 2 Corinthians 2, the Gospel also has a double-sided effect. To those who have trusted in Christ for their salvation, it is good news that prompts hope. To those who have not and are headed for God's judgment, Christianity is distasteful.

Christ Himself had that same effect on people. To some, He was the loving Savior whose forgiving words brought comfort and new life. But to others, He was a threatening figure they wanted out of the way badly enough to crucify Him.

As you grow in Christ, your life will take on a distinct flavor.

Some of your friends may find it pleasant; others may not like it.

Don't be discouraged; that will mean you are accurately representing Christ in your life!   —J.C.

Through preaching, teaching, and the Bible, God is telling me . . . _____

_____

Through nature and the lives of other believers, God is showing me . . . _____

_____

_____

I will respond by . . . _____

_____

Ya gotta have

The wrong channel

READ
Deuteronomy 18:9–22

MEDITATE
Isaiah 8:19
When men tell you to consult mediums . . . should not a people inquire of their God?

REFLECT
➡ What have I heard about channeling? Are my friends involved?
➡ Am I regularly reading the Bible and searching its pages for the answers I need about God and life?

CONSIDER
The only Spirit to guide us is the Holy Spirit.

Have you heard of "channeling"? No, it's not the annoying habit some people have of changing TV channels with the remote control every few minutes.

Channeling is more serious than that. It is a new way to describe an old practice—consulting spirits for information and guidance.

In channeling, a spiritual entity allegedly speaks (channels) his message through a human being. For example, J. Z. Knight of Yelma, Washington, supposedly channels a spirit named "Ramtha" who has attracted a large following, including many Hollywood biggies.

If spirits really are being contacted, is there anything wrong with it? Don't a lot of people claim to have been helped by the messages they've received? Yes. Aren't a number of otherwise sane people involved in this same stuff? Yes again. But be careful. It's a trap.

People involved in channeling are looking for answers to life's big questions of purpose, meaning, and fulfillment. And they are looking for spiritual experiences to fill a void in their lives. The problem is that they're looking in the wrong places—and getting the wrong answers.

These spirits are actually demonic deceivers who bait and hook people with some truth, then feed them lies. They consistently affirm pantheism (the teaching that all is God), and they reject what the Bible says about Jesus.

The Bible warns us about channeling (Deuteronomy 18:9–22; Isaiah 8:19–20), and tells us to stay away from people who follow the teaching of demons (1 Timothy 4:1).

We don't need channeling because the Bible gives us all the spiritual information we need. It has answers we can trust. And it points us to God and His truth. —K.D.

Through preaching, teaching, and the Bible, God is telling me . . . _____

_____

_____

Through nature and the lives of other believers, God is showing me . . . _____

_____

_____

I will respond by . . . _____

_____

A remarkable book

Ever wonder why we trust the Bible and not other "sacred" books? One reason is that only the Bible contains truths that have the power to produce a new birth.

When its truths are placed in the good soil of believing hearts, they produce spiritual fruit. The power of the Word transforms lives; those who were dead in their sins are made alive (Ephesians 2:4–5).

The Bible's uniqueness can be illustrated by what an old biology professor often told his students. He would hold a tiny brown seed in his hand and say, "I know precisely the composition of this little grain. It has in it nitrogen, hydrogen, and carbon. I know the exact proportions. I can make one that will look just like it. But if I plant my seed, nothing will happen. Its chemicals will simply be absorbed into the soil. If I plant the one God made, however, it will grow because it contains that mysterious element we call 'the life principle.'"

It's the Bible—not the Koran or Hindu scriptures—that contains this "life principle." Only the Bible has a divine origin: "All Scripture is God-breathed," Paul said in 2 Timothy 3:16. That's the reason he could tell his converts that what they held in their hands and hearts was the "word of life" (Philippians 2:16).

Mind if I ask you a very practical question? Has the living seed of God's Word taken root in your life and produced fruit? Do any of your friends and classmates know how important the "word of life" is to you? Take time today to think about the importance of the Bible in your Christian life. Then thank God for speaking to you in a way that you can understand.   —T.B.

Through preaching, teaching, and the Bible, God is telling me . . . _____

Through nature and the lives of other believers, God is showing me . . . _____

I will respond by . . . _____

Too busy

READ
Luke 5:12–26

MEDITATE
Luke 5:16
Jesus often withdrew to lonely places and prayed.

REFLECT
→ How is my prayer life? Am I satisfied with it? Why or why not?
→ Why is prayer important?
→ How can I keep from being too busy to pray?
→ What are several things I should be praying about?

CONSIDER
If you don't plan to pray, plan to fail.

I'm one of those people who would rather be "doing" than "planning" any day. My boss sometimes has to remind me that fifteen minutes of planning in the morning can make the rest of the workday that much more productive. He's right. When I plunge right into my work, things don't seem to go as well as when I sit down for a few minutes and plan my day.

This "planning vs. doing" battle applies where prayer is concerned too. Most Christians would rather "do" than "pray," even though the Bible reminds us of the importance of talking to God. Jesus Christ, during His three years of active ministry, would often retreat from a busy schedule of teaching, healing, and ministering, simply to pray.

History provides other examples. Martin Luther, the leader of the Reformation, reserved extra time for prayer when he was busy. "A wise man once said that he was too busy to be in a hurry; he meant that if he allowed himself to become hurried he could not do all that he had to do," wrote James L. Stalker in his book *Anthology of Jesus.*

So the question of prayer points back to you and me. Are we too busy to pray? The idea of talking to God on a one-to-one basis is such a privilege, but do we take advantage of it? Or do we use our God-given advantages as an excuse not to pray? Do we fail to pray because the job He gave us takes so much of our time? Do we neglect prayer because we spend too much time with a special friend He sent our way? Are we too busy preparing for service for the Lord to talk to Him?

If we're too busy to pray, we are definitely too busy!

—J.C.

Through preaching, teaching, and the Bible, God is telling me . . . _____

_____

_____

Through nature and the lives of other believers, God is showing me . . . _____

_____

_____

I will respond by . . . _____

_____

_____

Kan yu spel gud?

Americans can't spell very well. *The World Almanac and Book of Facts* reported that the Gallup polling agency tested people in Australia, Canada, the United Kingdom, and the United States. Guess who came in last. Americans. Asked to spell such common words as *magazine, sandwich, kerosene,* and *parallel,* Americans averaged 40 percent. Pretty embarrassing, isn't it?

But another kind of knowledge gap is even more distressing. It's in the area of Bible knowledge. A book by Jo Lewis and Gordon Palmer called *What Every Christian Should Know* gives some startling facts on how much Christian young people don't know. For instance, a Gallup poll revealed that one out of four churchgoing young people could not name one of the Ten Commandments. They also cited a sad-yet-funny story about biblical illiteracy. A student sent her teacher a card with the phrase "Thy word is a lamp unto my feet" on it. The student wrote a note explaining that the phrase was from a song by Amy Grant and Michael W. Smith. When the teacher mentioned that the words came from the Bible, the student was surprised. Yet there it is, in Psalm 119:105.

None of us will ever know everything we need to know about the Bible. But we need to have at least a working knowledge of its contents.

Don't wait till you're thirty to start learning. Start today. Begin a read-through-the-Bible program. (Four chapters a day will take you through it in a year, and you can take Sundays off.) Get some books that help explain what the Bible is all about. Buy a good study Bible. Ask your pastor for help. Don't get caught in the biblical knowledge gap.

—D.B.

Through preaching, teaching, and the Bible, God is telling me . . . _____

_____

Through nature and the lives of other believers, God is showing me . . . _____

_____

_____

I will respond by . . . _____

_____

_____

The phony phoner

READ
Matthew 7:15–20

MEDITATE
Matthew 7:15
"By their fruit you will recognize them."

REFLECT
➡ Do I know why I believe what I believe, or do I just take someone else's word for it? Am I vulnerable to error?

➡ Is my faith in Christ solid, or do I have some things I am questioning? How can I settle the issue?

CONSIDER
If something doesn't "ring true," it probably isn't.

Mmfftt! What's that sound? I know I should recognize it, but . . . Oh! It's the phone! But where is it? And what do I do with it?"

When the ringing phone woke me out of a sound sleep at 2:30 in the morning, I wasn't sure whether to pick up the receiver on the phone or hit the snooze button on my alarm.

"Hello," I said, sleep-talking. "Hello, Darrow, this is Dr. Balyo. How did you enjoy class today?" "Oh, fine, Dr. Balyo. I learned a lot." "Did you finish your assignment for tomorrow?" "Yes, I did." The conversation went on like this for about thirty seconds more. I had barely reached consciousness when the call was over and I was crawling back into bed.

The next day some of my friends asked me if I had gotten a call from Dr. Balyo during the night. Their laughter told me that I'd been had!

The call wasn't from Dr. Balyo at all. It was from a friend who imitated his voice.

Not being able to distinguish between real and phony cost me a little sleep and a lot of embarrassment.

There's something going on today in the world of "religion" that's much more dangerous than phony phone fun. The world is full of religious imitators who are trying to get us to believe "a different gospel—which is really no gospel at all" (Galatians 1:6–7).

That's why Christians need to know what's genuine and reject what isn't. "Watch out for false prophets. They come to you in sheep's clothing, but inwardly they are ferocious wolves. By their fruit you will recognize them" (Matthew 7:15). Whenever someone claims to represent God, check it out. Don't fall for a phony.   —D.P.

Through preaching, teaching, and the Bible, God is telling me . . . _____

_____

Through nature and the lives of other believers, God is showing me . . . _____

_____

I will respond by . . . _____

_____

The truth about lying

READ
Joshua 2:1–14

MEDITATE
Proverbs 12:19
Truthful lips endure forever, but a lying tongue lasts only a moment.

REFLECT
➡ When am I tempted to tell an outright lie or shade the truth a bit? Why?
➡ Have I told a lie recently? Do I need to go to the person I deceived and set the record straight?

CONSIDER
Tell the truth and trust God with the results.

Is it ever right to lie? That's a question ethics textbooks love to ask by citing rare cases in which truth seems to become less important than some other urgent need. As a student, you may be challenged to think about where truth fits on a scale of values. You'll struggle with situations in which you wonder if a lie might be the better choice.

Perhaps you've heard this example: If you had been living in Nazi Germany and you were hiding Jews in your home, what would you say to soldiers who pounded on the door? Would you lie to protect innocent lives?

That example sounds similar to the story we read in Joshua 2 today. Rahab hid some spies and then lied to the king's men who were looking for them. Did God like what she did?

God commended her faith (Hebrews 11:31), but He never commented on her lie. Rahab knew that God would give the Israelites the victory, and she welcomed the spies into her home. But even though she thought the lie was necessary, we have no evidence that God thought it was.

So where does that leave us? If we remember that our Lord is the God of truth (Psalm 31:5) and that Satan is the father of lies (John 8:44), we will realize the importance of always speaking the truth.

It is unlikely that you will ever face one of those cases in which a life depends on a lie, so you should be more concerned with being truthful to your friends, parents, roommates, and others. You'll have enough problems simply telling the truth without complicating things by lying and having to cover it up. Ask God to help you be a person of truth at all times. Even when a lie looks like a better option.   —K.D.

Through preaching, teaching, and the Bible, God is telling me . . . _____

_____

Through nature and the lives of other believers, God is showing me . . . _____

_____

_____

I will respond by . . . _____

_____

_____

This is reverence?

READ
Exodus 19:1–19

MEDITATE
Psalm 2:11
Serve the Lord with fear and rejoice with trembling.

REFLECT
➡ Do I treat God more like a buddy, a father, or a fearsome God?
➡ What impresses me most in today's passage about God?
➡ How can I develop more reverence toward God?

CONSIDER
True worship acknowledges God's "worthship."

Let's say you were honored with a personal, sixty-minute appointment with the main man, the President of the United States!

Would you show up in shorts and a tank top, plop your feet on his desk, and say, "What's up, Bill?" Or would you get decked out in your best clothes, walk respectfully into the room, speak when spoken to, and pretty much behave yourself?

So why do we treat our relationship with God so much more casually? People use His name in vain and we stand by silently. While other worshipers sing out in heartfelt praise, we're distracted by the ceiling fan. Our "appointments" with Him for prayer are ten-second wish lists.

God is our Father and He loves us, but He also is the Lord of the universe and Almighty God. He wants us to develop an intimate relationship with Him, but we must never forget the One we're relating to. Our attitude is to be one of reverence.

Reverence is a tough word to define. Gary Smalley said the fear of the Lord isn't the "AAH!" we scream at a horror movie. It's more the "aah" we whisper while gazing at something beautiful.

So how can you develop this reverence? Read the book of Exodus and notice the fire that rises from the top of a mountain, the violent earthquakes, the lightning and thunder. You serve the same God who made these things happen!

Balancing reverence with intimacy gives you that proper perspective. You'll be able to appreciate God for all He is: great enough to create a universe from nothing, but loving enough to seek a personal relationship with you. That's One who is worth worshiping!   —J.C.

Through preaching, teaching, and the Bible, God is telling me . . . _____

_____

Through nature and the lives of other believers, God is showing me . . . _____

_____

I will respond by . . . _____

_____

The biggest question

READ
Matthew 16:13–16

MEDITATE
Matthew 16:13
"Who do people say the Son of Man is?"

REFLECT

➧ What are some big questions I'll be facing in the next few weeks? At the end of the school year?

➧ What is my answer to life's most important question?

➧ Have I formulated answers to the important questions about my personal beliefs and morals?

CONSIDER
Life's most important question demands an answer.

It's crunch time in your English Lit. class. Because you want to major in English, you need a good grade. But you're on the bubble—if you do well on the exam you'll get an A; if you blow it, a C is a distinct possibility. The prof says that the last question will be an essay worth fifty points. If he asks the right question, you're okay. If not, you're in huge trouble. Right now it's looming as the most important question you've ever faced.

Life is full of gigantic questions: Where will I go to college? What should I major in? Should I study what I enjoy and am good at or what will offer the most job security when I graduate? How will I pay for college? Should I buy a car or not? Whom will I marry? What job should I take?

The answers often have important implications. But let's take it up a notch. Think about the question Jesus asked about Himself in today's Scripture. That's the most important of all. "Who do people say the Son of Man is?" A shining example? A great teacher? The Son of God and Savior of all?

Jesus was a good example for anyone to follow. He was a wise teacher. But here is the right answer to His question: "He is the Christ, the Son of the living God. He is my Savior and Lord." Can you honestly testify that you believe Jesus Christ is the Son of God and that He died for you? Have you said to Him, "I am a sinner. I know I cannot save myself. I believe You died to pay all the penalty for my sin, and I receive You as my Savior"? If so, you are forgiven of your sins and you are on your way to heaven.

If not, you need to say yes to Christ. That's the right answer to life's most important question. —D.E.

Through preaching, teaching, and the Bible, God is telling me . . . _____

_____

Through nature and the lives of other believers, God is showing me . . . _____

_____

I will respond by . . . _____

_____

Me? Do that?

READ
Hebrews 5:7–14

MEDITATE
2 Thessalonians 3:13
Never tire of doing what is right.

REFLECT

➡ Do I get involved in the Christian life or am I content to watch others live it?

➡ What "right things" do I get tired of doing? Why?

➡ What area could I start working on right now?

CONSIDER
Our place is on the frontlines, not the sidelines.

.

The Magnum. The Iron Wolf. Gemini. These are some of the most loved and feared theme park rides in the country. The adventurous flock to these rides. The more cautious act as spectators, choosing to watch others enjoy the experience. They have no intention of "getting involved."

But in some cases being a spectator can be more hazardous than being a participant? A New Jersey heart specialist, Dr. George Sheehan, using sports as an example, states that when you are a spectator rather than a participant, the wrong things go up, and the wrong things come down. Body weight, blood pressure, and heart rate go up. Flexibility, stamina, and strength go down. Yes, even at your age. Furthermore, Dr. Sheehan asks, "If the body goes, can the mind be far behind?" Maybe that's why you have a hard time concentrating in class!

Being a spectator in the arena of Christian living is a health hazard too. The wrong things go up, and the wrong things come down. Criticism, discouragement, and boredom go up. Sensitivity to sin, awareness of the needs of others, and desire for the Word of God go down. Sure, there's a certain amount of thrill and excitement in being a spectator, but there's nothing like the joy of being there yourself. Only by "constant use" can our spiritual senses be trained "to distinguish good from evil" (Hebrews 5:14). No, there's no substitute for personal experience—for sharing the Gospel with someone who doesn't know Christ, stepping out in faith and trusting God for something, using your God-given abilities to benefit someone else. These are the actions of a participant, not a spectator. Let's do it! —M.D.

Through preaching, teaching, and the Bible, God is telling me . . . _____

_____

Through nature and the lives of other believers, God is showing me . . . _____

_____

I will respond by . . . _____

_____

Think it over

Haggai 1:5–11

MEDITATE
Haggai 1:7
"Give careful thought to your ways."

REFLECT
➡ What area in my life needs "careful thought"?

➡ What do I see when I look honestly at how things are going with me?

➡ What mature Christian can I trust to help me see my life clearly?

➡ What can I do about my situation? What do I have to wait for God to do?

CONSIDER
Shallow thinking leads to shallow living.

If you've ever read the book of Haggai, raise your hand. Just as I thought. Nobody.

The pages of our Bibles are dog-eared and smudged in Philippians, John, and James, but they look brand-new in the general vicinity of Haggai. (It's in that part of the Bible called the minor prophets.)

Take four or five minutes (ten at the most) and read the thirty-eight verses of Haggai. You'll find one phrase repeated five times: "Give careful thought." The King James Version translates it: "Consider your ways."

The prophet was speaking for God to the Jews who had returned from Babylon. If he were writing today, he may have put it like this: "Think about it. You don't have enough to eat. Your clothing is threadbare. You are not prospering. The reason is that you have not obeyed Me. Now do what I said and rebuild the temple. Then you will experience My blessing."

Good advice! When life's a struggle, when it seems like you're in trouble all the time, the thing to do is to "give careful thought." Take time to evaluate why things are so difficult. You may need to change.

During one semester in college everything seemed to be going wrong. I got poorer grades than I ever had in my life. I was in trouble in the dorm. My job wasn't going well. My girlfriend broke up with me. Then the dean talked to me—gently, sincerely. I went back to my room and gave careful thought to the way I was living. I saw clearly that I had to be different. I got things right with the Lord.

How about you? In a slump? Struggling? The problem may be you. Take time to think it over! Then, with the help of Christ, do what has to be done. —D.E.

Through preaching, teaching, and the Bible, God is telling me . . . _____
_____
_____

Through nature and the lives of other believers, God is showing me . . . _____
_____
_____

I will respond by . . . _____
_____
_____

Unsafe sex

READ
1 Corinthians
6:12–20

MEDITATE
1 Corinthians 10:8
We should not commit sexual immorality.

REFLECT
→ What does it mean to me that my body is the "temple of the Holy Spirit"?
→ Why isn't my own power enough to conquer the desire to commit sexual sin?

CONSIDER
The best protection against unsafe sex is the word "no."

Life is full of contradictions. Like the people who diligently strap on their seat belts for safety today, then drive like there's no tomorrow. Maybe you're one of these deceived demolition-derby drivers. Before squealing out of the parking lot, you always buckle up.

Guess what. You're living under a false sense of security. A seat belt is no substitute for safe driving.

These days we're told that safe sex will protect us from sexually transmitted diseases. If we use proper protection, some say, we're safe sleeping with the partner of our choice. But this "protection" does not prevent the consequences of a dangerous practice. It doesn't stop the emotional, spiritual, and physical damage we do to ourselves. Sex outside of marriage violates God's holiness and, like all sin, invariably leads to death and destruction.

So how can we prevent sexual sin? The apostle Paul said, "Do you not know that your body is a temple of the Holy Spirit, who is in you, whom you have received from God? You are not your own; you were bought at a price. Therefore honor God with your body" (1 Corinthians 6:19–20).

That means God's Holy Spirit lives within you if you are a Christian—and to sin with your body is to bring shame to the place where God dwells. If you're thinking of having sex outside of marriage, stop and ask the Holy Spirit to help you keep from dishonoring God.

Don't play word games with your life. There is no such thing as safe sex outside of marriage. If you want protection, think about the Holy Spirit within. He will help keep you free of sexually transmitted diseases by keeping you free of sexual sin.   —T.F.

Through preaching, teaching, and the Bible, God is telling me . . . _____
_____
_____

Through nature and the lives of other believers, God is showing me . . . _____
_____
_____

I will respond by . . . _____
_____

Work on your offense!

MEDITATE
Mark 16:15
"Go into all the world."

REFLECT

➡ What does Ephesians 6:10–18 teach me about having an effective defense against Satan?

➡ How can I develop an offense that will help bring God the victory (Matthew 28:16–20)?

➡ In 1 Corinthians 9:24–27, what is Paul saying about competition, training, and winning?

CONSIDER
Let your lips as well as your life be a witness.

At a basketball game in Roxboro, North Carolina, Hillside High School took the opening tipoff and quickly scored two points. The other team, the Pearson High Rockets, then did something very odd. They decided to hang on to the ball and shoot only once at the end of each quarter. Hillside then went into a zone defense, allowing the Rockets to stall.

The only trouble was that the Rockets, who were effective in eating up the clock, missed their shots each of the four times they tried to score. They lost 2–0. Their game plan seemed good: control the ball, hold back, play it safe. But their strategy failed. They didn't get one hoop all night.

Many Christians follow a similar game plan; they do nothing but hold on to what they've got. They protect their faith, and they won't let anyone take it away.

But that's not the right strategy. In Jesus' assignment to the disciples, He made it clear that He didn't want them just to hang on. Notice that He didn't say, "Don't lose what I've given you." He told them to "preach the good news to all creation" (Mark 16:15). We shouldn't be satisfied to keep the enemy from scoring against us. We should be putting some points on the board ourselves.

With God's help, develop a strategy that includes both defense and offense. Defense: holy living and doctrinal purity. Offense: a willingness to tell others about the difference Jesus Christ has made in your life. Praise God! He has put you on the team so you can contribute to the ultimate victory!

—T.B.

Through preaching, teaching, and the Bible, God is telling me . . . _____

_____

Through nature and the lives of other believers, God is showing me . . . _____

_____

I will respond by . . . _____

_____

MARCH 21

Study the game plan

READ
James 1:22–27

MEDITATE
James 1:22
Do not merely listen to the word. . . . Do what it says.

REFLECT
→ How can I do what the Word says, instead of just hearing or reading it?
→ The next time I read a Bible principle that I should obey, I will write it down. And obey it.
→ What is God's "game plan" for my life?

CONSIDER
OBEY if you love Jesus.

For most pros, football is hardly a game. The four hours of "fun" on Sunday follow six days of hard work. The players practice many hours, repeating the same play over and over. They study complex game plans that fill thick notebooks. They watch films of opponents for hours.

Then some hot-shot quarterback strolls into camp and announces that he isn't going to practice, study game plans, or watch films. He's only going to show up on Sunday to play in the game.

How would his teammates respond? Well, he might want to think twice about stepping onto the field next week.

But isn't that our attitude about Bible study? We'd rather avoid the effort and rely on ourselves. But growing in Christ takes work. We have to study the Bible intently. Then we need to apply it to our lives. Application is the hard work that separates champions from talented people with unfulfilled potential.

Try this little test suggested by Becky Pippert in her book *Out of the Saltshaker and Into the World*. Next time you read your Bible, look for something you can obey. Maybe it will be a promise to believe, an order to carry out, or an example to follow. Whatever it is, decide that you will obey it.

Two things will happen. First, your faith in God will grow as you see His Word come alive in your life. Second, you will grow as a Christian, because maturity in Christ results from obedience.

Unless, of course, you don't want to put in the work. Maybe you would rather play the game of life on your abilities alone. If so, don't be surprised if you end up a loser. —J.C.

Through preaching, teaching, and the Bible, God is telling me . . . _____

Through nature and the lives of other believers, God is showing me . . . _____

I will respond by . . . _____

Help wanted

This ad ran in a number of Christian magazines:

Help Wanted

Volunteers willing to sell all they own and give proceeds to the poor, quit their job for full-time assignment, and leave home to work in other countries. Must be willing to postpone rewards until later. Possible loss of friendships and popularity. For more information see Matthew 19:21.

That challenging message points to an important truth—one we don't hear much about these days. The loving and kind invitation that Jesus gave to the people He asked to follow Him was never easy to accept. The rich young ruler, the fishermen who would become His disciples, and the tax collector were all asked to pay the high price.

If you are a Christian, you too must consider the cost. For example, to grow and prosper in your faith, you must learn, understand, and submit to the principles of Scripture. As one of Christ's disciples, you should maintain your relationship with Him by praying, studying His Word, fellowshiping with believers, and witnessing to your classmates. This will help sustain you when the pressure comes.

The apostle Paul reminds us of another cost. In 1 Corinthians 6:19–20 he wrote, "You are not your own; you were bought at a price." That price, of course, was the tormenting, agonizing death Jesus suffered so we would never have to pay the price of our own sin.

But what can we do in return for what He has done for us? Thank God we can answer Jesus' "help wanted" ad. It's the least we can do for the One who gave His all for us.   —T.B.

Through preaching, teaching, and the Bible, God is telling me . . . _____

_____

_____

Through nature and the lives of other believers, God is showing me . . . _____

_____

_____

I will respond by . . . _____

_____

_____

God or government?

READ
Romans 13:1–7

MEDITATE
Romans 13:1
The authorities that exist have been established by God.

REFLECT

➡ How can I show my support for the good things my government is doing?

➡ Would it honor God if I were to get involved in the political system on a local level?

➡ What is one issue about which I think my government has enacted legislation that does not honor God?

CONSIDER
A good Christian is a good citizen.

Did you ever wonder just how clean a returnable pop bottle has to be before the soft drink people can fill it up, cap it, and put it back on the shelf? Or have you pondered just what they do to meat before it gets to be a hot dog? And what about restaurants? How do you really know what goes into that vegetable soup? And by now you're probably wondering what any of this has to do with daily devotions.

Just this. The fact that we can drink soft drinks, buy red hots, and eat soup without worrying about getting ptomaine poisoning has a lot to do with Romans 13. Preserving the purity of our food system is just one of many valuable tasks done by a good government. But a government can enact health-promoting legislation and other essential services only if it has the support of the people. Therefore, Paul's request that people submit to governing authorities is vital to ensuring that a government can do the job it is ordained by God to do. And we should be thankful for the good work the government does.

But that brings to mind a follow-up question. Should we obey our government when it enacts legislation that goes contrary to God's moral code? Can we support the authorities when they protect us, yet resist them when they do something that clearly violates God's teaching?

Romans 13:3 seems to indicate that if a civil ruler oversteps proper authority we do have an option. We should obey God first and government second. So, while we are to thank God for and support the good our government does, we should also be aware that when God's standards are violated we have every right to push for change. —D.B.

Through preaching, teaching, and the Bible, God is telling me . . . _____

_____

Through nature and the lives of other believers, God is showing me . . . _____

_____

I will respond by . . . _____

_____

The worst trade

READ
1 Thessalonians
4:1–8

MEDITATE
1 Thessalonians 4:4
Each of you should learn to control his own body in a way that is holy.

REFLECT
➡ What influences make it hard for me to accept Paul's warning against sexual immorality? Are my friends a help or a hindrance in this matter?
➡ What would I lose if I were to have sex before marriage?

CONSIDER
Satan never makes an even trade.

How about making a couple of trades? I'll give you a 1978 rusted-out Mustang (top-speed 45 mph) in exchange for your high school diploma or college degree. (If you don't have it yet, I'll wait.) Or how about if I trade you my seven-can collection of vintage 1989 Coke cans for your baseball cards (or whatever else you collect)?

What? No takers? Well, congratulations. You have a lot more wisdom than a seven-year-old Toledo, Ohio, boy. He found a $100 bill at home and took off to spend it. But he didn't know what it was worth. All he knew was that he needed a quarter to buy a milkshake from the corner drugstore, so he talked a passerby into trading him a quarter for the seemingly worthless greenback. Nice trade, kid.

Here's one more trade possibility. But this one is a little different. It's a trade that you may have already been offered. One that is even more out of balance than the one the boy from Toledo made.

Yet it is a trade being grabbed up by young people every day. It is the offer of a few minutes of pleasure in exchange for your reputation, for your relationship with God, for a life of no regrets, for the full enjoyment of a pure relationship with the person you will marry, and possibly for your health. It's the offer of sex.

The apostle Paul knew it was a terrible trade. He commanded the Thessalonian believers to "avoid sexual immorality." He wanted them, in response to God's love and because of their relationship with Christ, to remain pure.

When you are offered this trade, don't fall for it. Guard your purity. It's worth keeping. —D.B.

Through preaching, teaching, and the Bible, God is telling me . . . _____
_____
_____

Through nature and the lives of other believers, God is showing me . . . _____
_____
_____

I will respond by . . . _____

I quit!

READ
Galatians 6:1–10

MEDITATE
Galatians 6:9
We will reap a harvest
if we do not give up.

REFLECT

➠ What am I tempted
to quit today?
School? My job?
One class with a
difficult prof? A
friendship that's
wearing me down?

➠ Why should I or
should I not quit in
each of the above
situations?

➠ What do the princi-
ples of God's Word
have to say about
what I should do?

CONSIDER
*To quit for the
right reasons is
hard work.*

It was one of my first jobs—groundskeeper for a motel in Florida.

After working there for several months, though, it seemed like my job title should have been Chief Weed Puller.

One day I decided that I had pulled enough weeds to last an entire lifetime. So I picked up the phone, called my boss, and told him that I quit, effective immediately. He offered to pay me more, but that wasn't the issue. (Although it did make me wish I had threatened to quit earlier!)

Then my dad found out what I had done. After his gentle lecture, I called my boss again and told him I was wrong to quit without notice and that I would work for him as long as he needed me.

That experience and many others since then have taught me a lot about quitting—whether it be a job,

school, or a relationship. Too often my desire to quit has been totally out of line. I'm tempted to quit for the wrong reasons.

Galatians 6 tells us about some occasions when it's wrong to quit. It tells us not to give up on a person who sins (v. 1), not to quit acting responsibly (vv. 1–5), not to quit supporting those who instruct us in the faith (v. 6), not to quit fighting the battle against sin (vv. 7–8), and not to quit doing good to people (vv. 9–10).

Is there something you are thinking about quitting today? Talk to God about it first. Make sure you're not just trying to avoid dealing with some hard issues. Honor the Lord by choosing to do what is right, not just what is easy.   —K.D.

Through preaching, teaching, and the Bible, God is telling me . . . _____

_____

_____

Through nature and the lives of other believers, God is showing me . . . _____

_____

_____

I will respond by . . . _____

_____

The dark heart mystery

READ
Jeremiah 17:5–9

READ
Jeremiah 17:5–9

MEDITATE
Jeremiah 17:9
"The heart is deceitful above all things and beyond cure."

REFLECT

➡ What do I think about the human condition? Are we basically good but tainted by our environment, or are we basically evil but offered hope of goodness by God?

➡ Is there some way I can write a paper in one of my classes that explores this question of the human condition?

CONSIDER
The problem of the heart is the heart of the problem.

The smoke-belching old steamer chugged its way downstream, parting the waters of the murky river that flowed through the dense African forest. Above the boat hung the overgrowth of tropical vegetation, shadowing the travelers as they journeyed into deepest Africa. The wary crew watched for signs of attack by ambushing warriors."

Joseph Conrad's haunting images, like the one above from *Heart of Darkness,* make him one of my favorite authors. Whether he was describing the mysterious yet strangely inviting isolation of "The Lagoon" or the sudden, mystifying appearance of a sailor's alter ego in *The Secret Sharer,* Conrad was a gripping storyteller.

One thing that makes *Heart of Darkness* great is that it explores a truth as old as life itself: the wickedness of the heart. Conrad peered into the human heart and found evil.

The basic human condition is evil. As the Lord said to Jeremiah, "The heart is deceitful above all things" (17:9). Yet, there is hope. "Blessed is the man who trusts in the Lord" (v. 7). That's the ultimate solution to the problem of a dark heart. Only those who put their trust in God can experience a goodness that can be called godliness.

Think about this: As wonderful as the books of Conrad, Golding, Faulkner, Twain, Dickens, and others may be in describing the human condition, they do no more than reveal what the Bible has already told us about it. That's why no matter how many other books we read, we must always go back to the Book—the one God gave us to tell us how to bring light to our own heart of darkness. —D.B.

Through preaching, teaching, and the Bible, God is telling me . . . _____

_____

Through nature and the lives of other believers, God is showing me . . . _____

_____

I will respond by . . . _____

_____

Hot items

MEDITATE
1 John 2:15
Do not love the world or anything in the world.

REFLECT
➡ What gives me more satisfaction: building my own little empire or helping God build His?

➡ Leading someone to Christ, serving in the church, modeling Christ in my home, school, and community—these are things that earn lasting rewards. Are these things really important to me?

CONSIDER
To be rich in God is better than to be rich in goods.

Bought a new car. Shiny red with a black top. Loved that car. Took good care of it. Didn't have it long. It burned up. No kidding. Actually burned up. And on Halloween night!

Seems that I parked on top of some leaves and the heat from the engine started the fire. As a result, I ended up with a really "hot" car. I got a replacement, but it was tan and shaped sort of like a football. Not exactly awesome.

Some years later, I got another new car. Well, it was really a used car, but it was new to me. This one was silver. And this time I watched out for smoking leaves. But soon the car began making some strange noises. I took it to the repair shop. Bad engine, they told me. I kept it for a while, but eventually it too gave up the ghost. Boy, for being so expensive, cars sure don't last very long.

The Bible says, "Do not love the world or anything in the world" (1 John 2:15). Loving "things" leads to idolatry, which means putting something ahead of God. In 2 Corinthians 4:18, the apostle Paul reminded us that the things of earth are temporary while the things of heaven are eternal. (And believe me, I know all about temporary.)

At this point in your life, you have a lot to look forward to. Owning a nice new car is probably one of them. But it's wise not to invest too much in or become too attached to earthly things. They don't last long. A much better investment is to "set your heart on things above" (Colossians 3:1). The things we store in heaven will never burn up, wear out, or become idols. —D.P.

Through preaching, teaching, and the Bible, God is telling me . . . _____

_____

Through nature and the lives of other believers, God is showing me . . . _____

_____

I will respond by . . . _____

_____

Listen to the music

READ
1 Samuel 16:14–23

MEDITATE
Psalm 33:3
Sing to him a new song.

REFLECT
➡ How can I test the theory that music affects my life whether I know it or not?

➡ Hearing a song like "Majesty" makes me want to . . .

➡ Hearing the theme song of my favorite TV show makes me want to . . .

CONSIDER
Get in tune with God before you choose your tunes.

It's time for the home version of "Who Said It?"—the game show that allows YOU to tell which person made an important statement.

Question 1: Who said, "Give me the making of the songs of a nation, and I care not who makes the laws." Was it (a) Paul McCartney, (b) Andrew Fletcher, (c) Michael Jackson?

The answer is (b), Andrew Fletcher. He was a seventeenth-century Scottish politician.

Question 2: Who said, "Find me someone who plays well and bring him to me." Was it (a) George Steinbrenner, (b) DeGarmo & Key, (c) Saul?

The answer is (c), Saul. When tormented by an evil spirit, he wanted someone to soothe him by playing the harp.

Question 3: Who said, "A number of people were exposed to a series of brief classical music excerpts that

moved from one mood to another. In every case the emotional response of the subject paralleled the spirit of the music." Was it (a) your mother, (b) a psychologist, (c) Ted Koppel?

The answer is (b), a psychologist. Research shows that music influences us whether we admit it or not.

Think about Fletcher's quote. What will be the result of a nation—or a church—whose people grow up listening to Madonna, 2 Live Crew, Prince? Think about Saul's request. When he wanted to get rid of an evil spirit that was tormenting him, he turned to music. It's ironic that people who turn to music today often invite in the spirit of evil.

Does the music you listen to help you sing to the Lord a new song?   —D.B.

Through preaching, teaching, and the Bible, God is telling me . . . _____
_____
_____

Through nature and the lives of other believers, God is showing me . . . _____
_____
_____

I will respond by . . . _____
_____

The right thing to do

READ
Philippians 2:1–4

MEDITATE
James 4:17
Anyone, then, who knows the good he ought to do and doesn't do it, sins.

REFLECT
➡ What three things has God made me aware of that could use my help? Who are three people I could do something for?
➡ How does Philippians 2 help me see my responsibility? What is my responsibility to others?

CONSIDER
Don't write people off, build them up.

An article in the *Chicago Tribune* told about a boy named Doug who learned that he had leukemia. The doctors were frank. Although there was a chance of remission, leukemia could be fatal, they told him.

On the day Douglas was admitted to the hospital, he looked around his room and said to his mother, "I thought you got flowers when you're in the hospital." An aunt called to order an arrangement. The salesclerk sounded young, and the aunt imagined someone inexperienced who wouldn't realize the arrangement's significance. "I want it to be especially attractive," she explained. "It's for my teenage nephew who has leukemia."

When the flowers arrived at the hospital, Douglas opened the envelope and read the card from his aunt. Then he saw another card. It said: "Douglas, I took your order. I work at the flower shop. I had leukemia when I was seven years old. I'm twenty-two now. Good luck. My heart goes out to you. Sincerely, Laura Bradley." For the first time since entering the hospital, Douglas was inspired.

"It's funny," concluded *Tribune* columnist Bob Greene. "Doug was in a hospital filled with millions of dollars of the most sophisticated medical equipment. He was being treated by expert doctors and nurses. But it was a salesclerk in a flower shop who, by taking time to care, gave Douglas hope and the will to carry on."

Do you know someone who is facing an uphill battle? Maybe it's a failure in an important class. Or a difficulty at home. Or a broken relationship. Like Laura Bradley, you can show that you care. Lift someone's spirit today.

—T.B.

Through preaching, teaching, and the Bible, God is telling me . . . _____

_____

_____

Through nature and the lives of other believers, God is showing me . . . _____

_____

_____

I will respond by . . . _____

_____

_____

A LOVING HEART

A cowardly Christian

READ
Joshua 1:1–16

MEDITATE
2 Timothy 1:7
God did not give us a spirit of timidity, but a spirit of power.

REFLECT

➡ Is there something in my life I don't want to face? Have I been putting it off because of fear?

➡ The Bible tells Christians that God will never leave nor forsake them. Do I really believe that?

CONSIDER
The reason people act cowardly is because they don't really believe God.

Sometimes I'm a lot like the Cowardly Lion in *The Wizard of Oz*. I lack courage. I know that the Bible says "God has not given us the spirit of timidity, but a spirit of power, of love and of self-discipline." But the fact is that I often find myself displaying spiritual cowardice rather than boldness. You want examples?

Instead of sharing my faith, I let witnessing opportunities go by (because I feel intimidated).

Instead of speaking out when someone is being unjustly criticized, I remain silent.

Instead of trusting the Lord completely, I worry a lot.

You wouldn't happen to have any of those problems, would you? Naah! Your roar reveals the heart of a spiritual lion, right? You've never sat around in the cafeteria and listened while the reputation of someone you know was

being seriously damaged. Sure, you felt funny about it, but you said nothing. What about that group of friends who don't know Christ? You've never held back from telling them the truth, have you? And you've never worried about a tuition payment coming due or a relationship going sour?

Let's remember God's encouragement. "Be strong and courageous . . . for the Lord your God will be with you" (Joshua 1:9). The Cowardly Lion found his courage when he recognized a cause and stood for something. We need to take a stand for Christ and trust Him to help us overcome our fears. "Stand firm in the faith; be men of courage; be strong" (1 Corinthians 16:13). Go ahead. Trust God. If there's something He's calling you to do, be brave! With Him by your side, you can do it! —D.P.

Through preaching, teaching, and the Bible, God is telling me . . . _____

_____

Through nature and the lives of other believers, God is showing me . . . _____

_____

I will respond by . . . _____

_____

Frail body; strong heart

MEDITATE
Psalm 41:3
The Lord will sustain him on his sickbed, and restore him from his bed of illness.

REFLECT

➡ Have I thanked God today for life and salvation?

➡ What has happened in my life that I wish the Lord would change but hasn't? Am I letting disappointment or bitterness touch my heart?

CONSIDER
What happens to us is not as important as what happens through us.

What makes Joni Eareckson Tada so special? It's more than her confinement in a wheelchair. It's more than her ability to draw fifty times better with her mouth than most of us draw with our hands. It's more than her talent for singing despite not having the use of muscles necessary to sing.

It's an attitude—a joy that comes from someone who has plunged to the depths of despair, has pleaded with God for restoration, and has found that even though physical healing will never come, God is sufficient. Because she never let her handicap touch her heart, she can touch our hearts.

This attitude is illustrated by a handicapped high school student. Although his crutches kept him from being physically active, he excelled in his studies and was popular with his classmates. For a long time nobody dared ask him why he couldn't use his legs. One day his closest friend finally asked. When the student explained the problem, his friend responded, "How do you keep from becoming bitter?" Tapping his chest, the young man replied, "I never let it touch my heart."

You probably don't think much about debilitating injuries. It could never happen to me, you say. But don't be too sure. For most of us, sickness—physical, mental, or emotional—crowds into our lives sooner or later. The Bible does not guarantee a life free from illness or disability. But it does tell us about spiritual strength.

If you are suffering from a long-term illness or injury, don't give in to bitterness, rebellion, or self-pity. When those emotions well up, be honest with God. Ask Him to protect you from letting those things touch your heart. —D.B.

Through preaching, teaching, and the Bible, God is telling me . . . _____

_____

Through nature and the lives of other believers, God is showing me . . . _____

_____

I will respond by . . . _____

_____

Fighting the foe

Pastor Tommy Barnett of Phoenix was tired of seeing pornographic literature at the barber shop and the grocery store. So he declared war on porn. And leading the way were the young people of his church. According to an article in the AFA Journal, the kids went to work trying to shut down adult bookstores and other immoral establishments.

They not only made their presence known at these places, they also passed out tracts and told the patrons about God's love. One young man handed out a tract and told the man he gave it to that Jesus loved him. The recipient thanked him by slugging him in the mouth. The young Christian picked himself up and replied, "Mister, Jesus still loves you!"

The story didn't end there. The slugger showed up at Pastor Barnett's church the next Wednesday and gave his life to the Lord. He couldn't shake the words of a dedicated young person: "Jesus still loves you."

Standing for what is right and true has always been dangerous. The apostle Paul was criticized, beaten up, and imprisoned. Jeremiah was made the laughingstock of Israel. Early Christians faced the lions. John Huss (1369–1415) and William Tyndale (1492–1536) were burned at the stake.

Your opportunities may not be as exciting and your results may not be as dramatic, but they will come. Maybe it will mean speaking up in class when a prof criticizes Christianity. Perhaps it will mean taking a stand against Christian friends who are planning a party that you know isn't right. It could even mean breaking off a romantic relationship before you do something you'll regret. Don't be afraid to fight the good fight.   —D.B.

Through preaching, teaching, and the Bible, God is telling me . . . _____

_____

_____

Through nature and the lives of other believers, God is showing me . . . _____

_____

_____

I will respond by . . . _____

_____

_____

Hangin' in there

READ
Psalm 84

MEDITATE
Psalm 84:12
O LORD Almighty, blessed is the man who trusts in you.

REFLECT
➡ The biggest burden facing me right now is . . .

➡ How can God make a difference in this situation?

➡ How does this keep me from getting too far down?

CONSIDER
The way to please God is to trust God.

In 1984, Paul Westphal's long, successful career in the NBA ended when he was cut by the Phoenix Suns. Although he was disappointed, Paul acknowledged that having been a pro athlete for so long kept him from facing the financial uncertainty other "un-employees" face when they lose their jobs.

"I don't want to pat myself on the back where there are a lot of factors in my favor," he said at the time. "It's easy to say you're living by faith when you have everything you want." (In case you're worried about what happened to Paul, he is now coaching for the Suns.)

Although we can't all share in Paul's financial security, we can all share his spiritual security. It comes from trusting God. When we trust Him, we can handle the tough times with confidence.

Another sports analogy can show how it works. Wise coaches try to keep their athletes on an even keel—never letting them get too high after a big win. Why? This keeps them from getting too low after a disappointing loss. The players concentrate on their ability and what they have learned from their coach, not their successes and failures.

Similarly, when we have confidence in God, we won't get carried away in the euphoria that comes from success. Nor will defeat pull us too low. Trusting in God gives life true stability.

What's dragging you down today? A low test grade? A tough loss in sports? Never enough money? Give today's passage a second look. Remember: Trusting in God will give you stability. And it will help you to hang in there when the going gets tough. —J.C.

Through preaching, teaching, and the Bible, God is telling me . . . _____

_____

Through nature and the lives of other believers, God is showing me . . . _____

_____

I will respond by . . . _____

_____

Bad case of butterflies

READ
Joshua 1:1–9

MEDITATE
Joshua 1:9

"Be strong and courageous. . . . God will be with you."

REFLECT

➡ What situations cause me to be fearful? Why?

➡ How has fear kept me from doing what I know I should?

➡ How has God helped me in the past when I trusted Him and did what was right? What good resulted?

CONSIDER
What God tells us to do, He gives us the power to do.

If anyone ever had a good reason to have a terminal case of the butterflies, it was Joshua. God told him that it was his job to take over where Moses left off as the leader of the Israelites (see Joshua 1). Suddenly, Joshua was in charge of more than a million nomads. And you know how hard it is to keep campers happy! It's enough to make anyone's stomach flutter.

Do the butterflies ever make you queasy and uneasy? Like before you have to give an oral report, perform as a musician or athlete, talk to someone about a date, interview for a job, begin a new semester, or take an exam? If so, then you know a little of how Joshua must have felt.

But he didn't have to face the challenge alone. Notice the encouraging things God promised to do for His leader. Things that could help anyone "be strong and courageous." God assured Joshua that no one would defeat him, that He would never leave him, and that He would go with him (v. 5). Yet it wasn't totally up to God. Joshua's part was to "obey all the law" and to meditate on the Book of the Law, God's Word (vv. 7–8).

What God said to Joshua emphasizes that His help comes to those who are on good terms with Him. And a big part of establishing that relationship with God is to get into the Bible. That's where we need to start in search for courage.

So, what does your day look like today? Are you fighting butterflies? Take a few minutes to review what God said to Joshua. Then trust Him. He can make you strong enough and courageous enough to do what is right—no matter what your stomach is telling you.

—K.D.

Through preaching, teaching, and the Bible, God is telling me . . . _____

_____

Through nature and the lives of other believers, God is showing me . . . _____

_____

I will respond by . . . _____

_____

When quitting is winning

READ
1 Timothy 4:7–16

MEDITATE
1 Timothy 4:8
Physical training is of some value, but godliness has value for all things.

REFLECT

➡ What activities crowd out time for prayer or church? Which of those activities could be cut back or eliminated to allow time for spiritual training and growth?

➡ What does the way I use my time say to others about what I believe is important?

CONSIDER
Quitters are winners when they quit for God's sake.

Bo Schembechler, the fiery head coach of the Michigan Wolverines for twenty years, learned early in his career that life is more than football.

In his first year at Michigan, he encouraged his staff to come up with a slogan to motivate the team. Above the locker room door the coaches put a sign that read: THOSE WHO STAY WILL BE CHAMPIONS. Later someone added, "And those who quit will be doctors, lawyers, and captains of industry."

Although quitting is often seen as a coward's escape hatch, quitters can sometimes be winners. Quitters become winners when they rearrange their priorities in life and stop spending too much time on things that have no eternal benefit.

The apostle Paul told Timothy that physical training has some value, but when compared with spiritual pursuits it was way down on his list of priorities. Godliness, though, has value "for both the present life and the life to come" (1 Timothy 4:8). That's why Paul told young Timothy to make his spiritual life a high priority.

Your efforts to read the Scripture today and even to read this article show that you are interested in developing your spiritual life. You're on the right track. But some days it's hard to know what activities to quit so you have time to "train yourself to be godly" (v. 7). School, work, family, recreation, and a social life fill your days. Is there still time for church, Bible reading, prayer, and trying to help others spiritually? Those are the real issues, the lasting matters of life.

Make choices that reflect a balanced view of life. Quit whatever blocks your spiritual progress. In God's record book you'll be a true champion!   —K.D.

Through preaching, teaching, and the Bible, God is telling me . . . ___

Through nature and the lives of other believers, God is showing me . . . ___

I will respond by . . . ___

Gossip section?

READ
Proverbs 11:9–13

MEDITATE
Leviticus 19:16
"Do not go about spreading slander."

REFLECT
➡ What is it about gossip that makes it enjoyable?
➡ How does it feel when someone spreads gossip about me?
➡ Why would I want to make someone else feel that way?
➡ When someone comes to me with gossip, what should I do?

CONSIDER
Gossips are full of hearsay. Everything they hear, they say.

A young man who worked as a busboy at a local restaurant told me that on Sunday the manager designates two extra non-smoking sections to accommodate the churchgoers who stop in after services. I was just starting to feel good about the good influence of the church people when the busboy added, "They may not smoke, but you ought to hear them gossip! They talk about the sermon, the pastor, the pastor's family, the people who were at church, the people who weren't, the pianist, everybody. If our restaurant had a non-gossip section, the church people couldn't sit in it."

Why do people gossip? Some may just want to stir up a little excitement. Others like the attention they get when they pass on "inside information" their friends don't know about. Some even use the old "prayer request" gimmick to spread their juicy tidbits. Others can't resist making themselves look good by making others look bad. And a few are simply malicious or are seeking revenge.

What's worse is that people who spread gossip—as well as those who eagerly listen—want to believe the bad stuff they hear about their brothers and sisters in Christ.

Proverbs 18:21 tells it straight: "The tongue has the power of life and death." You don't have to use poison to kill; you can do it with gossip.

What if restaurants actually did have nongossip sections? Would you and your friends be allowed to sit in it? Or do you need to ask the Holy Spirit to help you quit gossiping?   —D.E.

Through preaching, teaching, and the Bible, God is telling me . . . _____

_____

Through nature and the lives of other believers, God is showing me . . . _____

_____

I will respond by . . . _____

_____

Advantage of hard times

READ
Hebrews 4:14–5:10

MEDITATE
Hebrews 5:8
He learned obedience from what he suffered.

REFLECT
➡ How can hard times teach me obedience?

➡ What is the toughest thing I'm facing right now?

➡ How will obedience help me through it?

CONSIDER
Suffering teaches lessons we can't learn anywhere else.

I recently overheard the following exchange at Azusa Pacific University, where I work. Student (to friend): "Pray for me. I have a big exam tomorrow, and I haven't started studying yet." Friend (praying): "Lord, I pray that my friend will learn the value of hard work and discipline through this experience." Student: "Thanks a lot."

We know, of course, what that worried student meant. When we haven't studied as we should, we need all the divine intervention we can get. We see prayer as a possible shortcut. But the friend knew otherwise. In school, there is no substitute for hard work.

The same goes for obedience. It's a tough lesson, but we need to learn it. And just as there is no substitute for studying where school is concerned, there is no substitute for discipline where obedience is concerned.

According to Hebrews 5:8, Jesus learned obedience through suffering. The forty days He spent in the desert prepared Him for the deeper agony of dying on the cross. There was no other way to learn it.

In your life too you need to learn obedience. Going through hard times gives you that opportunity. How do you learn it? By hanging in there—by trusting God even when you feel like doubting.

A popular song at APU chapel services has these lyrics:

I'll obey and serve You.
I'll obey, because I love
    You.
I'll obey—
My life is in Your hands—
'Cause it's the way to
    prove my
love when feelings go away.
If it costs me everything,
I'll obey.

The person who wrote that song has obviously learned the lesson!   —J.C.

Through preaching, teaching, and the Bible, God is telling me . . . _____

_____

_____

Through nature and the lives of other believers, God is showing me . . . _____

_____

_____

I will respond by . . . _____

_____

_____

Up in flames!

MEDITATE
Psalm 32:8
I will instruct you and teach you in the way you should go.

REFLECT

➡ Sure, God talked to Abraham, Noah, and others, but how does God teach me in the way I should go?

➡ What part do these things have in God's guidance process for me: the Bible, friends, Christian books, prayer, parents?

CONSIDER
When you're looking for direction, look to God.

Okay, Future Teachers of America! What do you do with a stage full of grade school kids who are being rambunctious (and a little bit naughty) when they should be rehearsing for the all-important parents' night program? Well, Carol Pennington, music director and fourth grade teacher at Newark Christian School, hadn't been out of college too long, but she had a pretty good idea. She told them a story about how pros perform under pressure.

Miss Pennington was attending a performance of *Die Fledermaus* at the Metropolitan Opera in New York when the set behind the chorus caught fire. You've heard that "the show must go on." And it did. Not one performer turned around to watch the curtain and props being licked by tall, red flames, nor did they stop singing when NYC fire-fighters came on stage to

hose down the blaze. Instead, each professional focused on the director. And because the director saw that everything would be all right, the performers knew that in spite of the heat there was really nothing to get hot and bothered about.

That little story sure worked with those eager grade schoolers. And it made me think too. How many times do I take my eyes off the Director—even when things are going well. When the heat is on, how quickly I begin to worry. But how much better to keep my eyes on God, who said, "I will instruct you and teach you in the way you should go; I will counsel you and watch over you" (Psalm 32:8).

Make that your aim today! Forget the flames and focus on the Director's instructions.   —T.B.

Through preaching, teaching, and the Bible, God is telling me . . . NOT TO WORRY MYSELF, BUT TRUST IN GODS WISOM AND GUIDANCE. IF I LOOK TO HIM, HE WILL LEAD ME.

Through nature and the lives of other believers, God is showing me . . . THAT NOTHING CAN TAKE THE PLACE OF CHRISTIAN FELLOWSHIP AND IT IS A GIFT WE SHOULD VALUE

I will respond by . . . TREATING MY FRIENDS W/ LOVE, AND LOOKING TO GOD, AND SPENDING TIME IN PRAYER FOR WISDOM AND LET HIM SPEAK TO ME.

Quick! Get rid of it!

READ
1 Peter 2:1–3

MEDITATE
1 Peter 2:1
Therefore, rid your-selves of all malice and all deceit, hypocrisy, envy, and slander.

REFLECT
➡ In what ways do my words harm others?

➡ In what ways do my thoughts harm others?

➡ When I intentionally deceive or mislead someone, or covet what they have, or spread damaging information, how are others hurt? How am I hurt?

CONSIDER
If you think sin is right, your thinking is wrong.

When my son was a toddler, he was play-ing in the driveway alongside Grandpa's house. Spotting what he thought was a large gray ball stuck way back in the bushes, he went to get it. He tugged to get it out, but it wasn't a ball at all. It was a wasp's nest! Dean was attacked by hundreds of the angry critters, and his cries brought us all running. His clothes were full of wasps, so I ripped them off as fast as I could and threw them as far away as possible. We count-ed at least forty stings.

What I did with my son's clothes illustrates what Peter was calling for in 1 Peter 2:1. The words *rid yourselves* are not strong enough to describe what Peter really had in mind in dealing with the sins he named. In fact, the same word was used in another source from the same era to describe what a person would do if his long, flowing robes were to catch on fire. Frantically, he would rip them off and fling them as far away as he could.

This is a clear indication of what we are to do with the five deadly sins Peter named in this verse: malice (the intent to do harm), deceit (deliberately mislead-ing someone), hypocrisy (acting falsely), envy (feeling discontent because of what someone else has), and slan-der (hurting someone through lies and innuendo).

We are not to deal gently with these sins when they appear in our lives. We are not just to be "working on them." The moment we detect their presence, we need to ask the Lord to help us get rid of them. Each of these sins is terribly destruc-tive—to others and to our-selves. Like overalls full of wasps or a bathrobe on fire, we are to hurl them as far away as we can as quickly as possible! —D.E.

Through preaching, teaching, and the Bible, God is telling me . . . _____

Through nature and the lives of other believers, God is showing me . . . _____

I will respond by . . . _____

Really stretching it

READ
Genesis 1:20–26

MEDITATE
Revelation 4:11
"You created all things, and by your will they . . . have their being."

REFLECT
➡ Why is it important for me to stand up for creation? Why should I share my belief in the classroom?

➡ What difference does it make to me that God created all things?

CONSIDER
When God makes something, it works the first time.

Consider the giraffe. With its long neck, gangly legs, and spotted hide, the giraffe is one of nature's truly bizarre creatures. Some even say that giraffes prove that God has a sense of humor.

But, goofy appearance aside, the giraffe's stretched stature has a purpose. It lets it spot predators at a great distance. It also allows for serious chowing of nutritious leaves at the tops of trees. (Mmmm!)

Evolutionists would tell us that the giraffe we see today is the product of millions of years of mutations. (Remember learning this in Science 101?) They would say he adapted to his environment by growing tall and thin.

But there are serious problems with that theory. A giraffe's heart is not strong enough to pump blood all the way up his long neck. And he would faint if blood didn't reach his brain. Amazingly, there are valves

in his neck that assist the flow. And when he lowers his head, these "assist valves" stop the flow of blood so he doesn't blow his brains out getting a drink of water.

The evolutionist's mutation explanation cannot work with the giraffe. The giraffe's neck would have required countless mutations. But even that wouldn't work—all of the parts had to be in place the first time. No room for trial and error. This is a classic example of God's creation—everything in perfect form at first appearance.

The Bible tells us that God created the earth and everything on it. Scripture references from Genesis to Revelation proclaim this fact. Stand firm in your belief that creation is true. And look for evidence to support your belief—like the complex neck of the giraffe. Evolution and other deviations from creation only stretch the truth.

—T.F.

Through preaching, teaching, and the Bible, God is telling me . . . _____

Through nature and the lives of other believers, God is showing me . . . _____

I will respond by . . . _____

APRIL 10

Give it some time

READ
Psalm 90:1–12

MEDITATE
Ephesians 5:16
[Make] the most of every opportunity.

REFLECT

➡ What do I do that has no eternal value? Can I replace it with something that does? What? If not, how can my attitude about it make a difference for eternity?

➡ What has God's Spirit prodded me to do that I have not yet obeyed?

➡ What does it mean to "be very careful" how I live? (Ephesians 5:15).

CONSIDER
You can't kill time without injuring eternity.

Intellectual and moral considerations aside, what difference does it make if you spend a whole day watching "I Love Lucy," "Leave It to Beaver," and "Andy Griffith" reruns? Or if you spend five times more hours in the dorm lounge than you do in the library? Or if you make a habit of skipping your eight o'clock English class because you just can't go to sleep until after David Letterman? In other words, what difference does it make how you use your time?

While studying in Italy, I visited one of the great cathedrals in Milan. It has a beautiful triple-door entrance, and all three portals are crowned by splendid arches. Each arch is artistically carved with a thought-provoking inscription. Over one, etched in stone, is a wreath of roses with the words: *All which pleases is but for a moment.* Over another is sculpted the outline of a cross accompanied by this engraving: *All which troubles is but for a moment.* On the largest doorway—the great central entrance to the main sanctuary—is chiseled the most impressive thought of all: *That only is important which is eternal.*

Perhaps you are familiar with the verse, "Only one life, 'twill soon be past; only what's done for Christ will last." But have you ever pondered the significance of those words?

This is a weighty matter, so set aside some time to think about it. What you do next may have consequences not only now but throughout eternity. The next time you are deciding what to do, ask God to help you choose wisely, "making the most of every opportunity."

—T.B.

Through preaching, teaching, and the Bible, God is telling me . . . _____

Through nature and the lives of other believers, God is showing me . . . _____

I will respond by . . . _____

A SOUND MIND

Still guilty

READ
Jeremiah 3:11–15

MEDITATE
Proverbs 28:13
He who conceals his sins does not prosper.

REFLECT
- What temptation am I unable to get out of my mind?
- Which friend should I ask to pray for me?

CONSIDER
Why cover up what repentance can clear up?

Forty years. Seems like an eternity, doesn't it? Forty years ago Harry Truman was president (that's eight presidents ago). It was before space travel. Before Alaska and Hawaii were states.

How would you like to have a guilty conscience for forty years? A man from Washington State did. But after four decades of hauling around his guilt, he decided he couldn't drag it another day. So, after waking up more than 14,000 mornings with the undeniable, unrelenting knowledge that he had embezzled several thousand dollars, he confessed. When he was brought to trial, he told the judge, "After living with this thing hanging over my head for forty some years, it got heavier and heavier until I just couldn't stand it any longer."

The judge showed mercy. "Criminal charges are not warranted in this case," he said, as the old man, now hard of hearing, strained to catch his words.

So here you are with more than forty years ahead of you. Every day you are faced with choices about honesty, sexual purity, truth, kindness, and integrity.

You have two options. If you haven't already fallen into some serious sin, you can ask the Lord to help you stay clean.

If you have already done some things you regret, turn yourself over to the Lord. Don't try hiding your sin. Confess it to God. Ask His forgiveness. Then enjoy the freedom of a guilt-free conscience. You don't want to wake up some morning in the year 2030 still trying to cover up a forty-year-old problem.

—D.B.

Through preaching, teaching, and the Bible, God is telling me . . . _____

_____

Through nature and the lives of other believers, God is showing me . . . _____

_____

I will respond by . . . _____

_____

Truth and love

READ
Ephesians 4:1–16

MEDITATE
Ephesians 4:15
Speaking the truth in love, we will in all things grow up into him.

REFLECT
➡ Which do I lean toward: truth or love?
➡ How have I used the truth to hurt others. How would love have made a difference?

CONSIDER
When the truth hurts, cushion it with love.

Finish each of these pairs: salt and _____; Romeo and _____; Cagney and _____. Certain pairs are so inseparable that we can't think of one without thinking of the other.

Now try this pair: truth and love. You don't see them together too often, do you? They don't go together in practice very often either. It seems that when we speak the truth, we use it as a weapon. What God intends to be used as encouragement, we use to attack those who don't agree with us.

One of the members of our youth group designed a T-shirt that featured a skull and crossbones with the ominous message, "Repent or die." He intended the design to be an alternative to those heavy metal rock band insignias. But a lot of the kids took offense at the message's violence, even though it was doctrinally true.

That's why God reminds us to speak the truth in love. If we put these two concepts together we can achieve a dynamic balance. Truth without love hurts people. And the opposite, love without truth, also hurts, though in a subtle, slow-acting way. But truth with love changes people.

Churches have split and Christians have turned against each other in the name of truth. Just remember: Love of *seeking* the truth must not be separated from love in *speaking* the truth.

The next time a controversy erupts and someone threatens to hold others hostage to the truth, ask God to help you soften the truth with love.   —J.C.

Through preaching, teaching, and the Bible, God is telling me . . . _____
_____

Through nature and the lives of other believers, God is showing me . . . _____
_____

I will respond by . . . _____
_____

For sale: happiness

MEDITATE
Proverbs 3:13
Blessed is the man who finds wisdom.

REFLECT
➡ Am I happy? How can I tell?
➡ What do I think would make me happier? A date with the right person? Good grades? A better roommate?
➡ What part does my mind play in my happiness?
➡ What does the Bible say is the difference between blessed and happy?

CONSIDER
Happiness depends on whom you have—not what you have.

Now it's official. You can buy happiness. It says so right here on an envelope that landed on my desk this morning. I haven't opened it yet because I thought you might like to be on hand when I reach inside.

Okay, I've opened the envelope, and it does have something inside. A letter introducing me to an introduction service. If I were single (which I'm not), I could buy happiness by sending these folks a check and letting them pick out a date for me.

Things sure have changed. When I was in college, I could just walk up to a girl and ask her out. There weren't any middlepeople I had to pay to do the job for me. If happiness is found in being introduced to the right person, I guess happiness was free back then.

But wait! Maybe they're right—at least partly. Look at Proverbs 3:13. Blessed (or

happy) is the person who finds wisdom. And wisdom is personified as a woman. I wonder how many computers would crash if I asked for a date with wisdom.

Wisdom isn't really a person, however. By referring to it with feminine pronouns the author is using a literary device known as personification (ask your English prof).

So what then is this wisdom that Solomon speaks of as the source of blessedness? It is an acknowledgment of God's control and intervention in our lives. Verse 11 tells us to learn from the Lord's discipline and to listen to His rebukes. If we have the wisdom it takes to put our trust in God, we'll enjoy the pleasant ways and peace (v. 17) that He alone can give.

Can we really buy happiness? Of course not. But it does come from having a relationship with the right person: God.   —D.B.

Through preaching, teaching, and the Bible, God is telling me . . . _____
_____
_____

Through nature and the lives of other believers, God is showing me . . . _____
_____
_____

I will respond by . . . _____
_____
_____

The truth about Jesus

READ
John 5:17–30

MEDITATE
John 5:18
He was even calling God his own Father.

REFLECT

➠ What new things did I learn about Jesus today from John 5:17–30? Do I believe He is telling the truth?

➠ How well do I really know Jesus? What keeps me from knowing Him better?

CONSIDER
Do you know what the Bible says about Jesus?

If you wanted to find out the truth about Tom Cruise, where would you look? Would you read the *National Enquirer* and the *Star*? Of course not! You might find a lot of juicy tidbits, but not much that you could trust as true.

Would you watch one of his movies? Not much help either. Tom would be speaking as an actor. Nothing he said would be true about Tom Cruise the person.

To find out about Tom Cruise, you would need to spend time with him. As he talked, you would listen and observe to see if what he said matched what he did. If so, you would know that he was an honest person and that you could trust what he said about himself.

That's the route to follow in finding out about Jesus Christ: To find out the truth about Him, see what He says about Himself. For instance, today's Bible reading tells us a lot about Jesus. He is the source of eternal life (v. 21); He is in charge of all judgment (v. 22); He is deserving of the same honor people give God (v. 23).

These are bold claims. The Jews understood quite clearly what Jesus was saying; that's why they wanted to kill Him. After all, if Jesus wasn't God (and they were sure He wasn't), He deserved death because He was committing the terrible sin of blasphemy.

Spend some time in the four gospels: Matthew, Mark, Luke, and John. Notice what Jesus says about Himself. God wants us to become more like His Son (Romans 8:29). But to do that, we need to discover the truth about Jesus. —J.C.

Through preaching, teaching, and the Bible, God is telling me . . . _____

Through nature and the lives of other believers, God is showing me . . . _____

I will respond by . . . _____

Going down the tube

READ
Psalm 1

MEDITATE
Psalm 1:1
Blessed is the man who does not walk in the counsel of the wicked.

REFLECT
➡ What does Psalm 1 say I can do to make my life more prosperous in the right sense?

➡ If I were a parent, what programs would I not want my children to watch? Is it okay for me to watch them?

CONSIDER
Don't just watch the screen, screen what you watch.

What kind of a TV watcher are you? A channel flipper who wears out the remote control? Someone who checks out the TV listings in the paper first so you know what you're getting into? Or a Zombie-watcher who doesn't care what's on— you just plop down in front of the tube and stare?

Regardless of what type you are, there's something you should think about the next time you head for the TV lounge for an electronic study break.

Media analyst Kenneth Curtis, who has studied television for a decade, says that the virtually omnipresent, flickering screen underscores what is important, and what behavior and attitudes are desirable. In other words, the people who put together the TV programs you watch are conditioning you to think the way they think. That's a scary thought when you consider that Roseanne is one of the top-rated programs in America. Can you imagine millions of people thinking the way she does?

TV networks are not committed to biblical, Christian values. (Big revelation, right?) So if you are committed to following the Bible, you'll be receiving conflicting signals from television. And remember, the TV people are experts at influencing opinion, so don't think it won't affect you.

Television's excessive violence, emphasis on immoral sex, and glamorization of materialism can quickly distort our thinking.

Psalm 1:1 makes it clear that our counsel must not come from the ungodly. Think about that the next time you think about sitting down tubeside.   —M.D.

Through preaching, teaching, and the Bible, God is telling me . . . _____

_____

Through nature and the lives of other believers, God is showing me . . . _____

_____

I will respond by . . . _____

_____

The year of the cat

READ
James 1:12–18

MEDITATE
Proverbs 11:6
The unfaithful are trapped by evil desires.

REFLECT
➡ What temptations do I entertain rather than kick out of my mind?

➡ What is my plan for being less hospitable to sinful ideas and more so to holy ones?

CONSIDER
Sins once enjoyed are the most dangerous.

Just when a Soviet citizen thought his canaries were safe, there came the return of PAWS. Vladimir Dontsov had sent his pet cat, Murka, 400 miles away because she ate two of his little feathered friends. But the catty creature stayed only two days at her new home before she embarked on a long cat walk. One year later, she showed up at Donstov's fourth floor apartment with an injured ear and a mangled tail. This might sound like a pur-r-r-fect ending, but the faithful feline was expecting a litter of mini-Murkas. Now her master's problems were compounded. Not only had his canary-eating cat returned, she had brought along kitten reinforcements. Donstov learned a valuable lesson. You can't solve a problem by sending it away.

We do the same thing with sinful desires when we try to ignore them or push them out of our thoughts.

According to the New Testament, "each one is tempted when, by his own evil desire, he is dragged away and enticed" (James 1:14). We need to replace evil desires with wholesome thoughts. That's the only real solution to this stubborn problem. If we don't, James informs us, our evil desires will lead to sin and death.

Don't just chase your sinful desires away or they'll soon be scratching at your door again.   —T.F.

Through preaching, teaching, and the Bible, God is telling me . . . _____

_____

Through nature and the lives of other believers, God is showing me . . . _____

_____

I will respond by . . . _____

_____

Just do it!

MEDITATE
1 Timothy 4:12
Don't let anyone look down on you because you are young, but set an example for the believers.

REFLECT
➡ What are my reasons for not serving God?
➡ Are they valid reasons, or are most of them excuses?
➡ What are some of the things I fear when I don't do what I know I should? How can I give these fears to God and JUST DO IT for Him?

CONSIDER
Christianity is not a spectator sport.

Last year some of my favorite commercials came from Nike. They featured Bo Jackson, pro baseball and football player, competing in various other sports like running, cycling, and even hockey. (With Wayne Gretzky looking on stammering, "No . . . no.") I speculated how far they would take this concept. Would they show Bo deftly batting a birdie over a badminton net? Or maybe Bo performing a pile-driver to defeat Hulk Hogan?

Fortunately, they didn't. Each commercial ended with this simple slogan flashed on the screen, "Just do it!" In other words, don't just sit there and make a list of excuses as to why you can't participate. Get up and get into the game!

That's not bad advice, especially when we apply it to our spiritual lives. Because we're young, it's easy to hide behind the idea that we're not experienced enough to walk close to God or do great things for Him. We run out of fingers counting the reasons we're not ready to tell others about our faith or to be an inspiration to someone who is discouraged.

Wrong! A dedicated Christian can be a blessing no matter what his or her age may be. For example, read about Daniel and his friends in Daniel 1. Yes, they were young. But they were committed to God, and He gave them wisdom and understanding beyond their years.

Daniel's example makes us aware that it's wrong to sit back and leave the participating to others.

It's time to start pursuing God, growing in spiritual things, and setting a good example. So c'mon, JUST DO IT! —T.F.

Through preaching, teaching, and the Bible, God is telling me . . . _____

_____

Through nature and the lives of other believers, God is showing me . . . _____

_____

I will respond by . . . _____

_____

Price is right

READ
Colossians 3:15–23

MEDITATE
Colossians 3:17
And whatever you do . . . do it all in the name of the Lord Jesus.

REFLECT
➡ What pressures will I face in the next few days? In what ways can I glorify God in these circumstances?

➡ If I had a million dollars, would it be harder or easier to live for God?

➡ How do my words and actions reflect my desire to honor the Lord?

CONSIDER
Go for the glory—God's glory.

If you were a million-dollar-a-year professional basketball player, how would you spend your Saturday nights? Spinning Christian records and talking about Jesus on a small AM radio station? That's what Mark Price of the Cleveland Cavaliers did last season.

One evening, according to an article by Bob Dyer in the *Akron Beacon Journal*, Price was asked to answer this question: "How do you cope with the pressure you're under all the time?"

Now, the pressure Mark Price is under is different from what you face. While he has the burden of playing well enough to earn his megabucks, you may be trying to figure out how to scrape together enough minibucks to stay in school. While Mark has to guide his teammates through a tough 88-game schedule as the floor leader, you have to get along with your roommates for a couple hundred days. And while Mark has the pressure of living by God's moral standards on the road in the NBA, you have to try to live by those same standards as you mix with people who want you to live like the devil. (Some of your pressures are just like his, aren't they?)

So how does Mark Price survive? Here's what he told his radio audience: "I don't go out to try to please other people. I have a purpose for playing, and that's to honor and glorify God. If I go out and give the very best I can, then I don't have to worry about the outcome because I can look at myself in the mirror and say that I gave it my very best. I know that's all God has asked of me."

When NBA star Mark Price goes for God's glory, he can handle the pressure. And when our goal is to do "all in the name of the Lord Jesus," we can too.   —D.B.

Through preaching, teaching, and the Bible, God is telling me . . . _____

_____

_____

Through nature and the lives of other believers, God is showing me . . . _____

_____

_____

I will respond by . . . _____

_____

_____

Don't let it stop you

MEDITATE
2 Corinthians 4:7
We have this treasure in jars of clay.

REFLECT

➡ What Bible characters are good examples of overcoming obstacles? Joseph? Paul?

➡ Who do I know that I can look to as good examples of how to overcome obstacles?

➡ What obstacles do I face? A handicap? Bad home background? What can I do to overcome the limitations in my life?

CONSIDER
Trying times are times of trying.

I've never been one to read Ann Landers. And the thought of writing to Abigail Van Buren (Ann's sister) would never enter my mind. But I did run across a Dear Abby answer not long ago that made a lot of sense. She was illustrating the human capacity for overcoming obstacles. Abby wrote:

"Cripple a man, and you have a Sir Walter Scott.

"Bury him in the snows of Valley Forge, and you have a George Washington.

"Afflict him with asthma as a child, and you have a Theodore Roosevelt.

"Give him bad legs as a kid and you have an O.J. Simpson.

"Deny her the ability to see, hear, or speak, and you have a Helen Keller."

I'm sure you get the point. We are "jars of clay." Our bodies are weak. But we don't have to let a handicap or hardship stop us.

There are also several examples in the Bible. You can probably think of some. I have Moses in mind. Remember what happened when God called him in the burning bush episode? Moses responded with a whole grocery list of obstacles. "I'm not eloquent. I stutter. No one will listen to me. Nobody back in Egypt will ever believe that You sent me to help them get back to Canaan." But God wouldn't let Moses say no. He helped him, and Moses became Israel's greatest leader.

Do you have a limitation? A handicap? Don't let it keep you from reaching your potential. In the strength of God, and following the examples of others, don't let it stop you. For "Jesus' sake" (2 Corinthians 4:11) and to show God's "all-surpassing power" (v. 7), be an overcomer.   —D.E.

Through preaching, teaching, and the Bible, God is telling me . . . _____

_____

_____

Through nature and the lives of other believers, God is showing me . . . _____

_____

_____

I will respond by . . . _____

_____

Honestly now!

READ
Genesis 43:1–12

MEDITATE
Genesis 43:12
"You must return the silver."

REFLECT

➡ How honest am I in situations where I could gain more by being dishonest?

➡ What motivates me to be honest?

➡ How does my life indicate that I believe God sees everything I do?

➡ How can I be more honest with my friends, parents, employers, teachers?

CONSIDER
Some think they're honest because they've never been caught stealing.

How much money would it take to test your honesty? Is a fifty-cent undercharge important enough to mess with? Or are we honest only when somebody else knows about it?

Roger Young and William Taylor answered those questions with their actions.

Roger was a janitor in Charleston, West Virginia. One day he found a billfold on the shelf in a phone booth. He returned it to its owner at once, not realizing that it contained a thousand dollars. When he learned this, he said, "It wouldn't matter if it was one dollar or one million, I couldn't keep it." Now that's an honest man!

A similar incident took place in Washington, D.C., when William found a purse on the floor of his taxicab. Looking inside, he saw a lot of money, so he immediately turned it over to the police. They found nearly forty-two thousand dollars in cash, traveler's checks, and jewelry. The purse belonged to the wife of a retired General Motors executive.

Although both Young and Taylor received substantial rewards, that did not motivate their actions. They were simply being honest!

The statement by Jacob in Genesis 43, "You must return the silver," is remarkable. Years before, Jacob had thought nothing of stealing his brother's birthright by taking advantage of him in a moment of weakness. Later, he deceived his blind old father and cheated his brother out of the paternal blessing. But in Genesis 43 we see him instructing his sons to return some silver that did not belong to them. I like to think that his walk with God and growth in grace had made him truthful.

Can the same be said of us? Has our relationship to Christ made us totally honest?
—T.B.

Through preaching, teaching, and the Bible, God is telling me . . . _____

_____

_____

Through nature and the lives of other believers, God is showing me . . . _____

_____

_____

I will respond by . . . _____

_____

_____

Too bad?

READ
Psalm 130

MEDITATE
Psalm 130:4
But with you there is forgiveness.

REFLECT
➡ Who do I know that everyone has given up on? How can I help that person find God's forgiveness?
➡ What can I do to show the person that God cares, and that He is willing to forgive?

CONSIDER
Forgiveness is Christianity in action.

They gossip about Linda. She's an unwed mother. She's into drugs. She has attempted suicide. Her friends have no respect for her. Linda has no respect for herself.

Some ridicule her. "I've heard she comes from a good Christian family—but she's gone bad." Linda feels she deserves this label. "Christianity is for good people," she says. "But I'm anything but good." In her view, she's done too many things wrong. She feels God has given up on her. And she keeps plodding down the road to self-destruction.

She wants to get off that road. She desperately wants to change—to be accepted—to be loved. But that just doesn't seem possible. So she shakes off those feelings, pulls her protective shell back over her, and keeps going. Where she's headed, no one knows for sure. They're afraid to look.

People like Linda are all around us. They've given up on God. They're sure He wouldn't forgive them anyway. So they never ask. After all, who needs more rejection?

If only they would realize that God's heart aches for them! That He longs to release them from their self-imposed prison! Because of Jesus, they can know God's complete forgiveness. Freed from their bad habits and destructive way of life, they can have a future that is bright with promise. But they don't know. They just don't know.

God yearns to wrap His arms around every troubled and sinful person. But sometimes they need someone like you or me to look past what everyone else sees and see what God sees. They need a brave Christian who will turn them around and point them toward God's forgiveness.   —D.P.

Through preaching, teaching, and the Bible, God is telling me . . . _____

Through nature and the lives of other believers, God is showing me . . . _____

I will respond by . . . _____

The buddy system

READ
Hebrews 10:19–25

MEDITATE
Hebrews 10:24
And let us consider how we may spur one another on toward love and good deeds.

REFLECT
➡ Do I pride myself in being a lone ranger? Is that the biblical way to go?
➡ Two improvements I would like to make in my life are _____ and _____.

Who can I get to help me with these things?

CONSIDER
The best ability is accountability.

A few years ago, I got out of shape physically. Additional weight was making me into the kind of "bigger man" I didn't want to be. I knew I needed regular exercise to keep my mind clear and body healthy. But every time I started a new exercise program, I would soon quit. (Sound familiar?) My good intentions kept falling apart until a friend suggested that several of us at work begin running during our lunch break. We agreed to try it.

It worked! If I had run alone, I would have given up a hundred times for a hundred different reasons. Instead, my co-workers and I covered hundreds of miles. We could do it because we encouraged each other.

We got into shape. Our minds were clearer. Our stamina was up. Our waistlines were down. Things went so well that I even ran in a 25K race (and finished it).

That's what can happen when people band together to encourage each other to do something difficult. In the New Testament, we read that the early Christians worked together. By doing so, they were able to go further and rise higher in their Christian growth.

Do you need that kind of encouragement in your spiritual life? If you want to begin a daily time of prayer and Bible reading but you keep getting sidetracked, why not enlist a couple of Christian friends to do it with you. You'll "spur one another on." Or maybe you see a need at your school. Get a group of kids together to do something about it. Or is a fellow student lonely? Can you and your friends reach out to him or her?

Many things can't be tackled alone. So why not do what the early Christians did—work together. Then give God the glory.   —M.D.

Through preaching, teaching, and the Bible, God is telling me . . . _____
_____
_____

Through nature and the lives of other believers, God is showing me . . . _____
_____
_____

I will respond by . . . _____
_____

Is death the answer?

READ
Matthew 27:1–10

MEDITATE
Exodus 20:13
You shall not murder.

REFLECT
➠ Is there anything in my life that makes me think suicide is the only answer? What is it?

➠ Why is suicide never the best way to solve problems?

➠ Why is it important to talk about my feelings with a person who knows Christ?

➠ What would I say to someone who is considering suicide?

CONSIDER
The answers for life are found in Christ.

Raymond Belknap, 18, and James Vance, 20, made a suicide pact after drinking beer, smoking marijuana, and listening to British rock band Judas Priest's album *Stained Glass*. Raymond succeeded in his suicide attempt, but James blew away the lower portion of his face with a shotgun and lived for three painful years before dying of complications.

Lawyers for the two families claim that a subliminal message to "do it," or to commit suicide, exists in the band's song "Beyond the Realms of Death." Family members are convinced that the lyrics led James to conclude, as he told an investigator, that "the answer for life was death."

Whether or not the lyrics influenced these two young men no one will ever know. But when people thinking about suicide listen to rock music's message that they are worthless, that stress is too great, and that death will end their problems, they are in danger.

There is so much these young listeners never think about. For instance, what about facing God (Romans 13:9; 2 Corinthians 5:10)? And what about those left behind?

We may face situations that seem beyond our ability to cope. But with Christ we have the ability to deal with even the most severe situations (Ephesians 1:18–21; Philippians 4:19). The Lord will give us a way out of every type of temptation we face (1 Corinthians 10:13).

So when you hear musical messages to "end it all," concentrate on the truths about God's value on life. Remember the resources we have in the Lord Jesus. Reach out to someone you trust, someone who can help you see that you honor God best by living. For Him.   —K.D.

Through preaching, teaching, and the Bible, God is telling me . . . _____

_____

Through nature and the lives of other believers, God is showing me . . . _____

_____

I will respond by . . . _____

_____

What're you there for?

"Most church services start at eleven o'clock sharp and end at twelve noon dull," said Vance Havner, a Southern evangelist. Sunday mornings can seem pretty boring. But let's not put all the blame on the pastor. Church is not a spectator sport. If you think church means sitting in a pew and staring straight ahead through hymns, announcements, solos, offerings, and sermons, then of course you're bored.

Church is much more than that. The apostle Paul knew there was value in getting God's people together. He gave two reasons for looking forward to seeing his friends in Rome—two things you can look forward to in church:

1. Mutual encouragement. Paul couldn't wait to get to Rome, because when he and his Roman friends shared their spiritual gifts, both would be encouraged.

Paul, a dynamic Christian, found the company of his brothers and sisters in Christ very refreshing. And if he needed it, shouldn't you?

2. Spiritual harvest. Paul was also looking forward to a harvest among them (v. 13). He knew he would encounter people who were searching and would respond to the Gospel.

Sometimes, where evangelism is concerned, we miss the obvious. We think evangelism means bothering people who have no interest in Christianity. But people still turn up in church because they are searching. You can help them.

If your church seems dull, stop staring straight ahead! Start looking around you. You'll find, as Paul did, that people are what makes it an interesting place to serve and worship God! —J.C.

Through preaching, teaching, and the Bible, God is telling me . . . _____
_____
Through nature and the lives of other believers, God is showing me . . . _____
_____
I will respond by . . . _____
_____

Why kids drink

A25IL

READ
Proverbs 23:19–21

MEDITATE
Proverbs 23:20
Do not join those who drink too much wine.

REFLECT
→ What reasons do people give for drinking?
→ What reasons do people give for not drinking?
→ Which reasons fit better with what the Bible says?
→ How would it show more courage and confidence not to drink?

CONSIDER
A good reason not to drink is that you lose good reason when you drink.

Vanessa was a sophomore in high school. She and her two best friends had been drinking beer once in a while. Now they were getting ready for a big party. Some guys were going to be there they really wanted to impress.

Vanessa and her friends were afraid they wouldn't be accepted. "What we need is something to calm us down," she told her friends. "A drink will help us relax and be more fun to be with." But the only alcohol in the house was a bottle of scotch in her parents' cupboard. So they mixed it with some Pepsi and drank it. Within an hour Vanessa was in Intensive Care having her stomach pumped. She had consumed enough alcohol to make her pass out and stop her heart. Only quick action by the paramedics saved her life.

Vanessa thought a few ounces of alcohol would compensate for her lack of self-confidence and feelings of inadequacy. She had seen her parents mask their fear and pain with booze, so she tried to do the same.

There are other reasons kids drink: pressure from their friends, curiosity, influence of TV ads, and the lack of personal values.

Drinking is terribly dangerous, especially for young people. Instead of being a reduced-price ticket to self-confidence, it is a temporary and terribly dissatisfying escape from the pain and anxiety of life. It's the way of fear, not fortitude.

When we're honest, we see that the things we expect to get from drinking are the very things available to us through Jesus Christ.
—D.E.

Through preaching, teaching, and the Bible, God is telling me . . . ___

Through nature and the lives of other believers, God is showing me . . . ___

I will respond by . . . ___

A LOVING HEART

"I love you"

READ
Psalm 116

MEDITATE
Psalm 116:1
I love the Lord, for He heard my voice.

REFLECT
➡ How do I feel when someone says, "I love you"?
➡ What reasons do I have for telling God I love Him?

CONSIDER
If you love God, tell Him!

The sweetest words in the English language are "I love you." It's nice to hear Mom say it when you call home. And of course it is the "phrase most waited for" when you find that special person in your life.

"I love you" sounds nicest when it is a spontaneous, unrehearsed, voluntary expression of the heart. That's the long way of saying it means the most when someone says it because they want to, not because they have to.

Think about your relationship with God. When was the last time you told Him you love Him? And not because you were singing a Michael Card song and those happened to be the lyrics, or because your Bible study leader assigned you to write a paragraph on "Why I Love God." When was the last time your heart was so filled with love for the Lord that you said it to Him like you would say it to your boyfriend or girlfriend?

Although God is spirit (John 4:24), He is also a person with all the attributes of personality—including emotions. He can be angry (Exodus 32:11), grieved (Ephesians 4:30), and joyful (Zephaniah 3:17). And the love He feels for us is a deep, faithful love. It's a love that can see past all of our sins and forgive us. It's a love that sent His only Son to die for us.

You can respond to His love, both quietly and aloud. And just as we like to hear people tell us they love us, God likes to hear His children tell Him they love Him.

When was the last time you told God you loved Him? How about right now!
—J.C.

Through preaching, teaching, and the Bible, God is telling me . . . _____
_____
_____

Through nature and the lives of other believers, God is showing me . . . _____
_____
_____

I will respond by . . . _____
_____
_____

Synonym for happiness

Imagine that you're working a crossword puzzle and you come across the following clue:

Three-letter word for happiness, gladness, exhilaration of spirit.

What's the answer?

It's JOY—something we all like to experience. But where does it come from? What causes us to feel joy?

A DePaul University student told me that loving someone else is what brings joy into her life. Here's the way she put it. "Just thinking about it makes my heart beat faster. It's reaching a point when you realize that your own life might not necessarily be important. It's when you know that the other person is more important than you are."

I think she's hit on something. What she's talking about is selflessness, and it follows the thrust of Philippians 2:3. "In humility, consider others better than yourself." Paul told the Philippian people that if they did what he suggested, his joy would be complete. We can conclude that this kind of behavior would also give them joy—and us too, when we begin to consider others above ourselves.

If you want to experience joy, learn to love—selflessly.

If you like crossword puzzles, you probably like acrostics too. Here's one that can help you remember the formula for finding joy.

Jesus "Remain in My love" (John 15:10).

Others "Love each other" (John 15:12).

You "As the Father has loved Me, so have I loved you" (John 15:9).

That DePaul University student was right. Loving others brings us joy. Especially when we put Christ and others first.

—D.P.

Through preaching, teaching, and the Bible, God is telling me . . . _____

_____

Through nature and the lives of other believers, God is showing me . . . _____

_____

I will respond by . . . _____

_____

Safe terror

READ
Psalm 91

MEDITATE
Psalm 91:5
You will not fear the
terror of night.

REFLECT
➡ What scares me
about serving God?
Do I believe God
will help me over-
come those fears?
➡ Whom do I know
that has done
some scary things
in God's service?
What effect did it
have on that per-
son?

CONSIDER
*You are safer
with God in a
jungle than
without Him at
home.*

I only did it because my daughter talked me into it. She didn't want to go alone, and I didn't want to go at all. But you know how dads are. So we stood in line for over an hour for the opportunity to be terrorized by the Magnum, the tallest roller coaster in the world. Two hundred and five feet off the face of the planet. "On a clear day you can see Canada," posters promised. Not with your eyes shut, you can't.

We reached the front of the line, got on board, and hung on as the cars chugged to the top. Then suddenly we were hurtling over the precipice at seventy-five miles an hour. The death-defying ride tossed us and twisted us and took our breath away for the next two and a half minutes. We roared through dark tunnels and jerked around ninety-degree turns as the world screamed past and our lives flashed before our eyes.

When the final heart-pounding dive was over, we were thrilled to be alive.

It's funny, isn't it, how we'll do scary things as long as we know we won't actually get hurt. Yet we get scared away by things that seem frightening even though they shouldn't be.

Like missionary work. We're afraid to give ourselves to God because He might send us someplace where they have snakes. Or don't have malls.

Rachel Saint, a missionary in Ecuador for more than thirty years, knew she was going to a place where people might kill her (as they had her brother). Yet she went because she felt safe in God's hands.

Yes, there might be danger ahead if we do what God wants us to do. But we are safer doing that than anything else in the world. With God's loving care, those dangers are safe terrors. —D.B.

Through preaching, teaching, and the Bible, God is telling me . . . _____

_____

Through nature and the lives of other believers, God is showing me . . . _____

_____

I will respond by . . . _____

_____

"My buddy got saved!"

READ
John 1:43–51

MEDITATE
John 1:45
Philip found Nathanael and told him.

REFLECT
➡ In terms of importance, how do I rank these things: clothes, sports, job, car, studies, dating, having a friend trust Christ.

➡ Who was the last unsaved friend I invited to camp, youth group, church, or a Christian concert?

➡ Do I have any friends who are not Christians? Should I?

CONSIDER
Introduce your friends to your best Friend.

At age sixteen, Matt McCollum of Indianapolis, was 6'6" tall and an excellent basketball player. He could also hit a softball a mile. I know. I saw him do it. It was the staff-versus-campers softball game, and I was playing rover for the staff. The staff usually wins these games by 15 or 20 runs. But not this week. Not with Matt, Andy, Nathan, and their teammates. Especially Matt. The staff went out to a big lead. Then Matt went to work. He hit a home run. Then a double and a triple. Then another homer. The staff's lead dwindled until it was only five runs in the seventh inning. Matt came up with the bases loaded and hit another home run. The ball landed in the middle of the woods that most guys were just trying to reach!

Matt had become a Christian a year earlier at a camp in Ohio. He talked about his high school and his church. This year he had brought some of his high school teammates to camp with him, including Andy.

When I asked him what the highlight of the week had been for him, I thought he would mention his blacktop basketball game, his big home run, or the stirring youth messages.

I was wrong. Pointing to Andy, he said, "My buddy on my basketball team at school got saved Monday night. That's the best part!"

Sports are important. Athletic achievements can mean a lot. It's nice to be able to say, "I hit three homers in one game." Or "I scored thirty points in basketball." But you've got the right perspective when, like Matt McCollum, the most important thing of all is Christ. And it's a bonus when you can say with rejoicing, "My buddy got saved!"   —D.E.

Through preaching, teaching, and the Bible, God is telling me . . . _____

_____

_____

Through nature and the lives of other believers, God is showing me . . . _____

_____

_____

I will respond by . . . _____

_____

A rough way to go

READ
Hebrews 12:1–11

MEDITATE
Hebrews 12:11
No discipline seems pleasant at the time.

REFLECT
➡ How do I react to the nicks and scrapes I receive?

➡ What kinds of experiences have I had in the past week that could be used to "rough me up" so I can sprout?

➡ Is it easier for me to point out the lessons others should learn than to see my own?

CONSIDER
Suffering isn't cruel, it's corrective.

Some kinds of seeds need to be roughed up before they can grow up. Seeds of certain desert bushes are covered with hard shells that keep water out. They can lie dormant on the sand for several seasons, but when heavy rains finally come, the little seeds are carried away in flash floods and bashed against sand, gravel, and rocks. If they are deposited where the soil is damp, moisture is absorbed through the nicks and scratches they suffered during their rough ride through the flood waters. Only then do they begin to sprout and grow.

Christians can be like those stubborn little seeds. We have tough hides that need to be bruised and skinned before we can grow. The Lord does not allow His children to suffer needlessly, but sometimes we need to be scraped against difficulties before we start to absorb the Living Water and begin to grow into mature believers.

A stack of unpaid bills, a disappointing relationship, a balky car, or an instructor who makes unreasonable demands can help to change us from seeds that are languishing in the desert into beautiful, fruit-bearing trees. It's not easy to think of our problems as opportunities for the Lord to prod us to spiritual growth. It's no fun to have our ego nicked, our patience tested, or our motives challenged. But when we feel the discipline of our loving Father, we know our faith is beginning to sprout and grow. —M.D.

Through preaching, teaching, and the Bible, God is telling me . . . _____

_____

_____

Through nature and the lives of other believers, God is showing me . . . _____

_____

I will respond by . . . _____

_____

_____

Ya gotta have

The trouble with towers

READ
Genesis 11:1–9

MEDITATE
Genesis 11:4

"Let us build ourselves . . . a tower that reaches to the heavens, so that we may make a name for ourselves."

REFLECT

➡ What towers in my life need to be bulldozed?

➡ What values do I have that contradict the Lord's claims on my life?

➡ How can I guard against the drive to achieve personal acclaim, wealth, and prominence?

CONSIDER
Getting down on your knees is better than getting up in the world.

Maybe he had always been a daredevil—the kind of kid who swam out beyond the buoy or drove too fast. But one escapade was certainly "tops." The young acrobat climbed up the steel and glass surface of the world's tallest building: Chicago's 110-story Sears Tower. It took him seven and a half hours carrying fifty pounds of climbing equipment and battling forty-mile-an-hour winds. When he reached the top, he got a warm reception—the police! His reward? Criminal charges, including citations for disorderly conduct, trespassing, and property damage. He had made a name for himself, but he also placed it on the police records of the Windy City.

The tower of Babel was built by a group of people who wanted to make a name for themselves. In a warped effort at civic pride, they constructed a magnificent tower to symbolize their unity and opposition to God. But God was waiting at the top. He saw their competitive, aggressive natures, and He stopped them cold by dispersing them all over the world, confusing their language, and thwarting their self-serving ambitions.

It's human nature to want to make our names and our faces and our deeds prominent. We are easily drawn into the fast lane of academic or business success and social status. Yet God tells us clearly that none of those things are to take His place in our lives. Ambition is something we must yield to the Lord. When He molds and shapes our abilities and talents to His plans, we are free to climb the ladders He provides, confident that what awaits us at the top is a reward for faithful service.

—M.D.

Through preaching, teaching, and the Bible, God is telling me . . . _____

_____

Through nature and the lives of other believers, God is showing me . . . _____

_____

I will respond by . . . _____

_____

Missing the mark

READ
1 John 4:7–12

MEDITATE
Romans 3:25
God presented him as a sacrifice of atonement.

REFLECT

➡ Have I prayed to receive Christ as my Savior?

➡ Am I trying to pay the cost of my sin? Do I realize that Christ has done everything necessary for me to be forgiven by God?

➡ How can I let go of the guilt I've been holding on to for so long?

CONSIDER
If we could pay for salvation, Jesus wouldn't have died to pay for it.

"Mischief, thou art afoot; take what course thou wilt." As you literary types know, that statement was made by Marc Antony in *Julius Caesar*. But a few years ago I would have thought it was what Ben's parents (neighbors of mine) said every time they sent their rambunctious little guy out to play. With Ben, you never knew what to expect.

One day while Ben was playing in our backyard, the inevitable happened. CRASH! The unmistakable sound of breaking glass! Ben had tossed a baseball and missed his target—but not our window.

Knowing that Ben couldn't possibly pay for the damage he had done, I offered to pay for the window for him. Disbelief covered his face. You would have thought someone had just given him tickets to Disney World.

It was a great opportunity to tell Ben that he could be forgiven by God and go to heaven if he would do what he had done with me—accept someone else's payment for his wrong. So that day, Ben prayed to receive Christ as his Savior.

We are all like Ben. We've blown it. We've missed the mark. In the classroom, at home, on a date, we've messed things up pretty badly. As a result, something was broken—our relationship with God. And no matter how hard we try, we can never pay for the damage we've done. But Romans 3:25 says that "God presented [Christ] as a sacrifice of atonement." He paid the penalty for our sins by His death on the cross. Salvation is not a matter of what we can do for ourselves but what Christ has done for us. We need only follow Ben's example and accept God's payment for our sins. —D.P.

Through preaching, teaching, and the Bible, God is telling me . . . _____

_____

Through nature and the lives of other believers, God is showing me . . . _____

_____

I will respond by . . . _____

_____

Second thoughts

READ
Matthew 14:22–33

MEDITATE
Matthew 14:30
But when he saw the wind, he was afraid.

REFLECT
➡ What kinds of things cause me to have second thoughts about following the Lord Jesus?

➡ Is there something I know I should be doing for Christ that I've stopped doing because of second thoughts? How can I get started again?

CONSIDER
Believe your beliefs and doubt your doubts.

Sandy had answered the call of Christ to enter missionary service, so she enrolled in Bible school. But halfway through her sophomore year she began to have second thoughts. She was doing well in her courses, but she wondered if she was doing the right thing. Guys with no interest in missions wanted to date her. She began to see that missionary work would be really difficult. And she started to think about the things she would have to do without if she left the United States. Sandy wondered if it truly was the voice of God she had responded to as a junior in high school.

Sandy's not the only follower of Christ to have second thoughts. Peter did too. He was out in a boat on the Sea of Galilee and a huge storm was raging. Suddenly Jesus appeared, walking on the water. He commanded, "Don't be afraid!" Then to Peter He said, "Come" (v. 29). Peter stepped out of the boat and began walking across the water, just like Jesus. But the powerful wind and high waves made him doubt. The next thing he knew, he was sinking.

When Peter left the boat to follow Jesus, he never saw the wind or waves. And when Sandy first told the Lord she would be a missionary, she didn't think about the obstacles. But later she had second thoughts. Jesus rescued Peter. And Sandy, after several weeks of struggle, recommitted her life to Christ and went on to become an effective missionary in Kenya.

Now that you understand more of what it means to follow Jesus, are you having doubts? Ask the Holy Spirit to renew and direct you. Wrestle it through. Then, as you find and do the will of God, He'll take care of your second thoughts.   —D.E.

Through preaching, teaching, and the Bible, God is telling me . . . _____

_____

_____

Through nature and the lives of other believers, God is showing me . . . _____

_____

_____

I will respond by . . . _____

MA4Y

READ
1 Corinthians
9:24–27

MEDITATE
1 Corinthians 9:26
I do not run like a man
running aimlessly.

REFLECT
➡ How am I doing?
What is my spiritual strategy?
➡ What steps should I take to correct my plan? What habits or friends or situations should I change?

CONSIDER
Not planning to win means planning to fail.

Do you know people who seem to have everything going for them yet still don't quite have it all together? I read about a champion boxer like that. He was young; he was strong; he was a power hitter; he held a world title. But not for long. Although he knew how to hit, he hadn't quite mastered the art of avoiding getting hit. Besides, he couldn't control his personal life—too many late nights, too many broken training rules, too much junk food. No one who knew him was surprised when he lost his title. He had great potential but no plan.

We can be just like that boxer. We make a commitment to Christ, and for a while we bask in the glow of a fresh and vibrant faith. We feel like champions for Him. But we don't have a plan to keep the tempter away, and we soon find ourselves discouraged and defeated. Bible study and prayer get nudged out of our schedules. We give little time to building relationships with the Christian friends who were so important when we first came to know the Lord. We set ourselves up for a big downfall.

What we need is a plan for battling Satan. Through careful attention to the instruction of Scripture, involvement in church, fellowship with other believers, and a consistent prayer life, we can stay in shape spiritually and avoid Satan's attacks. Without that kind of strategy, we'll waste our time "running aimlessly."

Our relationship with the Lord is like all the other relationships in life—it grows and develops only as we spend time getting to know Him and finding out what He wants to do in our lives. Guard that friendship like a treasure. It's the key to a truly successful life. —M.D.

Through preaching, teaching, and the Bible, God is telling me . . . _____

_____

_____

Through nature and the lives of other believers, God is showing me . . . _____

_____

_____

I will respond by . . . _____

_____

_____

READ
Matthew 18:1–4

MEDITATE
Matthew 18:3
"Unless you change and become like little children, you will never enter the kingdom of heaven."

REFLECT
➦ Am I sure that I have been forgiven of my sin? Why?

➦ Have I expressed childlike trust in Christ?

➦ Am I continuing to live in humble faith?

CONSIDER
To become God's child, you must have childlike trust.

When the number two high-gain antenna on the $1.5 billion Hubble Space Telescope jammed during startup operations, one NASA engineer began acting like a little kid. He ran out to the store and bought two boxes of Tinkertoys, a lamp cord, some glue, and a roll of masking tape. Then he built a model of the telescope. Using the Tinkertoys, engineers were able to visualize how an inch-thick electrical cable was interfering with the movement of the dish-shaped antenna. (I bet they didn't teach them how to do *that* in college!)

David Skillman, the grown man who built the Tinkertoy model, commented, "The moral of the story is that there is no solution that's too humble."

But some people don't like simple solutions—like the one Jesus offered to restore our communication with God. It seems too easy for many. So they look elsewhere. Some religions even have complex systems for earning God's approval. But such systems are about as good as doing twenty extra-credit projects to compensate for getting F's on all your exams—painful, frustrating, and impossible.

Jesus' answer contrasts sharply with the solutions world religions offer. For instance, He said we need to become like children. We have to stop thinking of the solution as being so complicated that we have to figure it out or so demanding that we have to work to earn it.

The only solution is childlike trust in God. We need to be humble enough to accept His simple plan of salvation. Jesus died in our place on the cross and offers forgiveness and new spiritual life to all who will trust Him.

Like the Tinkertoy solution, it may seem simple. But it works!　　—K.D.

Through preaching, teaching, and the Bible, God is telling me . . . _____

_____

_____

Through nature and the lives of other believers, God is showing me . . . _____

_____

_____

I will respond by . . . _____

_____

_____

READ
John 11:1–26

MEDITATE
John 5:24
"Whoever hears my word and believes him who sent me has eternal life."

REFLECT
➡ Am I like the "fool" in Luke 12? Am I prepared for death? Do I know for sure where I am going when I die?

➡ Have I received Christ as my Savior? Am I living for Him? Do I want to live—or die— out of fellowship with my Lord?

CONSIDER
Living without God means dying without hope.

It was a tragedy of the worst kind. Eighty-seven people died in a nightclub fire in New York City. Most were young people about your age. While fire officials searched for a cause, grieving families searched for a way to deal with the nightmare. As it turned out, the fire was no accident. It was arson. And the motive? Revenge. An angry man wanted to get back at his girlfriend, so he set fire to Happy Land. Happy Land. What an ironic name! Eighty-seven people looking for the time of their life, found instead their time to die.

Death is something we'd rather not think about. There's so much life to live. Friends, family, graduation, careers, marriage, having children, having fun—these things are about life, not death. But death can't be ignored. Hebrews 9:27 tells us that we are all destined to die. And it would be a mistake to be so busy living that we don't plan for dying. "You fool! This very night your life will be demanded from you" (Luke 12:20). Jesus said this to a man who planned well for life but not at all for the life after.

I know, this is tough stuff, serious stuff. But don't turn away. Don't close the book and find something else to do. Not yet. Stop and think about it. Better yet, think about what Jesus said. "He who believes in me will live, even though he dies; and whoever lives and believes in me will never die" (John 11:25–26).

You are not prepared for death until you receive life through Jesus. "Whoever believes in the Son has eternal life" (John 3:36).

Think it over. It's a matter of life and death.　　—D.P.

Through preaching, teaching, and the Bible, God is telling me . . . _____

_____

_____

Through nature and the lives of other believers, God is showing me . . . _____

_____

_____

I will respond by . . . _____

_____

_____

Momentary madness

MEDITATE
Proverbs 14:29
A quick-tempered man displays folly.

REFLECT

➡ What damage might I cause by spouting off? Can I afford it? How will I repair it?

➡ "A man's wisdom gives him patience; it is to his glory to overlook an offense" (Proverbs 19:11). What does that verse mean to me?

➡ Does it suggest any changes I need to make in the way I react to things?

CONSIDER
Got a temper? Keep it!

If you don't control your passion, it will control you." Now, is that a true statement or what?

I saw this demonstrated in the life of a young student named Beckie. She's normally an even-tempered person. Unlike most of us, she doesn't have to put on the facade of being composed. That's just the way she is—cool, calm, and collected.

Except for one day. The day everything seemed to bother her, especially her nine-year-old brother. As usual, he was wired for activity and pranks. And on this day, when she was trying to study for exams, he was especially mischievous. What he did to set her off, I'm not sure. But Beckie exploded. She screamed at him, jumped up, spun around, and . . . THUD!

You know how comedians kick a door with their foot to make it sound as if they've walked into it head-

first? Well, Beckie wasn't pretending. And she didn't hit the door with her foot. In her blind anger, she walked into the door headfirst. Her brother was now bent over with laughter, and Beckie was even more angry. Now she was angry with her brother, the door, and herself.

Someone once wrote, "An angry man is angry again with himself when he returns to reason." I now understand what he meant. Proverbs 14:29 says, "A patient man has great understanding, but a quick-tempered man displays folly." That says it pretty well, doesn't it?

Everything we do reflects on God, and losing control of our temper reflects badly on Him. So stay calm. If you run into too many doors you might cause permanent damage!   —D.P.

Through preaching, teaching, and the Bible, God is telling me . . . _____

_____

_____

Through nature and the lives of other believers, God is showing me . . . _____

_____

_____

I will respond by . . . _____

_____

_____

Enough already!

READ
John 8:31–36

MEDITATE
John 8:32
"The truth will set you free."

REFLECT
➡ When I read the Bible, what can I do to keep from getting bogged down by things I don't understand? Read smaller portions? Read something basic like one of the gospels? Get a commentary? Buy a study Bible?

➡ Where can I go to find answers to help me know what the Bible says?

CONSIDER
Don't trust religion; trust Christ.

When it comes to religion, I hear so many different and contradictory messages that I'm confused about what's really true." The college sophomore who told me this was expressing the feelings of a lot of people. They're having problems sorting out the true from the false in religion.

He appeared to be sincere. He wasn't angry. He wasn't a skeptic. He was just confused. He had heard enough about religion to make his head spin. It was as if he had been placed in a room full of radios with each one tuned to a different station. That makes it pretty hard to get things straight. He had so many questions: Is New Age the way to go? What about reincarnation? Is Christ really the only way to God? Does God really exist? Could the atheist be right?

To add to the confusion caused by so many religious claims, other people (like your philosophy prof maybe?) are telling you that there is no spiritual truth and that all truth is relative. It would be easy to throw up your hands and say, "Forget it. They can fight it out among themselves. I'm not going to believe anything!"

If you have ever felt this way, I have a suggestion. Turn to a source you can trust. A source that has been proven to be accurate and full of integrity. A source that has stood the test of time and scrutiny. Turn to the Bible, the Book of Truth. Open it and read it for yourself. Let it straighten out the confusion for you.   —D.P.

Through preaching, teaching, and the Bible, God is telling me . . . _____
_____
_____

Through nature and the lives of other believers, God is showing me . . . _____
_____
_____

I will respond by . . . _____
_____
_____

The treasure hunter

READ
Proverbs 2:1–8

MEDITATE
Proverbs 2:4
Search for [wisdom] as for hidden treasure.

REFLECT
➡ What could I learn by reading a chapter of Proverbs each day?
➡ What criteria do I use for judging the wisdom of the world? What my parents say? What my professors say? What my friends say? What musicians say? What talk-show hosts say? What the Bible says?

CONSIDER
A millionaire without wisdom is a pauper.

You gotta admire Mel Fisher. He's a treasure hunter who searched for gold and found it! His first find was some gold coins scattered on the ocean floor. From then on, Mel dreamed about hunting for lost treasure. And dreams are not all he ended up with. After sixteen years of looking for the Spanish wreck *Nuestra Senora de Atocha,* he found it in fifty-five feet of water near Key West, Florida. His divers salvaged millions of dollars worth of treasure from this sunken ship—but it didn't come easy. They toiled long and hard with metal detectors, diving to investigate every metallic "blip." But the work finally paid off, and today Fisher is rich!

The good fortune of that treasure hunter made me think of some verses that speak of a treasure "more precious than rubies" (Proverbs 3:15). The treasure is wisdom—the ability to know right from wrong and to apply that knowledge to life.

I know what you're thinking. Mel Fisher's millions sound a lot more valuable than Solomon's wisdom. But think about this: When Solomon had a chance to ask for anything he wanted from God, he asked for wisdom. And after getting it, he still spoke highly of it. He recommended wisdom as something to seek with all the persistence of a treasure hunter (2:4).

Think about the things you'll have to deal with in years to come: jobs, relationships, finances. And think about some of the struggles you are having today. You can't find a better resource for working through them than godly wisdom.

Would you like to find a hundred million dollars worth of treasure? I would. But wisdom from God is the only treasure worth searching for! —M.D.

Through preaching, teaching, and the Bible, God is telling me . . . _____

_____

Through nature and the lives of other believers, God is showing me . . . _____

_____

I will respond by . . . _____

Free coke!

MEDITATE
James 4:7
Resist the devil, and he will flee from you.

REFLECT

➡ When was the last time I fell for one of Satan's lies?

➡ What one is he trying to get me to believe right now?

➡ What do I use as a basis for making decisions? Feelings? Desires? Other people's opinions? The Bible?

CONSIDER
What Satan offers, you pay for.

Everywhere I went I saw students carrying a two-liter bottle of the real thing. What in the world was coming off? Had a Coke truck dropped its load on the small college town of Morgantown, West Virginia. Did they receive a visit from the Coke fairy? Had the students started a new prohibition against alcohol?

Hardly.

I discovered that free cola was being given away in exchange for a credit card application. "Just fill out the form and the Coke is yours."

Was it a case of getting something for nothing? Not on your life. The credit card people were spending money on the students because they wanted them to use their credit card.

Get the picture? It's really all about putting temptation in front of the students and letting human nature take its course. They didn't seem to be asking for much. But hidden in their generosity was a financial hazard.

Satan takes this same approach with us. He doesn't seem to be asking for much. Just one touch, just one drink, just one hit. In reality, though, he's asking for a lot more than that. He's asking us to sign over our reputation, our self-respect, maybe even our lives.

Don't do it. Don't sign. Don't give in to the temptation. Think about what you might be getting into. Satan's contracts always have hidden language, so read the fine print.

Jesus didn't fall for it. When Satan asked Him to become a free agent and switch teams, Jesus refused. He knew only too well the character of Satan: that he "prowls around like a roaring lion looking for someone to devour" (1 Peter 5:8). You know it too. Don't fall for his tricks. With Satan, there are no freebies.   —D.P.

Through preaching, teaching, and the Bible, God is telling me . . . _____

_____

Through nature and the lives of other believers, God is showing me . . . _____

_____

I will respond by . . . _____

_____

Killed by a mermaid

MAY 14

READ
1 Corinthians
15:1–11

MEDITATE
1 Corinthians 15:17
If Christ has not been raised, your faith is futile.

REFLECT

→ Why is Jesus worthy of my trust? Do I live like I really believe He is alive in heaven?

→ What would I tell a skeptic who said that the stories about Jesus are simply a bunch of fairy tales?

→ Am I ready for Christ's return?

CONSIDER
Jesus didn't just make claims—He proved them.

A religious leader in southwest Zimbabwe was killed by a mermaid. At least that's what his relatives think. According to the *Associated Press,* police say he drowned.

When Lovemore Mpofu didn't surface after diving into water near a dam during a cleansing ritual, his followers thought it was part of the ceremony. In fact, some believe he probably had the ability to breathe under water. They sang and danced for two days before it dawned on them that he might have drowned. That's when Mpofu's relatives came up with the theory that he was killed by a mermaid who lives in the dam.

Ridiculous? Sure is. Why would anyone believe that stuff? But wait a minute. Have you ever wondered if what you believe might sound a little weird to someone else? After all, if you accept what the Bible says,

you believe that your leader, Jesus, disappeared one day, but that He now lives in heaven and will one day come back to earth for you. Talk about bizarre!

Do you really believe that stuff? I do. Here's why.

His arrival on earth was the culmination of hundreds of years of prophecy. He actually did have supernatural abilities. He died on the cross just as He said He would, and then three days later He was alive! The tomb that had been guarded by Roman soldiers was empty. And Jesus personally appeared to hundreds of people before He went to heaven.

We would be foolish to believe in a religious leader who could not back up his claims. And we would be foolish not to follow the One who demonstrated that He was and is all He claimed to be.   —K.D.

Through preaching, teaching, and the Bible, God is telling me . . . _____

_____

Through nature and the lives of other believers, God is showing me . . . _____

_____

I will respond by . . . _____

_____

You make the call!

READ
Genesis 39:1–15

MEDITATE
1 Corinthians 6:18
Flee from sexual immorality.

REFLECT

➡ I've been in that situation and I failed. Now what is my next step as a believer in Jesus?

➡ Perhaps I need to write a vow before God right now that I will not be involved in premarital sex.

➡ What can I learn from Hebrews 13:4 and Matthew 15:19–20?

CONSIDER
Don't let your date go out of bounds.

Perhaps you've seen the little sports spots during the World Series or an NFL game. Over a game-action clip, an announcer says something like, "Jose Canseco hits a high fly to center field. As the ball arrives at the fence, so does Ken Griffey, Jr. Griffey leaps and grabs the ball. But as he does, he tumbles over the fence, still holding the ball. Is it a home run or an out? You make the call!"

This mini-feature is a challenge. You don't have some umpire telling you what the ruling is. Instead, using your knowledge of the rulebook, you have a chance to make the decision.

Here's another time when you need to make the call. You're out on a date with someone you've had your eye on for a long time. Things are going really well. You've been to a basketball game and you've had a great time yelling and screaming

and generally acting like a kid. But now your date wants to play a different game and starts pressuring you to do things sexually that you know are not right.

"You make the call!" There's nobody around to decide for you. Using God's standards (found in His rule-book, the Bible), you know what call you have to make. And you have to make it just as firmly and assuredly as a major league umpire. You need to make the same smart call Joseph did. He headed for the exits when Potiphar's wife started messing around.

It's your body, and it is the temple of the Holy Spirit. Don't let anyone make a decision about your body that would bring dishonor to you and to the testimony of Jesus Christ. You make the call.   —D.B.

Through preaching, teaching, and the Bible, God is telling me . . . _____

Through nature and the lives of other believers, God is showing me . . . _____

I will respond by . . . _____

The love of money

READ
1 Timothy 6:3–10

MEDITATE
1 Timothy 6:10
The love of money is a root of all kinds of evil.

REFLECT
➡ Have I compromised biblical standards for the sake of money?
➡ When? Why?
➡ When have I chosen to do what is right rather than what is profitable?
➡ What do my goals for the future tell me about the importance of money in my life?

CONSIDER
Money ceases to be good when it becomes a god.

Robert Pilatus and Fabrice Morvan, better known as Milli Vanilli, won a Grammy in 1989 for Best New Artist. Their debut album sold seven million copies.

But they were frauds. In late 1990, the producer who had turned them into stars decided to turn them in to the public. He revealed that Rob and Fab hadn't sung a single note on their blockbuster album. Neither had they used their own voices in concert appearances or on music videos. All they had done was look good and move their lips. Fans were justifiably disgusted. They had been defrauded. Why? Because Milli Vanilli and their producer saw a way to make a lot of money in a short amount of time.

Money has a strange way of warping morals and priorities. For money, people will steal, lie, misrepresent, and even kill.

The apostle Paul warned Timothy about the lure of money. Paul knew that people of all kinds could get infected by a lust for wealth.

When that happens, they become willing to trade away their integrity and even their relationship with God (1 Timothy 6:10).

Instead of choosing what will please the Lord, we choose what has the most potential for financial gain. The author of Proverbs 30 prayed, ". . . give me neither poverty nor riches, but give me only my daily bread. Otherwise, I may have too much and disown you. . . . Or I may become poor and steal, and so dishonor the name of my God"(vv. 8–9).

How much influence does money have in your life? Sure, you need it for clothes, transportation, books, tuition, food, a place to live. But are you in control of your money? Or is your money in control of you?

—K.D.

Through preaching, teaching, and the Bible, God is telling me . . . _____

_____

Through nature and the lives of other believers, God is showing me . . . _____

_____

I will respond by . . . _____

_____

One long look

READ
1 Thessalonians 4:3–8

MEDITATE
2 Timothy 2:22
Flee the evil desires of youth, and pursue righteousness . . .

REFLECT
➡ What do the words "rejecting God" mean to me?
➡ If my thoughts were broadcast over a loudspeaker today, what would people hear? How would I feel?

CONSIDER
What comes in through the eye stays in the mind.

Camp is a place for making memories. Memories of new friends, the same old food, and ancient (some even thirty years old) counselors trying to relate to kids half their age. I have a memory of one such counselor.

"Andy" was explaining the definition of lust to me and to the other attentive adolescents in my cabin. This was our nighttime devotions—just before "lights out." He began, "Well, when I was in the Army, I was stationed overseas where they allowed, uh, colorful billboards. One board that I drove by had the picture of a beautiful, scantily dressed woman on it. I figured if I looked once at it, it was okay. But if I looked twice it was definitely "lust." At that point, one of the more mischievous campers asked, "But what if you took one long look?"

We all broke up in laughter. But lust is no laughing matter. In 1 Thessalonians 4 we are told to control our own bodies (and minds) "in a way that is holy and honorable, not in passionate lust" (vv. 4–5). And what is the reason for avoiding untamed sexual thoughts? It's found later in the passage: "Therefore, he who rejects this instruction does not reject man but God" (v. 8). In other words, if lust-filled thoughts are running wildly through your head, you're running from God at the same time. This is serious business. God doesn't want us to give in to impure thoughts. He wants us to give them up so that He can fill our minds with His holiness.

So before taking "one long look" at something you should look away from—take a long, hard look at what God has to say about lust.

—T.F.

Through preaching, teaching, and the Bible, God is telling me . . . _____

_____

_____

Through nature and the lives of other believers, God is showing me . . . _____

_____

_____

I will respond by . . . _____

_____

_____

How to spell success

READ
1 John 2:15–17

MEDITATE
1 John 2:17
The man who does the will of God lives forever.

REFLECT
→ What have I been using as my success guideline? Is it anywhere close to God's guideline?

→ How can a person who died in a foreign land at a relatively young age be considered successful?

CONSIDER
Outside God's will is no success. Inside is no failure.

I have an assignment for you. Don't get all worked up; it won't be graded. Ask five people what it means to be a success. Any five. Not including your dog. Go ahead. When you come back with your answers, I've got two stories for you.

Well, what did people say? Did they agree? Look at these two success stories to see if they verify what you discovered.

Success story number one: John W. Yates was so poor he had to put cardboard in his shoes to cover up the holes. (No kidding!) Yet when he opened a bank account at the age of fifteen, he deposited his tiny earnings under the name "John W. Yates and Company." The "and Company" part referred to the Lord. He named the Lord as his partner and manager. He wanted to do only what would please Him. Guided by this philosophy, he went on to become a multimillionaire.

Success story number two: Oswald Chambers showed so much artistic promise that at age eighteen he was invited to study under Europe's greatest masters. But he declined the offer and went to a Bible college, where he eventually became a teacher. Later, Chambers went to Egypt and ministered to the spiritual needs of British soldiers. When he died there in his forties, he left behind devotional classics like *My Utmost for His Highest*.

The stories have few apparent similarities—except this: Both men made doing God's will their prime objective. And both were successful in doing that.

Success is different things to different people. But in God's economy, it means one thing: Doing His will. Is that your goal?   —D.B.

Through preaching, teaching, and the Bible, God is telling me . . . _____

_____

Through nature and the lives of other believers, God is showing me . . . _____

_____

I will respond by . . . _____

_____

The healthiest place

READ
1 John 3:16–19

MEDITATE
1 Thessalonians
3:12
May the Lord make your love increase and overflow.

REFLECT

➡ How can I help my church warm up to unbelievers who are searching as well as to believers who are hurting?

➡ What might happen if I were to model Christ's love—even if no one else does?

CONSIDER
To warm up your church, let the Son shine.

If *Time* magazine came out with a cover story identifying the healthiest place on earth, people would be falling all over themselves to move there. Right? Not necessarily. Especially if that place was the South Pole!

The world's southernmost point might also be its cleanest with no pollution, no dust, and very few people to bring such things in. The air there is as fresh and clean as it must have been all over the world before we began pouring industrial wastes into the atmosphere.

It's also one of the few locations where people are not bombarded by germs. Not only is it too cold for them to be active, but there's nothing for them to live on. And since winds start at the South Pole and move northward, they tend to keep away any contaminants.

But with temperatures that drop to 100 degrees below zero, it's just too cold for us to pack up and move there!

Sometimes our churches resemble the South Pole. There's no pollution: the truth of God is boldly preached. Error has no chance to survive. And Scriptures are meticulously quoted. That's great! That's how it should be. But sometimes they're so cold no one wants to go there. The spiritual temperature is sub-zero.

There should be a huge difference between the church and the South Pole. Our Lord designed the church to be one of the warmest places on earth—a place where the love of Christ is to warm the hearts of all who attend.

What can you do to help your church "warm up" and become a friendly place—a place where people feel accepted and where God is pleased to meet with sincere, caring believers in an atmosphere of Christian love?

—T.B.

Through preaching, teaching, and the Bible, God is telling me . . . _____

_____

_____

Through nature and the lives of other believers, God is showing me . . . _____

_____

_____

I will respond by . . . _____

_____

_____

Ya gotta have

Strength training

READ
2 Samuel 22:21–37

MEDITATE
2 Samuel 22:33
"It is God who arms me with strength."

REFLECT
➡ Why do I need God's strength today?
➡ How can I become spiritually stronger?

CONSIDER
Flex your faith; it builds strength where it counts.

How strong are you? Is your book-carrying arm twice the size of your other one? Could you win an arm-wrestling match with your grandmother?

At least one million Americans don't think they're strong enough, so they spend four hundred million dollars a year for black-market anabolic steroids. Among them are 250,000 high school seniors who want to improve their athletic statistics and be better prepared physically for collegiate competition.

But these athletes pay a high price. Psychiatrists at the Yale University School of Medicine report that steroid users can become addicted and they can suffer from irritability, anxiety, paranoia, and impaired judgment. Also, they are more likely to attempt suicide.

With those types of side-effects, why would anyone choose this kind of strength?

Stronger in body but weaker in mind doesn't seem to be a very good trade-off.

In 2 Samuel 22 (you did read it, didn't you?), David sang about a strength you can't get by injection or pills. You don't even have to exercise a lot. And you end up stronger where it counts—in your ability to cope with the real issues of life. God's infusion of strength into our lives has nothing but positive side effects.

So how do we build spiritual muscles? God's strength comes to those who are obedient (vv. 21–25), faithful (v. 26), blameless (v. 26), pure (v. 27), humble (v. 28), and who take refuge in Him (v. 31).

You'll need godly strength if you want to fight off the temptations and problems ahead. Let God "inject" you with His strength. That will do more for you than bulging biceps ever could. —K.D.

Through preaching, teaching, and the Bible, God is telling me . . . _____

Through nature and the lives of other believers, God is showing me . . . _____

I will respond by . . . _____

Enough for today

READ
Matthew 6:9–13

MEDITATE
Matthew 6:11
"Give us today our daily bread."

REFLECT

➡ What worries me about tomorrow? How should I handle that concern?

➡ What spiritual needs should I ask the Lord to meet today?

➡ How has God proved Himself to me in the past few weeks by meeting my needs?

CONSIDER
Don't use up today's strength on tomorrow's needs.

When my wife and I visited Brazil, we enjoyed going to the *fedas*, or open-air markets. The aisles between the stalls were always jammed with shoppers buying everything from parasols to pineapples. They were also buying their groceries for the day, including meat freshly butchered and laid out for display. We learned from our missionary friends that for many Brazilian's shopping is a daily task. They do not own refrigerators and have no way to keep food fresh. Besides, some husbands are day laborers and receive payment for their work at the end of every day. Since it is barely enough for one day's provision, they have no money to shop ahead.

That's how things were done in Jesus' day too. Most people were poor. They worked all day, received their low pay at the end of the day, and used the money to purchase the next day's food. Life was perilous. They were always one day from hunger. An illness or injury would be devastating. So, when Jesus told them to pray for daily bread, He was saying, "Give us our bread for today."

What is true of these people physically is true for all of us spiritually. We need "food" from God every day. Each day brings different demands that draw on our strength. It may be telling someone about Christ. Or helping a friend through a crisis. Or taking a hard test. Or resisting a powerful temptation. Whatever it is, God has promised us strength for today. What we need He will supply. Before we start any day, we should pause and pray, "Give us today our daily bread."

—D.E.

Through preaching, teaching, and the Bible, God is telling me . . . _____

_____

Through nature and the lives of other believers, God is showing me . . . _____

_____

_____

I will respond by . . . _____

Comeback player

READ
Acts:15:36–41

MEDITATE
2 Timothy 4:11
Mark . . . is helpful to
me in my ministry.

REFLECT

➡ My current spiritual
condition is _____
_____.

➡ What can I do to
keep from letting
early failures drag
down the rest of
my life?

➡ How can I be more
useful to God?

CONSIDER
*It's never too
late to come
back to God.*

Baseball season is in full swing (unless the players are on strike). For me and a few of my diehard-baseball-fan friends, it means we have already started our annual Rotisserie League.

In this fantasy baseball game, each of us becomes a team owner. We meet to draft a complete roster from the active American and National League players. A player's hitting or pitching statistics for the year determine his worth. Total statistics determine the standings.

The most fun is the draft—trying to decide which player is on the verge of a great season and predicting which player would not help your team. We like to think it's as intense and scientific as the real thing.

In Acts 15, Barnabas and Paul got into a disagreement about the potential of one of their team members: John Mark. Paul remembered how Mark had deserted them on an earlier road trip. But Barnabas thought Mark deserved to be put back on the active roster. "They had such a sharp disagreement that they parted company" (v. 39). It probably made Mark feel responsible for the whole mess.

But Mark's story doesn't end there. In fact, toward the end of Paul's life, he urged Timothy to bring Mark with him, "because he is helpful to me in my ministry" (2 Timothy 4:11). The young man who had failed so miserably in Paul's eyes earlier was now a valued member of the team.

In baseball terms, how is your Christian life? Are you coming off a bad season? One filled with disappointments and missed opportunities? Are you in a spiritual slump?

Take heart. As Mark proved, with Christ's help you can always make a great comeback! —J.C.

Through preaching, teaching, and the Bible, God is telling me . . . _____
_____
_____

Through nature and the lives of other believers, God is showing me . . . _____
_____
_____

I will respond by . . . _____
_____
_____

Bugs and booze

READ
Proverbs 23:29–35

MEDITATE
Proverbs 20:1
Wine is a mocker and beer a brawler; whoever is led astray by them is not wise.

REFLECT
➡ Why would I want to drink? What's the real purpose?
➡ What would God think about me if I got drunk?

CONSIDER
Only weak characters depend on strong drink.

Have you ever seen a major-league cockroach? I mean the kind that opens refrigerator doors and can't be killed. You spray it with industrial-strength Raid and it asks, "What is that—Glade Forest Fresh Scent?" Even worse than one Rambo roach, however, is an entire infantry of the things.

One man, for sure, would attest to that. A thirty-one-year-old construction worker returned home one night after drinking to find cockroaches "in great numbers" parading around his apartment. He was drunk. He overreacted. He pulled out his lighter and set the place on fire, nearly turning the whole complex into a towering inferno. Then he got so upset by his actions that he slit his wrists. Fortunately, other residents of the building put out the fire, and his suicide attempt resulted only in minor injuries. But this story could have had a tragic ending. Many people could have lost their lives because of one man's alcohol-induced foolishness.

Alcohol abuse kills. You probably know of someone who was killed or injured in an alcohol-related car wreck. A local TV station carries "DON'T DRINK AND DRIVE" public service videos done by high school students. One video shows students dressed in professional clothes saying, "I could have been a doctor" and "I could have been a teacher" and "I could have been a father." Why the past tense? They represent young people who have lost their lives in senseless drunk-driving accidents.

Don't become a statistic. Don't "linger over wine" (Proverbs 23:30). For "it bites like a snake and poisons like a viper" (v. 32). And it leads to destruction. If you have the Holy Spirit inside, you don't need outside stimulants. —T.F.

Through preaching, teaching, and the Bible, God is telling me . . . _____

_____

_____

Through nature and the lives of other believers, God is showing me . . . _____

_____

_____

I will respond by . . . _____

_____

When life hurts

READ
2 Corinthians 1:1–7

MEDITATE
2 Corinthians 1:5
Through Christ our comfort overflows.

REFLECT

➡ I (know/don't know) what it is like to lose a family member or friend to death. How should I view God as my comforter?

➡ When I think about death, what is the most comforting hope I have?

CONSIDER
If you've been comforted, comfort someone else.

She was a marvelous person. A loving mother to her teenage sons. A faithful, gracious wife. A woman who trusted God completely. Her gentle spirit was admired by all who knew her. And her sense of humor made her fun to talk to.

But I can't talk to her anymore. While still in her thirties, my sister died of cancer—devastating, unrelenting cancer. And even though it happened several years ago, it still hurts me.

Perhaps you know what I mean. Maybe you too have lost someone you were close to. A parent, a sister, a brother, a friend. I know that nothing I could say in this devotional article could ever take away that pain.

Yet through the pain of death we learn. We grow. We discover again what God can do for us in our struggles. One thing that really helps is something Paul said in 2 Corinthians. He called God "the Father of compassion and the God of all comfort." Remember, God knows about grief. He knew the agony of Jesus' painful death. He understands exactly what we are going through when we face life without someone special.

Notice, though, that Paul took this idea of comfort a step further. He pointed out that when we endure suffering, we learn how to help others. To put it in personal terms, I have suffered the death of my sister, and now I should be willing to help you find comfort in a similar sorrow.

"Through Christ our comfort overflows," Paul said. When you think about it, it's an amazing system because it can bring comfort to all who need it.

Seek God's comfort. He will give it to you. And He will also make you a comforter. —D.B.

Through preaching, teaching, and the Bible, God is telling me . . . _____

_____

Through nature and the lives of other believers, God is showing me . . . _____

_____

I will respond by . . . _____

_____

Ya gotta have

Other side of the fence

READ
Hebrews 13:5–8

MEDITATE
Hebrews 13:5
Keep your lives free from the love of money and be content with what you have.

REFLECT
➠ What do I envy most about my friends?
➠ How can I change that envy to contentment toward God!

CONSIDER
Contentment is wanting what you have, not having what you want.

A friend and I were talking recently and I mentioned to him how I envied his family ties. I'm still single, and he has a great wife and two wonderful daughters. He said he sometimes wished he could be free and single again. We both laughed. Each of us envied what the other had!

But it's not completely funny. Discontent is what our society is all about. We're always looking for a faster car, a better job, a bigger house. We never seem to be happy with what we have, and we're willing to do anything to get more.

A man envied his friends because they had bought bigger and better homes. So he put his home up for sale and prepared to move his family. As he read the classified ads, he came across a home that seemed just right. Excited, he phoned his realtor. "Let's check out that house," he said quickly. The realtor laughed. "That's your house you're reading about."

It's easy to look at our friends with envy. One seems to have lots of money; another seems to have lots of boyfriends; another drives the baddest car in town. Everyone seems to have a perfect life except you. But chances are, if you were to ask your friends, they would probably come up with things about you that they envy!

There is nothing wrong with trying to make life better. (That's why you're in school, after all!) But if our point of reference is what other people have, we need to rethink our priorities. We need to remember that God has made us who we are and put us where we are for a reason. That will help us see that the grass is green on our side of the fence too! —J.C.

Through preaching, teaching, and the Bible, God is telling me . . . _____

_____

Through nature and the lives of other believers, God is showing me . . . _____

_____

I will respond by . . . _____

_____

What am I doing?

READ
Romans 7:15–25

MEDITATE
Romans 7:15
I do not understand what I do.

REFLECT

➡ As important as it is to do the right thing, it's more important to rely on Christ for the power to do it. Am I?

➡ Do I fill my mind with the right things by reading the Bible and spending time in prayer? How does what I think about determine what I do?

CONSIDER
No one knows how bad he is until he has tried to be good.
—C. S. Lewis

"Straighten up!" You've heard that message a few times, haven't you? Well, as you know all too well, the order to "straighten up" has nothing to do with posture. It's all about behavior. In other words, somebody wanted you to stop doing what's wrong and start doing what's right.

Could it be that you're struggling with that very problem right now? Only this time it's not Mom or Dad telling you to "straighten up," it's your conscience. You know that what you are doing (or not doing) is wrong. And you'd like to break the negative cycle. But it's tough. You made promises—even kept them for a while. But then, there they are again. Those same old bad choices or habits.

If the apostle Paul were here, he could relate to your problem. He once said, "For I have the desire to do what is good, but I cannot carry it out. For what I do is not the good I want to do; no, the evil I do not want to do—this I keep on doing. . . . What a wretched man I am! Who will rescue me from this body of death?" (Romans 7:18–19, 24).

It sounds like Paul wanted to straighten up. And he did. But first he had to surrender his life to the only One who could change him from being a victim to a victor. And guess what. Paul's source of victory is our source of victory. When Paul figured out how to lick the problem, he exclaimed, "Thanks be to God—through Jesus Christ our Lord!" (Romans 7:25).

Are you trying to straighten up? Then turn your life over to Christ and serve Him with your whole heart. That should straighten things out for you.   —D.P.

Through preaching, teaching, and the Bible, God is telling me . . . _____
_____
_____

Through nature and the lives of other believers, God is showing me . . . _____
_____
_____

I will respond by . . . _____
_____
_____

Oh, no! Cyberphobia!

READ
Isaiah 51:7–9

MEDITATE
Isaiah 51:12
"Who are you that you fear mortal men . . . who are but grass?"

REFLECT

➡ When the Bible tells us to fear the Lord, what does that mean? Terror? Respect and reverence? Awe?

➡ When I'm making a decision, whom do I think about? Am I always afraid of what one person will say? Is that right?

CONSIDER
If you fear God, you don't have to be afraid of people.

Help! I've got cyberphobia!"

"Too bad. I hope there's a cure for it."

"Whatever it is, don't get too close to me."

Cyberphobia is the name psychologists have given to a relatively new phobia—the fear of computers.

That's right. According to a team of business professors at George Mason University, many people have a serious fear of computers. Just being in the same room with one makes them panic. Their heartbeat becomes irregular, they feel like they can't breathe, they get dizzy, and they tremble all over. This would be especially serious at colleges that install computers in every dorm room. ("Is it still here?" "Yes!" "Agggh!!! I can't sleep with that thing staring at me!")

One therapist said these people are afraid that when they try to learn how to operate a computer, they'll fail— that when they sit down at the keyboard and look into the screen, they're going to pass out or go blank.

Does it make sense? No. But phobias never do. They are irrational yet very real fears.

Another kind of phobia is the fear of the opinions and actions of others. Because we're afraid of what Mom or Dad or a sister or our best friend may say, we do what they want us to do. But how does that look to God? How must He feel when we are so much under the control of others? When we act as if our fate and well-being rest only on their approval? When we are so afraid of someone that we panic and forget to trust only in Him?

Isaiah reminded his readers that they shouldn't fear people. God is the One who has the last word on our future, and we need to depend on Him alone.

—M.D.

Through preaching, teaching, and the Bible, God is telling me . . . _____

_____

Through nature and the lives of other believers, God is showing me . . . _____

_____

I will respond by . . . _____

_____

High tech, gentle touch

READ
1 Thessalonians
2:1–9

MEDITATE
Philippians 4:5
Let your gentleness be
evident to all.

REFLECT
→ Do I respond better
to condemnation or
gentleness? What
does that tell me
about getting along
with others?

→ What situations call
for confrontation?
How should I pro-
ceed?

→ What can I learn
about effective
confrontation from
2 Samuel 12:7?

CONSIDER
*People don't
care how much
you know until
they know how
much you care.*

A youth pastor was on his way to visit one of his young people in the hospital. Although he had warned her of danger, she had continued to hang around with some rather wild kids. Now she was suffering the horrible consequences of a toxic overdose.

As he rode up the elevator, he mulled over how he should approach her. He knew that she had willfully and knowingly violated the moral law of God and was paying the price. He would be theologically correct to point out her sin, harshly condemn her, and demand that she repent or else face the further judgment of God. But was that the best approach?

As he got off the elevator, the youth pastor saw a sign by the nurses' station that said, "High tech, gentle touch." The intensive care unit was filled with complicated, state-of-the-art equipment. There were monitors and respirators and machines of all types to keep people alive and bring them healing. But the words "gentle touch" reminded the patients and their families that even though a lot of advanced technology was involved, the nurses and doctors still cared very much about their patients.

"That's what Christ did," he thought, as he made his way to the young patient's room. He reflected on how gently the Lord Jesus treated the woman by the well. Now he knew what he should do. When he talked with the teenager, he tempered the tough biblical truth with a gentle and loving manner. And the girl listened as she had never done before.

As we deal with our friends, we must be gentle and Christlike. It's the gentle touch that counts.   —D.E.

Through preaching, teaching, and the Bible, God is telling me . . . _____

_____

Through nature and the lives of other believers, God is showing me . . . _____

_____

I will respond by . . . _____

_____

Chizburger, pliz

READ
Luke 12:13–21

MEDITATE
Luke 12:15

"A man's life does not consist in the abundance of his possessions."

REFLECT

➡ How have my summer jobs shaped my attitude about my career goals?

➡ Is it wrong to want to make a lot of money? Why or why not?

➡ How could I glorify God and be a success in business at the same time?

CONSIDER

It's not how much you possess but what possesses you that counts.

Sergei attends college in the Soviet Union. During a summer break he worked at the huge new McDonald's in Moscow and earned 350 rubles a month. He made more money serving up *chizburgers* and *big maks* than his dad made as a teacher. And now, after a taste of capitalism, he wants to be a businessman.

In the USA, a lot of students know all too well what it is like to work at a fast-food place, but they probably wouldn't want to compare their wages with what their dads make. Although the pay isn't great, employees in a fast-food place can get a fast education in capitalism: Get other people to work fast and you can make a fast buck.

So if you're figuring out what you want to be when you grow up (I'm still wondering about that myself), think about this: Money often has a lot to say about what kind of major you choose in college, how many degrees you're going to shoot for, and where you send your resumes when you're all done.

Is it wrong to want to have a good-paying job? To build a business? Let's answer by asking another question. What about the farmer in today's Bible reading? What was his problem? Jesus zeroed in on the man's selfishness and self-sufficiency.

As we evaluate our career goals we need to evaluate our attitude at the same time. If our reasons for wanting a hefty bank account are pride, self-esteem, and security, we'd better start over. These things come only from God, and if we look for them any other place we're going to be taking orders from the wrong boss. —K.D.

Through preaching, teaching, and the Bible, God is telling me . . . _____

_____

Through nature and the lives of other believers, God is showing me . . . _____

_____

_____

I will respond by . . . _____

_____

A LOVING HEART

Multiculturalism?

READ
Galatians 3:26–4:7

MEDITATE
Galatians 3:28
There is neither Jew nor Greek . . . male nor female, for you are all one in Christ Jesus.

REFLECT

➡ In what ways do I show prejudice against others? What does God think about my thoughts and actions?

➡ What does it mean to be colorblind in the racial sense? How can I develop that kind of outlook?

CONSIDER
The best place for prejudice is in the past.

Don't tell me you've never heard the word *multiculturalism.* Even though this new buzzword looks imposing, its definition is simple. It's "the concept of seeing the world through the eyes of more than one culture."

Multiculturalism is happening in the United States. Instead of citizens becoming more alike, we are staying different—while continually experiencing the culture of others. Think about your fellow students. Even if you don't attend a school like some in Los Angeles where ninety foreign languages are spoken, it's likely that your classmates have many different skin colors and accents.

A *Time* magazine article proclaimed, "By 2056, when someone born today will be 65 years old, the 'average' U.S. resident will trace his or her descent to Africa, Asia, the Hispanic world, the Pacific Islands, Arabia—almost anywhere but white Europe." The point is, we will experience more and more cultures in the future.

As our community becomes more "colorful," it's important that we remember the words of Paul: "There is neither Jew nor Greek, slave nor free, male nor female, for you are all one in Christ Jesus" (Galatians 3:28). There's no room for prejudice in a heart touched by Christ.

God is not the least bit concerned about the color, language, or multiculturalism of His children. He looks at the heart. So should we.

—T.F.

Through preaching, teaching, and the Bible, God is telling me . . . _____

_____

_____

Through nature and the lives of other believers, God is showing me . . . _____

_____

_____

I will respond by . . . _____

_____

M28Y

Bound to be free

READ
Galatians 4:28–5:1

MEDITATE
John 8:36
"If the Son sets you free, you will be free indeed."

REFLECT
➡ In what ways does pride keep me from enjoying the full benefits of belonging to Christ?

CONSIDER
The only way to be free is to let Christ take hold of you.

When a Canada goose flew into Wisconsin with an arrow lodged in her body, she refused to be helped. She dodged game wardens who tried to catch her, avoided the tranquilizer-laced grain they tried to feed her, and even evaded the cannon-fired nets they hurled at her.

Finally, after a month or so of evasive maneuvers, she grew so exhausted that they were able to catch her with a fishing net. Surgery was performed to remove the arrow, she recovered, and she was returned to freedom. If geese could think, she probably would have wondered why she had stayed away from those nice people for so long.

She was not much different from the people Jesus spoke to (John 8). They were trapped by sin and needed to be set free, but they didn't trust Jesus. They didn't understand that He wanted to set them free from the sin they couldn't escape on their own (see Galatians 5:1). They mistook His motives for those of a captor. What He was asking them to do sure sounded like slavery to them. And no self-respecting sons of Abraham were about to become slaves. What they failed to see was that only in giving up control of their lives could they be truly free.

Being Christ's followers means becoming a slave in order to be free; becoming weak so that through His strength we may become strong. Following Christ is not struggling to stay aloft with a broken wing or a serious wound. It is being secure in the One who loves us enough to capture us and cure us, even when we want to go the other way. —M.D.

Through preaching, teaching, and the Bible, God is telling me . . . _____

Through nature and the lives of other believers, God is showing me . . . _____

I will respond by . . . _____

Chowing down

READ
John 4:27–34

MEDITATE
John 4:34

"My food . . . is to do the will of him who sent me."

REFLECT

➠ What does my spiritual diet consist of? Music? Reading? Listening to sermons? What else?

➠ Do I try to obey God every day or do I get distracted for days and weeks at a time?

➠ How can I measure my spiritual strength?

CONSIDER
Undeserved goodness from God should lead to unreserved obedience from us.

Whether it's due to a "Big Mac Attack," a "Burger King Craving," or a "Taco Bell Run for the Border," we've all hopped in the car and beat it to our favorite "quick stop" and gorged ourselves on fast food. I mean, it's the American way, right?

The really weird thing is that many of us are overeating and starving at the same time. That's because the fatty meats, oversalted french fries, and syrupy soft drinks we enjoy don't carry the full nutritional value our bodies need. Burgers, fries, and drinks are convenient and may even have their place as an occasional change of pace. But when they are substituted for the fresh fruits and vegetables that are essential for good health, we're headed for trouble.

There's a parallel in the area of spiritual health. Some of the most undernourished believers are those who stuff themselves with religious activities. They dine on good preaching. They sample every gospel recording artist that comes along. They feed on good literature from solid Christian authors. And though there's certainly nothing wrong with these elements, they make up too much of their spiritual diet. By themselves, these snacks, or "fast foods," are incomplete. Unless believers combine them with obedience to God, they will be undernourished and weak.

It's not hard to imagine Jesus enjoying music and good preaching and reading material while He was here on earth. But His "food" was doing the will of His Father (John 4:34).

Follow His example. Don't just snack. Chow down on obedience to God. And enjoy it!   —M.D.

Through preaching, teaching, and the Bible, God is telling me . . . _____
_____
_____

Through nature and the lives of other believers, God is showing me . . . _____
_____
_____

I will respond by . . . _____
_____
_____

Redeeming the scraps

READ
1 Peter 4:12–16

MEDITATE
Job 23:10
"When he has tested me, I will come forth as gold."

REFLECT
➡ One tough time I am going through right now is . . .
➡ It burns me because . . .
➡ Through it, God is building in me . . .

CONSIDER
Great trials are opportunities for great triumphs.

Compare a hunk of scrap metal to a car (this does not work if your car *is* a hunk of scrap metal). Both are made of the same substance: steel. But the car is more valuable than the scrap. Why? Because the steel has been molded under intense heat into the form of an automobile. As scrap, it's almost worthless. As the body of a Miata or a BMW, it's expensive (and very costly to insure!).

This reminds me of the Christian life. The heat of tough times can mold us into something as valuable as gold. But if we keep our original shape, the only place for us is the scrap heap.

In the fourth chapter of his first letter, Peter wrote to encourage his fellow Christians. They were undergoing persecution—so much that they definitely felt as if they had been thrown into the fire. But Peter encouraged them with a promise. He said that fiery trials develop character. Because of their hardship, the people would come out of it much better.

But that often doesn't convince us. We don't go around looking for tough situations. We prefer comfort to character. We're not stupid. But as Peter reminds us, some qualities can be molded into our lives only through the fire of tough times.

How about you? What tough times are you facing? A difficult class? Friends who don't seem to care? A parent who doesn't understand? Are you tempted to just get out of town? Be encouraged. God is allowing that ordeal to build your character—and to keep you off the scrap heap.　　　—J.C.

Through preaching, teaching, and the Bible, God is telling me . . . _____

_____

_____

Through nature and the lives of other believers, God is showing me . . . _____

_____

_____

I will respond by . . . _____

_____

_____

Better than a bungee

MEDITATE
Deuteronomy 33:27
"The eternal God is your refuge, and underneath are the everlasting arms."

REFLECT
➡ Why do I have a hard time trusting God?

➡ In which area of my life is God telling me to take a leap of faith? How am I going to respond?

CONSIDER
If you can't trust God, you can't trust.

One of my friends is always challenging me to go "bungee-jumping" with him. Supposedly, the sensation of falling is quite stimulating. I probably won't take my friend up on his offer. The sensation of smashing into the ground worries me.

God calls us to take a risk in our faith. In trusting Him for our salvation, we do take a "leap of faith," believing that He will catch us. And we can be certain—no matter what we encounter in life—that He always will; He won't let us fall.

Throughout the Bible, God promises strength and support for those who trust Him. "I will strengthen you and help you," He assures us in Isaiah 41:10, "I will uphold you with my righteous right hand."

Author Ben Patterson tells about a young father who was awakened by the smell of smoke. He quickly gathered his family and they ran outside. Suddenly, before he could stop her, his daughter ran back in to rescue her teddy bear.

Soon she appeared at a second-floor window. The father yelled to her to jump. "But Daddy, I can't see you," the girl responded. "That's okay, Honey, I can see you," the father reassured her.

That's God's encouragement to us. We may not be able to see Him, but He can see us.

Are you having a hard time figuring out what's going on in your life? Does the future look like a maze? Relax. God sees the big picture. Trust Him. His everlasting arms are there to catch you.

—J.C.

Through preaching, teaching, and the Bible, God is telling me . . . _____

_____

Through nature and the lives of other believers, God is showing me . . . _____

_____

I will respond by . . . _____

_____

Hand-in-the-bucket test

MEDITATE
Romans 12:3
Do not think of yourself more highly than you ought.

REFLECT
➡ In which areas of my life is pride a problem? What evidence is there that I think too highly of myself?
➡ How can I show God's strength through my own weakness?

CONSIDER
It takes more courage to be humble than to be proud.

A few years ago, I interviewed former major league pitcher Don Sutton on the topic of athletes and their egos. Don's advice: "If you think you're important, stick your hand in a pail of water, then pull it out. See how long it takes the water to forget you were there."

Now, there's nothing wrong with being confident. Don had to believe he could get the job done out on the mound. (And with 324 wins and 3,574 strike-outs, he was right!) But when confidence becomes pride, we're in dangerous territory.

Pride can take many forms. You might be proud that your dorm room is fixed up nicer than any other. Or perhaps your good grades make you feel superior to those who have to struggle to get C's. Or your athletic ability might cause you to look down on those poor unfortunates who can only look on from the bleachers.

Such attitudes are dangerous, because pride stunts our spiritual growth. When we become overly impressed with our own abilities, God can't work through us. Paul understood how the system works: "When I am weak, then I am strong" (2 Corinthians 12:10). Why? Because when Paul recognized his own weakness and depended on God, God's power was unleashed through him.

How would you rate yourself on the pride scale?

If you rate yourself too highly, it might be time for Don Sutton's "hand-in-the-bucket" test. Use the results as a reminder to depend on God's strength, not your own.   —J.C.

Through preaching, teaching, and the Bible, God is telling me . . . _____

Through nature and the lives of other believers, God is showing me . . . _____

I will respond by . . . _____

Acting the part

READ
Mark 12:35–40

MEDITATE
Proverbs 8:13
"I hate pride and arrogance."

REFLECT

➡ What do I want God to see when He looks at me?

➡ What do I want others to believe when they watch me?

➡ What keeps me from being honest with my parents and my friends?

➡ What difference would it make to others if they knew me the way I know myself?

CONSIDER
If you are true to God, you won't seem false to your friends.

A young attorney just out of law school was sitting behind her desk gazing proudly at the diplomas on the wall of her new office. When she heard a knock at the door, she quickly reached for the phone and started talking. The door opened, and she assumed the person standing there was her first client. She motioned for him to come in and continued talking into the phone. After hanging up, she asked the man how she could help him. "I've come to hook up your telephone, ma'am," he replied.

The attorney's attempt to make herself look important made her look foolish instead.

The desire to feel important is nothing new. It was a problem with the teachers of the law in Jesus' day. They showed their self-importance in the way they dressed and prayed. But they didn't engage God in real conversation any more than that young attorney engaged anyone on her not-yet-connected phone.

Aren't we all a little bit like these folks? We dress and act to fit certain roles. But one problem is, "We may fool some of the people some of the time, but we can't fool all of the people all of the time." (No, I didn't make that up.) And we certainly won't fool God. He hates hypocrisy. In fact, Jesus said some pretty harsh things about those who fake it. "Such [people] will be punished most severely" (Mark 12:40).

What will help us avoid pride? Integrity. Simply put, we have this quality when what we do and say matches what we think and feel.

Make the tough choice. Get real. Before God, admit it when you're wrong, and say, "I don't know" when you don't. You'll be glad you did. (And so will everyone else!)   —T.B.

Through preaching, teaching, and the Bible, God is telling me . . . _____

_____

_____

Through nature and the lives of other believers, God is showing me . . . _____

_____

_____

I will respond by . . . _____

_____

_____

Dirty versus clean

READ
Psalm 15

MEDITATE
Psalm 24:3–4

Who may stand in his holy place? He who has clean hands and a pure heart.

REFLECT

➡ What percentage of the stuff I've been watching and listening to recently could be called dirty?

➡ How much sin is too much if I want the "clean hands" and "pure heart" that Psalm 24:3–4 talks about?

CONSIDER
No sin is little.

irty movies. Dirty dancing. Dirty clothes. Which bothers you more? Although the people who sell Tide have always bragged, "Tides in; Dirt's out," to sell their soap, our society uses a different selling slogan these days: "Dirt's in; Clean's out."

It's no wonder, then, that a movie about basketball great Pete Maravich never made it into theaters. "Too soft," distributors said of its "G" rating. In other words, it's too clean.

And it's no wonder that people like Tone Loc, whose popular rap songs have been banned as obscene, can say, "Kids like it because it's dirty. If it was clean, who'd play it?"

So the battle rages between clean and dirty.

Which side of the battle are you on? The Bible says God's people have a responsibility to keep clean. David made it clear that clean living is the standard for someone who wants to be accepted in the holy presence of God (Psalm 15).

If you have questions about the difference between clean and dirty, notice David's advice for remaining unspotted:

- Stay blameless.
- Do what is right.
- Tell the truth.
- Don't slander others.
- Don't mistreat your neighbor (or suitemate).
- Don't associate with immoral people.
- Honor those who fear God.
- Keep your word.
- Be generous.
- Don't sell yourself.

Now there's a checklist you can use. Take a minute to evaluate your performance in each area. How'd you do last year, last month, last week? Are you moving in the direction of clean or dirty? What will you do about it?   —D.B.

Through preaching, teaching, and the Bible, God is telling me . . . _____

_____

Through nature and the lives of other believers, God is showing me . . . _____

_____

_____

I will respond by . . . _____

_____

_____

A RESPONSIVE SOUL

People with pull

READ
Titus 2:1–8

MEDITATE
1 Corinthians 11:1
Follow my example.

REFLECT

➡ In what ways do I lead others? Who might be looking to me as an example of how to live?

➡ How can I learn more about Christ's example? How important is His example to my own ability to lead wisely?

➡ What earthly example of good leadership can I look to?

CONSIDER
Good leaders don't push their weight around; they point the way around.

Remember playing "follow the leader"? One person would get up and do silly things and everyone else had to follow exactly. Now that you're beyond silly preschool games, do you find yourself in leadership—at the head of the class, president of the youth group, student council officer? Ever wonder about your authority? Or question how to manage? Or wonder what to do? Where to start?

Dwight D. Eisenhower did some serious leading. As Supreme Commander of the Allied troops during World War II, and as President of the United States from 1953 to 1961, he managed quite successfully. To illustrate how he did it, he used a simple demonstration. He would place a single piece of string on a table and say, "Pull it and it follows wherever you want it to go; but push it, and it goes nowhere."

You may be able to push people around for a while and get them to do what you want, but in the long run the people you lead in such a way will become disillusioned and resentful.

To earn the respect of those you lead, you need to model honesty and commitment. That's exactly what Paul did. He encouraged others to follow him because he had confidence in the One he followed: Christ (1 Corinthians 11:1).

So if your goal is to lead others, your task will be a demanding one. But one thing is sure—leaders who know how to pull have a lot greater chance of success than those who only know how to push. —T.B.

Through preaching, teaching, and the Bible, God is telling me . . . _____

_____

_____

Through nature and the lives of other believers, God is showing me . . . _____

_____

_____

I will respond by . . . _____

_____

_____

Ya gotta have

JU5NE

Taking the challenge

READ
Psalm 16

MEDITATE
Psalm 16:8
I have set the Lord always before me.

REFLECT

➡ Do I think and pray before the day begins or do I plunge into it?

➡ What situations are particularly tough for me? How would it help me to think and pray beforehand?

➡ How will these verses help me? Ephesians 4:23; Philippians 2:1–5; Colossians 3:2.

CONSIDER
When you plan your day, include God.

Athletes talk about getting "psyched up" for big games. It's the process they go through to get into the right mental attitude. One college football player spends two hours doing this on the day of the game. He says, "I think about the good plays I could make. In my mind I jump around and ward off blockers, then I tackle the quarterback for a loss." Many golf pros do the same thing in getting ready for a tournament. They sit back and imagine themselves making a perfect drive or iron shot that drops the ball a few inches from the flag.

Mental preparation can also help us get ready for the challenges of living for Christ. It's a way of preparing spiritually for the specific needs we have. Instead of praying the general "bless me" and "use me" prayers, picture yourself making the kind of Christian response the situation calls for.

Maybe you'll see yourself faced with another tough Friday. You planned to get up early and look over your notes one more time before the exam, but you slept through the alarm. You can't find your good pen, and you're out of clean socks.

Okay. There's nothing you can do to change your circumstances, so you'll have to make the best of them. How? By not compounding your problems by going into the day already stressed out. So sit back and relax. That's right. Even if you're already running late. Now, as the psalmist did, set the Lord before you. Picture Him at your right hand, keeping you from falling out of character. Imagine Jesus walking with you and claim the power of the Holy Spirit. Then you'll not merely be "psyched up," you'll be mentally and spiritually prepared to meet the challenges in ways that honor the Lord.   —M.D.

Through preaching, teaching, and the Bible, God is telling me . . . _____

_____

Through nature and the lives of other believers, God is showing me . . . _____

_____

I will respond by . . . _____

_____

A SOUND MIND

167

JU6NE

News you can trust

READ
Nehemiah 6:1–14

MEDITATE
Nehemiah 6:19
And Tobiah sent letters to intimidate me.

REFLECT

➡ Why am I sometimes quick to believe bad news about people?

➡ Am I ever guilty of spreading false or misleading information? Of talking before I have all the facts?

CONSIDER
Compare bad news with the Good Book.

If you can trust anything, you can trust the newspaper, right? Day after day it arrives at your door (or on the porch roof, depending on the aim of your paper carrier). It tells you about the events of the day and the people who made them happen. It uncovers scandal, warns of danger, reports on international news, and gives you the scores. Without its daily summary of government, business, sports, and world affairs, you'd be the odd person out in many conversations.

But a strange thing happened to me on my way to my easy chair one day. I knew the inside story about an event that made front-page news, and I was interested to read what the newspaper would say about it. To my disappointment, I found out that my "trusted newspaper" was not so trustworthy after all. The core of the story was accurate but

many of the details were not. It was obvious that whoever gave information to the reporter did not have the facts straight. The readers, of course, had no idea they were getting misleading and wrong information.

Nehemiah received wrong information too. His came in the form of untrue and threatening letters from Tobiah. He recognized the letters as a deliberate attempt to get him to stop rebuilding the walls of Jerusalem, and he had enough sense to ignore them and keep on doing what was right.

Are we as discerning as Nehemiah? What do we do when someone sidles up to us with a major league rumor? Can we tell when someone is using "news" to manipulate us?

Test the news you hear. Compare it with the truth of God. Then you'll know if you have news you can trust!
—M.D.

Through preaching, teaching, and the Bible, God is telling me . . . _____

_____

Through nature and the lives of other believers, God is showing me . . . _____

_____

I will respond by . . . _____

_____

Rot and squish

READ
Philippians 4:4–8

MEDITATE
Ecclesiastes 1:8
The eye never has enough of seeing nor the ear its fill of hearing.

REFLECT

➡ Do I think much about the things I listen to on the radio and watch on TV? And what about the videos I choose? What are they saying to me? What am I doing to myself?

➡ Where do I really stand on this issue? Do I have a stand? Do I need to take one?

CONSIDER
It matters what goes into your mind.

If you become a couch potato, will you rot and be thrown away? And if you turn into a radio bug, will you get squashed?

Huh?

Okay. Let me ask it another way. Do you think you are being shaped by the programs you watch on TV and the kind of music you listen to? I posed this question to a group of college students recently and here are some of their comments:

First student: "Only if you let yourself. If you're not looking to be influenced by something, you won't be. I knew a person who considered himself to be born again. I talked about rock music with him, and he said he used to listen to it but it made him do certain things, and I laughed at him because it can't make you do anything. It's not hypnotic."

Second student: "I disagree. The advertising industry wouldn't spend 70 billion dollars a year to put ads on TV if they didn't influence people. I believe hearing a song over and over again is going to influence people. Not overtly but maybe subvertly."

Third student: "I don't get influenced by music unless I want to be."

Second student (again): "You're not like the rest of the world or me. I'm talking about it subtly modifying your attitude and the way you look at life. I think music could do that."

Now, what do you think? And what about the Bible? Does it say anything about what we should allow into our minds? Yes!

Read Philippians 4:8. (Yes, right now.) Look at the description of the things we should have on our minds: True. Noble. Right. Pure. Lovely. Admirable. Excellent. Praiseworthy. That ought to make us think.   —D.P.

Through preaching, teaching, and the Bible, God is telling me . . . _____

_____

Through nature and the lives of other believers, God is showing me . . . _____

_____

I will respond by . . . _____

_____

How smart are you?

The history prof strode into the classroom engulfed in a cloud of arrogance. He was the teacher; we were the lowly, ignorant scum of the earth who signed up for his required course. He not only knew a lot, but he also knew he knew it—and that's what irritated me the most, I guess. Maybe that's part of the reason I reacted so strongly one day when he talked about Jesus Christ.

This prof treated the Bible as if it were myth and referred to Christ as just one of many so-called messiahs. The teacher's lecture left Jesus in the grave—with no mention of a resurrection.

I couldn't stand it, so I raised my hand and asked about the reported resurrection of Jesus and His uniqueness. You would have thought that I had publicly slandered the prof's mother! He went into a verbal tirade until the class ended.

I may not have handled the situation very well. I know now that I could have stated my question in a less threatening manner. In fact, I realize that my arrogance about my knowledge of Christ was just as obnoxious as my prof's arrogance about all he knew.

In those kinds of situations it's important not to misuse the statement, "I have more insight than all my teachers" (Psalm 119:99). The psalmist, though, was not thumbing his nose at godless teachers; he was rejoicing over the rich truths of God's Word. He knew that by studying the Bible he would gain the most important knowledge of life. And he was not being arrogant. Rather, he had a quiet confidence that the best education comes from personal study of God's Word. How smart do you want to be?   —K.D.

Through preaching, teaching, and the Bible, God is telling me . . . _____
_____
_____

Through nature and the lives of other believers, God is showing me . . . _____
_____
_____

I will respond by . . . _____

The nightmare

READ
Proverbs 4:1–15

MEDITATE
Hebrews 2:1
We must pay more careful attention . . . so that we do not drift away.

REFLECT
➡ Do I pay attention to what is being taught in church? What about this past Sunday? What was the lesson about? What did I get out of it? Was I tuned in or tuned out?
➡ Am I growing as a Christian? If not, could it be I've not applied what I've been taught?

CONSIDER
If you're not listening, you're not learning.

It's a recurring nightmare on the college campus. And it's one that most students (except for those all-A brainiacs) have experienced. You sit through class for what seems like an eternity listening to another in an endless string of less-than-thrilling lectures.

Well, almost listening. You catch an occasional word or phrase, but basically you're tuned out. You think about everything except what's being taught. The same thing happens when you read the boring textbook.

Then, the next time you show up for class, the nightmare begins. Instead of picking up where he left off, wherever that was, the instructor says, "Okay, get out pencil and paper and put your textbooks away. We're going to have a test."

A test! You've gotta be kidding. You tell yourself not to panic. You did attend class, so you probably know more than you think. There's nothing to worry about. I mean, how bad could it be?

The test lands on your desk. Oh, that bad. You realize that you know even less than you thought you did. And what you do know is slipping away fast. You'll be lucky to pass. "If only I had paid attention!" you say to yourself.

What's true of the classroom is true of church. If we are to get anything out of it, we have to pay attention. "We must pay more careful attention, therefore, to what we have heard, so that we do not drift away" (Hebrews 2:1).

So the next time someone speaks about God, don't sleepwalk through what is being taught. It could turn out to be a nightmare.

—D.P.

Through preaching, teaching, and the Bible, God is telling me . . . _____

_____

Through nature and the lives of other believers, God is showing me . . . _____

_____

I will respond by . . . _____

Asleep on the job

READ
Revelation 3:1–6

MEDITATE
Revelation 3:2
"Wake up!"

REFLECT
➡ If serving and pleasing God is my number one goal, do I spend enough time each day making sure I accomplish that?

➡ What good things can distract my attention from God?

➡ Satan is a master of distraction. How does he distract me from my goal of following Christ?

CONSIDER
To avoid distractions, keep your eyes on Jesus.

One thing an umpire is supposed to do is pay attention. He can't be day-dreaming or scanning the stands for his wife or figuring his income tax with his ball/strike counter. It's his job to keep his eye on the ball at all times. When he doesn't, a fiasco follows.

It was a minor league game somewhere in Texas. The score was tied in the bottom of the ninth. Texarkana had a runner at third and the batter had two strikes on him. As the Sherman pitcher came to the plate with the pitch, the runner at third took off for home. Quickly the home plate area was a swirl of activity as the ball, the runner, the batter, and the umpire all congregated amid the flying dust. The runner appeared to slide across the plate with the winning run. But wait! No sooner had the safe call been given than the Sherman manager was nose-to-nose with the umpire. If the pitch is a strike, he explained, then the batter is out and the run doesn't count. When he asked the umpire if the pitch was a ball or strike, all the befuddled masked man could say was, "I don't know. I was watching the runner and I didn't pay attention to the pitch." You can imagine the scene that followed. Being distracted caused the umpire a lot of grief.

We're often like that umpire. The distractions of daily living, even though they are not bad, keep us from accomplishing our primary goal: serving Christ and living for Him. It's tough to keep our eyes on the Lord while taking care of everything else. But we can do it if we don't get distracted by the flurry of activity all around us.   —D.B.

Through preaching, teaching, and the Bible, God is telling me . . . _____
_____
_____

Through nature and the lives of other believers, God is showing me . . . _____
_____
_____

I will respond by . . . _____
_____
_____

Today's widows

READ
**Deuteronomy
10:17–21**

MEDITATE
Jeremiah 49:11
"Your widows too can
trust in me."

REFLECT
➡ I think it would be
tough to raise kids
alone because . . .
➡ Who is one single
mother I know?
➡ How can I help
her?

CONSIDER
*A sympathetic
heart is proven
by helpful
hands.*

A major trend in society during the 1980s was the emergence of the single-parent family. According to a *Newsweek* article, 5.6 million children under the age of fifteen lived in homes without a father in 1988.

For the young mother who has lost her husband, whether through death or divorce, life is tough. In cases of divorce, the *Newsweek* article added, only one-third of all divorced mothers receive any financial support from their former husbands. As for help in raising the kids, a 1981 study by the National Survey of Children found that nearly half of all children between the ages of eleven and sixteen living with their mothers hadn't seen their fathers for a year.

Thus, the single mother has to raise her children with little help and go out and find a job to pay the bills. During the time her youngsters need her the most, financial realities force her to be away from them.

A consistent theme in both the Old and New Testament is that God's people need to help widows and orphans. They represent some of society's most helpless people. A similar challenge could be issued to the church concerning single moms. As the statistics demonstrate, they too need our help. Whether mowing a lawn, joining with friends to perform minor home or car repairs, or babysitting, we can help single mothers.

True, God, more than anyone else, is there to support those who must go through life alone. But when you read verses such as James 1:27, ". . . look after orphans and widows," you don't have to wonder how to be God's hands and feet. And you don't need to look any further than your own church to find someone you can help!   —J.C.

Through preaching, teaching, and the Bible, God is telling me . . . _____
_____
_____

Through nature and the lives of other believers, God is showing me . . . _____
_____

I will respond by . . . _____
_____
_____

JUNE 12

Against the odds

READ
Judges 7:1–8

MEDITATE
Zechariah 4:6
"Not by might nor by power, but by my Spirit."

REFLECT
➡ At what times do I sense a need for God's help in my life?
➡ What situations make me retreat in fear if I am not trusting the Lord?
➡ What was a recent situation in which I saw God at work?

CONSIDER
If we are on God's side, we can't lose.

How would you like to compete against the best tennis players in the world on center court at Wimbledon? Would you like to step into the boxing ring with Mike Tyson? Do you think you could win a one-on-one basketball game with Michael Jordan? How well would your church slowpitch softball team do in a showdown with the Oakland Athletics?

What's the matter? Are you chicken or something? Afraid of a little challenge?

That's how Gideon must have felt when the Lord told him to battle the huge Midianite army with only three hundred men. Why did God make the odds so impossible? He explained, "In order that Israel may not boast against me that her own strength has saved her" (Judges 7:2). The Lord wanted everyone to know where the real power was.

God likes it when we are forced to depend on Him. That's when we begin to understand how weak and helpless we are against everything we face in life. And that's when we find out that He is all we need in all the battles of life.

What odds are against you today? Whom do you fear? Unreasonable teachers? A hostile roommate? An abusively anti-Christian fellow student who will verbally attack you if he or she hears you talk about Jesus to anyone? Tough co-workers who flaunt their immorality?

We all need to learn from Gideon. God can take care of us no matter what the odds are against us. As we learn to trust Him, He will also show that it is His strength working in us and for us. —K.D.

Through preaching, teaching, and the Bible, God is telling me . . . _____

Through nature and the lives of other believers, God is showing me . . . _____

I will respond by . . . _____

Ya gotta have

The greatest of all

MEDITATE
Isaiah 9:6
He will be called
Wonderful Counselor.

REFLECT

➡ Why do some people not want to discuss Jesus whey they talk about the other great figures of history?

➡ What about Jesus makes Him great to me?

CONSIDER
*Wise men still
seek Jesus.*

Who's the greatest person you've ever studied? Aristotle? Julius Caesar? Joan of Arc? Michelangelo? Queen Elizabeth I? Shakespeare? Abraham Lincoln? Martin Luther King, Jr.? Winston Churchill?

These were truly remarkable people. What they accomplished went far beyond the normal. They led nations or sparked revolutions in thinking, politics, or the arts.

One other name surpasses them all, but it is generally overlooked in classroom discussions of great people. The name is Jesus.

Look at what eyewitnesses said about Him: "This man has done nothing wrong" (Luke 23:41). "No one ever spoke the way this man does" (John 7:46). "I find no basis for a charge against this man" (Luke 23:4). "Surely this was a righteous man" (Luke 23:47).

But those comments in response to some false charges reflect only a part of His greatness. God Himself declared from heaven, "This is my Son, whom I love. Listen to him!" (Mark 9:7). That's the real reason Jesus is unique. In the history of the world, only Jesus was both divine and human.

Think about what Jesus accomplished. "He never wrote a book; yet the libraries of the world are filled with volumes written about Him. He never penned a musical note; yet He is the theme of more songs than any other subject in the world. Great men have come and gone; yet He lives on. All others have failed in some way, but not Jesus!"

In your quiet moments of reflection, do you think about Jesus? Contemplate the difference between Him and others. Then thank God that you can know the greatest Person of all.   —D.B.

Through preaching, teaching, and the Bible, God is telling me . . . _____

_____

Through nature and the lives of other believers, God is showing me . . . _____

_____

I will respond by . . . _____

_____

Out of the saltbox

READ
Matthew 5:13;
Luke 14:34–35

MEDITATE
Matthew 5:13
"You are the salt of the earth."

REFLECT
➡ How might my voice make a difference in the morality of my school?
➡ What wrongs am I aware of in my world that need correcting?
➡ What can I do about it?

CONSIDER
Salt does no good if it stays in the shaker.

Here's a quick quiz. Name five uses for salt. Ready for answers?

(1) Season food. (2) Melt ice. (3) Make ice cream. (4) Preserve meat. (5) Gargle.

Did I say preserve meat? Sure did. Although we don't think much about it in our day of refrigeration, it was important in Jesus' day. Suppose Peter and John have a good day on the lake and catch sixty-two fish. To get them ready for market in Jerusalem, sixty miles away, and to keep the fish from spoiling on the journey, they rub them heavily with salt. The salt will slow down the decaying process, so the fish will still be good when Peter and John finally get them to market.

Jesus talked about salt. He said that you are the salt of the earth. He meant that His followers are to perform the same function in the spiritual world that salt does in the natural world. Let's face it.

We live in a rotten world. Our righteousness, our stand for truth and right, our resistance to corrupting influence, is essential. We preserve our world from rotting within.

In the eighteenth century, France and England were both morally degenerate. France had a terrible, bloody revolution; England did not. Why? Historians say it was because of the powerful moral influence of one man—John Wesley. His preaching and the witness of his followers made the difference. He was salt.

You are the salt of your school, your workplace, your dorm, maybe even your family. Your life and witness can help preserve it from rotting. But to do so, you must get out of the saltbox. Isn't that exactly what Jesus was talking about?   —D.E.

Through preaching, teaching, and the Bible, God is telling me . . . _____
_____
_____

Through nature and the lives of other believers, God is showing me . . . _____
_____
_____

I will respond by . . . _____
_____

Who owns me?

READ
1 Corinthians
6:18–20

MEDITATE
1 Corinthians 7:23
You were bought at a price; do not become slaves of men.

REFLECT

➡ In what ways do I acknowledge that Christ owns me?

➡ What other things make claims of ownership on me?

➡ What decision have I made about my body? Do I consider it mine to do with as I please? Or do I consider it God's to do with as He pleases?

CONSIDER
*Our Father
knows best.*

The Humane Society was looking for new owners for unwanted cats and dogs. So it ran an ad with a picture of a lovable puppy and a cute little kitten. Over the page were printed these words: "It's who owns them that makes them important."

Who owns you? That's an important question for the Christian. The answer has a direct bearing on how we make our moral choices and what we do with our bodies.

Terry Hershey, Executive Director of Christian Focus, wrote, "To answer [the question of ownership] requires honesty and healthy introspection. I can be owned by my need to be needed, my need to rescue, my addiction to the 'high' of the conquest, my need to be held, my need to prove my masculinity or femininity. It is in coming to terms with this area of neediness that we begin to address the issue of our decision-making."

Okay, so who owns you? You belong to your parents, but they do not own you. Nor does a boyfriend or girlfriend. He or she has no right to demand full possession—especially if it involves a violation of your personal or moral boundaries to gratify a need for sex or power.

As Christians, we belong to God. He bought us with a heavy price—the life of His own Son. We are His. And when we accept His authority regarding right and wrong, we will make right moral choices.

As with the puppy and kitten in the animal shelter ad, it's who owns us that makes us important! —D.E.

Through preaching, teaching, and the Bible, God is telling me . . . _____

_____

_____

Through nature and the lives of other believers, God is showing me . . . _____

_____

_____

I will respond by . . . _____

_____

Dying inside

READ
John 6:35–40

MEDITATE
John 6:37
Whoever comes to me I will never drive away.

REFLECT
➡ Whose influence shapes my self-image the most? God's or someone else's?
➡ Whose acceptance do I want most?

CONSIDER
Don't try to earn what God has already given.

"Five more pounds, Mom. Just five more pounds." These were the words of a young woman, just out of high school, who was trying to find a way to fit into her world. She thought her problem was her weight. So she went on a diet. And it seemed to work. She lost fifteen pounds.

But that wasn't enough. Not nearly enough. So she continued to diet. Soon this was no longer a diet; it was an obsession. She lost more than weight. She lost her perspective.

She thought losing weight would solve her problems. It didn't. She went too far. Her weight dropped to seventy-five pounds. She died at the age of twenty-one.

This young woman was like a lot of today's college-age adults. Somewhere along the line they've picked up the message that they are unacceptable. And that message plays over and over in their heads. "You're too fat," it says. Or too thin. Or too short. Or too lanky. They just can't seem to get it right. Personal satisfaction is always on the other side of the window. And there they stand—hands cupped around their eyes, nose pressed against the glass, looking in.

It's lonely on the outside looking in. But that happens when we look to people for approval instead of to the Lord Jesus Christ. Making Him the most important person means we can stop killing ourselves to be accepted. We don't need to be thinner, smarter, more attractive, or more talented. We only need to come to Jesus Christ in faith and then live to please Him. "Whoever comes to me I will never drive away," He promises (John 6:37). Now, that's the kind of acceptance we all need.
—D.P.

Through preaching, teaching, and the Bible, God is telling me . . . _____
_____
_____

Through nature and the lives of other believers, God is showing me . . . _____
_____
_____

I will respond by . . . _____
_____
_____

Beyond destruction

READ
James 1:2–8, 12

MEDITATE
James 1:12
Blessed is the man who perseveres under trial.

REFLECT
➥ What is the hardest thing I have to do? School? Work? Practice? Resist a certain temptation?
➥ What keeps me from going to Christ and asking for the strength to handle it?
➥ How will this help me in the future?

CONSIDER
Don't settle for easy when hard is better.

You're climbing in the Central Cascade Mountains of Washington, and it's cold. You're following a mountain stream to Rachel Lake at the 6,000-foot level. It's September, and an early winterlike wind is blowing. Night comes. You camp. You decide to build a fire. You get out your saw, cut up some fallen limbs, and build a roaring fire to keep warm, right? Wrong!

You gather the wood all right, get lots of tinder, and set it all on fire—but the wood refuses to burn. Then you remember that the limbs seemed unusually heavy. And they were hard to cut, even with a sharp saw. You also noticed that the rings were very close together. Then you realize what has happened. Because of the harsh conditions—high altitude, strong winds, intense cold—the wood is extremely dense and strong. It's nearly impossible to destroy.

Living through tough conditions makes Christians durable and strong too. The harder the teacher, the more we learn. The more demanding the coach, the better we play. The more the music instructor expects, the better we perform. The harder we work, the stronger we become.

James was writing to believers who were being persecuted for their faith. I don't mean being mocked in the school lunch room (although that can be tough). I mean getting beat up, losing their jobs, having their homes burned down, being thrown into prison. Some even died.

With the Lord's help, hardship can make us tough—too tough to be destroyed by Satan and his forces. —D.E.

Through preaching, teaching, and the Bible, God is telling me . . . _____

_____

Through nature and the lives of other believers, God is showing me . . . _____

_____

I will respond by . . . _____

_____

A STRONG CHARACTER

JUNE

Dumping garbage

READ
Proverbs 12:6–19

MEDITATE
James 1:19
Everyone should be quick to listen, slow to speak.

REFLECT
➡ What situations are dangerous to me because they make me say things I regret later?
➡ What can I learn from these verses, which talk about how to control my tongue? Psalm 120:2; Proverbs 10:19; 18:6–7; 21:6; Ecclesiastes 10:12–14.

CONSIDER
A temporary outburst can do permanent damage.

We grew up with this philosophy:
Sticks and stones may break my bones, But words will never hurt me.
I knew it must have been true because Mom said it, and she was always right. Her kitchen wisdom helped me cope with a lot of trials and tribulations of growing up.

But now that I'm older, I know that this little saying is not really true. Although words cannot cause the same pain that a rock or a 2-by-4 does, they sure can hurt! Unkind words can inflict mental and emotional damage that can last a lifetime. I can still remember some very painful words said to me while I was growing up. And I'm sure I said some things that people are still trying to recover from.

In regard to our words, the apostle James said, "Be quick to listen, slow to speak and slow to become angry" (1:19). Sure. Nothing to it, right? Wrong. We all say things in frustration or anger that we regret later. The big question is, "How can I keep from saying things that hurt people?" When someone shortsheets my bed or trashes my favorite tape, how can I keep from saying something that will hurt?

Maybe it will help you to think of angry words as a pile of garbage. You've got it in the plastic bag of your mind and you're headed to the dumpster. But someone sets you off and BOOM! You dump that garbage all over the floor. Your stinking, hurtful words are everywhere. They're difficult to clean up, and some of the stains may be permanent.

I guess Mom was wrong. Words can hurt. Ask Christ to help you to be quick to listen. And think long and hard before you talk. Then you won't have a lot of garbage to clean up.   —D.E.

Through preaching, teaching, and the Bible, God is telling me . . . _____

Through nature and the lives of other believers, God is showing me . . . _____

I will respond by . . . _____

Follow your heart?

READ
Jeremiah 17:5–10

MEDITATE
Jeremiah 17:9
The heart is deceitful above all things and beyond cure.

REFLECT
➡ How is the following saying true in my life? *Sow a thought—reap an act. Sow an act—reap a habit. Sow a habit—reap a character. Sow a character—reap your destiny.*
➡ What good things can I do to keep myself so busy that I won't have time to get into the wrong situations?

CONSIDER
Trust God, not your emotions.

Have you ever felt torn between obeying your conscience and following the advice of friends? Are you resting on the horns of that dilemma right now? (And resting quite uncomfortably, I would guess.)

Your mind is telling you one thing, but your heart sends a different message. You can feel the war going on. If you decide to go through with it (experiment with drugs, surrender your body, read that questionable magazine), you'll be ignoring everything you know about right and wrong. But if you don't do it, you'll lose face with your friends. And even worse, you'll be MISSING SOMETHING. There's nothing worse than that!

So what are you going to do? It probably depends on whose advice you follow—whose voice you're listening to. A friend might say, "Come on, don't be such a dork. Live a little. You don't want to miss anything. Go for it. Follow your heart." (And by the way, people who say things like that aren't real friends.) But another voice tells you that following your heart can be a bad idea. That's the voice of God speaking to you.

"The heart is deceitful above all things and beyond cure" (Jeremiah 17:9).

"Out of the heart come evil thoughts, . . . sexual immorality, . . . false testimony . . ." (Matthew 15:19).

In life you make decisions, then those decisions turn around and make you. That's why it is always good to think things through before you act.

Don't follow your emotions. You can't always trust them. And don't do everything your friends tell you to do. You can't always trust them either. But you can always trust God. Follow Him. He won't lead you into trouble. —D.P.

Through preaching, teaching, and the Bible, God is telling me . . . _____
_____
_____

Through nature and the lives of other believers, God is showing me . . . _____
_____
_____

I will respond by . . . _____
_____

I sure fooled God!

READ
Acts 8:18–24

MEDITATE
Acts 8:21–22
"Your heart is not right before God. Repent of this wickedness."

REFLECT
➡ What are some wrong motives I have for doing things for the Lord? Specifically, why do I pray? Give? Attend church? Read the Bible?
➡ Is it possible to do anything with completely pure motives? Why?

CONSIDER
If you try to fool God, you'll be the fool.

Last week I volunteered to pick up the dry-cleaning so my wife wouldn't have to make the trip. It was a nice thing for me to do, but I didn't do it to be nice. I really wanted to check out the new fishing lures at the sporting goods store next door.

Have you ever offered to do something unselfish when you actually had a selfish motive in mind? We all do.

A little girl was kneeling beside her bed saying her goodnight prayers. "Dear Lord, she began, "now I lay me down to sleep." But before she said "Amen," she added a line to the familiar bedtime prayer. "And dear Jesus, please send the lovely snow to keep the flowers warm in winter." Her parents nearly burst with pride at the thoughtfulness and devotion of their little daughter. But then she looked at them mischievously. "I sure fooled the Lord that time. I really wanted the snow to come so I could play with my new sled."

We smile at such naïveté. But before we get too pious, we need to check our own intentions. It's easy to fall into the trap of doing good deeds with wrong motives. To make a new friend when what we're really after is a chance to meet her cute brother. Or to sing in church, not to glorify God but to get on Mom and Dad's good side. We can even put money in the offering for selfish reasons.

Acts 8 tells about Simon the Sorcerer who wanted the apostles' gift of healing. But he didn't want it so he could bring other people blessing; he wanted to use it to make money. Imagine such crass selfishness!

Let's be honest about our reasons for doing things. It's always a good idea to check our motives.　—D.E.

Through preaching, teaching, and the Bible, God is telling me . . . _____

_____

Through nature and the lives of other believers, God is showing me . . . _____

_____

I will respond by . . . _____

_____

DEAR LORD, GRANT ME THAT MANSION BY THE LAKE SO I CAN MORE ABLY MINISTER TO THE INCREDIBLY WEALTHY.

A LOVING HEART

Technical!

READ
Galatians 5:16–26

MEDITATE
Proverbs 14:29
A quick-tempered man displays folly.

REFLECT

➡ What makes me angry? Is my anger righteous? Does it honor or dishonor God?

➡ Is my anger a problem? Does the presence of the Spirit in my life (Galatians 5:22–23) leave room for things like anger?

CONSIDER
When you lose your temper, you always find trouble.

It was a hard-fought match between two evenly skilled professional tennis players. One of them was known for his temper. Losing it, that is. So you knew it had to happen. The line judge made a call that the player disagreed with. That's all it took. His racket went crashing to the ground and the air was filled with expletives. It turned out to be an expensive tirade. Not only did he lose an important point, the argument, and respect, he was also heavily fined for his behavior. "Better a patient man than a warrior, a man who controls his temper than one who takes a city" (Proverbs 16:32).

This is true in any sport. A head basketball coach should do more than just show his players how to play good defense. He's expected to show them how to be good people. One particular coach, however, became known as much for flying off the handle as for his winning teams. In one big game, he verbally abused an official for missing a big call. But the ref didn't miss the abuse. "Technical!" he signaled. The two free throws awarded to the other team proved to be costly. The angry coach's team lost by one point. "A quick-tempered man displays folly" (Proverbs 14:29).

We often watch people like these and think, "What losers!" But are we any better? When a friend does something we don't like, when our employer makes unfair demands, or when we get a lower grade than we think we deserve, do we always respond graciously?

We can—if we let the Holy Spirit control us. Let's be known by this verse: "The fruit of the Spirit is . . . self-control" (Galatians 5:22–23).
—D.P.

Through preaching, teaching, and the Bible, God is telling me . . . _____

_____

_____

Through nature and the lives of other believers, God is showing me . . . _____

_____

_____

I will respond by . . . _____

_____

_____

Ya gotta have

Mouthwashing

READ
Proverbs 16:18–24

MEDITATE
Proverbs 16:23
A wise man's heart guards his mouth.

REFLECT

➡ What words of wisdom can I find in Proverbs 16 about controlling what I say?

➡ Do I ever use God's name in vain? What does swearing do for me? What does it do to God?

➡ How can I have more control over what I say? How can I control my mouth?

CONSIDER
Our words reveal what is hiding in our hearts.

They've been doing it in Asia for centuries. Now they are doing it in the United States. What is it? Eating curry? Riding in rickshaws? Using chopsticks? No. Cleaning their tongues.

Studies at an American university show that if you will take the time (and can stand it) to clean your tongue every day, you will reduce the build-up of dental plaque that leads to tooth decay. (As news goes, this isn't big, but your teeth would appreciate it.) So an enterprising businessman has manufactured a tongue-cleaning tool and is marketing it through a major drugstore chain. If the idea catches on, he says, Americans will soon have clean tongues.

I have vivid memories of something else that cleans mouths. As a child, I once used the Lord's name in vain at the dinner table. Big mistake! Big, big mistake! I had my mouth washed out with soap. And guess what. It worked. I never did that again.

I wish keeping my mouth clean were as easy as using a tongue-cleaner or a bar of Ivory soap. Just think of what it would mean to have tongues that didn't gossip, tell lies, criticize friends, speak unloving words, spew out anger, or reveal secrets. It sure would be an effective way to keep from saying too much when we should keep quiet or saying too little when we should speak up.

The Bible says we can have more careful speech if we have a wise heart. And how do we get a wise heart? By yielding to the will and control of the Lord. Only He can help us keep our tongue clean.   —M.D.

Through preaching, teaching, and the Bible, God is telling me . . . _____

_____

_____

Through nature and the lives of other believers, God is showing me . . . _____

_____

_____

I will respond by . . . _____

_____

_____

A LOVING HEART

Love attack

READ
1 Peter 3:8–13

MEDITATE
1 Peter 3:8
Be sympathetic, love as brothers, be compassionate.

REFLECT
➡ Do I have a friend or acquaintance who needs someone to show some love and care? What is one thing I can do to show true compassion?

CONSIDER
Love breaks down the barrier of fear.

Something had attacked Erica's body, and doctors weren't sure what it was. For a week, things like walking, combing her hair, and talking on the phone were almost impossible.

Erica needed prayer, love, and patience. And she received it in abundance—especially from her parents, her church, and her teachers. And from Lisa, her close friend.

Lisa's love and acceptance were remarkable. While Erica's other friends weren't quite sure how to relate to her, Lisa called her on the phone every day, starting with her first day in the hospital. Although Erica's speech was slow and halting, Lisa would wait patiently for her to talk, and she never mentioned how difficult it was to understand Erica. She laughed with her sick friend, talked about normal things, and offered to help her in any way she could. To Lisa, Erica was still Erica, even if she was sick.

Lisa's love was therapeutic. She didn't allow Erica to feel alone. She was exactly what Christ expects His followers to be. Selfless. She wasn't expecting anything in return. She simply recognized the need and responded. Erica has recovered—partly because Lisa made sure she came down with a sudden attack of love.

With Lisa's example in mind, let's think about how we love others. Do we look out for the needs of our friends, or do we leave that for someone else? Is there someone at school or church who needs love and acceptance? Peter's assignment, "Be sympathetic, love as brothers, be compassionate" is still due.

We do a lot of talking about love and compassion. Let's put it into practice. There are a lot of hurting people out there.   —D.P.

Through preaching, teaching, and the Bible, God is telling me . . . _____

_____

_____

Through nature and the lives of other believers, God is showing me . . . _____

_____

_____

I will respond by . . . _____

_____

J24E Reality of rejection

READ
Matthew 27:27–46

MEDITATE
Matthew 27:46
"My God, my God, why have you forsaken me?"

REFLECT

➡ When do I feel the most alone? The most forsaken? What can I do about it?

➡ Rejection is a part of life, so what can I do to handle it better?

➡ Whom do I know that needs a friend? How can I help that person overcome feelings of rejection?

CONSIDER
Jesus was rejected so that we might never be.

I'm sorry. You're just not working out. We're going to have to let you go."

"We've been talking it over. Next fall we're going to ask Carrie Wilson to be our roommate. You're going to have to find someone else to live with."

"Our car's filled up. Sorry. You'll have to go to the game with someone else."

Are these awful situations, or what? We'd rather have almost anything happen to us than to be rejected by people we thought had accepted us.

Perhaps you've been feeling a lot of rejection lately, and it hurts. It seems that nobody understands.

Not true. One Person does understand: the Lord Jesus. Look at the rejections He faced during the final hours of His life. Judas, His disciple, sold Him out (Matthew 26:14–15). The other disciples forsook Him (26:56). The religious leaders

of Israel lined up against Him (26:59; 27:41). Peter, one of the inner three, denied Him (26:69–75). And finally, even His heavenly Father turned His face from Him (27:46), causing Him to cry, "My God, why have you forsaken me!"

Yes, Jesus was "despised and rejected" (Isaiah 53:3). Yet He suffered that humiliation, that terrible aloneness, so that He could bring us forgiveness. But there's more. Because He suffered, He can understand the pain of our rejection.

Sure you feel alone, forsaken, hurt. But the Lord Jesus will never, never, NEVER forsake you. Because of Him, you have help when you face even the toughest of rejections.   —D.E.

Through preaching, teaching, and the Bible, God is telling me . . . _____
_____
_____

Through nature and the lives of other believers, God is showing me . . . _____
_____
_____

I will respond by . . . _____

Dealing with bears

READ
Psalm 34

MEDITATE
Psalm 34:4
He delivered me from all my fears.

REFLECT

➡ What tough situations have I faced recently? Did I try to avoid them or trust the Lord and confront them head-on?

➡ Why is it so hard to trust in God for help?

➡ What can I do to learn to trust Him more?

CONSIDER
Fear the Lord and you won't fear anything else.

A nyone with half a brain would think twice about charging a large black bear. Yet that's the latest advice from someone who should know. Lynn Rogers, a wildlife ecologist, has been studying bears for most of his life. He claims that black bears are timid animals who will clack their teeth, blow air, moan, slap the ground, and even rush briefly at people—all as a bluff. His advice? Next time you are camping and a black bear confronts you, don't drop your backpack and run for a tree; instead, wave your arms, throw rocks, and scream! Any volunteers?

Maybe you don't do a lot of camping, but I'm sure you confront some pretty ferocious "bears" during the week. A tough assignment. A difficult roommate. A blustery coach. A sudden illness. Ridicule from a nonbelieving coworker.

Maybe you've already learned that you can't outrun these bears either. So what're you supposed to do?

Confront them!

Confront a bear? Thanks for the great advice.

It's true. God wants you to stand up for what is right and not cower and quake when you meet a bearlike challenge.

David wrote that the person who trusts in God cannot lose. "I sought the Lord, and he answered me; he delivered me from all my fears" (Psalm 34:4). David knew that "the angel of the Lord encamps around those who fear him" (v. 7), and that "the eyes of the Lord are on the righteous and his ears are attentive to their cry" (v. 15).

When you meet a bear today, do what is right and be assured that the Lord is watching out for you. —K.D.

Through preaching, teaching, and the Bible, God is telling me . . . _____

_____

Through nature and the lives of other believers, God is showing me . . . _____

_____

I will respond by . . . _____

_____

Partnership with God

READ
Luke 11:1–10

MEDITATE
Luke 11:1

"Lord, teach us to pray."

REFLECT

→ What do I find especially satisfying, or particularly uninteresting, about prayer?

→ How can I benefit by putting Jesus' model in my own words and by praying persistently? How will others benefit? What will happen to my relationship with Jesus?

CONSIDER
Before making plans, talk to the architect.

Just in case you missed the August 1990 issue of the *Journal of the American Medical Association,* here's some information you might be interested in knowing.

The AMA studied a group of 200 hospitalized heart patients to evaluate the power of prayer. That's right. Doctors studied prayer! The patients were divided into two control groups. One group was not prayed for, and the other group was prayed for regularly by some Christians. None of the patients was told of the experiment. The results were startling: The patients who were prayed for had significantly fewer complications than those who were not.

It's difficult to say exactly what happens when people pray, but the really neat thing is that everyone benefits. In his book *Only a Prayer Away,* John Guest writes, "It is remarkable to think that God has given us a partnership with Him in directing the course of human events. It is extraordinary to realize that our prayer can change events and circumstances in the world around us. But what is just as remarkable is that when we pray, we change. More often than not we become the answer to our own prayers as we open up ourselves to God in prayer."

The Bible is full of examples of prayers and instructions for believers to pray. In Luke 11 we have the privilege of learning Jesus' response to the disciples' request, "Teach us to pray." He responded by providing a model for prayer (vv. 2–4), and by stressing the importance of persistence in praying (vv. 5–10).

Prayer is no experiment. Put it into practice.   —T.B.

Through preaching, teaching, and the Bible, God is telling me . . . _____

_____

Through nature and the lives of other believers, God is showing me . . . _____

_____

I will respond by . . . _____

_____

Finish what you start

READ
2 Timothy 4:6–8

MEDITATE
2 Timothy 4:7
I have finished the race.

REFLECT
→ Have I slowed down in my Christian development? Did I stop growing? When? Why?
→ What kinds of things stop me spiritually? Disappointment? Temptation? Peer pressure? Money problems?

CONSIDER
Ending well is better than starting fast.

For a long time the racing cars built by Mickey Thompson were the fastest in the world. He was a wizard at getting peak performance out of an engine. Mickey Thompson cars were great starters.

But not one of them was a winner! That's right. Thompson's racers did not get a single checkered flag. Why?

None of them finished. Although Thompson could build the fastest automobiles in the world, he couldn't build one to run an entire race. Each of those twenty-nine cars was leading the race when it broke down and had to pull out. Sometimes it was a blown engine. Other times it was a broken gearbox or steering problem. Mickey Thompson's cars had great beginnings. But they never made it to the finish line.

Know anybody who starts things with enthusiasm but somewhere before the finish line loses it and lets the project die? Could that person be you?

Believers in Jesus need to be both good starters and good finishers. The apostle Paul is a good example. He started well by responding immediately to Christ on the Damascus road. He learned about Christ in the seminary of the desert. He spearheaded the European missionary effort. Along with joys and successes, he had disappointments, persecutions, and pressures. Then when Paul was about to be martyred, he said that he had finished the race. And he did so having "kept the faith."

Perhaps you had a good start with the Lord. You've been making progress. But now you're struggling. Discouragement has come over you. Or temptation. Call on the Lord for help. Christ can make you a good finisher.   —D.E.

Through preaching, teaching, and the Bible, God is telling me . . . _____
_____
_____

Through nature and the lives of other believers, God is showing me . . . _____
_____
_____

I will respond by . . . _____
_____
_____

Running on empty

READ
Isaiah 40:28–31

MEDITATE
Isaiah 40:31
Those who hope in the Lord will renew their strength.

REFLECT
➡ Why do I seem to have so little time for fellowship, Bible reading, and prayer?
➡ What does that tell me about what's important to me?
➡ What should I do to keep my spiritual tanks full?

CONSIDER
Is it time for a spiritual fill-up?

"We won't run out," I said confidently. "There's enough gas to get you home and me too. I know the gas gauge on this car."

My new girlfriend and I were on our way home after a big date, and it was close to midnight. She had seen that the needle was past empty and had let me know that she had no intention of walking the rest of the way home.

As usual, I was running on empty. It's not that I didn't have the money. I simply didn't leave myself enough time to stop for gas.

Looking at the gauge, I knew she had reason to worry; but I didn't admit it to her, and I didn't let her hear my huge sigh of relief when we pulled into her driveway. Nor did I ever tell her that I ran out of gas less than three blocks from her house and had to walk more than a mile to get more.

I sometimes do the same thing spiritually. I keep myself running at top speed, barely slowing down to say hello to the Lord at the end of the day. I get up late the next morning, rush headlong into the day, and keep repeating the cycle. I allow no time for reading the Bible or anything more than a ten-second "thanks for the food" prayer. There's certainly no time for reflecting on the character of God or carrying on an extended conversation with Him. Spiritually speaking, I'm running on empty, putting myself at risk of becoming stranded in some spiritual wasteland.

So what's the answer? Keep the spiritual energy flowing through fellowship with believers, quality time in the Word, and deep, honest prayer. Meditate on God's truth. If you use these spiritual tank-fillers, you won't find yourself running out of gas. —D.E.

Through preaching, teaching, and the Bible, God is telling me . . . _____

_____

_____

Through nature and the lives of other believers, God is showing me . . . _____

_____

_____

I will respond by . . . _____

_____

READ
Matthew 23:23–28

MEDITATE
Matthew 23:26
"Clean the inside . . . and then the outside also will be clean."

REFLECT
➡ Why do I sometimes pretend to be spiritual when I'm really not?

➡ God makes it clear that He doesn't respect fakers. What can I do to make my devotion to Him more true?

CONSIDER
Looking good is no substitute for being good.

N ow for something completely different:

"Hey-y-y-y dudes and dudettes. This is veejay TeleTom coming to you on CJTV—your daily video devotional station. Let's kick back and take in some awesome sights and sounds from that totally cosmic group, C.J. Staph & The Infections. But before that, remember this: We're your only 24-hour, high-power, sun or shower, 'quiet time' channel. And we're geared to give you the hottest in videovotions. Ready, get set, let's . . ."

Due to a serious lack of reality (and technical difficulties), CJTV has mercifully been canned. Please ignore the previous paragraph.

I tried, but I just couldn't do it. Fake video, that is. No matter which way I strike the keys on my Macintosh, the words come out in black and white type—not full color video. And pseudo-video just doesn't cut it.

Neither does pseudo-Christianity. Jesus got after the Pharisees for trying to fake their way to heaven. They were hypocrites—people who acted out the righteous life. And Jesus wouldn't buy it.

You may have said "Whoa!" to all the "woes" in today's Bible reading. But they're important.

The Pharisees were condemned by Jesus for this reason: although they put on a pretty face, they were full of "greed and self-indulgence" and "hypocrisy and wickedness." Not exactly the fruit of the Spirit.

Does the Pharisee condition exist today? You better believe it. But God has a better plan. He wants us to live for Him and love Him with all our heart, soul, and mind. He doesn't want "Joe Christians" who just look good. Get the picture? It's time to tune in.   —T.F.

Through preaching, teaching, and the Bible, God is telling me . . . _____

_____

_____

Through nature and the lives of other believers, God is showing me . . . _____

_____

_____

I will respond by . . . _____

_____

_____

Still a kid

READ
Hebrews 5:12–6:3

MEDITATE
Hebrews 6:1
Let us . . . go on to maturity.

REFLECT

➡ What is my spiritual age? If others knew how long I've been a Christian would they consider me mature or immature in my faith? Why?

➡ What can I do to increase my spiritual maturity? Why should I go to the trouble?

➡ How can I encourage other believers to grow?

CONSIDER
You should never stop growing— spiritually.

He celebrated his twenty-fifth birthday in September of 1990, but he never attended high school or college. In fact, he still acts like a kid.

Who is this guy? You've probably seen him on TV. He's cute, a little pudgy, and giggles a lot—especially when you poke him in the stomach. In 1987, *Advertising Age* declared him to be America's most loved character.

Still wondering who I'm describing? Here are a few more hints: He hangs out in the refrigerated section at grocery stores, he makes a lot of dough, and he wears a chef's hat.

Now do you know? Yeah, yeah, he's the Pillsbury Doughboy, alias "Poppin' Fresh."

Despite all his cuteness, the Doughboy can really get on my nerves. He's such a kid. I mean, how deep can a guy be who has spent twenty-five years giggling about dinner rolls? Ever had a roommate like that?

The Pillsbury Doughboy can get us thinking about our own age and spiritual maturity. Do we have any depth to our knowledge of the Bible or our relationship with God? Or have we remained pretty much the same as we were after one year of trusting Christ?

The writer of Hebrews challenged his readers to grow up in the faith, to dig into the "meat" of God's Word, and not be satisfied with the important but elementary truths (Hebrews 6:1).

Are you growing up in your spiritual knowledge and in your relationship to Christ? How have you grown this year? This week? —K.D.

Through preaching, teaching, and the Bible, God is telling me . . . _____

_____

Through nature and the lives of other believers, God is showing me . . . _____

_____

I will respond by . . . _____

_____

Do the rich rule?

READ
Psalm 72:8–14

MEDITATE
Psalm 72:13
He will take pity on the weak and the needy.

REFLECT
➡ What do I like least about politics?
➡ Why do the poor and helpless need God's help (and mine)?

CONSIDER
Salvation puts us all on level ground.

In our society, money and power seem to go hand in hand. The "golden rule" seems to be that those who have the gold make the rules. Businesses and special interest groups stuff the campaign coffers of politicians, who then repay their political debt in the form of favorable votes.

Even though this sounds depressing (and maybe a bit cynical), we can take heart that it's not God's way of running a nation. Look at today's Scripture reading. It's drawn from a prayer written by Solomon concerning his own rule, but it's also a prophecy about Jesus Christ's righteous rule.

The first four verses (8–11) talk about the kings of the earth bowing down to Israel's king. They bring gifts and tribute; these powerful rulers serve the righteous ruler. But who holds the special place in the ruler's heart? Look at verses 12–14. The needy, the afflicted, the weak—they receive pity from the king. He rushes to their aid.

When Jesus came to earth, He followed those principles. When He taught in His hometown synagogue (Luke 4:14–30), He chose to read from Isaiah 61:1–2: "The Spirit of the Lord is on me because he has anointed me to preach good news to the poor" (Luke 4:18). Throughout His ministry, Jesus showed pity toward those too powerless—whether physically, economically, or politically—to defend themselves.

What are your "politics" like? Do the rich get special treatment from you? Are you more likely to make friends on the basis of social status? Then you may be responding to the wrong "constituency"! —J.C.

Through preaching, teaching, and the Bible, God is telling me . . . _____

_____

_____

Through nature and the lives of other believers, God is showing me . . . _____

_____

_____

I will respond by . . . _____

_____

_____

194

Ya gotta have

What do you know?

READ
Proverbs 2:1–11

MEDITATE
1 Corinthians 8:1
Knowledge puffs up.

REFLECT

➡ My field of greatest knowledge is _____ _____.

➡ How can I use that for God's glory?

➡ What kinds of things could the right kind of knowledge help me avoid (see Proverbs 2)?

➡ In what areas would I like to increase my knowledge?

CONSIDER
Let what you know reflect the One you know.

A senior had backed a meek little freshman into a corner and was bombarding him with an impressive string of scientific facts. He said, "Did you know that . . . ? Are you aware of . . . ? Does it interest you . . . ?" Finally, the beleaguered freshman got a word in edgewise. "Well, there is one thing you do not know," he squeaked out. The senior glared at the frosh and snapped, "And just what is it I don't know?" "You don't know that you are standing on my sore foot!"

Knowledge is good, and we should accumulate as much of it as possible. But it is not good if we use it to hurt or intimidate others.

I've had professors who knew so much it made my head hurt just to think about it. But they had the personality of Attila the Hun, so they had a tough time transferring any of that knowledge to students. And as a teacher, I've had students who were smarter than I am—and acted like it too. The first part I could handle, but not the arrogance. I'd rather be around people who know a little less and care a little more.

As Solomon said, "Knowledge will be pleasant to your soul" (Proverbs 2:10). It keeps you out of trouble at times, Proverbs 2 suggests. The right kind of knowledge can help you know what is right and what is wrong. It is something you need to pursue with enthusiasm.

But once you get a little of it, be careful how you use it. Never use knowledge as a club to pound over people or as a wedge to separate friends. Keep in mind that our knowledge, as great as it might seem, is nothing compared with God's.

What do you know? Probably many, many things. But don't let it go to your head. —D.B.

Through preaching, teaching, and the Bible, God is telling me . . . _____

_____

_____

Through nature and the lives of other believers, God is showing me . . . _____

_____

I will respond by . . . _____

_____

No hype

READ
Luke 3:1–18

MEDITATE
Luke 3:4
"Prepare the way for the Lord."

REFLECT
→ Why would it be easy for the world to associate Christians with hype?
→ How can I spread the Gospel without hype?

CONSIDER
The Gospel—the whole truth and nothing but the truth.

I teach a course in public relations at Azusa Pacific University. One topic that always causes a lot of discussion is hype, which means to create excitement about an event long before it happens.

For example, P.T. Barnum, hype's founding father, would stage wild publicity stunts to draw attention to his entertainments. Hype is used today as well—by rock stars seeking publicity, by movie people trying to create advance excitement for a flick. (Remember seeing those dinosaur symbols everywhere?)

One public relations firm president made the following statement: "John the Baptist himself did superb advance work for Jesus of Nazareth."

I know PR has been practiced throughout history, but John the Baptist? I don't think so! Even the most casual reading of today's Scripture reading shows that his ministry was not just PR. And his choice of words like *repent* would make any PR practitioner turn pale.

John the Baptist's ministry was to call Israel to repentance in preparation to receive her Messiah. Advance work? Perhaps. Hype? No way!

You might think you are practicing PR by sharing your faith. You are, but in a different, more important sense than you might think, and with greater consequences. You are helping the public relate to the God of the universe—something that can be done only through His Son, Jesus Christ.

Hype implies that there's no steak—just sizzle. The Gospel goes much further. It's lifechanging, it's eternal, it's real . . . in other words, it ain't hype!   —J.C.

Through preaching, teaching, and the Bible, God is telling me . . . _____
_____
_____

Through nature and the lives of other believers, God is showing me . . . _____
_____
_____

I will respond by . . . _____
_____
_____

Know what?

MEDITATE
2 Peter 1:5
Make every effort to add to your faith goodness; and to goodness, knowledge.

REFLECT
➡ What is the difference between knowing about God and knowing God?

➡ What can I learn from Paul's deep desire to know Christ (Philippians 3:10)?

CONSIDER
Knowing about God is different from knowing God.

While interviewing students at Santa Monica College, I met one young man who told me that he was interested in finding out all he could about God and religion. At first, I was encouraged.

But then I asked him why he wanted to learn about religion, and he said that he wanted to expand his education on this subject. He was curious about what motivates religious people. He was interested in studying the differences in their beliefs and in their religious practices.

Now I was disappointed in his answer. He did not want to learn more about God so he could do His will. For him, knowing God was not a spiritual quest but an intellectual one.

I wonder. Are you trying to learn more about God? Are you seeking to understand the way the Holy Spirit works? Do you read Christian books? Go to youth conferences? If so, why? Is it possible that you think like the student in California? That you want to learn more about God only to satisfy your curiosity?

The apostle Peter said to a group of first-century Christians that this knowledge of Christ could be "ineffective" (2 Peter 1:8). To avoid that, he told them to add to their faith such things as goodness, knowledge, self-control, perseverance, godliness, brotherly kindness, and love (vv. 5–9). These qualities will help us use our knowledge of God properly. He doesn't want us to increase our knowledge about Him just so we can be smarter. He wants us to learn about Him so we can become loving, productive Christians.   —M.D.

Through preaching, teaching, and the Bible, God is telling me . . . _____

_____

_____

Through nature and the lives of other believers, God is showing me . . . _____

_____

_____

I will respond by . . . _____

_____

_____

Stay where it's safe

READ
Proverbs 8:32–36

MEDITATE
Proverbs 8:36

"All who hate me [wisdom] love death."

REFLECT

➡ How well do I know the principles for Christian living found in the Bible? Am I willing to live by them?

➡ What might Satan use to get me to self-destruct?

➡ If I'm on a self-destructive course, what will it take to get me back on track?

CONSIDER
Wisdom loves life; foolishness despises it.

On a lonely stretch of Florida beach, 100 pilot whales hurled themselves onto dry ground in an apparent mass suicide. It was another example of self-destructive behavior that continues to baffle marine biologists.

These huge creatures had "followed the leader" and beached themselves. They were sure to die in the Florida sun. People came from all over the country to try to get them to go back into the sea. No amount of coaxing and pushing was successful. The people formed a human fence between the whales and the shoreline. But it didn't work. The sea mammals tore through them and hurled themselves onto dry ground anyway.

Do you suppose that to angels human beings sometimes look like these misguided whales? They must wonder what strange urges cause humans to self-destruct, even while God is doing so many good things for us.

Like unreasoning animals, we keep trying to break out of the safe environment God created for us. Instead of staying in the security of loving submission to God and His principles, we throw ourselves onto the arid ground of sin and disobedience.

Next time your worldly wisdom causes you to consider ungodly behavior, think of those beached whales. That's the predicament we get ourselves into when we disobey God. —M.D.

Through preaching, teaching, and the Bible, God is telling me . . . _____

Through nature and the lives of other believers, God is showing me . . . _____

I will respond by . . . _____

The party's over!

READ
Daniel 5:1–6, 25–31

MEDITATE
Daniel 5:1

King Belshazzar gave a great banquet for a thousand of his nobles.

REFLECT

➡ This world is throwing a party that will one day end in destruction. What parts of the "party" do I enjoy and not want to give up?

➡ In light of the Lord's return, what is my responsibility to those around me?

CONSIDER
At the end of every person's life stands God.

The party had been going on for three days while the boys' parents were in Acapulco. At first the teenage brothers had just invited a few of their friends over to their secluded house. But the rumor of a booze party raced through their school, and soon lots of people were coming. They brought beer, then hard stuff, then drugs. Sex was rampant. Then, on a drunken dare, a girl tried to chug-a-lug a fifth of scotch. She vomited and passed out. Then she convulsed and stopped breathing. Someone was sober enough to call the E-unit. As they rushed her out to the ambulance, one of the paramedics said, "You'd better pray. It's the only chance she's got." One by one the scared, sobered kids left. The party was over.

A similar thing happened in the Old Testament, only on a bigger scale. King Belshazzar threw a wild party, and at the height of it he brought in the sacred utensils from the temple.

That was as far as God was going to let them go. A hand appeared and started writing on the wall. The reveling stopped. The king was terrified. He called Daniel to interpret the message. In essence, God told the king that He was going to divide his kingdom. It happened that very night! The party was over.

Our society has been in the middle of a decades-long party. Ignoring God. Oblivious to His laws and His ways. On a binge of materialism and selfishness and sexual perverseness, our generation has tried to satisfy every desire. But the handwriting's on the wall—in the pages of the Bible. One day, perhaps soon, God's judgment will begin. Then it will be abundantly clear to everybody that the party's over! —D.E.

Through preaching, teaching, and the Bible, God is telling me . . . _____

_____

_____

Through nature and the lives of other believers, God is showing me . . . _____

_____

_____

I will respond by . . . _____

_____

_____

Dangerous knowledge

READ
Proverbs 12:20–23

MEDITATE
Proverbs 12:23
A prudent man keeps his knowledge to himself.

REFLECT
➡ What is the difference between knowledge that is earthly and that which comes "from above" (see James 3:13–18)?
➡ Have I been humiliated by someone who knows more about the Bible than I do? When?
➡ In what situations am I tempted to misuse knowledge?

CONSIDER
If you don't use your head, you'll waste your knowledge.

A Bible study was started among some young women in a college dorm. Some were not Christians; others were new believers. The leader didn't know much about the Bible, so she was glad when a new girl started coming who really understood the Scriptures. Now we'll all learn faster, she thought.

Wrong! The new girl did have superior Bible knowledge, but she didn't know how to use it very well. When one of the girls volunteered an answer that turned out to be incorrect, she would roll her eyes and sigh. Then she would give the right answer with a tone of impatient superiority.

You can guess what happened. One by one the unsaved girls dropped out. Then the new Christians stopped coming. Before long the group disbanded, just because one know-it-all girl would not change.

At times we are tempted to use our Bible knowledge inappropriately. But the following pointers may help us. First, James warns against using knowledge out of bitter envy or to promote ourselves (3:14). He calls it "earthly, unspiritual, of the devil" (3:15).

Second, no matter how much we may know, it isn't very much. Robert Oppenheimer, the brilliant scientist who helped develop the atom bomb, said, "What we know is really like a cup of water in the ocean. What we know is the cup. What we don't know is the ocean."

Solomon said, "A prudent man keeps his knowledge to himself." No need to flaunt it, nor to use it as a weapon. When we do that, we impress no one but ourselves.
—D.E.

Through preaching, teaching, and the Bible, God is telling me . . . _____

_____

Through nature and the lives of other believers, God is showing me . . . _____

_____

I will respond by . . . _____

_____

Freud fraud

JULY 8

READ
Matthew 23:1–15

MEDITATE
Psalm 119:29
Keep me from deceitful ways.

REFLECT
➡ What are cults? What's wrong with them?
➡ Do I know enough Bible truth to be able to detect religious fraud?

CONSIDER
To avoid fraud, listen to God.

Freud was a fraud—that's what a group of researchers has concluded. But before we find out why he has come under attack, let's find out who he is and why anybody cares.

If you've ever taken a psychology course, the name Sigmund Freud should ring a bell. (The bell, of course, was Pavlov's thing, but that's another story.) Freud is the correct answer for these questions:

1. Who was the father of psycho-analysis?

2. What Austrian physician lived from 1856 to 1939?

3. Who developed the treatment of mental illness that has been dubbed the "talking cure"?

At a 1991 meeting of the American Association for the Advancement of Science, experts presented evidence that Freud falsified his reports and made exaggerated claims for his methods.

According to a professor of science history at MIT, Freud's case studies "are rampant with censorship, distortions, highly dubious reconstructions, and exaggerated clinical claims."

Researchers are concluding that Freud's method may not have a scientific leg to stand on. If they're correct, Freud won't be the first person in history to turn out to be a fraud. Take the Pharisees, for example. (Please, take them!) They worked very hard to develop a system for dealing with spiritual problems. But one day Jesus came along and announced that they were frauds.

This all raises a big question: How do we know who's leading us in the right direction? The time-tested manual is the Word of God. When we use the Bible to show us how to live, we won't waste our time following frauds.   —K.D.

Through preaching, teaching, and the Bible, God is telling me . . . _____

_____

Through nature and the lives of other believers, God is showing me . . . _____

_____

_____

I will respond by . . . _____

_____

_____

Don't lose your head

READ
Proverbs 6:20–35

MEDITATE
Proverbs 6:26
The adulteress preys upon your very life.

REFLECT
➡ On a scale of 1 to 10 (with 10 being the highest), how would I rate my susceptibility to impure thinking or actions?

➡ What are three things I can do to get out of a relationship that is harmful to my moral well-being?

➡ What can I do to avoid unhealthy relationships?

CONSIDER
Sin's hook is often hidden in an attractive package.

A praying mantis is to the garden what Mike Tyson is to boxing: elusive, dominant, and fierce. And both have had their problems with members of the opposite sex.

Consider the mantis. The instinct that sends the male in pursuit of a mate often results in his untimely death. I watched this happen on a TV nature special that portrayed the unusual habits of this remarkable insect. In one instance, a male tried to show affection for a female mantis, but in return she viciously attacked him. And in another case, a female actually accepted the attention of her "lover," but then suddenly turned cannibal. (Make that "preying" mantis!) In the most literal way, the male mantis lost his head in the pursuit of love.

That's why a mantis "in love" is a lot like a man "in lust."

A similar thing happens to us if we let our natural drives steer us in the wrong direction. If the author of Proverbs had been writing to his daughter, he probably would have warned her about the many "lines" a man might use to gain her affection. He would have cautioned her never to act against her better judgment. But the author was writing to his son. Five times in the first nine chapters of Proverbs he told his son that a man can lose his head, heart, and body to the power of seduction. The wrong woman is an overwhelming magnet to wrong desire.

We need to listen to those pointed warnings, remembering that even strong people can be carried away by lust, lose their heads, and ruin their lives. But it doesn't have to happen. By following God we can avoid people who "prey upon our lives" through sexual seduction.   —T.B.

Through preaching, teaching, and the Bible, God is telling me . . . _____

_____

_____

Through nature and the lives of other believers, God is showing me . . . _____

_____

_____

I will respond by . . . _____

_____

_____

Video resumes

MEDITATE
Matthew 23:28
"On the outside you appear to people as righteous."

REFLECT

➡ What areas of my life am I afraid to talk to God about? Why?

➡ When was the last time I asked another believer to help me with a problem in my life?

➡ How can I develop greater honesty with God and others?

CONSIDER
Don't pretend to be what you don't intend to be.

If job-hunting isn't tough enough these days, now we have video resumes to contend with. I don't know about you, but I'd be afraid that if I made a videotape resume it would end up on "America's Funniest Home Videos."

Kathryn Troutman, owner of The Resume Place in Washington, D.C., would probably agree with me. Commenting on the video-resume idea, she said, "The rare person, maybe in advertising or something, can come across as a dynamo. Most people look like a jerk on videotape."

Trying to "look good" on videotape can be a difficult task. And the tape would probably not be all that accurate in determining a person's ability to perform a job.

But in a culture that thrives on superficiality, "looking good" counts for a whole lot in trying to get approval, prestige, or most important—a job.

The religious leaders in Jesus' time on earth were experts at making a good appearance. They wore the right kind of robes, put on the right kinds of holy-looking accessories, and talked and walked like people who knew God and were obedient to Him.

But the Pharisees' "resume" didn't impress Jesus. He could hear the emptiness in their pious voices, see the meaninglessness in their holy gesturing and their meticulous ritual-keeping. Though they looked great on the outside, He knew they were rotten as death itself on the inside.

How often do we "put on a good appearance" for those around us or try to impress people with our religious achievements without letting them see that we are struggling? Do we think we are fooling God too? —K.D.

Through preaching, teaching, and the Bible, God is telling me . . . _____
_____
_____

Through nature and the lives of other believers, God is showing me . . . _____
_____
_____

I will respond by . . . _____
_____
_____

If the shoe fits

READ
Matthew 5:43–48

MEDITATE
Matthew 5:46
"If you love those who love you, what reward will you get?"

REFLECT
➡ What do I do that shows others that my faith in Christ is genuine?
➡ The Christian journey requires that I take the higher, less-traveled road. Am I doing that or am I taking the same route as everyone else?

CONSIDER
Would you want someone to represent you like you represent Jesus?

You're walking through the mall checking out all the great stuff in the display windows. You're interested in a lot of the things you see, but you know you can't buy anything because you're broke. Flat busted. So you make up your mind to be happy just looking.

One store lures you inside with its display of new athletic footwear that pumps air into your shoes (and pumps money out of your wallet at the same time). Quicker than you can say, "I'm just looking, thank you," the salesperson tells you that these shoes are the latest "in" item. "Sure, they're a little more expensive," he says. "But they're worth it."

As he steers you toward the cash register a funny thing happens. You notice that the shoes he's wearing aren't much better than the pair you have on—and they aren't the pumped-up brand he's trying to sell to you. To

yourself you say, "Yeah, right, everybody should own a pair." To him you say, "No thanks," and turn around and walk out.

Our efforts to interest our friends in the Christian life are sometimes just as unconvincing. Too often we want them to accept Christ and pay the higher price of identifying with Him when we show no visible evidence that we're willing to pay it ourselves.

So how can we establish our credibility? By loving people as Christ loved them. Which means that we don't reject people who are different. We do good when it's not expected. We're kind even when kindness is undeserved.

That will show people we have found something that really does make a difference in the way we walk. —M.D.

Through preaching, teaching, and the Bible, God is telling me . . . _____

_____

Through nature and the lives of other believers, God is showing me . . . _____

_____

I will respond by . . . _____

_____

Time to rock the boat?

READ
Acts 16:16–34

MEDITATE
Acts 16:20

"These men . . . are throwing our city into an uproar."

REFLECT
➡ What are some things worth getting excited about?

➡ Have I ever felt deeply enough about Christ to rock the boat a little for Him?

➡ What are the appropriate channels to follow in the issues I feel strongly about?

CONSIDER
If you want things to get moving, you may have to push.

We were anchored in the Bay of Finn in the North Channel. A large two-masted square rigger sailed around a bend and into a narrow channel. The good ship *Fairplay* was manned by twenty-six teenagers from Toronto who were sailing exactly as sailors did in the nineteenth century. The ship slowed to a snail's pace as it threaded its way through the tight inlet. Suddenly a gust of wind blew it onto the rocks below the surface of the water.

The captain called his young crew to deck and gave clear orders. They were to run together from port to starboard at his command. He commanded; the loyal crew obeyed. As they ran from side to side, the ship began to rock. Finally it broke free.

Sometimes young people need to "rock the boat" in churches that have run aground. They're not mov-ing forward and haven't been for years. They need zealous, devoted, sincere young people to "rock the boat" and get them unstuck. Enthusiasm is catching. And sometimes we need to ask hard questions and apply tough tests to things that haven't been changed for thirty-five years.

Paul and Silas had Philippi in an uproar. They "rocked the boat" of religious tradition with their enthusiastic witness for the Lord Jesus. Maybe it's time for you and your friends, turned on by the Lord and led by the Spirit, to rock the boat for Christ in your school, your church, your world.   —D.E.

Through preaching, teaching, and the Bible, God is telling me . . . _____

_____

_____

Through nature and the lives of other believers, God is showing me . . . _____

_____

_____

I will respond by . . . _____

Odd fellow

READ
James 2:1–9

MEDITATE
James 2:1
Don't show favoritism.

REFLECT
➡ What unspoken (and unimportant) criteria do I expect others to meet before I accept them into my circle of friends?

➡ What is my attitude toward people of different races, denominations, or economic backgrounds? Do I love them as I love myself?

CONSIDER
Prejudice is the lazy person's substitute for thinking.

Met a guy recently. Maybe eighteen or nineteen years old. Seemed like a peculiar sort of guy. I didn't know quite what to think of him. Odd would be the best word to use, I guess. He looked kind of like an unmade bed.

I decided to talk with him, find out about him, and maybe help him out. After all, I'm a Christian and Christians are supposed to share Christ's love with others. Especially those who are down and out. And this guy seemed way out!

So, I spent some time talking with him. And I discovered something I didn't expect—he wasn't weird at all. He was just a little different. In fact, he really had his head on straight. He was quite intelligent. And you know what else? He was a Christian. Suddenly his hair didn't seem all that long anymore.

That incident taught me a lot—about myself. And I thought I'd come further than that in my Christian development!

I began wondering, do people have to come in plain manila envelopes for me to accept them? Don't I realize that when I prejudge people I do them a terrible disservice? Isn't prejudging a close cousin to prejudice?

Notice how James put it. "My brothers . . . don't show favoritism. . . . Love your neighbor as yourself. . . . If you show favoritism, you sin" (James 2:1, 8–9).

Think about it. Do we base our response to others purely on external factors? How can we honor God in the way we treat people who are different from us? —D.P.

Through preaching, teaching, and the Bible, God is telling me . . . _____

_____

Through nature and the lives of other believers, God is showing me . . . _____

_____

I will respond by . . . _____

_____

Poison ivy paranoia

14

READ
1 John 3:1–10

MEDITATE
James 1:15
Sin, when it is full-grown, gives birth to death.

REFLECT
➡ What are some places at my school where I "get the itch to sin" if I hang around?
➡ Some argue that to reach sinners you have to go where they are. How does that correspond with biblical warnings to stay away from sin?

CONSIDER
It's never wrong to fear sin.

W hat started as a great experience ended in one of the worst weeks of my life.

I was a sophomore in college and had recently started dating the most wonderful girl in school. (She's now my wife.) One Saturday we headed off to a local park for a nice autumn walk. We enjoyed strolling the paths, talking, and getting better acquainted. Something special was in the air.

On Monday I found out what it was.

Poison ivy. By Monday morning my face, hands, and arms were covered with that dreaded, unmistakable, unbearable rash. It wasn't long before I looked like the monster from the lost lagoon as my skin swelled and . . . well, I'll skip the details.

For a whole week I stayed in my room behind a curtain, unable to go to classes, attend basketball practice, or do anything but try not to scratch. I was one miserable sophomore.

And now I have poison ivy paranoia. I wouldn't step into a patch of weeds to pick up a hundred dollar bill. And as for exploring the woods— that's a joy I've given up forever. I know what damage the enemy can do. And even if I don't know exactly how it might attack, I refuse to go where it lives. I will not fall prey to its venom again.

What's true of poison ivy is also true of sin. We know exactly what kind of damage it causes when it is "full grown." And we don't know when we might run into it. But one thing is sure. We can avoid going to the places where it's known to be.

We need a healthy case of sin paranoia. It will keep us away from the places where it grows.   —D.B.

Through preaching, teaching, and the Bible, God is telling me . . . _____

_____

Through nature and the lives of other believers, God is showing me . . . _____

_____

I will respond by . . . _____

Down—but not out

READ
Acts 15:36–41

MEDITATE
2 Timothy 4:11
Get Mark . . . because he is helpful to me.

REFLECT
➡ What was the first thought that crossed my mind the last time I let someone down or made a bad decision? How can I handle the situation differently next time?
➡ What can I learn from failure that I can't discover any other way?
➡ In reading Acts 15:36–41, what do I observe?

CONSIDER
Our weakness displays God's strength.

I've done it again," you moan, "I'm sure to win the Jerk of the Year Award." You didn't mean to drive away and leave your little sister at the mall or crunch the fender of your parents' car on the way home or close the garage door on the family cat. It just kind of happened.

It's not hard to be forgetful or careless or clumsy. Most of us can do it with our eyes open. But messing up—even on a regular basis—never has to be the end of the world.

Even John Mark, Paul's associate, failed to come through (see Acts 13:13). His motto could have been: "When the going gets tough, the weak get out of here." He deserted Paul and Barnabas shortly after starting out with them on their first world missionary tour.

John Mark may have failed the first time, but he was willing to try again. Later he went with Barnabas to Cyprus and became a valuable assistant to him and to the work. And Paul was so convinced of his value that when he was in a dungeon in Rome, he wrote Timothy, "Get Mark and bring him with you, because he is helpful to me in my ministry."

Failure is never final. The Bible makes it clear that heaven will be full of people like you and me (2 Corinthians 4:7). So if you are down on yourself because of a failure, don't give up now. Call on the Lord Jesus for help. You may be down, but you're not out unless you give in to defeat.   —T.B.

Through preaching, teaching, and the Bible, God is telling me . . . _____

_____

Through nature and the lives of other believers, God is showing me . . . _____

_____

I will respond by . . . _____

_____

Face the wind

READ
Proverbs 14:22–26

MEDITATE
Proverbs 14:26
He who fears the Lord has a secure fortress.

REFLECT
→ What promises of Christ will help me when I am afraid?

→ What am I most afraid of right now? What will help me face it?

→ What was I afraid of in the past that no longer scares me? How did I overcome it?

CONSIDER
Face your fear and it will flee.

Time out for a little literature. First, American. Ralph Waldo Emerson wrote, "Fear always springs from ignorance." Now, British. Twentieth-century author Rudyard Kipling said, "Of all the liars in the world, the worst is your own fear."

Fear. We all have it. Those who say they don't are just afraid to admit it. In reality, fear is a God-given gift. That's right, *gift.* Soldiers who admit their fear as they go into battle, for example, have a far better chance of surviving than those who brag that they have no fear.

Fear is "a strong emotion caused by impending evil." Fear is always of the future. It's too late to be afraid of the past or even the immediate present. It's the tornado that might strike. The job we might lose. The class we might fail. Or the people who might laugh if we tell them about Christ.

The way to overcome fear is to understand it and to face it. When a sailor takes a sailboat out to sea and is hit by a sudden gale, what does he do? He turns his boat into the storm. He points its prow right into the wind and waves. It's his best chance of surviving.

"Do the thing you fear the most," said another writer (an anonymous one), "and the death of fear is certain." So, learn all you can about what is frightening you, then take action. When you understand the thing you are afraid of, it shrinks. And when you walk toward it, it begins to fade away. Talk to that difficult professor. Make that speech. Stand in that batter's box. Give that person you've been wanting to date a call. Tell Mom or Dad what you've been so afraid to tell them.

If you're afraid, learn the lesson of the sea. Face the "wind" and watch your fear vanish.   —D.E.

Through preaching, teaching, and the Bible, God is telling me . . . _____
_____
_____

Through nature and the lives of other believers, God is showing me . . . _____
_____
_____

I will respond by . . . _____
_____
_____

Time to let it go!

READ
Ephesians 4:29–32

MEDITATE
Luke 6:37
"Forgive, and you will be forgiven."

REFLECT

➡ Am I generally a forgiving person or do I remember insults and hurts for a long time?

➡ Have I told someone I've forgiven them when I really haven't? What can I do to get forgiveness beyond my lips and into my heart?

CONSIDER
It's foolish to hold on to what's destroying you.

Megan was miserable. Every so often she would cut down her best friend, Sarah. They had been friends since fifth grade and now they were attending the same college. They had a couple of the same classes, and they were in the same Bible study group. They did a lot of things together. But Megan was sometimes mean to Sarah, and Sarah couldn't understand why.

Megan knew, though. Two years earlier Sarah had gone through a stage of spiritual rebellion. She did some pretty wild things, and Megan had tried to talk to her about it. But Sarah insulted her and told her to mind her own business. A few months later, Sarah came back to the Lord—and became a stronger Christian than ever. As soon as she could, she went to Megan and apologized for the way she had treated her. "Oh, that's okay," Megan had responded. But in her heart she had not forgiven her, and she was still carrying the anger and bitterness around with her—after two years!

In Luke 6:37, forgive means "to let loose, to let go." It refers to things we would be better off without.

Are you, like Megan, making yourself (and maybe others) miserable because you can't forgive and forget? Let it go. As God has forgiven your offenses, you must be willing to forgive those who have offended you. It's time to turn it loose!

—D.E

Through preaching, teaching, and the Bible, God is telling me . . . _____

_____

Through nature and the lives of other believers, God is showing me . . . _____

_____

I will respond by . . . _____

_____

Why shoot the wounded?

READ
Psalm 109:1–6,
14–21

MEDITATE
Psalm 109:16
For he . . . hounded to
death the poor and
the needy and the
brokenhearted.

REFLECT
➡ What is my first
response when I
hear about a
believer who has
fallen into sin?
➡ Whom do I know
that needs my
understanding and
encouragement?
What will I do?

CONSIDER
*A hurting person
needs a helping
hand.*

They were shocked at Mt. Carmel Mercy Hospital on Detroit's northwest side. A young gunshot victim had been brought in a few days before. He was recovering quickly from his wounds. His condition had been upgraded to fair, and he was looking forward to going home before long. But then someone walked into his room, shot him again, and killed him. Patients and staff were horrified. A spokesperson said that nothing like that had ever happened in the hospital's fifty-year history.

Wouldn't it be wonderful if we could say that about our churches? Wouldn't it be great if we could honestly say that in fifty years of meeting together for fellowship and spiritual healing, we had not had a single wounded member cut down by another Christian? Or a fragile new believer trampled by criticism or judgment?

David was talking about this problem in Psalm 109. When he was hurt and vulnerable, some insensitive people took advantage of his weakness. If he had sinned, what he needed was their loving correction. If he was ill, he needed their comfort and encouragement. What he didn't need was scorn, gossip, and ridicule.

How is it where you worship? With your campus study group? At your youth meetings? How could you make it better? Do you know any "wounded" Christian soldiers? Ask God for the mercy to show them kindness, love, and compassion. They don't need to be shot at.   —M.D.

Through preaching, teaching, and the Bible, God is telling me . . . _____

_____

_____

Through nature and the lives of other believers, God is showing me . . . _____

_____

_____

I will respond by . . . _____

_____

_____

In concert with Paul

READ
Philippians 4:8–9

MEDITATE
Philippians 4:8
If anything is excellent or praiseworthy— think about such things.

REFLECT
➡ What guidelines do I use for judging the music I listen to?
➡ What are my ten favorite music groups? Which ones don't pass the Philippians 4:8 guidelines?

CONSIDER
Tune in to God's guidelines before you turn on the radio.

"Turn that thing down!" Those words could come from any irritated parent who doesn't enjoy sounds that make her think a 747 is taxiing on her roof. Or from the guy down the hall who hasn't learned to study with Rez band blasting through the dorm.

Music brings out the emotions in people. And there's more to it than volume control. The more important consideration is the kind of music you listen to. That's what gets folks really emotional. When you tell people they're listening to the wrong kind of music, they'll defend it like a pit bull.

The music question has been under discussion among Christians before Bill Haley and the Comets, Elvis Presley, and U2 came along. Even old Gospel favorites such as "Amazing Grace" and "Revive us Again" had detractors at first. There are no easy answers.

But there are guidelines. Composer Don Wyrtzen, writing in *Moody Monthly*, lists some principles he has devised for judging music. He said, "Eight adjectives from Philippians 4:8 give us a biblical standard for evaluation. Is this music true? Is it noble and right? Is the lyric morally pure? Is the music lovely and admirable? Only what is excellent and worthy of praise should pervade the thoughts and feelings of God's children. Whether it's Fleetwood Mac, Kenny Rogers, Amy Grant, or George Beverly Shea [ask Mom and Dad who he is]— these adjectives of excellence should control the performing and listening habits of those who love Christ."

Music is one of the hardest areas of life for Christians to control. But when we seek the Holy Spirit's help and listen to Paul, we'll be "in concert" with God's guidelines.
—D.B.

Through preaching, teaching, and the Bible, God is telling me . . . _____

_____

Through nature and the lives of other believers, God is showing me . . . _____

_____

I will respond by . . . _____

_____

Ya gotta have

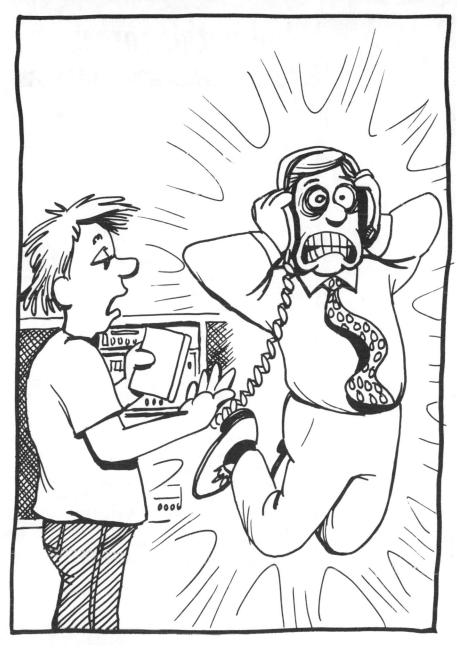

BUT JOHNNY CHAINSAW AND THE PURPLE
SCREAMERS **IS** MY MOST MELLOW MUSIC, DAD.

A LOVING HEART

And in this corner . . .

20

READ
James 4:1–12

MEDITATE
James 4:1
What causes fights and quarrels among you? Don't they come from your desires?

REFLECT
➡ How do I respond when I don't get what I want?
➡ What types of things do I want but can't have? Are my desires consistent with what God wants for me?
➡ How can I respond to those who bully me with their selfishness?

CONSIDER
Fights begin when selfishness steps into the ring.

Forty fourth-graders from Midland, Michigan, had a more exciting field trip than they expected. During a visit to the state capitol to see their legislators in action, they had ringside seats for an impromptu fistfight between two senators.

It seems that the two men had been in a heated debate over property tax cuts. After one senator lost a key vote on an amendment, the other one (according to news reports) "needled him with an epithet." The other senator shot back, "Any time, any place!" Then the battle began. Other senators hurried to separate the two men as they exchanged punches and wrestled on the floor.

Although this isn't what political science textbooks mean when they talk about "floor fights," those involved in politics are all too familiar with the sound of verbal battles and personal attacks.

You don't have to be a legislator to know that people who don't get what they want will fight about it. If not physically, perhaps verbally or by holding a grudge or by giving the silent treatment.

Think about the last disagreement you had with someone. What were the real issues? Do the words of James 4 accurately describe what happened? Did the fight begin because one person failed to get what he or she wanted?

To keep fights from breaking out, we need to determine the root problem of disagreement and work on that. Is it pride? Selfishness? Covetousness? Lust? Then we must talk to the Lord about our desires if we find them faulty, and ask Him to purify our motives (vv. 2–3). When we get angry because we don't get what we want, we need to ask the Lord for the strength to give selfishness a knockout punch. —K.D.

Through preaching, teaching, and the Bible, God is telling me . . . _____

_____

_____

Through nature and the lives of other believers, God is showing me . . . _____

_____

_____

I will respond by . . . _____

_____

_____

Ya gotta have

Bummed out

READ
Jeremiah 20:7–13

MEDITATE
Jeremiah 20:11
The Lord is with me like a mighty warrior.

REFLECT
➡ Am I happy with the way my life has been going? How does my attitude affect my relationship with God? I want to: (a) Continue to feel this way; (b) Forget about God for what He's allowed to happen to me; (c) Turn back to God and ask for strength to stay true to Him.

CONSIDER
Either succeed with God or fail without Him.

Feeling bummed out? Thinking that God has let you down? I mean, you came to school full of hopes and dreams. You prayed about the right school. And you're sure He led you to where you are. So why has it been so difficult? Your grades are the pits. You're close to making the Dean's List all right—but it's the wrong list. Your social life is about as exciting as a salt-free diet. That special person "God brought into your life" has bailed out. And you've been left alone. Again. And to top it all off, you're doing a lousy job of witnessing for Christ. You're about as likely to win someone to Christ as you are to win the Publishers' Clearing House grand prize.

Well, slide over. You've got company. Jeremiah, a great man of God, felt that he was getting less than a "fair deal" too. He wrote, "O Lord, you deceived me, and I was deceived; you overpowered me and prevailed. . . . The word of the Lord has brought me insult and reproach" (Jeremiah 20:7–8).

Jeremiah was bummed out. Things hadn't gone the way he had expected them to go. And he felt deceived, misled, confused, and beaten. But he didn't quit. Despite his pain and confusion, he kept trusting God. He knew in his heart that God hadn't abandoned him. "The Lord is with me like a mighty warrior" (v. 11), he said. And his advice was to "Sing to the Lord" (v. 13).

So what are you going to do? Where do you go from here? Do you leave school? Give up on relationships? Give up on God? Not on your life! Do what Jeremiah did. Even though he continued to struggle, he kept on trying. And he turned to God. So should you.   —D.P.

Through preaching, teaching, and the Bible, God is telling me . . . _____

_____

_____

Through nature and the lives of other believers, God is showing me . . . _____

_____

_____

I will respond by . . . _____

_____

_____

"I love being a turtle!"

READ
Romans 1:1–17

MEDITATE
Romans 1:16
I am not ashamed of the gospel.

REFLECT
→ Have I been unhappy with my Christian life lately? Discouraged?
→ Do I know why? Is it some sin?
→ What kinds of things take the joy out of my Christian life? Why do they depress me so much?
→ Do I know a Christian friend who needs cheering up? What can I do to help?

CONSIDER
Enjoy Jesus!

Okay, I admit it. Once in a while (only when I'm around little kids, of course), I watch those lovable, heroic creatures from the sewers of New York, the Teenage Mutant Ninja Turtles. These courageous little fellows with the names of famous Renaissance painters thrill young viewers with their mighty deeds of valor.

I especially like Raphael because of one line he says every so often. He may say it in the midst of battle. Or perhaps after a mean villain has just been vanquished. Or even after downing another pizza. Raphael will throw wide his arms, lift his head proudly, and say, "I just love being a turtle!"

We should all be proud of who we are. We should all say with pride, "I love being a Smith or a Carlson!" Or "I love being Asian!" Or "I love being a student at Idaho State University!" Or "I love being a woman!"

Most of all, those of us who believe in the saving power of Jesus should say, "I love being a Christian!" It could be in the soaring moments of a worship and praise service, or during the quiet stillness of prayer on a beautiful fall evening. It could even occur in the midst of an intense spiritual struggle, while we are being opposed for our faith.

But maybe you're not feeling that way right now. You're not so sure about Christ and Christianity. Is your faith kind of shaky? Perhaps you need to talk things over with a campus ministry worker. Or a youth pastor. Or a dependable Christian friend. Or the Lord. Find out what might be holding you back from experiencing the kind of confidence as a believer that makes you say, "I love being a Christian!" —D.E.

Through preaching, teaching, and the Bible, God is telling me . . . _____

_____

Through nature and the lives of other believers, God is showing me . . . _____

_____

I will respond by . . . _____

_____

The secret of courage

123

MEDITATE
1 Corinthians 2:3
I came to you in weakness and fear.

REFLECT

➡ I'm not afraid to admit that I'm afraid of _____
_____.

➡ What am I going to do about it?

➡ Do I really believe that God can help me in any situation? How am I going to show Him today that I trust Him?

CONSIDER
Trust turns fear into triumph.

For some people, it's spiders. For others, heights. We're talking fear here. Maybe arachnids or skyscrapers don't scare you. But what about making a speech, or going out on a date, or calling a potential employer. If you are normal, you probably fear something.

Walter Anderson, editor of *Parade* magazine, wrote a book about coping with anxiety. It's called *Courage Is a Three Letter Word*.

No, the word isn't *run*. It's *yes*. To Anderson, real courage means saying "yes" to life instead of backing down or running away. He says that courage is acting when there is fear, not waiting until there isn't any. He wrote, "Of all the successful people I've known and written about in the book, it's not just that they learned to live with or cope with anxiety, they've learned to live better because of their fear." He illustrated by pointing to a nationally known figure who was humiliated before the entire country. But that person showed great character and courage by saying "yes" to life and coming back from the disaster.

By Anderson's definition, the apostle Paul was a true man of courage. He admitted that he went to Corinth with his message "in fear, and with much trembling." (Read about it in 1 Corinthians 2.) But in spite of that fear, he did the Lord's work. And he did it by depending on the power of the Spirit of God (v. 4).

Think about what you are afraid of. Who intimidates you? Is there something you can't handle? Admit that you are scared, call on God for help, and face it anyway. Your weakness is a great opportunity for God to show you His strength. And that, after all, is the true source of courage for any of us.

—M.D.

Through preaching, teaching, and the Bible, God is telling me . . . _____

_____

Through nature and the lives of other believers, God is showing me . . . _____

_____

I will respond by . . . _____

Yawn yawn yawn

READ
Ecclesiastes 2:1–11

MEDITATE
Ecclesiastes 2:20
So my heart began to despair over all my toilsome labor.

REFLECT
→ When was the last thing that got me really excited? How long did my excitement last? What took its place?
→ Does it take more and more to make me happy? To give me the feeling that life is worth living?
→ Do I try to see beyond the immediate and consider the eternal?

CONSIDER
Christ makes an empty life full.

According to the *Guinness Book of World Records*, a fifteen-year-old girl once yawned for five weeks straight! No reasons were given. Maybe it was grammar class. Or TV reruns. Or perhaps her telephone was out of order.

Her long yawn got me to wondering, "Why do people yawn?" Why do we suddenly contort our faces, stretch our mouths wide open, take a deep breath, and make weird sighing noises? I did a little research and found out. Shallow breathing, warm stuffy air, or nervousness can deplete the oxygen in our body. So our Creator-Designer has equipped us with a deep-breath reflex response that sends a rush of oxygen to the rescue. That's the technical explanation, but a yawn or a sigh is usually a signal of nervousness, tiredness, or boredom.

When we read Ecclesiastes, we can almost hear Solomon sigh as he tries one thing after another in an effort to find meaning in life. Time after time his spirit reacted to various and exciting experiences with the cry, "All is vanity." During one long period, everything he touched produced only sighs of emptiness (1:2; 2:11). He finally realized that nothing truly satisfies a person except fearing God and keeping His commandments (12:13).

Are a lot of your friends bored with life? Have they tried popular pleasures only to have them grow old and tiresome? Have you done that? There's a reason why our souls "yawn and sigh"— to remind us that God alone can satisfy.　　—M.D.

Through preaching, teaching, and the Bible, God is telling me . . . _____
_____
_____

Through nature and the lives of other believers, God is showing me . . . _____
_____
_____

I will respond by . . . _____
_____
_____

Ya gotta have

Occupation: page turner

READ
Romans 16:21–27

MEDITATE
Galatians 5:13
Serve one another in love.

REFLECT

➡ Do I receive enough recognition for my work? How much would be enough?

➡ How do I feel about people "on center stage"?

➡ How can I serve someone "in love" today?

CONSIDER
We serve Christ best when we love others first.

When Elmer Booze walks on stage for a virtuoso piano performance, nobody applauds. That's because he's not a concert pianist, he's a professional page turner.

Although he has music degrees from two universities and plays the piano very well himself, Elmer has been sitting in the shadows for twenty-five years. In Washington, D.C., he is a regular at the Kennedy Center, the National Gallery of Art, the Canadian Embassy, and the Library of Congress. He has turned pages at the White House and at concerts in New York and London.

Many great pianists depend on people like Elmer to make their performance the best it can be. And while they take their bows, the Elmers of the world are in the background smiling—content with the part they had in the performance.

In the closing sentences of Paul's letter to the Romans, we meet another man who worked behind the scenes (see v. 22). His name was Tertius, and he was a highly skilled secretary who wrote while Paul dictated. Like Elmer, Tertius was content to "turn pages" (or in his case, roll a scroll) to help someone else.

I wonder, would I get enough satisfaction for a job well done if I never got any recognition? Would I do my best if it meant that someone else was going to get credit? How about you?

Few of us can be the soloist. Most of us work behind the scenes and watch other people take the bows.

The issue for us is this: Will we resent the lack of recognition and envy the person on center stage? Or will we be able to "serve one another in love" because our highest goal is to glorify Christ? —K.D.

Through preaching, teaching, and the Bible, God is telling me . . . _____

_____

Through nature and the lives of other believers, God is showing me . . . _____

_____

I will respond by . . . _____

_____

Julie's secret

READ
Psalm 65:5–13

MEDITATE
Psalm 62:8
Trust in him at all times . . . pour out your hearts to him.

REFLECT
➡ What is there that I've been holding inside because it hurts too much to face it?
➡ Besides God, what other person could I go to with this problem?

CONSIDER
Your troubles are no secret to God.

Julie is involved in a cover-up. Keep that in mind as I tell you more about her.

Julie is a bright, energetic, socially outgoing college student. Her life is full of the same kinds of activities most students are involved in. Enough dating to keep life interesting, more studies than she can handle, and plenty of career planning to keep her serious. She seems normal and reasonably well adjusted.

But that's only on the surface. Inside Julie's heart rests a secret. A terrible secret that ravages her mind and tears away at her self-image. It makes her feel guilty one moment and angry the next. And worst of all, her secret has caused her to question God and be suspicious of people. Julie is a victim of incest. Her father sexually abused her when she was a young girl. She's undergoing counseling—but it's a long road back.

Where do people like Julie go when they have been misused so callously? To whom does a person turn when he or she is struggling with problems for which there are no easy answers? It's good that Julie's getting counseling. But according to the Bible, she can also turn to God. He is compassionate, and He understands as no one else does.

He is the one who is able to "sympathize with our weaknesses." That helps us know that we can "approach the throne of grace with confidence, so that we may receive mercy and find grace to help us in our time of need" (Hebrews 4:15–16).

What are you struggling with? Perhaps you, like Julie, are trying to deal with a tragedy by covering it up. That won't help. Open up to God. He understands and He can help you. Trust Him.

—D.P.

Through preaching, teaching, and the Bible, God is telling me . . . _____

_____

Through nature and the lives of other believers, God is showing me . . . _____

_____

I will respond by . . . _____

_____

Worth bragging about

J27Y

READ
**1 Corinthians
1:26–31**

MEDITATE
1 Corinthians 1:31
"Let him who boasts
boast in the Lord."

REFLECT
➡ What Christian
principle do I find
in Matthew 23:12?
How does it go
against my culture?

➡ Should I ever feel
any spiritual pride?

➡ What do I do (or
not do) that I feel
good about? Is it
because I am glory-
ing in myself? Or
am I glorying in
Christ?

CONSIDER
*Bragging about
anything but
God is empty
boasting.*

My school, Colorado, has a better football team than Notre Dame.

My Shadow is better than your Honda.

I look better in my clothes than she does in hers.

I can have all the dates I want.

Boasting. What we're proud of. When you stop to think about it, we brag about some pretty shallow things—like the kind of car we own. (You'd think we designed it or built it. Most of us didn't even pay for it!) Or the grades we get. We even boast about things we have no control over, like the basketball team we happen to support. We may even brag about our church or our particular Christian lifestyle.

Paul the apostle had a lot to say about boasting. Most of it was directed to the proud people of Corinth. He identified some of the wrong things they were boasting about, which we might be tempted to brag about as well: ourselves (1 Corinthians 1:29); certain people in the church (1 Corinthians 3:21); and how good they looked (2 Corinthians 5:12). It's wrong to beat the drum about ourselves, someone we heroize, or something physical and external.

This doesn't mean we have nothing to crow about. Paul mentions some things for which believers can have bragging rights: when we go through suffering (Romans 5:3); our weaknesses (2 Corinthians 12:5) and the Lord Himself (1 Corinthians 1:31; 2 Corinthians 10:17). Paul also found glory in the cross (Galatians 6:14).

Feeling a little cocky? Doing a little boasting, even if only to yourself? Stop! Listen to the Word of God. If you're going to brag at all, brag about the Lord.   —D.E.

Through preaching, teaching, and the Bible, God is telling me . . . _____
_____

Through nature and the lives of other believers, God is showing me . . . _____
_____

I will respond by . . . _____
_____

Pizza guilt

READ
Haggai 1

MEDITATE
Haggai 1:5
"Give careful thought to your ways."

REFLECT
→ If I were a multimillionaire would I feel right about spending $5 million of it to build a home for myself? Why or why not?
→ How do my spending choices reflect God's values? How can they?

CONSIDER
Being self-indulgent is the opposite of being God-honoring.

Ever feel guilty after pork-ing out on pizza? While you're wiping the pizza sauce out of your hair (flung there during your feeding frenzy), has someone ever had the nerve to mention starving babies in Africa?

Tom Monaghan, owner of Domino's Pizza, could probably identify with the feeling. The source of his guilt, though, was not how much pizza he had eaten or even how much his customers had eaten. The guilt eating at Mr. Monaghan was related to the $5 million mansion he started to build.

While reading C. S. Lewis's *Mere Christianity*, Monaghan decided he just couldn't go through with the project and ordered work stopped on his cavernous, partially-completed home. He said, "I began thinking. Am I building this out of pride, or what?" He has given away a lot of money to charities and he apparently couldn't reconcile his charity work with an extravagant home for himself.

The personal evaluation that Monaghan went through is the kind of thinking we all need to be doing.

The prophet Haggai confronted the Jews about their misplaced values. He accused them of building luxurious homes (Haggai 1:4) instead of a place of worship.

Holed up in that tiny dorm room for nine months of the year, you probably can't relate to a multimillion-dollar home. But you don't have to be building a palace to have mixed-up priorities. You can have mixed up priorities earning five dollars an hour. The question is, Do your values and actions accurately reflect your calling as a follower of Christ? Are your career goals, spending habits, and concern for the disadvantaged consistent with how Christ wants you to live?　—K.D.

Through preaching, teaching, and the Bible, God is telling me . . . _____
_____
_____

Through nature and the lives of other believers, God is showing me . . . _____
_____
_____

I will respond by . . . _____
_____

The geek magnet

READ
James 2:1–13

MEDITATE
James 2:1
Don't show favoritism.

REFLECT

➡ When I'm in a group, do I notice those who might feel left out? Do I try to draw them in or do I allow them to remain "outside"? Why?

➡ Am I so concerned about my reputation with the popular group that I avoid those who might be considered "different"?

➡ How can I be more sensitive to the needs of others?

CONSIDER
How can we reject someone Jesus died for?

According to a South Carolina college student, a geek magnet is a person who attracts people who are—well, let's just say . . . unpopular. They're not part of the "in crowd." I guess you'd say they're a part of the "out crowd." In fact, way out. A year or two ago these people would have been called nerds. Now, they're geeks. And if you seem to attract them, you probably wonder what that says about you.

That was the problem troubling a young woman. She wanted to know what was wrong with her that made her attract the unattractive?

I'll tell you what was wrong: Absolutely nothing!

People who are lonely, who feel left out, and who sometimes have a poor concept of themselves need the acceptance of someone like this friendly college student.

So, what faults does she have that contribute to the situation? She's extremely nice and makes others feel comfortable. She's honest and doesn't put on airs. She accepts others and is not pretentious or cliquish.

As she matures, she'll begin to see that her problem is really a blessing—a compliment. Imagine how valuable she will be as a teacher or social worker or psychologist!

In James 2 we are warned not to show favoritism. That's because we're really no better than anyone else. We are all sinners in need of God's grace. So what right do we have to think we can accept some people and snub others on the basis of such weak stuff as appearance? Think about it. From God's perspective being a geek magnet is a pretty good thing.   —D.P.

Through preaching, teaching, and the Bible, God is telling me . . . _____

_____

_____

Through nature and the lives of other believers, God is showing me . . . _____

_____

_____

I will respond by . . . _____

_____

_____

Grand prize: nothing!

READ
Jeremiah 2:4–13

MEDITATE
Jeremiah 2:11
"My people have ex-changed their Glory for worthless idols."

REFLECT
➡ How does 1 Corin-thians 3:10–15 refer to works done for the Lord? Works done for ourselves?
➡ What priority do I give to obeying the Lord?
➡ What spiritual value do I give to my weekend activi-ties?

CONSIDER
The world's rewards are all consolation prizes.

How would you like to win a free shopping spree? You know how they work. The winner gets to take home all the stuff he or she can accumulate in five minutes.

So get your shopping carts ready. The gong goes off and you race through the aisles, clearing the shelves of all the pizza and soda you can load into your carts. When the time is up, the cost of the items is tallied and you get to keep every-thing you gathered. And it doesn't cost you a cent.

If I won a prize like that, I'd first go through the store and find out where all the expensive items were. When the spree began, I'd head for those items first. Then I'd go to the munchies.

Now, suppose your best friend wins one of those shopping sprees and invites you along. The gong gongs, and she races through the store throwing empty boxes and cartons into her carts. What would you think? What would you say? "Hey, air-head, this is ridiculous! Why don't you take the valuable stuff?"

The Israelites did some-thing equally foolish. They could have been enjoying the blessings and benefits of a close relationship with God, but instead they wor-shiped idols of clay and wood that couldn't do a thing for them.

If you're a Christian, life is a great prize that offers all kinds of opportunities to serve the Lord and earn the gold, silver, and precious stones of Christ's reward. Don't waste your time serv-ing the gods of this age. What's so great about being a winner if the prize is noth-ing?   —M.D.

Through preaching, teaching, and the Bible, God is telling me . . . _____

_____

_____

Through nature and the lives of other believers, God is showing me . . . _____

_____

_____

I will respond by . . . _____

_____

_____

It doesn't work!

READ
Ecclesiastes 2:1–11

MEDITATE
Ecclesiastes 2:3
I tried cheering myself with wine, and embracing folly.

REFLECT
➡ What advice does Ephesians 5:18 have for followers of Christ?
➡ Does drinking really do for people what they say it does?
➡ What can I do to relax? How can I deal with my problems? How can I gain social confidence?

CONSIDER
Drinking doesn't solve problems, it creates them.

Lots of college freshmen drink. A comparatively high percentage of them subsequently crack up their cars. Many of them have serious injuries; too many die.

A major automobile insurance agency, tired of all this, wanted to find out why these students drink. So they conducted a survey. The results, published in *USA Today*, gave the following reasons for why college freshmen drink:

1. To relax (53% of men; 49% of women).
2. To feel less tense in social situations (40%; 37%).
3. To get drunk (39%; 34%).
4. To keep friends company (23%; 17%).
5. To forget problems (19%; 20%).

Does alcohol do what these freshmen expect? Well, it does relax some people and help break down their inhibitions. But some inhibitions need to remain standing. And it does help people forget their problems. But what good is that? The problems are still there when the person wakes up the next morning. And by then they may even be worse. Getting drunk has never solved a problem, but it has certainly complicated many.

Solomon, the wisest man who ever lived, agreed. In fact, he said, "I tried cheering myself with wine." But when it was over, he called it "meaningless" (v. 11). He went on to give strong warnings against alcohol abuse (Proverbs 20:1; 23:20–21).

Before you are tempted to try alcohol, stop and think. Think seriously about why you are drinking. Does alcohol really do what you are hoping it will do? Listen to God's warning. Then look honestly at those who are drinking. Then I think you'll agree that it doesn't work!
—D.E.

Through preaching, teaching, and the Bible, God is telling me . . . _____

Through nature and the lives of other believers, God is showing me . . . _____

I will respond by . . . _____

How to look smart

READ
Deuteronomy 4:1–8

MEDITATE
Deuteronomy 4:6
"Surely this great nation is a wise and understanding people."

REFLECT
➡ "People can respect you even if they don't like you." I agree/disagree with that statement because:

_____

_____.

➡ How am I going to show God's wisdom in my life today?

CONSIDER
True wisdom comes from God.

Do you want people to think you're intelligent? Try the following suggestions:

Raise your hand every time the instructor asks a question. (Dangerous. You might get called on to answer.)

Carry around books by Herman Hesse. (Again, dangerous. You might get into a conversation with someone who has actually read Hesse.)

Go to Harvard. (The problem with this is getting accepted—and then paying for it!)

Follow God.

Believe it or not, following God is even tougher than getting into Harvard. But ironically it's your best chance for success in your quest for intelligence. That's because God has promised to help.

God calls on us to obey His commandments and live out our faith within society.

He wants us not only to know His law but to follow it. Throughout the Bible, knowledge and obedience are woven tightly together.

Moses suggested to the people of Israel that if they would obey God's commands, the other nations would be impressed (Deuteronomy 4).

You may not have experienced this, but it's true. People can respect you even if they don't agree with you. They may choose not to obey God—and seeing someone who does may make them feel guilty—but even non-Christians know that it takes courage and inner strength to be a Christian.

So, you can not only look smart, you can be smart without resorting to deceitful methods. Just obey the all-wise God, no matter what the cost. You'll quickly develop a reputation for being a real wise guy! —J.C.

Through preaching, teaching, and the Bible, God is telling me . . . _____

_____

_____

Through nature and the lives of other believers, God is showing me . . . _____

_____

_____

I will respond by . . . _____

_____

_____

Lunchpail geniuses

READ
**Ecclesiastes
1:12–18; 2:12–16**

MEDITATE
Ecclesiastes 2:16
Like the fool, the wise
man too must die!

REFLECT
➡ What kind of
grades am I
capable of earning?
➡ What are my career
goals? Why?
➡ Where does God fit
into my grades and
my goals?

CONSIDER
*Better than a
high IQ is a high
view of God.*

Do you know your IQ? Are you proud of how high it is? Or worried about how low it is? Do you use it as a guage for how well you're going to do in life?

Surprisingly, people with high IQs don't necessarily find happiness in high-paying, mind-stretching careers. We might expect a person with genius-level intelligence to be dissatisfied with anything less than daily disscussions of E=MC^2 or subatomic particles. But many highly intelligent folks find all the fulfillment they need while working in blue-collar jobs.

According to Peter Kizilos in an article in the *Detroit News,* many high-IQ types are plumbers, construction workers, firefighters, store clerks, bus drivers, and garbage collectors. Hans Arlton, for example, has scored as high as 160 on intelligence tests, yet he's happy to be a Minneapolis construction worker. His job leaves him time for things he loves to do: woodworking and playing the trombone.

Frank is a firefighter with an IQ of 137. He has never taken promotional tests because success would mean moving from the neighborhood and his friends. He says, "I consider myself a success in life at only one thing. That's being a father to my kids."

Now let's talk about your IQ. If you're pulling in good grades, great—keep at it. If you'd like to get good grades or pass a tough class, go for it. Just remember the words of the author of Ecclesiastes. Although knowing a lot of information has some value (2:13–14), it won't make any eternal difference (vv. 15–16).

What matters eternally is how we honor God with what we know. True wisdom begins with proper respect for God and doing what He wants us to do—no matter what our IQ says.   —K.D.

Through preaching, teaching, and the Bible, God is telling me . . . _____

_____

Through nature and the lives of other believers, God is showing me . . . _____

_____

I will respond by . . . _____

_____

Personal struggles

READ
Proverbs 6:20–23

MEDITATE
Psalm 119:74
I have put my hope in your word.

REFLECT

➡ Am I honest about the confusion and struggles I have in being a Christian? Why or why not?

➡ How much time do I spend each day in God's Word? Is that enough?

➡ During the next two weeks I will read the Bible for _____ minutes each day.

CONSIDER
God's truth is the answer to our confusion.

Often, when a person contemplates our hectic and bewildering society, he can become confused—even in his walk with the Lord. I am a struggling college student . . ."

These words are from a letter written by a young man I'll call Jim. My heart went out to him because I could feel his pain. He's struggling to make sense out of this morally twisted mess of a world while trying to live in a way that pleases the Lord.

Chances are, you know firsthand what he's talking about. I've been in and out of that place too. And we're not alone.

Solomon pictured God's Word as a father's commands and a mother's teachings. He told us, "Bind them upon your heart forever; fasten them around your neck. [In other words, take them into your heart and mind and carry them with you at all times.] When you walk, they will guide you; when you sleep, they will watch over you; when you awake, they will speak to you" (Proverbs 6:20–22).

Guidance, protection, and companionship. That's what we need when we lose our way. So let's get into God's Word and let it get into us. Then we can experience God at work, not just through the Bible, but also in our lives.

Are you facing personal struggles regarding life or faith? Are you looking for a deeper and stronger relationship with God? Open up that Book again and say to God, "I have put my hope in your word." —D.P.

Through preaching, teaching, and the Bible, God is telling me . . . _____
_____
_____

Through nature and the lives of other believers, God is showing me . . . _____
_____
_____

I will respond by . . . _____
_____

Traps, tapes, and TV

READ
Psalm 140

MEDITATE
Psalm 140:5
Proud men have hidden a snare for me.

REFLECT
➡ I agree or disagree that TV and videos influence me. What evidence do I have that I am right?

➡ In what situations do I need to pray, as David did, "Rescue me, O Lord, from evil men"?

CONSIDER
Let the Bible be your TV guide.

D id you ever see a McDonald's restaurant that's as clean and friendly as the ones in commercials? Or how about those Domino's commercials with the dancing delivery person? If that's a dose of reality, then I'm in the Baseball Hall of Fame.

You know what those commercials are doing, I'm sure. They're not concerned about reality; they're creating an idealized image of their product to make us feel good about it. Over time, we forget about reality and begin to see only the idealized version. We begin to think of these places as an extension of our home. After all, the people sang and smiled and waved at us in our own family room. Companies know that if they build an image, we will believe.

This idea of media influence would be harmless if it went no further than where we get our pizza. But in between those clever commercials are TV shows. When we watch them, we subject our minds to their influences.

As do commercials, programs slowly influence us to their way of thinking. A constant visual diet of idealized, risk-free, morality-free scenes of drinking, drugs, sex, lying, bad language, and disrespect can lead us to think of these things as harmless. But they're not. And these programs lure us into activities that are not God-honoring.

The major difference between today's threats via video and the threats facing David (Psalm 140) is that we are often unaware of the danger. We don't see the snares even as we are walking right into them.

We need to pray as David did: "Keep me, O Lord, from the hands of the wicked" (v. 4). And we may have to turn off the TV before we get trapped in ungodly ways of thinking.   —D.B.

Through preaching, teaching, and the Bible, God is telling me . . . _____
_____
_____

Through nature and the lives of other believers, God is showing me . . . _____
_____
_____

I will respond by . . . _____
_____
_____

Who me? In charge?

READ
Daniel 1

MEDITATE
Daniel 1:17
To these four young men God gave knowledge and understanding.

REFLECT
➡ Which of my friends are good leaders? What characteristics make me think so?

➡ What traits did Daniel have that made him a good leader?

CONSIDER
God makes leaders out of ordinary people.

How many times have you heard someone say, "Someday you will be the leaders in the church." It's one of those irritating phrases adults say to drive young people crazy.

The problem is—whether you like it or not—this saying is painfully true. It dawned on me the other day that it has indeed happened to people my age. The people I went to school with are taking over. A couple of them are presidents of Christian colleges. Another is a psychologist. Others are pastors. Some are missionaries. One is a college football coach. One is a seminary professor. And on it goes.

When you're in college, it is hard to picture that person sitting next to you in American Lit as a school superintendent. Or that roommate of yours as chairman of the board of education. Or yourself as . . . What role will you have in the next fifteen years

or so when the mantle of control is passed along to you and your friends? As you think about this, I hope it stirs up a desire to make the following decisions:

To live for Jesus each day now, so you'll know how to live for Him when you have people looking up to you.

To live in God's will each day so you are ready to accept His assignment for you.

To prepare mentally for your role by learning all you can.

To develop the people skills needed to get along with others.

It's true. If Jesus doesn't return first, that gang sitting around in the lounge watching Dick Van Dyke reruns will someday be in charge. Now's the time for you to seek God's help and to get ready for your role as a leader.

—D.B.

Through preaching, teaching, and the Bible, God is telling me . . . _____

_____

_____

Through nature and the lives of other believers, God is showing me . . . _____

_____

_____

I will respond by . . . _____

_____

_____

Door of indifference

MEDITATE
1 Peter 2:15
By doing good you should silence the ignorant talk of foolish men.

REFLECT

➡ What principles of good citizenship do I see in 1 Peter 2:13–17?

➡ If I am going to practice good citizenship, I need to be better informed. What are my best sources?

➡ If I want to get involved in the political process, whom do I call?

CONSIDER
Be a part of the process, not a part of the problem.

Would you ever consider running for political office, circulating a petition, writing a letter to your congressperson or governor, or attending a rally in support of an issue?

Before you say no, look at some statistics compiled by the Times Mirror Center for the People and the Press. According to their findings, today's young adults couldn't care less about what is going on in the political arena. They may be big *Current Affair* fans, but don't bring up current events.

Less than 40 percent of the eligible voters between eighteen and twenty-four said they vote in state, local, or national elections. Less than 30 percent of people under age thirty-five who were polled read the newspaper. And when the polling agency went to Columbus, Ohio, to talk to young adults about their view of citizenship, no one they asked believed that good citizenship included attending a community board meeting, running for elected office, signing a petition, or writing a letter to the governor.

So what does all this mean? It means you have a golden opportunity to make a difference in your community by making your views known and showing people that Christian young people do care.

How do you start? Why not work for a local politician in a campaign? Or get behind an important petition drive. Or write a well-thought-out letter to the editor of your local newspaper. Or run for the student senate.

Today, more than ever, our society needs to hear the voices of young people who love and honor God and want to influence their community with what is good and right.   —D.B.

Through preaching, teaching, and the Bible, God is telling me . . . _____

Through nature and the lives of other believers, God is showing me . . . _____

I will respond by . . . _____

Loosen the noose!

READ
Romans 6:11–18

MEDITATE
Romans 6:18
You have been set free from sin and have become slaves to righteousness.

REFLECT

➡ Where did I get the idea that the Bible is just a lot of rules to take the fun out of life?

➡ When I am tempted to do something the Bible says is wrong, what will help me resist?

➡ What things threaten to make me their slave? How can God help me avoid them?

CONSIDER
Your greatest freedom is freedom from sin.

Why can't I live my life the way I want to? Why all the rules? Adults are cramping my style. Why should I have to worry about curfews? And why shouldn't I be able to date anyone I want to and listen to any kind of music I like? I mean really, folks, take off the noose!

Ever felt this way? At one time or another, all of us struggle with rules that limit our freedom. In fact, that's the very reason some people reject Christ.

College students often tell me that Christianity doesn't appeal to them because it has too many don'ts. Having to obey all of those rules in the Bible is about as pleasant to them as being bound and gagged. But what these students fail to realize is that the principles of the Bible don't enslave us—they set us free. Living within God's will prevents us from being held captive by sin.

Look at what Paul said about sin: "Do not let sin reign in your mortal body so that you obey its evil desires" (Romans 6:12). He was indicating that if we let it, sin will become king, leading us to do evil. But there is a way to avoid that: "But thanks be to God. . . . You have been set free from sin and have become slaves to righteousness" (vv. 17–18). "Slaves to righteousness." Now that's a unique way to be free!

Whether we realize it or not, it is the *absence* of principles and guidelines—rules if you will—that binds us. You've seen that concept at work in friends who are trapped by alcohol or pornography or drugs. By obeying Christ we can avoid that kind of imprisonment. That's the way to make sure the noose is loose!   —D.P.

Through preaching, teaching, and the Bible, God is telling me . . . _____

_____

Through nature and the lives of other believers, God is showing me . . . _____

_____

I will respond by . . . _____

_____

Where to put the light

READ
Philippians 2:12–16

MEDITATE
Philippians 2:15
You shine like stars in the universe.

REFLECT
➤ In which places that I go am I the only light shining?
➤ What are some dark places where God does not want me to go?
➤ What can I do to make sure my light is as bright as it can possibly be?
➤ What other truths can I get out of Philippians 2:12–16?

CONSIDER
You need to glow in the dark.

Here's a question for all you electrical engineering majors. If you were designing the electrical scheme for a building, where would you put the lights?

Instead of complaining that you need more information, read the following story for some insight on lights.

A woman felt really alone at her place of employment because she was the only Christian. To make matters worse, she was often ridiculed for her faith and accused of being narrow-minded. Finally she was so discouraged that she considered quitting.

But before going that far, she made a wise move; she went to her pastor for advice. After listening to her complaints, he asked, "Where do people usually put lights?"

"In dark places," she replied. Immediately she knew she had her answer. Her place of work was indeed a "dark place" where "light" was vitally needed. She decided to stay where she was. It wasn't long before a number of her fellow employees came to know Christ as their Savior.

So, the answer to that electrical engineering question was really quite simple. You put lights where it is dark. And guess who the lights are in our dark world: you and me.

As stars in the universe brighten the blackened nighttime sky, so we light up the places of spiritual darkness where God puts us.

If you are in a job or school or home where it seems especially dark, now you know why. You are the only light those around you may ever see. —D.B.

Through preaching, teaching, and the Bible, God is telling me . . . _____

_____

Through nature and the lives of other believers, God is showing me . . . _____

_____

I will respond by . . . _____

_____

Don't quit now!

READ
James 1:2–4, 12

MEDITATE
James 1:3
The testing of your faith develops perseverance.

REFLECT

➡ On a scale of 1 to 10 (with 10 being the highest), how do I measure up when it comes to perseverance? Am I a spiritual quitter?

➡ What are some of the things that cause me to give up?

➡ What does Hebrews 12:1–2 tell me about perseverance?

CONSIDER
Why quit when you still might win.

Cecil Fielder had hit forty-nine home runs, and he wanted to become the eleventh man in major league history to hit fifty in a single season. But he hadn't been swinging the bat very well, and it came down to the last game of the season. He'd been under enormous media pressure. No one would have blamed him if he sat out game 162, perhaps coming in only to pinch-hit. But he would not give up. He was going for it.

In his first at-bat he hit a weak pop-up. Then in the fourth inning Cecil drove a fastball into the left-field seats. He had done it! In the seventh he hit number fifty-one. Because he refused to quit, Cecil Fielder wrote his name in the record books.

The Bible calls this quality perseverance. And it means remaining faithful to God's will until the end.

That kind of commitment eliminates a lot of people.

There's no room for wimps or crybabies. And people always looking for excuses aren't welcome either. Nor are those who just won't put forth the effort to keep going.

Note the people who stuck it out in tough circumstances. Noah in the ark. Joseph in prison. Shadrach, Meshach, and Abednego in the fiery furnace. Daniel in the lions' den. Paul in his beatings. Christ on the cross.

What tough circumstances are you in? Are people at work making fun of your faith? Does a science instructor think Christians are relics of antiquity? Does it sometimes seem that it's you versus the world?

So why bother? Here's what James said before he was killed for his faith: A crown of life has been promised for those who love God enough to stay true to Him (1:12). There's the motive: love for God. That's why you shouldn't quit. —D.E.

Through preaching, teaching, and the Bible, God is telling me . . . _____

_____

Through nature and the lives of other believers, God is showing me . . . _____

_____

I will respond by . . . _____

_____

Muffler shop meditation

READ
Psalm 138:7–8

MEDITATE
Psalm 138:7
Though I walk in the midst of trouble, you preserve my life.

REFLECT

➡ Is God punishing me when my car won't start or when somebody gets ink on my new coat?

➡ Who do I know who seems to sail through life without difficulty?

➡ How does God "preserve my life" even in the "midst of trouble"?

➡ What will be the ultimate measure of my success?

CONSIDER
No problems; no successes.

As I write this article, I'm sitting in the waiting room at The Muffler Man. I don't normally write in muffler shop lounges. I prefer quieter, less smoky areas. Like my office.

But my catalytic converter quit converting, and it has to be replaced. So here I am wondering why things like this keep happening. I have become all too familiar with items I never wanted to know about—like automatic transmissions, washing machines, and kitchen faucets. Things that keep falling apart.

I try to be a good person. I love my wife and kids. I pay my taxes. I go to church. Yet my muffler still fell off. On the way to church no less.

But it isn't just me. The other day I saw a brand-new Cadillac sitting beside the road with its hood up and its forlorn driver staring helplessly at the engine. Imagine spending thirty thousand dollars for a car and still having to get the thing towed!

As you prepare yourself for a career, keep in mind that you are not going to be able to avoid problems. Perhaps you're thinking that you can earn enough money to avoid the difficulties that come from having old cars and inexpensive homes. Don't count on it. BMW dealers have service departments too. And the bigger and fancier the house, the more things there are to break. Even Jacuzzis go on the fritz.

So don't put your trust in things that break down, need repairs, and go out of style.

Instead, put your trust in God and consider the things of the world to be tools—not the final prize. If God wants to accomplish something worthwhile in your life, He can do it even when you are in the "midst of trouble."

—D.B.

Through preaching, teaching, and the Bible, God is telling me . . . _____

_____

Through nature and the lives of other believers, God is showing me . . . _____

_____

I will respond by . . . _____

_____

Get out of my ear!

MEDITATE
Psalm 119:10

I seek you with all my heart; do not let me stray.

REFLECT

➡ What spiritual activities do I replace with things of less importance: How can I change this?

➡ In what areas has laziness entered my Christian life? Have I become less involved in prayer, Bible reading, and church attendance? Why have I allowed this to happen?

CONSIDER
Complacency is one step from losing.

Congratulations! You did it. You overcame one of the great enemies of the Christian life: *Complacency.* He's that little guy who crawls into your ear and tries to convince you that because you're doing so well you can ignore things like prayer, reading the Bible, and going to church.

But you are too smart for that old trick. You know his strategy. He's just trying to get you out of a positive habit or prevent you from developing one. And when you've listened to him in the past, he laughed your ear off and said something like, "Got you again, turkey!"

How do I know that this happens to you? Because it happens to me. In fact, it almost happened this morning. I sat down to write some devotional articles. However, I hadn't had my own devotions yet, and I felt I needed to do that first. But then that little guy named Complacency

told me I didn't need devotions today. You don't have time for devotions this morning, his voice said softly. You have too much work to do. You can have them tomorrow. But I shook him out of my head and opened *Our Daily Bread* (another devotional publication produced by Radio Bible Class). These are the first words I read from writer Dave Egner: "Every believer in Christ is involved in spiritual warfare every day. We cannot afford, therefore, to enter the day complacently." I got the message.

I get the feeling that Mr. Complacency will be back. Maybe today. Maybe tomorrow. And I'll bet he's planning to pay you a little visit too. But if we seek God with our whole heart and make Him the priority in our life, His voice will drown out the self-destructive advice of old man Complacency.   —D.P.

Through preaching, teaching, and the Bible, God is telling me . . . _____

_____

_____

Through nature and the lives of other believers, God is showing me . . . _____

_____

_____

I will respond by . . . _____

_____

_____

Holy hurricanes

READ
Psalm 119:65–75

MEDITATE
Psalm 119:75
In faithfulness you have afflicted me.

REFLECT
➡ When I'm in the eye of the storm, it's impossible to see my way out. How can Psalm 119 and James 1 help me navigate?
➡ What are some lessons I have learned from times of difficulty in the past?

CONSIDER
Don't back down when difficulties come up.

I had always thought of hurricanes as something people could do without, but I recently learned that they are necessary to keep nature in balance.

These tropical storms, with winds up to 150 miles per hour and accompanied by torrential rains, flashing lightning, and rumbling thunder, can be devastating. Yet scientists tell us they are tremendously valuable. They release much of the oppressive heat that builds up at the equator, and they are indirectly responsible for much of the rainfall in North and South America. Meteorologists are convinced that hurricanes actually do more good than harm.

The Bible teaches us that the hurricanes (i.e., difficulties) that strike believers are like that. Although they bring temporary pain and grief, they can produce long-term benefits. A person's character is more likely to be strengthened in the heat of suffering than in times of ease and prosperity. Sometimes God allows us to endure tough times even though it is within His power to prevent them. He does not shield us from the inevitable results of our own foolishness. As a matter of fact, we need difficulties and afflictions for our development as well as for our correction.

If you care at all about the kind of person you are becoming (and I have a strong hunch you do), take the advice of James: "Consider it pure joy . . . whenever you face trials of many kinds" (1:2). Why? "Because you know that the testing of your faith develops perseverance" (v. 3). As a part of the maturing process, let perseverance work on you. It may feel like a hurricane, but the results will be worth it.

—T.B.

Through preaching, teaching, and the Bible, God is telling me . . . _____
_____
_____

Through nature and the lives of other believers, God is showing me . . . _____
_____
_____

I will respond by . . . _____
_____

No hand-me-downs

Some things have to be tried to be enjoyed.

For example, how do you describe a T-bone steak to a person who has never eaten anything but hot dogs? And what words would you use to tell someone who has never been in an airplane about the breathtaking wonder of flying over the Rocky Mountains? Or how do you make another person understand the sudden rush of adrenalin you felt in a crisis situation.

It's just as difficult to explain the joys of walking with Jesus to people who have never done so. Try describing it to them and they might think only about all the "fun" things they won't be able to do anymore. About all you can do is assure them that it's a wonderful life (no, not the one with Jimmy Stewart) and that you're praying for them to trust Christ and find out for themselves.

The delights of knowing God and the joy of living in fellowship with Him cannot be hand-me-downs. A relationship with God is a first-hand experience. Only the upright can enjoy the confidence of the Lord (Proverbs 3:32).

When David described the blessings of the life of faith, he urged others to "taste and see that the Lord is good." He knew that God's love can only be experienced firsthand.

Have you experienced the good life for yourself? Do you know the joy of having your sins forgiven? Can you feel the strength that comes from relying on God? If not, taste for yourself and see that the Lord is good. Accept Jesus as your Savior and begin to walk with Him. It's not something you can pick up secondhand.   —M.D.

Through preaching, teaching, and the Bible, God is telling me . . . _____
_____
_____

Through nature and the lives of other believers, God is showing me . . . _____
_____
_____

I will respond by . . . _____
_____
_____

Breaking bad news

READ
Proverbs 27:1–9

MEDITATE
Proverbs 27:5
Better is open rebuke than hidden love.

REFLECT

➡ What are some ways people have told me news that was hard to swallow?

➡ When I correct people, do my words follow the principles of Proverbs 27?

CONSIDER
Break bad news as if you were on the receiving end.

How do you tell someone bad news?

What do you say when: (a) You notice that someone sat on a humongous wad of gum? (b) The friend who is talking to you has incredibly bad breath? (c) You just ruined a borrowed sweater? (d) You smashed your parents' car? (e) You want to break up with the person you've been dating? (f) You just ruined your chemistry lab project and your lab partner doesn't know it yet?

Telling people what they don't want to hear isn't easy—but it's often the necessary and loving thing to do.

Proverbs 27 offers some principles of good communication. Perhaps they can help us when we have to be bearers of bad news.

1. Don't provoke the other person (v. 3). Only a fool goes around looking for trouble.

2. Keep your cool (v. 4). If you are out of control, you'll probably say the wrong thing.

3. Don't be motivated by jealousy (v. 4). Resist the temptation to point out the faults in a person you envy.

4. Be open and honest (v. 5). The best way to show that you care is to tell the truth.

5. Speak as a loving friend (v. 6). An enemy will flatter you in order to take advantage of you, but a friend will tell you what you need to hear to become better.

6. Give genuine, earnest advice (v. 9). Loving words are like perfume to the soul.

If you keep these principles in mind, you'll be more tactful and more loving even when you have to break unpleasant news.   —K.D.

Through preaching, teaching, and the Bible, God is telling me . . . _____

_____

_____

Through nature and the lives of other believers, God is showing me . . . _____

_____

_____

I will respond by . . . _____

_____

_____

"I hate that!"

READ
Proverbs 6:16–19

MEDITATE
Proverbs 6:16
There are six things the Lord hates.

REFLECT
➡ What happened yesterday that made me feel hatred toward someone?

➡ What kinds of things typically make me mad?

➡ Which of the seven things in Proverbs 6 have made me angry lately? Do I love the opposite of each?

CONSIDER
What we hate reflects what we love.

The tough-looking hombre walked up to the table and picked up a taco. Just as he bit into it, the taco shell shattered, spilling stuff all over him. At that, he said, "Oh, I hate that! I hate it when that happens!"

That scene, if you don't remember, is from a TV commercial. After seeing it a few times, I found myself repeating "I hate that! I hate it when that happens!" when something occurred that I didn't like.

I admit, I say "I hate that" about some pretty insignificant things—ketchup that won't come out of a bottle, stale potato chips, tough pizza crust, and catching a red light when I'm in a hurry. It's unbelievable how such simple irritations can bug me.

God hates things too. But He doesn't do so in a comical or petty way. He hates what deserves to be hated. Proverbs 6 lists seven things that the Lord finds detestable. They are (1) a big ego, (2) lying, (3) murder, (4) evil scheming, (5) rushing into evil, (6) lying in court, (7) troublemaking.

If the Lord hates those things, it makes sense to stay about a thousand miles away from them. But it also makes sense to understand why God feels so strongly about them.

God hates those things because they are the exact opposite of what He loves: (1) humility, (2) honesty, (3) respect for human life, (4) a desire to please Him, (5) eagerness to do what is right, (6) justice, and (7) peacemaking.

Are those attitudes and actions important to you? Do you love what the Lord loves and hate what He hates? This is no trivial matter. After all, what we hate reveals what we love. —K.D.

Through preaching, teaching, and the Bible, God is telling me . . . _____

_____

_____

Through nature and the lives of other believers, God is showing me . . . _____

_____

_____

I will respond by . . . _____

_____

_____

Pay attention!

READ
Proverbs 18:1–2,
13, 17, 24

MEDITATE
Proverbs 27:9
The pleasantness of one's friend springs from his earnest counsel.

REFLECT
➡ How do I behave when someone else is speaking?
➡ Do I appear interested or bored?
➡ Do I feel that I'm a little better than most people? A little worse? How do I let that feeling show with my body language?

CONSIDER
I can't hear you if I'm thinking about me.

The young man sitting across from me as we ate lunch was frustrated. "How can I make friends?" he asked. "I just can't seem to keep friends. I'm tired of being so lonely." As I munched on my fries and listened, it became obvious that he simply did not know how to make and maintain close relationships.

Sound familiar? Maybe I can help.

One thing that's important in making and keeping friendships is to focus directly on the person who is talking to you. In other words, pay attention. How? By doing these things: Maintain eye contact; lean forward a little; follow closely; and ask occasional questions. This will send the person an important message. You will be saying, in effect, "I really am interested in you."

In addition, avoid actions that say you are emotionally disconnecting with the other person. These actions send the signal that you are more interested in your own agenda than in what that person is saying. Some of these negative actions are: turning your body slightly away; glancing at your watch; yawning or sighing; looking at the door; playing with a pencil; interrupting in mid-sentence with another topic. Any of these minor distractions can lead the potential friend to think you don't care about him or her.

Are you having trouble making friends? It could be that you're turning people off when they are talking to you. You'll have a lot better chance at connecting if you learn to pay attention. Let people experience the "pleasantness" of your friendship. —D.E.

Through preaching, teaching, and the Bible, God is telling me . . . _____
_____
_____

Through nature and the lives of other believers, God is showing me . . . _____
_____
_____

I will respond by . . . _____
_____

Porcupine personality

READ
James 3:13–18

MEDITATE
James 1:19
Everyone should be . . . slow to become angry.

REFLECT
➡ How do I respond to criticism? Do I enjoy firing quills at people? What should I do about it?
➡ Could I be unaware of my own quills? How? Why?

CONSIDER
A good friend won't stick others, but sticks with them.

It's hard to cuddle a porcupine. When you try to get close, you get poked by quills. That's probably why no porcupine has been a serious challenger for pet-of-the-year honors.

According to people who follow these heavy-set, short-legged rodents through the woods, porcupines have few natural enemies. But I can't imagine them having very many close friends either.

If you approach a porcupine, it will turn away from you and prepare to drive its tail quills into your flesh. One expert has described the porcupine as "a solitary but not antisocial animal."

The porcupine reminds me of some people I have known. They're quite civil until they feel threatened. But if someone questions their views on an issue, offers some criticism, or asks them a personal question, they turn and point their "quills" at the threatening person.

In contrast, James encourages us to "relax our quills," so to speak, and not to be so defensive. He says we should "be slow to speak and slow to become angry" (1:19), love our neighbor as ourselves (2:8), be merciful and slow to judge (v. 13; 4:11–12), rid ourselves of bitterness and selfish ambition (3:14), seek to be peaceful, considerate, submissive, and merciful (v. 17), be open with God and others about our faults (4:6–10; 5:16), and stop grumbling about others (5:9). As you think about the past few days with instructors, deans, dorm advisors, parents, teammates, coaches, roommates, and your boyfriend or girlfriend, have those shining characteristics been evident?

Or have some of those people been poked by your quills? Sometimes we're not very cuddly, are we? —K.D.

Through preaching, teaching, and the Bible, God is telling me . . . _____

_____

_____

Through nature and the lives of other believers, God is showing me . . . _____

_____

_____

I will respond by . . . _____

_____

_____

AUGUST 18

Wish you weren't here

READ
Isaiah 1:10–17

MEDITATE
Isaiah 1:13
I cannot bear your evil assemblies.

REFLECT
➡ I think parents should/should not force kids to go to church because . . .
➡ How do I need to change my attitude toward things like church and Bible study?

CONSIDER
Even at church, worship takes place in the heart.

You plop down into the pew, wishing you were somewhere else. Then you mumble toward heaven, "I hope You're happy."

The answer: "I'm no happier than you are."

For some reason, we have the idea that God is pleased by our actions. We think He is quite moved when we do "righteous" things like going to church, giving money to worthy causes, or reading our Bibles—even when we don't want to.

But God is not impressed by outward actions. He is much more concerned about our inward motives. The people of Israel thought they were pleasing God by fulfilling their ceremonial responsibilities. God's response: "They have become a burden to me" (v. 14).

So what am I suggesting? Am I saying that next time Mom wants you to go to church and you don't feel like it, you should say, "Hey, my devotional book says that God hates it when I go when I don't feel like it. So I'm staying home to please God"?

Not exactly. I'm suggesting a different approach. Work on your heart and your attitude!

God didn't tell the Jews to stop their religious ceremonies. Instead, He said, "Stop doing wrong, learn to do right!" (vv. 16–17). Once your attitude is right, you approach things like church and Bible study in a whole different way.

If the activities that help you grow as a Christian have started to grow tiresome, change your focus. Think about God before going to church; how Bible study helps you apply your faith to your everyday life; how getting together with other Christians can teach you more about Jesus Christ. You'll get more out of it . . . and God will be a lot happier to see you there!   —J.C.

Through preaching, teaching, and the Bible, God is telling me . . . _____
_____
_____

Through nature and the lives of other believers, God is showing me . . . _____
_____
_____

I will respond by . . . _____
_____

A LOVING HEART

Fight together!

READ
Ephesians 4:17–28

MEDITATE
Ephesians 4:27
Do not give the devil a foothold.

REFLECT

➡ Do I see myself as a member of Christ's army, fighting against the devil?

➡ Am I squabbling with some fellow member of that army? How do I suppose Satan feels about that?

➡ Am I often offended by other Christians? Easily hurt? Holding grudges? What should I do about it?

CONSIDER
If you have to fight someone, fight Satan.

It was early morning. The racket outside was so loud I rolled out of bed and went to the front door to see what was happening. I knew about their longstanding feud. I'd heard them yell at one another before, but I'd never heard them go at it like this.

There in the trees in front of our house the crows and the blue jays were quarreling again. But their war of noise and wings had escalated. I watched the reserves fly in and take positions in the branches. The actual bombing and strafing was concentrated in the upper branches of a big oak.

Then I saw something I hadn't expected. A bird with big brown wings retreated to a nearby elm. That was no crow! And this was no longer a spat between the blues and the blacks. They had stopped fighting one another. They now had a common enemy, an owl. The crows

and blue jays combined forces against the owl.

Like crows and blue jays, believers in Christ have a common enemy—Satan. He is reason enough to make us forget our differences. That's what Paul was talking about in Ephesians 4. He told us to put aside our personal dislikes, our anger, and our self-centered interests and concentrate on doing right. When we fight one another, we "give the devil a foothold."

When people observe you and your friends, do they see squabbling or cooperation? Why not show them what the forces of good can do when they work together!
—M.D.

Through preaching, teaching, and the Bible, God is telling me . . . _____
_____
_____

Through nature and the lives of other believers, God is showing me . . . _____
_____
_____

I will respond by . . . _____
_____
_____

What now?

READ
James 1:1–8

MEDITATE
James 1:5
If any of you lacks wisdom, he should ask God.

REFLECT
→ How well do I respond in crises? Why?
→ What problems do I face today?
→ How has God answered other times I have prayed for wisdom?
→ Do I believe He can truly help me? Why?

CONSIDER
A breakdown is a good time to look up.

I used to wonder what it would be like to have my car break down hundreds of miles from home. But not anymore. Now I know.

My family was traveling from Michigan to Alabama to visit Grandpa and Grandma. The car cruised along quite well until we were about two hours away from our destination. Then I began to hear a noise that I was sure I wasn't supposed to be hearing. I pulled onto the shoulder to investigate.

After peering under the hood and poking around for several minutes, I knew nothing more than when I first stopped the car. So I let the engine cool down and drove slowly along the shoulder to an exit. The mechanic at the service station listened, pulled some things off the engine, and calmly let me know that minor surgery would not be the solution. I needed a new engine. Welcome to Alabama.

The apostle James knew nothing about Oldsmobiles, but he knew what Oldsmobile drivers need to do when their cars break down. He said they're to "believe and not doubt" (1:6).

To steady my own weak faith as my car was being hauled away, I recalled times in the past when God had met my needs in answer to my prayers. Even though I was emotionally frazzled, my faith grew stronger.

So what should you do the next time your car dies, your roommate treats you badly, your instructor pops a quiz in your hardest class, or something worse happens? Remember what James said. Ask God for wisdom. And if your faith is a little wobbly, remind yourself why God can be trusted. If you can do that, you can have the joy of watching God at work, even in your trials.   —K.D.

Through preaching, teaching, and the Bible, God is telling me . . . _____

_____

_____

Through nature and the lives of other believers, God is showing me . . . _____

_____

_____

I will respond by . . . _____

_____

The results of asking

READ
1 Samuel 1:1–20

MEDITATE
1 Samuel 1:15
"I was pouring out my soul to the Lord."

REFLECT
➡ What was the last thing I prayed about specifically? How did God answer my prayer?
➡ How long am I willing to wait for an answer?

CONSIDER
Prayer works.

Phyllis Jones knew exactly what she wanted—a husband—but she didn't know where to look. So she prayed. Pat Kelly knew what he wanted too—a good time—and he went looking for it in a Chicago night spot not far from where Phyllis was praying.

Phyllis Jones was a Christian, the daughter of an evangelist and a member of the Jones Sisters gospel singing group. She wanted a husband who shared her love for Jesus Christ. Pat Kelly was an outfielder for the Chicago White Sox and brother of NFL great Leroy Kelly. He was not a Christian.

Eventually Pat Kelly became a Christian through the influence of a Chicago businessman. And Phyllis's sister Gail married baseball player André Thornton. Then Pat was traded to Cleveland, where he became Thornton's teammate. Soon André was introducing Pat to his sister-in-law Phyllis. Her four-year-old Chicago prayer was answered when she married the man who had danced the night away while she prayed.

One awesome thing about being a child of God is the surprises He has in store for us. Because we can't see the whole picture, we sometimes wonder what He is doing. But if we are faithful in praying for His guidance, we will eventually get what we want—or something even better.

Phyllis Jones was doing what a great woman of the Bible had done thousands of years before. Hannah, like Phyllis, had a problem—a void in her life. She wanted a baby. So she prayed. And you know what surprise God had in store for her—Samuel, who would become a courageous prophet and priest of God.

What is the empty spot in your life? Have you asked God to fill it?   —D.B.

Through preaching, teaching, and the Bible, God is telling me . . . _____

_____

Through nature and the lives of other believers, God is showing me . . . _____

_____

I will respond by . . . _____

A limo ride

READ
Matthew 21:1–11

MEDITATE
Matthew 21:5
"See, your king comes to you . . . riding on a donkey."

REFLECT

➡ Why were some people turned off by Jesus' lack of pomp?

➡ How can I praise Jesus right now and throughout the day?

➡ What will our Lord's second coming be like? What aspect of Jesus will the world see then?

CONSIDER
Jesus did not come to impress us but to redeem us.

Jay Leno has one. So does Queen Elizabeth II. And Zsa Zsa Gabor had one that she was driving erratically just before a Beverly Hills cop pulled her over.

What am I talking about? A Rolls-Royce. These long, sleek apartments-on-wheels are a symbol of wealth, status, and power.

No one expects you to come riding onto campus in a stretched-out luxury limo. But people would think it odd if the President of the United States were to drive up in your rusted-out Chevette.

With that in mind, think about the time Jesus entered Jerusalem and crowds of people gathered to welcome Him. They were so happy to see Him that they spread branches on the road and shouted, "Blessed is he who comes in the name of the Lord!" Wouldn't it have been fitting for Him to arrive in a limo (if they'd been around back then)? After all, He was

the King of Glory, the Son of God. If anyone deserved the best transportation money could buy, it was Jesus.

Instead, Jesus came into town riding—of all things—a donkey. But there is more going on here than meets the eye. While earthly kings usually came to power through the use of swords and strong horses, Jesus used peace and humility. He called for willing submission to His rule. What at first seems peculiar to us actually was quite fitting.

If we evaluate Jesus on the basis of human standards of wealth and power, we'll have a flawed understanding. His mission was not to impress people with His riches or to force people to worship Him. He came in poverty to solve our spiritual bankruptcy and to free us from our bondage to sin. Blessed is He who came—riding on a donkey—to bring us the riches of eternal life! —K.D.

Through preaching, teaching, and the Bible, God is telling me . . . _____

_____

_____

Through nature and the lives of other believers, God is showing me . . . _____

_____

_____

I will respond by . . . _____

_____

_____

The hardest thing to do

READ
1 Samuel 12:16–25

MEDITATE
James 5:16
Pray for each other.

REFLECT
➡ In an average week, how much time do I spend in prayer?
➡ Looking forward to next week, what hours will I set aside for prayer?
➡ What are three prayer requests that I will bring before God this week?

CONSIDER
Praying is hard; living without it is a lot harder.

Let's assume you are open to anything God asks you to do. You'd be willing to lead a Bible study, work on a construction project in Africa, or (perish the thought) be a recreation leader for some junior highers.

But what about the work of praying? Is that too much to ask? In terms of pure effort, praying doesn't seem all that difficult. Yet look back on the past week. You may have spent two hours preparing for a Sunday school lesson, or a couple of hours at a youth group outreach. But how much time did you spend in prayer?

This is not to say that we should be legalistic about it. One sixteenth-century pastor got so caught up in church responsibilities that he fell behind in his prayers. So he prayed for three days straight, going without food and sleep! It took him five days in bed to recover from that marathon (and it was probably a lot longer before he felt like praying again).

Somewhere between his "too much" and our "too little" is the proper balance. We need to spend time in prayer. In fact, it is commanded in Scripture. We need to talk to our heavenly Father about what's happening in our lives. Some situations can be resolved only by God's intervention, and we should talk to Him about them.

But prayer takes discipline. It requires faith to leave situations in God's hands rather than try to solve them ourselves. It requires patience to leave a prayer request to God's timing.

When Samuel turned Israel over to the authority of King Saul, he assured the people, "Far be it from me that I should sin against the Lord by failing to pray for you" (v. 23). Forget the failure part. Make it a point to start spending more time with God in prayer.   —J.C.

Through preaching, teaching, and the Bible, God is telling me . . . _____

_____

_____

Through nature and the lives of other believers, God is showing me . . . _____

_____

_____

I will respond by . . . _____

_____

_____

WELL, WE,VE GOT TWO MINUTES LEFT. WHO HAS
SOME HEARTFELT PRAYER REQUESTS WE CAN LIFT
UP TO THE LORD?

A RESPONSIVE SOUL

You were there!

READ
Romans 6:1–14

MEDITATE
Romans 6:7
Anyone who has died has been freed from sin.

REFLECT
➡ If my sin nature was crucified with Christ, why is it so easy to sin?
➡ In what area will I consider myself dead to sin but alive to Christ today?

CONSIDER
I died in Christ; He lives in me.

Imagine that your father is a judge and you are nabbed by the police for speeding. (You? Never!) When you arrive in court, you find out that the judge assigned to your case is your dad! As you stand before the bench, Dad says, "You are my child, and I love you so much." (Under your breath, you say, "Keep talking, Dad!")

"But," he continues, "I am also sworn to uphold justice. You have broken the law, and you must pay the full consequences." (Scratch the "keep talking" comment.) But then your father does the unexpected. He takes off his robe and comes around to the front of the bench. Then he pulls out his wallet and pays your fine. This is a perfect combination of mercy and justice.

That's exactly what God did when He sent His Son, Jesus Christ, to die for our sins. Jesus came "down from the bench" and took our place. He paid our "fine" in full. Even more, when He rose again, He brought us new life. He gave us a "clean record," complete with power over our sin nature.

A Christian visiting Israel walked to the hill thought to be the place where Christ was crucified. His guide asked, "Have you been here before, sir?" "Yes," the man answered. "About 2,000 years ago."

We were all there, in a sense, when Christ died because our sin sent Him there. But the good news is, those of us who believe in Him were also there three days later when He conquered sin and death once and for all. Praise God!

—J.C.

Through preaching, teaching, and the Bible, God is telling me . . . _____
_____
_____

Through nature and the lives of other believers, God is showing me . . . _____
_____
_____

I will respond by . . . _____
_____
_____

Is it live? . . .

READ
Acts 12:18–24

MEDITATE
Ephesians 4:2
Be completely humble and gentle; be patient, bearing with one another in love.

REFLECT

➡ How can I keep from developing a proud heart?

➡ What are some areas in my life that I haven't turned over to God? What keeps me from letting go?

➡ What are five ways I can be more patient and humble today than I was yesterday?

CONSIDER
Don't take credit for what God has given you.

O r is it Milli Vanilli? "Musically, we are more talented than Bob Dylan. Musically, we are more talented than Paul McCartney. Mick Jagger, his lines are not clear. He don't know how he should produce a sound. I'm the new Elvis." Thus spoke Rob Pilatus of the pop group Milli Vanilli.

That was before Milli's manager told the world that good-looking Rob and his partner Fab had merely lip-synched to studio singers' voices during their concerts and music videos. Shortly thereafter, they were stripped of the Grammy they had won for their hot debut album. As the music industry and fans rejected him, Rob had to scarf down some bitter humble pie.

But let's watch the finger-pointing here. How many of us have never overstated our own abilities and accomplishments?

King Herod committed this sin big time. When his subjects called him a god, he "did not give praise to God" (Acts 12:23). Because of this arrogance, according to the historian Josephus, he was seized with violent pains and died within the week and "was eaten by worms" (Acts 12:23). (I hope you're not reading this over breakfast. If you are, sorry for wasting that bowl of Apple Jacks.)

God wants us to find our self-worth in Him, not in our own gifts or great deeds. He knows that we are too weak to handle praise from others. If we don't deflect praise from ourselves and direct it to God, it will lead to pride—the original sin.

We need to be "completely humble" in all that we do. By daily thanking God for everything He has done, we acknowledge that only He is worthy of praise and adoration. And that will keep us from pride.   —T.F.

Through preaching, teaching, and the Bible, God is telling me . . . _____

_____

_____

Through nature and the lives of other believers, God is showing me . . . _____

_____

_____

I will respond by . . . _____

_____

_____

What can I say?

Here's the scene. You're minding your own business, literally. You've stopped by the administration building to pay a bill. You drop off your check with the bursar (real colleges use this mysterious title for people who take your money), and you head for the elevator. The door opens and there stands the president of the college. You and the prez are about to take a little ride to the lobby.

What do you say to the president? "Nice weather, isn't it?" is too superficial. "How's the budget?" is too nosy. Do you introduce yourself? Do you study your shoes? What do you say so this dignified, sophisticated person won't think, "How'd this deadhead ever get into college?"

Life sometimes presents some pretty awkward moments. It happens when we talk to someone we've just met, when we talk to professors, when we talk to prospective employers. And when we talk to God.

You put down your devotional book and your Bible after your quiet time, you bow your head to pray, but you can't think of a word to say. It's just you and God and you are speechless. Nothing you can think of seems lofty enough.

Try doing what David did in Psalm 145. He heaped praise on God. Listen. "I will exalt you . . . I will praise your name . . . great is the Lord." Then think about some of these things: God's unfathomable greatness; His glorious splendor; His wonderful works; His power; His great deeds; His abundant goodness; His righteousness; His graciousness and compassion. When you start praising God you'll never run out of things to say.   —D.B.

Through preaching, teaching, and the Bible, God is telling me . . . _____

Through nature and the lives of other believers, God is showing me . . . _____

I will respond by . . . _____

Something stinks

READ
2 Corinthians
2:12–17

MEDITATE
2 Corinthians 2:14
God . . . spreads everywhere the fragrance of the knowledge of him.

REFLECT

➡ The quickest way I know to spoil my testimony for God is by _____.

➡ What can I do to "smell better" to those who now think I smell like death?

➡ What part of my life needs freshening up the most?

CONSIDER
Keeping your Christian testimony strong makes good "scents."

E ver get the impression after watching television that something's desperately wrong with you? It's no wonder. Ninety percent of commercials are focused on one message: you STINK!

Oh, they're polite about it, but the insult is still there. The flawless female smiles into the camera and whispers, "Use Ultra Swish mouthwash" (because your breath stinks). The magnificent male stares into the camera and chortles, "Try Dr. Droll's shoe inserts" (because your feet stink). Your armpits stink, your bathroom stinks, even your clothes stink. You have a problem; they have a solution. And if you'll just part with some of your cash, you can fix it.

But there's some good news the ad people aren't telling you— your life doesn't have to stink. The message of 2 Corinthians 2 is different from all those commercials.

By being part of God's family, Paul said, believers in Christ can be confident that their life "smells good." He called it "the fragrance."

But there is one catch. The fragrance is the knowledge of Christ, and some people are not going to like it. Paul explained that "we are to God the aroma of Christ" (v. 15). To friends and classmates who accept the Gospel of God's grace, you will be "the fragrance of life" (v. 16). But to those who reject the life-giving grace of God, you are the "smell of death" (v. 16).

You can keep your life smelling good. The Holy Spirit will help you spread the knowledge and fragrance of Christ in the way you walk and talk. Then no one around you can say, "Something stinks."　　　—T.B.

Through preaching, teaching, and the Bible, God is telling me . . . _____

Through nature and the lives of other believers, God is showing me . . . _____

I will respond by . . . _____

It can happen to you!

READ
Proverbs 23:29–35

MEDITATE
Proverbs 23:29–30
Who has woe? . . .
Those who linger over
wine.

REFLECT
- Do I believe I am invincible? Do I see bad things happen to others but believe they will never happen to me?
- In what areas of my life am I "playing with fire"? How can I put it out?
- When have I had to pay the price for bad decisions?

CONSIDER
If you sow wild oats, don't expect things to come up roses.

Steve Zandy is speaking to the juniors and seniors at his high school alma mater. To be given this privilege, he must be a real success in life, right? Maybe he's a great quarterback. Or a powerful motivational speaker who waxes eloquent about reaching beyond your potential.

But when Steve begins his speech, the students at East know that neither of those things is true. His whole body quakes, and his efforts to speak require great concentration. There are uneasy moments of silence while he struggles to get the next sentence out. Yet the students listen carefully. Why? Because of his story. And because he's only a couple of years older than they are.

"I did just what you guys do to fit in," Steve says haltingly. "I went to parties. I drank. I acted like a jerk. Then one night when I was a sophomore, I got drunk. I got in my sister's car. I hit a tree and ended up in a coma. Now look at me. . . . You can't afford to take life lightly," concluded Zandy, who has endured five years of intensive therapy to get where he is. "If you do, the price could be very heavy."

Steve Zandy is trying to get kids to see the consequences of driving while drunk. He is a living testimony that the biblical principle of sowing and reaping applies to teenagers as well as adults (Galatians 6:7). Like most young people, Steve thought it could never happen to him.

It may not be alcohol with you. It may be drugs. Or sex. Or playing chicken with pickup trucks. If you think you're getting away with something, you need to wise up and give serious thought to what Steve Zandy and the Bible say: You sow; you reap . . . and you weep. —D.E.

Through preaching, teaching, and the Bible, God is telling me . . . _____

_____

_____

Through nature and the lives of other believers, God is showing me . . . _____

_____

_____

I will respond by . . . _____

_____

_____

My teacher flunked!

READ
1 Timothy 4

MEDITATE
1 Timothy 4:15
Be diligent in these matters; give yourself wholly to them.

REFLECT
➤ What are the characteristics of a good teacher? A good pastor?
➤ What are the characteristics of a good student? A good church member?
➤ Am I growing in my spiritual knowledge and character? Why or why not?

CONSIDER
Yearn to learn—and what you know will grow.

In the opinion of Vartan Gregorian, president of Brown University, "Students don't fail, teachers fail."

Those words sound appealing, don't they? Particularly if you've just bombed a pop quiz or flunked that big term paper! If I were a student again, I would like to hear someone tell my profs that it's their fault I didn't do well in class.

Imagine this: You just received a failing grade in a required course for your major. You go home and tell your parents, "Guess what, folks. My instructor flunked one of the courses I have to have to graduate!" Would they buy that excuse? Sure. Right after they bought some swampland in Florida.

What Dr. Gregorian said is true to an extent. Teachers have to do all they can to motivate students, and they must present the material clearly.

On the other hand, students have to be responsible for how much they learn—no matter how good or bad the teacher. The desire to learn has to come from within.

The same is true in the pastor/church member relationship. Pastors need to see the importance of their role in setting an example, in exciting their "class" about the study of God's Word. If pastors fail, churches will struggle.

But that doesn't mean church members are off the hook. We've got a lot to learn. If we fail to grow in our Christian life, we have no one to blame but ourselves. We have Bibles. We have access to the truth. We have the Holy Spirit to guide our study and empower our lives.

In the spiritual as well as the intellectual realm, good learning requires good teachers and good students.

—K.D.

Through preaching, teaching, and the Bible, God is telling me . . . _____

_____

_____

Through nature and the lives of other believers, God is showing me . . . _____

_____

_____

I will respond by . . . _____

_____

_____

AUGUST 30

Dumb graduates?

READ
Proverbs 1:1–7

MEDITATE
Proverbs 1:5
Let the wise listen and add to their learning.

REFLECT
- How would I describe my growth as a Christian: Steady? Sporadic? Minimal? Dramatic?
- What causes me to stagnate in my spiritual life?
- What helps me to keep growing and learning?

CONSIDER
The more you follow Christ the more you have to learn.

James Lehrer stood before rows of graduating seniors at a commencement and said: "A college diploma does not mean you are educated." Perhaps not the most popular thing to say to folks who just invested four years and thousands of dollars, but true nonetheless. He went on to explain that a diploma "means that you have been opened up to a perpetual state of ignorance and thus a lifelong hunger for more—more ideas, more knowledge, more good thoughts, more challenges.

"Some of the dumbest people I know," he continued, "went to prestigious colleges and universities. They walked across a stage, took diploma in hot little hand, pronounced themselves well-educated, and proceeded to never read another book, entertain another fresh idea, or tax their minds in any way."

Lehrer's comments can also be applied to Christians. Paul said, "I keep asking that the God of our Lord Jesus Christ . . . may give you the Spirit of wisdom and revelation, so that you may know him better" (Ephesians 1:17).

Jesus told His disciples, "This is to my Father's glory, that you bear much fruit" (John 15:8).

Peter said, "Grow in the grace and knowledge of our Lord and Savior Jesus Christ!" (2 Peter 3:18).

And Paul told the Philippians, "This is my prayer: that your love may abound more and more in knowledge and depth of insight" (1:9).

Getting saved is a bit like graduating. It's a commencement—a beginning. "Let the wise listen and add to their learning." —K.D.

Through preaching, teaching, and the Bible, God is telling me . . . __________

Through nature and the lives of other believers, God is showing me . . . __________

I will respond by . . . __________

A walk on the beach

READ
Proverbs 14:12–19

MEDITATE
Proverbs 14:15
A prudent man gives thought to his steps.

REFLECT
➡ How good am I at thinking things through before taking action?
➡ What have been some things I goofed up because I failed to think about the consequences first?
➡ What trouble have I avoided because I did think something through?

CONSIDER
Right thinking leads to right living.

A statement made by Senator Ted Kennedy during his nephew's rape trial in Florida struck me as noteworthy. When asked about his decision to go out to a bar with his son and nephew in the wee hours of the morning, Kennedy said, "I wish I had stayed home and taken a long walk on the beach."

We would all be better off sometimes if we took that advice. Anytime we consider doing something that is either sinful or unwise, we need to have an alternative—something that gives us a chance to clear our minds and consider the consequences of our actions. As Proverbs 14:15 puts it, "A prudent man gives thought to his steps."

Our "long walk on the beach" might be a talk with a roommate or a drive in the car or a trip to some quiet corner of the campus where we can collect our thoughts.

Whenever we're faced with a choice of doing something wrong or questionable, we need to get away from the scene so we can think.

If your experience is anything like mine, most of the things you regret are things you did hastily and without sufficient thought. Life is too short to mess it up with bad decisions about things we can avoid.

The wise person "fears the Lord and shuns evil, but a fool is hotheaded and reckless" (Proverbs 14:16).

It's hard to be reckless after a long walk on the beach—alone. —D.B.

Through preaching, teaching, and the Bible, God is telling me . . . _____

Through nature and the lives of other believers, God is showing me . . . _____

I will respond by . . . _____

The only sure answer

READ
Psalm 111

MEDITATE
Psalm 111:7
The works of his hands are faithful.

REFLECT
➡ How have I seen God at work in my life? How do I know that He will never fail me?

➡ What words in Psalm 111 describe God? How has He demonstrated those attributes to me?

➡ What do I need to give over to God right now and trust Him for?

CONSIDER
God's failure rate is zero.

If you're preparing for a career behind a television camera, this will not be good news. While visiting the news studio of one of Chicago's largest TV stations, I was surprised to discover that when the news anchors sit behind their desks, no one is behind the three cameras focused on them! The cameras are run completely by computers.

I know what you're thinking. What happens if something goes wrong with the computer? When asked that question the person showing us around the studio replied quickly and boldly, "It won't. The computer will not fail."

Being confident is a good thing, and it's nice that the TV people aren't worried about technological glitches, but let's have a bit of realism here. Nobody can be sure that anything made by human hands will work every time. Everything we touch is subject to failure. No one can guarantee perfection.

No one but God, that is. He alone never, never fails.

And because God is perfect in every aspect of His existence, we can trust Him without reservation. When we are trying to figure out what career path to follow, we can ask Him to guide us. When we are faced with tough questions of right and wrong, we can trust God's Word to give us clear direction.

People, machines, computers, and institutions—as good as they might be—will fail. But not God. That's why He alone deserves our absolute, unfaltering trust.

—D.B.

Through preaching, teaching, and the Bible, God is telling me . . . _____

_____

_____

Through nature and the lives of other believers, God is showing me . . . _____

_____

_____

I will respond by . . . _____

_____

_____

Get it in writing

READ
Psalm 40

MEDITATE
Psalm 38:9
All my longings lie open before you, O Lord.

REFLECT

➤ Why do I like/not like keeping a journal?

➤ If I'm not the journaling type, what other method can I use for personal reflection about my relationship with God?

➤ What can I learn from Psalm 40?

CONSIDER
A journal can help you stay on the "write" path.

What is the longest paper you've ever written? A research paper on the Spanish Inquisition? Something for English 101? Did you enjoy it? Or did you strain to get the minimum number of required words?

Edward Ellis wouldn't have any trouble getting enough words. He actually enjoys writing. Did I say enjoy? Perhaps it would be more accurate to say that he is obsessed with writing.

He began keeping a journal when he was sixteen years old. He and two friends made a bet to see who could keep a journal longer. Sixty-four years and twenty million words later, Ed is still writing. That's right; it's not a misprint. This guy has written twenty million words. That's nearly half the length of the forty-four-million-word *Encyclopedia Britannica*.

When asked, Edward Ellis gives a little free advice to would-be journal keepers. He says, "There's no value to a diary unless it's sincere."

Many parts of the Psalms sound a lot like personal journals. In Psalm 40, for example, David exposed his inner struggles, his frustrations, and his strong desire to continue trusting the Lord.

You will probably never write as much as Edward Ellis, but a little bit of writing is good for you. Take a few moments to write down how you identify with David in Psalm 40. Or write out your personal thoughts in response to what God is teaching you.   —K.D.

Through preaching, teaching, and the Bible, God is telling me . . . _____

_____

_____

Through nature and the lives of other believers, God is showing me . . . _____

_____

_____

I will respond by . . . _____

_____

Crazy drivers

READ
2 Kings 10:28–36

MEDITATE
2 Kings 10:31
Jehu was not careful to keep the law of the Lord.

REFLECT
➡ What kind of driver am I? How is my life similar to the way I drive? How is it different?

➡ What part of my life do I tend to keep for myself instead of devoting it to the Lord? What risks am I taking?

CONSIDER
A reckless life is a sign of a divided heart.

Jehu, king of Israel, was a crazy driver. When he first became king, someone who saw him coming in a chariot said, "The driving is like that of Jehu son of Nimshi—he drives like a madman" (2 Kings 9:20).

Do you know anyone who disregards speed limits, stop signs, and the common courtesy of the road?

The newspaper carried the story of a bus driver who must have cheated his way through driver's ed. He took his terrified passengers on a three-hour ordeal across western Montana and northern Idaho. Passengers reported that the driver nearly sideswiped several trucks, sped 20 mph over the speed limit around a tight curve, tailgated slower drivers, got the bus stuck in a driveway, and cursed passengers who complained about his driving. To one passenger, the driver said, "I haven't killed anybody yet," as if he could excuse his recklessness as long as he didn't have a serious accident.

Jehu ruled over Israel for twenty-eight years. For the most part he did well, but at times he was careless. Driving like a madman was only one of his problems. In summarizing his life, the Bible tells us that "Jehu was not careful to keep the law of the Lord, the God of Israel, with all his heart."

What about you? What would the Lord say about your life? Could He say that you have followed Him with all your heart? Or are there some areas where you are careless, even reckless in how you behave? Are you hurting yourself, endangering others, or both?   —K.D.

Through preaching, teaching, and the Bible, God is telling me . . . _____

Through nature and the lives of other believers, God is showing me . . . _____

I will respond by . . . _____

Fair? Who says?

READ
Hosea 1:2–11

MEDITATE
Hosea 3:1
"Go, show your love to your wife again."

REFLECT
→ I don't think it's fair that _____.

→ What could God be teaching me through this situation?

→ What is my reaction when things don't go my way? (a) I bail out; (b) I dig in and make the best of it; (c) I cry and fuss and complain to anybody who will listen; (d) I ask God to help me grow.

CONSIDER
With God, life isn't just fair— it's great!

Big news! Life does not come out even!

Some people have it all— good looks, money, good grades, talent. Others have to scrape by on average or even less-than-average allotments of those things.

My daughter doesn't think it's fair that she got her finger smashed in the car door. A parent I know doesn't think it's fair that his daughter didn't make the high school basketball team. Another student doesn't think it's fair that he got disciplined for what he thought was a harmless prank.

So get used to it. Life isn't fair. But if you think you've got problems with fairness, read about Hosea and his wife, Gomer. Having a wife named Gomer was not Hosea's worst problem.

Hosea was the nicest guy you could ever meet. Kind, generous, loving. But his wife! We're talking big-time trouble here. She was as unfaithful as a spouse could be. Yet Hosea didn't storm off and criticize her— demanding that God explain why he got stuck with her. No, despite the unfairness of it all, Hosea continued to do all he could to win Gomer back. He did what God wanted him to do.

Does life seem unfair to you? Are you upset that your roommate seems to get all the good dates? Or that your prayers don't seem to do as much good as someone else's? Or that no matter how hard you work you never seem to have any money?

Yes, life is unfair. So the best thing to do is to follow Hosea's example: Do what is right anyway. Whether or not life is fair, our duty is to follow God's leading. He alone knows what is ultimately right.   —D.B.

Through preaching, teaching, and the Bible, God is telling me . . . _____

Through nature and the lives of other believers, God is showing me . . . _____

I will respond by . . . _____

A STRONG CHARACTER   **261**

Back on the path

READ
Psalm 1

MEDITATE
Proverbs 4:14–15
Do not set foot on the path of the wicked. . . . Avoid it, do not travel on it.

REFLECT
➡ I'm on the wrong path. How can I get right with the Lord?

➡ What promise in 1 John 1:9 can I claim for myself?

➡ I'm on the right path, but my friend isn't. Do I have the courage, faith, and love to help steer the person back?

CONSIDER
If you're traveling on the wrong track, you'll get derailed.

You got off to a good start this semester. You turned your assignments in on time. You kept up on your rest. But then you started to sleep in, goof off, and miss deadlines. You got off the path of self-discipline and into trouble.

The same can happen spiritually. A section of *Pilgrim's Progress* illustrates the truth that to stray off the path of God's will is to invite disaster. Christian and Hopeful are walking the King's Highway to the Celestial City. But the path, once smooth and easy, becomes rough and hard. It hurts their feet. Then they come to a lovely field called Bypath Meadow. They cross the fence into it and find an easy path.

Then that path becomes rugged and steep. A terrible storm comes up. Flood waters rise. Exhausted, the two lost and weary pilgrims fall asleep. They are rudely awakened by the owner of the meadow, the Giant Despair. He drags them to Doubting Castle and throws them into a stinking dungeon. The giant taunts, starves, and beats them. Their spirits sink. They are hurt, confused, despairing.

Finally Christian and Hopeful begin to pray. While they are praying, Christian remembers that he is carrying a key called Promise. He uses it to open the dungeon door and the gate of Doubting Castle. They are free! And soon they find their way back to the King's Highway.

Are you filled with doubt? Thinking of giving up? Perhaps it's because somewhere along the way you left God's path to wander along some pleasant-looking bypath. If so, use the key of promise (1 John 1:9) to unlock the doors of your prison and come back to Jesus.   —D.E.

Through preaching, teaching, and the Bible, God is telling me . . . _____

_____

Through nature and the lives of other believers, God is showing me . . . _____

_____

_____

I will respond by . . . _____

Ya gotta have

In need of repair

READ
Nehemiah 1

MEDITATE
Nehemiah 1:6
"I confess the sins
we . . . have commit-
ted against you."

REFLECT

➡ How would I rate
the condition of
my spiritual life?
___ excellent
___ good
___ fair
___ poor
Why?

➡ What areas of my
life need attention?

➡ What sin am I slow
to confess and for-
sake?

CONSIDER
*A life that isn't
maintained will
need to be
restored.*

Even if you hate memoriz-
ing dates and learning
about people from the past,
you probably enjoy history
when your teacher says two
magic words: Field Trip. Even
history buffs would rather
visit a historical site than sit
in a room and read about it.

But if you are planning a
field trip, you'd better go
soon. Many historical sites in
the States are falling apart.
Some are being forced to
close. The National Park
Service doesn't have enough
money to keep up repairs.

According to a Newhouse
News Service report, a thirty-
pound chunk of marble
broke off a column at the
Jefferson Memorial and fell
sixty feet. Several buildings
in historic Independence
Park in Philadelphia have
been closed because of
maintenance problems. And
the seventeenth-century
Spanish fort in St. Augustine,
Florida, has serious structural
problems.

Nehemiah had his share
of maintenance problems
too. The walls around Jerusalem were crumbling. They
had been destroyed by
invaders many years before,
and resettlers didn't have the
resources to make repairs. It
was enough to make Nehe-
miah cry. He wept not merely for the city walls but for
the people. He knew that the
bigger problem was the spiritual apathy and sin of the
citizens. Their spiritual lives
were also in disrepair. So he
did something about both.

What's the condition of
your spiritual life? Are any
parts of it crumbling from
lack of attention? Was the
enemy able to knock down
your defenses while you
were distracted by some
momentary pleasure? If so,
pray Nehemiah's prayer of
confession. Then get on with
rebuilding your life. Ask the
Lord to guide you and give
you strength.   —K.D.

Through preaching, teaching, and the Bible, God is telling me . . . _____

_____

Through nature and the lives of other believers, God is showing me . . . _____

_____

I will respond by . . . _____

Making things happen

READ
Galatians 6:1–5

MEDITATE
Galatians 6:5
Each one should carry his own load.

REFLECT
➡ How often do I do things for others without being prompted? Am I a "make it happen" person, a "watch it happen" person, or a "wonder what happened" person?

➡ How do I put Galatians 6:2 into action?

CONSIDER
Spectators never get the trophies.

And now something from one of the great philosophers of our time, Los Angeles Dodgers' manager Tommy Lasorda, someone who never fails to brighten interviews with his optimism and enthusiasm. After years of managing, he has developed a distinctive viewpoint about baseball players. "There are three types of baseball players," Lasorda says, "Those who make it happen, those who watch it happen, and those who wonder what happens."

If you were putting together a team, you would want to get as many make-it-happen athletes as possible. Players like Joe Montana, Larry Bird, Rickey Henderson, and Wayne Gretzky are the take-charge type. They don't sit back and wait for the action to come to them.

You would also want a few watch-it-happen players. They're the observant types. They can't get enough of the game. They always know how many outs there are, who's up next, what the count is on the batter, and what the pitcher's ERA is.

The third group of players you would option off to a minor league team or send home. They are in a fog about the game, and they are always about two steps behind the action.

But you are not putting a sports team together, you are putting your life together. And the best way to do that is to be someone who makes things happen. Don't go through life passively. Get involved. Start a prayer group. Volunteer to feed the hungry. Tutor a younger student. Don't sit on the curb and watch life pass by like a parade. You are responsible for the skills God has given you. Use them. Make things happen. —D.B.

Through preaching, teaching, and the Bible, God is telling me . . . _____

_____

Through nature and the lives of other believers, God is showing me . . . _____

_____

I will respond by . . . _____

_____

Ya gotta have

The bachelor party

READ
James 2:14–26

MEDITATE
James 2:18
I will show you my faith by what I do.

REFLECT
➥ What does 1 Thessalonians 4:3–8 tell me about sexual purity?
➥ Have I clearly defined right and wrong in my own mind? Am I still undecided about some issues?
➥ What issue do I need to take a stand on? How can I get the courage and strength to stand up for my convictions?

CONSIDER
What you do outshouts what you say.

Tom Rademacher, a columnist for the *Grand Rapids Press,* wrote an article about a bachelor party he attended. After a great afternoon of golf and pizza, the time came for the evening's special entertainment—a stripper. The guys all rushed into the living room to get a good seat. All except one. The groom. He went quietly out to the kitchen so he wouldn't have to watch.

Later, he said to Rademacher, "It was my personal choice. I didn't want to embarrass anybody, nor was I judging anyone." Then he explained. "My friends are important to me. I don't ever want to let them down. But my relationship with God is even more important."

He went on to tell the reporter that if Jesus were in the kitchen, he could not have taken Him into the living room. "That's the biggest reason," he concluded.

"Because He was right in there with me."

The reporter concluded his column with some personal observations. First, we all have someone—spouse, children, parents—to whom we are answerable. Would we take them everywhere we go? Second, in spite of what society may try to get us to believe, not everybody's "doing it." There are young people who have the guts to say no to behavior they know is wrong.

Congrats to the man in the kitchen! He stuck to his convictions. And he made a strong impact for Christ, not only on the reporter and his friends at the party but also on the people of the city who read the article.

"I will show you my faith by what I do," wrote James. And the Grand Rapids groom followed his advice. Would things have been different if you'd been in his situation?
—D.E.

Through preaching, teaching, and the Bible, God is telling me . . . _____

_____

_____

Through nature and the lives of other believers, God is showing me . . . _____

_____

_____

I will respond by . . . _____

_____

"Come and die"

READ
Mark 8:27–9:1

MEDITATE
Mark 8:35
"Whoever loses his life for me and for the gospel will save it."

REFLECT

➡ To identify with Christ is to identify with His death. If that were to put me in danger, what would I do?

➡ Have I left myself a "back door" in my commitment to Christ? Do I plan to stick with Him forever or only as long as He makes my life easier?

CONSIDER
If you are worth dying for, Jesus is worth living for.

With the buildup of forces in the Middle East during Operation Desert Shield and Desert Storm, a number of National Guard units were called into active duty. After a few weeks of intensive training in desert warfare, they were sent to Saudi Arabia.

A news item I read during the buildup told about a man who had been in a National Guard unit for seven years, but who refused to report for duty when his outfit was called. He had been against war all along, he claimed, and never thought he'd be called on for actual combat. When faced with the prospect of facing a live enemy with real bullets, he decided not to report. His case was heard by a military tribunal, and he was sentenced to jail for refusing to obey orders.

He's a lot like some Christians. They are willing to serve the Lord faithfully every weekend among friends. They'll stay true to Him as long as things are going well. But as soon as the going gets rough, as soon as they sense any personal danger or inconvenience, they back out. They will take no risks or abuse for their faith. "I didn't think it would come to this," they say.

Dietrich Bonhoffer, one of the few pastors in Nazi Germany who stood up against Hitler, wrote, "When Christ calls a man, He bids him come and die." That's what it means to take up our cross, to lose our lives so that we can save our lives. No backing out for those in the army of the Lord. No running away. In our battle against the world, the flesh, and the devil, we need to follow Christ's example and be willing to "come and die."
—D.E.

Through preaching, teaching, and the Bible, God is telling me . . . _____
_____
_____

Through nature and the lives of other believers, God is showing me . . . _____
_____
_____

I will respond by . . . _____
_____
_____

Checkup for lovers

READ
1 Corinthians 13

MEDITATE
1 Corinthians 14:1
Follow the way of love.

REFLECT
➡ What messages about love do I hear from TV programs and commercials? How do they correspond with what the Bible says about love?

➡ How can I make sure I use 1 Corinthians 13 as my test for love?

CONSIDER
Love, like Jesus, puts others first.

What kind of lover are you? TV commercials, magazine ads, and billboards bombard us and tempt us with suggestions about what it takes to be a good lover—the right clothes, the right drink, the right car. Maybe the people who make these ads don't think we're smart enough to know that those things have absolutely nothing to do with love.

Our focus shouldn't be on being a good lover anyway. We should be more concerned with how to be loving. There's a major difference here.

To become a loving person we first have to fill our minds with wholesome thoughts. Second, we have to understand that being loving means treating others in a way that pleases them—not ourselves.

What the thirty-second ads on TV don't even try to tell us is that love is so much more than a physical thing.

In the greater sense, loving is a spiritual matter. And when it comes to being the kind of lover that pleases God, there is no better example than Jesus Christ. His entire life was spent loving others. From washing the disciples' feet to dying on the cross in our place, Jesus was showing us that loving others costs something. He was a living example of 1 Corinthians 13:5, "[Love] is not self-seeking." His primary interest was seeking the good of others.

Can that be said of us? Do we love the people in our dorm the way Jesus would? Do we seek the best for our friends? Is our love for our boyfriend or girlfriend selfish or selfless?

Paul wrote, "I will show you the most excellent way" (1 Corinthians 12:31). And that way was the way of love, explained in detail in chapter 13. Take Paul's love checkup and find out what kind of lover you are. —D.P.

Through preaching, teaching, and the Bible, God is telling me . . . _____

_____

Through nature and the lives of other believers, God is showing me . . . _____

_____

I will respond by . . . _____

Where's the love now?

READ
Jeremiah 2:1–7

MEDITATE
Revelation 2:4
"You have forsaken
your first love."

REFLECT
➡ Do I love Christ as
much as when I
first was saved?
More?

➡ In what ways have
I been disappoint-
ed by Christ? Was I
expecting too
much? The wrong
thing?

➡ What can I do to
regain my first love
for the Lord Jesus?

CONSIDER
*If you're not in
touch with Jesus,
guess whose
fault it is.*

Nothing is as exciting as new love. If you haven't experienced it yourself, you've seen it in the faces and lives of friends who are newly married. When they look at each other, their faces glow. They laugh a lot. There's a spring in their step and joy in their hearts.

It's not only true of marriages. Remember when your friend bought his first new sports car? He washed it every day. He polished it once a week. You sometimes caught him just looking at it, his eyes filled with pride.

And what about the day you moved into your first dorm room? No, it wasn't the Taj Mahal or a suite at the Sheraton, but it was yours (and your roommate's, of course). You had that feeling of exhilaration of being on your own. You loved that place!

But as time passes, so does excitement. Newly married couples find that marriage isn't perfect, and neither are they. The sports car gets a couple of scratches and goes for weeks without getting washed. And your dorm room seems to be getting smaller, and why doesn't your roommate take care of that pile of laundry that's starting to throb over in the corner.

Whenever we set our whole hearts on a person or object, we're bound to be disappointed. Except when that Person is the Lord Jesus. If we lose that first love for Him, the fault is not with Him but with us. It's probably a breakdown in our communication. Has your love for Jesus cooled? It's not Him; His love for you is the same. Get back in touch with Him, and ignite the flames of love again.   —M.D.

Through preaching, teaching, and the Bible, God is telling me . . . _____
_____
_____

Through nature and the lives of other believers, God is showing me . . . _____
_____
_____

I will respond by . . . _____
_____
_____

Real-life cookie monster

MEDITATE
Luke 6:28
Bless those who curse you, pray for those who mistreat you.

REFLECT

➡ When was the last time someone got what should have been mine? How did I respond?

➡ What would happen if I began to show Christ's love to those who have hurt me? Whom will I start with today?

CONSIDER
Love your enemies:
Jesus did.

It all started at the airport. A woman waiting to "wing it" decided to buy a best-selling paperback book and a box of Oreos. She settled into her seat and waited for the announcement to board her flight. As she started to read, she noticed a man one seat away starting to nibble oreos from the box on the chair between them. She couldn't believe that this guy had the nerve to scarf down her snack. So-o-o-o, she reached over, took one of the icing-filled wonders, and popped it into her mouth.

The man said nothing. He simply took out another cookie and began to munch. The woman couldn't believe it. She grabbed another and glared at him. The great cookie war continued until one lone Oreo remained in the package. The man took it, broke it in two, gave her half, and got up and left.

A bit later when the disgruntled woman reached into her purse for a tissue, her hand came across a cellophane package. She looked down and stared in disbelief at her box of Oreos— unopened! Oops!

What if this had happened to you? Would you have responded like the woman trying to get what she thought was hers or like the man who was willing to share what he knew was his? More important, how do you respond daily when it appears that others are taking what belongs to you?

Jesus instructs us to love and bless those who mistreat us. He wants us to be "merciful, just as your Father is merciful" (Luke 6:36). By doing this we will not only end some nasty skirmishes on earth, but also our "reward will be great" (v. 35) in heaven. Show love when it's least expected and you'll be blessed unexpectedly. That's the way the cookie crumbles.

—T.F.

Through preaching, teaching, and the Bible, God is telling me . . . _____

Through nature and the lives of other believers, God is showing me . . . _____

I will respond by . . . _____

A LOVING HEART

What makes you happy?

READ
Luke 15:11–32

MEDITATE
Luke 15:32

"We had to celebrate and be glad, because this brother of yours was dead and is alive again."

REFLECT
➡ Do I rejoice when I hear of someone who comes to God from a life of sin? Or do I resent it?

➡ Do I direct people toward God and encourage their spiritual growth?

CONSIDER
Love those most who deserve it least.

Mr. Mactavish was gone. I wanted to wait until morning to see if he would come back on his own. But the look on the other family members' faces vetoed that idea big time. So we climbed into the car and began looking for our stubborn Scottish Terrier, who was far more interested in being lost than found.

As we slowly drove down street after street, we called his name and peered out into the darkness. No response. We imagined all kinds of terrible things happening to good ol' Mactavish. Even I became sentimental. What if he'd been hit by a car? What if someone else picked him up? What if we never saw him again?

Then we found him. And by the time we did, I was as happy as the rest of the family to see him. Mac was a sight for sore eyes—soaked with mud and smelling rotten. But at that moment all three of us—my wife, Diane, my son, Ben, and I— appeared to be happier about being with that dirty little dog than we were about being with one another.

Does that mean we loved Mac more than we loved one another? Of course not. Neither does showing special affection for a classmate who turns to Christ, forsakes a sinful habit, or asks God to forgive some wrong behavior mean that we love others any less. It means that we have enough of God's love to celebrate with Him when one of His rebellious children comes home.

Are you waiting till later to look for the lost or wandering? Or do you love them enough to go out looking for them now?   —M.D.

Through preaching, teaching, and the Bible, God is telling me . . . _____

_____

_____

Through nature and the lives of other believers, God is showing me . . . _____

_____

_____

I will respond by . . . _____

_____

_____

Peace for Parkening

READ
Romans 2:5–11

MEDITATE
Romans 2:9–10
There will be . . . glory, honor and peace for everyone who does good.

REFLECT
➡ Do I live for God's glory or for my own?

➡ Why is peace so elusive?

➡ What would happen if I could get my eyes off myself and keep them on God?

CONSIDER
No God, no peace. Know God, know peace.

Who's the greatest guitarist to rip a riff in the last thirty years? Jimi Hendrix? Eddie VanHalen? Phil Keaggy? Christopher Parkening?

Christopher Parkening. Yes—he may be the best. He is one of the top classical guitarists in the world. He's played his instrument in every major city around the globe. He has strummed and picked at the White House and on network TV.

But Chris will tell you that all that globetrotting and showstopping comes out a weak second to something else that happened to him. He says that coming to Christ is the most important event in his life. It was then that he finally realized why God had given him this amazing ability.

"When I came across the passage in 1 Corinthians that says, 'Whatever you do, do it all for the glory of God'" [10:31], he says, "I went back to playing the guitar, but this time with a different purpose. As Bach said, 'The aim and final reason of all music is none else but the glory of God.'"

This discovery helped him just before he and singer Kathleen Battle were to perform at the Grammy Awards. A stage director said, "In twenty seconds you'll be performing for over 200 million people—live." Instead of getting uptight, Chris turned to Kathleen and said, "The important thing is for us to play and sing for the Lord, right?"

And now, each time he plays, he knows where to turn for peace. "To handle my weaknesses and the pressures, I seek God's grace every time I walk on stage."

Got some challenges facing you today? God promises "glory, honor, and peace for everyone who does good" (Romans 2:10). And the best way to do good is to do it all for God.   —T.F.

Through preaching, teaching, and the Bible, God is telling me . . . _____

_____

_____

Through nature and the lives of other believers, God is showing me . . . _____

_____

_____

I will respond by . . . _____

_____

Doing the right thing

READ
Mark 12:28–34

MEDITATE
Mark 12:31
"Love your neighbor as yourself."

REFLECT
➡ How does the explanation of love in 1 Corinthians 13 help me make ethical decisions?
➡ What do the Ten Commandments (Exodus 20) add to my understanding of God's will for my moral decisions?

CONSIDER
If you're right with God, you'll be right with others.

Your friend parades in front of the full-length mirror and says, "New outfit. How does it look?" You think it looks awful. Do you tell her or do you spare her feelings?

You've been on the job only two months but you've discovered that the office sales leader is padding his expense account. Do you overlook it or do you tell the sales manager?

The cashier gave you too much change. Do you return the money or keep it?

These are just a sample of the kinds of questions being discussed in new courses on ethics at universities across the country. An issue of Western Michigan University's alumni magazine carried the headline, "Ethics Becoming Standard Discussion Topic in Tomorrow's College Classroom." The article quoted Samuel Florman, a prominent ethics theorist, who said that "most evil acts are committed not by villains but rather by decent human beings—in desperation, momentary weakness, or any inability to discern what is morally right."

I can appreciate the problem. Finding the wise, honest course of action can be like trying to find a missing contact lens in a moonlit swimming pool.

When we examine the words and life of Jesus, however, we find a clue to making sound moral choices—regardless of the circumstances or consequences. The key principle is simple and universal: "Love your neighbor as yourself." When we do so, we will find a tactful yet honest way to discuss a friend's new outfit; we will be compassionate yet forthright with a cheating co-worker; and we will know what to do with money that belongs to someone else. Right ethics start with right relationships—first with God and then with others. —T.B.

Through preaching, teaching, and the Bible, God is telling me . . . _____

_____

_____

Through nature and the lives of other believers, God is showing me . . . _____

_____

_____

I will respond by . . . _____

_____

_____

Ya gotta have

SEPTEMBER 16

It's gr-r-r-eat!

READ
Psalm 34:1–9

MEDITATE
Psalm 34:8
Taste and see that the
Lord is good.

REFLECT
➡ When I talk about
Christ with some-
one, Christian or
non-Christian, do I
give the impression
that my salvation is
something I'm
enthusiastic about?
Or do I sound as if
there are a lot
more important
things in life?

CONSIDER
*If you must
spread some-
thing, spread
enthusiasm.*

Back in the fifties, an enthusiastic little tiger named Tony made the phrase "It's Gr-r-r-reat!" famous. He still spends all his time on TV commercials trying to get folks to fork over three bucks for a breakfast cereal called Sugar Frosted Flakes. To Tony, this stuff is the best thing since, well, corn flakes.

To some people, Tony is a little fanatical. I mean, all he ever does is talk about how great this cereal is—insinuating that you're a loser if you don't try it. Maybe it works. Maybe we want to find out why this cartoon tiger is busy touting cereal instead of out chasing antelope or African wildebeest. So we taste the sugary morning treat for ourselves.

Enthusiasm. It always gets our attention.

With his sincere belief and contagious enthusiasm, Tony reminds me of someone in the Bible. David was a bit of a tiger himself. Like Tony, he seemed to have a one-track mind. "I will extol the Lord at all times; his praise will always be on my lips" (Psalm 34:1). And also like Tony, David believed in the power of personal experience. He wrote, "Taste and see that the Lord is good" (v. 8).

According to the dictionary, enthusiasm means "to be inspired or possessed by God." That sounds like David, don't you think?

Who today should be more inspired—more enthusiastic—than Christians who have God's Spirit living within them?

Look, you're young and full of life. So show some life in your youth group. You don't have to be as loud as Tony the Tiger or as poetic as David. But you do need to be sincere and enthusiastic. After all, if you're not excited about Christ, how can you expect others to be? —D.P.

Through preaching, teaching, and the Bible, God is telling me . . . _____
_____
_____

Through nature and the lives of other believers, God is showing me . . . _____
_____
_____

I will respond by . . . _____
_____
_____

A LOVING HEART   273

The last will be first

READ
Mark 9:33–37

MEDITATE
Mark 9:35
"If anyone wants to be first, he must be the very last."

REFLECT
➡ Where does the drive to become Number One come from? Have I picked it up from my parents? The world? My church?
➡ How difficult is it for me to serve others? Am I willing to set up chairs for people or wash dishes?

CONSIDER
Last place is sometimes the way to reach first place.

It was at the Daytona 500—the biggest race on the stock car circuit. "King Richard" Petty was about to lose his thirty-eighth straight race. Going into the last lap, he was running thirty seconds behind the leaders—an insurmountable difference in racing.

All of a sudden, as they entered the backstretch, the car in second place bumped the leader, forcing him onto the edge of the infield grass. Furious, the offended driver pulled his car back onto the track, caught up with the new leader, and forced him against the outside wall. The cars careened and screeched to a stop, locked together. The two drivers jumped out of their cars and got into a brawl. While all of this was going on, Richard Petty streaked by for the win, pocketing stock car racing's biggest payoff.

This made me think of what Jesus said to His disciples after their argument about which of them was number one. Jesus told them that the believer who struggles for first place now is sure to lose it later.

Christ's followers operate on a set of principles different from the world's. We are not like race car drivers. We don't have to come in first to be important. We can hand out programs at the play and glorify God by doing our best. We can help in the nursing home and honor God by doing a humble task with a cheerful heart. We can serve without complaint because we are doing it for the Lord.

This is meekness, not weakness. From God's point of view, serving in positions of less honor or importance is not self-defeating behavior. That's what Jesus did, and it's the only way to keep from coming in last. —M.D.

Through preaching, teaching, and the Bible, God is telling me . . . _____

_____

Through nature and the lives of other believers, God is showing me . . . _____

_____

I will respond by . . . _____

_____

Ya gotta have

SEPTEMBER 18

Satisfaction guaranteed

READ
**2 Corinthians
5:1–10**

MEDITATE
2 Corinthians 5:6
We are always confident.

REFLECT
➡ Have you been influenced to investigate some religions other than Christianity (e.g., Eastern or New Age)? What makes you curious about them?

➡ What is the basic difference between Christianity and other faiths?

CONSIDER
Christ gives what religion only promises.

Despite the apparent apathy toward religion in many universities, most people in the world have an interest in it. According to the *World Almanac and Book of Facts,* our world has 860 million Muslims, 655 million Hindus, 300 million Buddhists, 1.6 billion Christians (used in the broad sense; i.e., anyone who expresses interest in a religion based on Jesus), 18 million Jews, and 94 million tribal religionists. Of the 5 billion people in the world, only 4 percent say they do not believe in God.

The fact that so many people are interested in religion might be good news— if there weren't so many religions that offer so little. Most world religions offer little hope, require lots of work, and give no guarantee of receiving anything for the trouble.

In China, for example, devout religious pilgrims ascend a sacred mountain called Taishan. They climb 7,000 steps to its summit. At the end, they reach one of the most beautiful buildings in all of China—the Temple of the Azure Cloud. Here they offer sacrifices, which the worshipers believe will gain God's favor. These poor folks take those 7,000 steps to nowhere without any assurance that their efforts are doing them any good.

Faith in Jesus Christ is so different! He did all the work; we receive all the benefit. All we have to do is trust Him. And the best part is the guarantee that our faith leads to eternal life. So why trust anything but Jesus. Christianity is the only religion in the world that comes with a guarantee!   —D.B.

Through preaching, teaching, and the Bible, God is telling me . . . _____
_____
_____

Through nature and the lives of other believers, God is showing me . . . _____
_____
_____

I will respond by . . . _____
_____

Quick fixes

Boy, it's been a rough day! First, I goofed up an exam. Then I yelled at my friend. I can't wait till I get to my room. I'll grab a Coke, put on my favorite tape, and mellow out for a while. Then maybe things will be better."

But is that the answer? Or could it be that your escape to the sanctuary of your room is just a quick fix for a more deepseated problem?

Our society is hooked on quick fixes. We move through life so fast that we don't take the time to deal adequately with anything. Then, when something goes wrong, we look for a fast cure so we don't mess up our crammed schedules.

Looking for quick fixes is a problem spiritually too. We let ourselves drift farther and farther from God. If we feel guilty about it, we try to make it okay by sending up a quick prayer and trying to convince ourselves that God understands.

But quick fixes don't work. They're like putting ice on a broken leg. It may diminish the pain and reduce the swelling, but it doesn't solve the problem. Eventually, the bone is going to have to be set and a cast applied.

If we're doing poorly in school and snapping at our friends, we won't solve the problem with a jolt of caffeine and some mellow music. And we surely won't restore our relationship with God with a hastily offered generic prayer.

Slow down. Stop running so fast. Take time to deal with matters completely. Repair those broken relationships with people and God by repentance and confession. Spend time in Bible reading. Adjust your schedule so you have time to study. Communicate with your friends—don't snap at them. Ask God to help you stop relying on quick fixes.

—D.E.

Through preaching, teaching, and the Bible, God is telling me . . . _____

_____

_____

Through nature and the lives of other believers, God is showing me . . . _____

_____

_____

I will respond by . . . _____

_____

_____

I AM NOT SELF-CENTERED. I JUST WANT TO
KNOW WHO GAVE PERMISSION FOR ALL THESE
PEOPLE TO BE BORN AND WHAT ARE THEY DOING
ON MY PLANET?

A RESPONSIVE SOUL

Sugar high

READ
Proverbs
25:14–16, 27, 28

MEDITATE
Proverbs 25:27
It is not good to eat
too much honey.

REFLECT
➡ Do I ever indulge
in self-congratula-
tions? Do I make
sure others know
of my accomplish-
ments?
➡ What motivates my
Christian service?
➡ What light do
these verses shed
on this topic?
Proverbs 3:34;
Matthew 23:12;
1 Peter 5:5.

CONSIDER
*When pride
steps out, faith
steps in.*

It's the middle of the afternoon and you're sagging. You need a lift to get you through the next class. You need some sugar, quick! So you get a Snickers bar from the machine. Or a Coke. Or some Oreos you stashed away from lunch. Now you can make it. Right?

Wrong! A study by researchers at Montana State University has challenged the popular idea that a high-sugar snack will give you a spurt of energy. The scientists tested long-distance runners on stationary exercise bikes. Athletes who had a sugar-free drink before the workout were able to pedal 25 percent longer than those who had a drink loaded with sugar. The study concluded that "athletes may be well-advised to abstain from high-sugar snacks."

Centuries before Montana State University enrolled its first student, the Bible warned that too much sugar can affect our well-being. Solomon used the danger of too much honey to point to matters more serious: the problems that occur when we overindulge in the "sugar highs" of self-glory. The wise king warned about the dangers of pride (Proverbs 25:14, 27), and the reason is clear. Looking for attention and bragging about our accomplishments might taste sweet for a moment. But in the long run, bragging does to the character what eating M&M's does to the body.

Few things weaken believers more than a diet of pride and self-centeredness (Proverbs 16:18). All our energy is used up on ourselves. Instead of wasting our energy patting ourselves on the back, let's hand over all our praises to God.   —M.D.

Through preaching, teaching, and the Bible, God is telling me . . . _____

_____

_____

Through nature and the lives of other believers, God is showing me . . . _____

_____

_____

I will respond by . . . _____

_____

_____

Ya gotta have

The end of the world?

READ
John 21:15–19

MEDITATE
Mark 14:71

"I don't know this man you're talking about."

REFLECT

➡ In what area of my spiritual life am I failing?

➡ Have I let past failures keep me from making spiritual progress?

CONSIDER
Successful people stop at nothing—not even failures.

We'd rather do anything than fail! I mean, what's worse than falling on your face before the whole world? Or going for something really big—like being on the homecoming court or making the basketball team or going for the lead in the school play—and not making it?

And it's not just in school stuff that we hate to fail. We have spiritual failures too. We feel guilty because we don't read the Bible enough. We pray only at meals. We have opportunities to witness, but we can't seem to open our mouths. We keep falling into the same sinful habit over and over and over.

So we come up with a solution: We give up. We just stop trying. Because we failed once, or because we keep on failing in one area, we assume we're hopeless, that God got tired of watching us drop the ball and gave up on us. But that's not the way it is with God. He does not abandon us just because we fail. If you don't believe me, ask Peter.

You see, Peter failed Him—big time! On that crucial night before Jesus' death, Peter denied that he ever knew the Lord. When he said, "I don't know this man," he swore that he was telling the truth. But Jesus forgave Peter and tenderly and compassionately restored His repentant, sorrowful disciple (John 21). And the rest of the New Testament contains the record of Peter's vital and heroic role in the founding of the church.

Have you failed at something big? Feel like quitting? Don't! Ask Jesus for help—again and again if you have to. He'll be there to forgive you and restore you and help you. It's not the end of the world! —D.E.

Through preaching, teaching, and the Bible, God is telling me . . . _____

_____

Through nature and the lives of other believers, God is showing me . . . _____

_____

I will respond by . . . _____

_____

Dare to be different

READ
1 Chronicles 4:3–10

MEDITATE
1 Chronicles 4:10
"Let your hand be with me."

REFLECT
➡ Do I make compromises in areas I know I shouldn't just to be like everyone else?
➡ Could I honestly say that I stand out for God?

CONSIDER
It's better to stand out than to fit in.

The more time I spend on college campuses, the more I realize that some things haven't changed all that much since I was in college. For example, young people today are as concerned as ever about fitting in. And what are they trying to fit into? Usually it's a pair of jeans, a great-looking, loose-fitting T-shirt, and (if someone in the family can afford them) appropriate athletic shoes—sneakers that are too expensive to buy but too important to be without.

For whatever reason, people don't like to be different.

Christians, however, need to be careful about fitting in too well. In fact, there are things about which we must dare to be different.

Jabez dared to be different. Jay who? Jabez. Jabez didn't seem to be overly concerned about being like everyone else. He knew that many of the everyone elses of his day weren't following God. He was more honorable than those around him (1 Chronicles 4:9). In fact, his character probably was the reason God answered his prayer. He prayed that God would bless him (we often worry more about our friends' approval than God's) and that God would keep him from harm (if we are doing something worthwhile, we can freely ask God to protect us). Jabez, it seems, was not concerned with fitting in. His strength came in standing out—for God.

By following the example of Jabez we can be more honorable than the world around us. And if we're willing to not fit in with the world, we can really stand out for God! —D.P.

Through preaching, teaching, and the Bible, God is telling me . . . _____
_____
_____

Through nature and the lives of other believers, God is showing me . . . _____
_____
_____

I will respond by . . . _____
_____

Beyond the shadows

READ
Psalm 121

MEDITATE
Psalm 121:1
I lift up my eyes to the hills.

REFLECT
➡ What makes me doubt God? What makes me discouraged?
➡ What makes me lose confidence in the Lord?
➡ What causes me to take my eyes off Jesus? What can I do to keep my faith focused on Christ?

CONSIDER
Nothing is hopeless when your hope is in God.

If you're a booster of the Buffaloes or a backer of the Broncos, I envy you because you probably live on the eastern slope of the Colorado Rockies. All you need to do for inspiration is look west and there you see Pike's Peak, Mount Evans, Long's Peak—all beckoning you to come and enjoy their purple mountain majesties.

One of the most awesome sights I've ever seen was in the Rockies. One morning I looked to the west and noticed that the foothills were covered with thick, low clouds. My son and I were planning to hike in the mountains, but they were swathed in foreboding darkness. The foothills looked treacherous, and anyone wanting to begin a westward trek would sense danger. But then, with sudden splendor, the mountains beyond were flooded with bright sunlight. Their snow-capped, gleaming peaks, towering above the deeply shadowed lower hills, beckoned us with the promise of a safe journey.

Sometimes life is like that. The trail ahead looks dark and dangerous (especially if finals are looming). You may even have trouble finding your way because the shadows are so dark. Your heart seems weak; your steps falter; your faith is small. When that happens, lift your eyes! Ahead, above the shadows, the bright sunlight of God's promises will light the path for you. Hope and confidence will return.

Are you slowed down in your walk with Christ? Caught in the gloomy foothills of drudgery or fear? Then look up. With eyes of faith, look beyond the shadows!
—D.E.

Through preaching, teaching, and the Bible, God is telling me . . . _____

Through nature and the lives of other believers, God is showing me . . . _____

I will respond by . . . _____

The junk drawer

READ
Luke 21:29–36

MEDITATE
Luke 21:34
"Be careful, or your hearts will be weighed down."

REFLECT
➡ What do I need to get rid of today so I can be better used by God?

➡ If Christ came back today, would I be proud of the state of my life? How can I put things in order?

CONSIDER
Hidden sin never goes away.

Do you have a junk drawer? You know—a place where everything from dead batteries to old ticket stubs to expired Burger King coupons ends up. I do. I often turn to it in a last ditch effort to locate a missing something. But it's frustrating. I sort and sift. Rifle and toss. And the stuff just seems to multiply. And even if I find the Hefty twist ties or the birthday candles or whatever treasure I was looking for, the time I spent looking was wasted. I need to get rid of the unneeded stuff so that the good stuff is readily accessible.

Our minds and hearts can be a lot like a junk drawer. If we don't remove the clutter that accumulates in them we'll have difficulty functioning effectively. Christ asked us to "be careful, or your hearts will be weighed down with . . . the anxieties of life" (Luke 21:34). Of course, the "anxieties of life" are different for each of us. But whatever they are—bitter memories, grudges, overcommitted schedules, or things we love—they can use up time and energy that should be directed somewhere else. Did you ever try sorting the items on your mind? How many are like dead radio batteries or tickets to a 1989 major league baseball game—no longer useful and just taking up space? To be ready when Jesus returns we need to clear away what is not important and concentrate on what is.

If we remove the junk from our minds and hearts, keeping careful watch over what we think and do, we will be more useful to God. The things God wants in our lives will stand out like a fifty-cent piece in a drawer full of bottle caps. —T.F.

Through preaching, teaching, and the Bible, God is telling me . . . _____
_____
_____

Through nature and the lives of other believers, God is showing me . . . _____
_____
_____

I will respond by . . . _____
_____
_____

Growing up or old?

READ
1 Corinthians
13:9–13

MEDITATE
1 Corinthians 13:11
When I became a man, I put childish ways behind me.

REFLECT
➡ How has my thinking about Christ and His kingdom changed in the last year?
➡ How has my behavior changed that shows I really am growing up?

CONSIDER
What is your spiritual age?

At 65, I am in far better shape than I was at 25. At that age I was a mass of bad habits. I smoked foolishly, drank to excess, slept little, and popped Benzedrine tablets to keep myself awake. Looking back on all this, I suppose that what has taken place principally is a shift in emphasis from the instinctive physical drives to the mental ones. When I was young, my body controlled my mind in a runaway fashion. It has taken forty years of experience—sometimes painful, often dismaying—to put my mind in charge of the rest of me.

"It is not easy to learn about the 'tyranny of what feels good.' Slouching in a soft armchair. . . , watching a baseball game for two hours is pleasant. It feels good, but there are other things that feel good too: The discipline of work, the joy of creating, and the ecstasy of learning, always learning, continually learning."

Garson Kanin wrote these words in *Flight Time* magazine. Some people grow up, and others just grow old. It would appear that the difference lies in how we use our heads. Paul wrote, "When I was a child . . . I reasoned like a child. When I became a man, I put childish ways behind me" (1 Corinthians 13:11). What does it mean to grow up? Those who grow up learn the importance of putting others first; those who grow old live only to gratify their physical desires. Christian maturity means keeping the body under the control of the mind, and the mind under the control of the Holy Spirit.

Ask God today to help you "put away childish ways."

—T.B.

Through preaching, teaching, and the Bible, God is telling me . . . _____

_____

_____

Through nature and the lives of other believers, God is showing me . . . _____

_____

_____

I will respond by . . . _____

_____

Foolish demands

READ
Exodus 17:1–7

MEDITATE
Exodus 17:6
"Strike the rock, and water will come out of it."

REFLECT
→ In what ways am I influenced by the thinking of the world?

→ Do the demands of Christ for kindness or moral purity seem foolish to me?

→ Will I do whatever God asks? Or do I reserve the right to pick which of His commands I will obey?

CONSIDER
God's commands always make sense.

Darkness was settling in as we visited with our friends, so I reached over to turn on the lamp setting on the table beside my chair. To my frustration, I could find no switch. After watching me fumble, our hostess said, "Just touch the base of the lamp and the light will go on." I had never seen one of those magic-touch lamps, so her instructions seemed foolish to me. I expressed my doubts but did what she said. Of course the light came on.

Some of the things the Lord asks us to do seem equally foolish by human understanding. He asks us, for example, to serve Him—not money—even though many consider money as the best way to gain comfort and pleasure (Matthew 6:19–24). He tells us to be forgiving—even of roommates who enjoy making life miserable—as Christ forgave us (Ephesians 4:32). And if someone asks to borrow something, we're to offer the person more than he or she asks. To people who live by human thinking alone, the responses God expects seem foolish.

Moses probably felt that way too when God asked him to hit a rock with his staff to get water to satisfy a couple of million thirsty Israelites. Yet Moses did as God asked, and he got the water he had asked God for.

If we refuse to look at things as God does, then obeying Him will seem foolish. But when we look at money, friends, relationships, and values through the eyes of God, the demands that seem foolish will begin to make a whole lot of sense.
—D.E.

Through preaching, teaching, and the Bible, God is telling me . . . _____

Through nature and the lives of other believers, God is showing me . . . _____

I will respond by . . . _____

The dreaded misnomer

READ
Isaiah 5:18–25

MEDITATE
Isaiah 5:20
Woe to those who call evil good and good evil.

REFLECT

➡ What person deliberately uses a misnomer to cover up the seriousness of his or her behavior? Do I do that? With what?

➡ What things does society call by the wrong name to make them more acceptable?

➡ How can I best learn how God views what is going on in my world?

CONSIDER
Satan doesn't want us to call sin "sin."

A writer for the *Detroit News* expressed astonishment at the way the truth is often stretched in advertising. While visiting in New England, she went to an exclusive Cape Cod restaurant and ordered a "fresh fruit salad" from the menu. But when it came, it was anything but fresh. The peaches, pineapples, pears, grapes, and maraschino cherries had spent many months wallowing in their own juice in a can before being served. When the writer asked the waitress what happened to the fresh fruit, she was told, "Oh, honey, that's just what they call it."

Later, the same columnist stopped at a Hot Pie cart at a sporting event. When she bit into her piece of cherry pie, it was ice cold. So she complained. The pie seller told her brusquely, "Hot Pie is just the name of the pie."

Deliberately giving something the wrong name doesn't happen only in advertising. It happens whenever people turn their backs on truth and "call evil good and good evil."

For example, people who use pornography call themselves openminded. Those who spend an afternoon drinking alcohol call it stopping for "happy hour." And those who steal from their employers claim they are just "getting some of what they owe me."

But God is not fooled by misnomers. He sees our deeds for what they really are, not what we call them. Don't accept the world's designations—or even your own. Accept God's verdict of truth. He never uses misnomers.

—M.D.

Through preaching, teaching, and the Bible, God is telling me . . . _____
_____
_____

Through nature and the lives of other believers, God is showing me . . . _____
_____
_____

I will respond by . . . _____
_____
_____

Which rights are right?

SEPTEMBER 28

READ
Hosea 14:1–9

MEDITATE
Hosea 14:9
The ways of the Lord are right.

REFLECT
➧ What do I fear about sharing my faith at school? How much does it really matter to me whether I do or don't?
➧ Which rights should I begin exercising at school?

CONSIDER
You can't use your rights until you know them.

You may not know it, but if you are a Christian in a secular educational setting, you have rights that need to be protected. To help you stand up for what is rightfully yours, here's a "bill of rights for Christians in public schools" compiled by attorney John Whitehead:

1. Right to equal access: Christian student organizations must be afforded the same rights as other non-curricular student groups.

2. Right to read the Bible: Students can read their Bible during free times at school.

3. Right to express views: Students can express their religious views during class discussions.

4. Right to distribute literature: Students can pass out literature if done in a non-disruptive way.

5. Right to pray: Students can pray during noninstructional times.

6. Right to express beliefs: Students and teachers can discuss religious matters on an individual basis.

7. Right to have religious beliefs: Teachers can't be excluded from teaching based on their religious beliefs.

8. Right to teach about religion: Teachers can teach about religious beliefs that are relevant to the subject matter.

9. Right to access literature: School officials can't remove literature from the library solely because of its religious content.

10. Right to excuse students: Parents can excuse their children from objectionable material being taught.

God's ways are right. And now you know what rights you have to share God with others at school. To miss your chance just wouldn't be—uh—right. —T.F.

Through preaching, teaching, and the Bible, God is telling me . . . _____

_____

Through nature and the lives of other believers, God is showing me . . . _____

_____

I will respond by . . . _____

_____

No-no to the yo-yo

READ
**Colossians
2:20–3:17**

MEDITATE
Colossians 3:2
Set your minds on
things above.

REFLECT
➡ What habits in
Colossians 3:5–9
do I have the most
trouble with?
➡ Why do I have
trouble breaking
bad habits?
➡ What steps can I
take to replace
wrong behavior
with what is right?

CONSIDER
*To break a
habit, first fix
your thinking.*

It may not look like it when you are standing in line at Wendy's, but nearly half of all women and a quarter of all men are dieting at any one time.

Yale University psychologist Kelly Brownell has discovered that most people fall into a yo-yo pattern—they regain weight within six months to a year after losing it. As soon as they hit their weight-loss goal, they tend to return to their old habits.

This yo-yo pattern is not only frustrating, it is also unhealthy. It contributes to a higher risk of heart disease and premature death. The best solution to a weight problem, according to Brownell, is not simply dieting, but developing lifelong, healthful eating habits.

The apostle Paul didn't specifically address weight loss, but he did write some good words of advice for anyone trying to break an unhealthy habit. He gave a long-range solution that would produce spiritual health.

Paul put it all in perspective when he said, "Set your minds on things above, not on earthly things. For you died, and your life is now hidden with Christ in God. When Christ, who is your life, appears, then you also will appear with him in glory" (3:2–4). Paul also identified what habits we are to break (vv. 5–9) and what kinds of new, holy habits we are to put in their place (vv. 12–17). Just as the long-range solution for weight control calls for eating less, choosing the right foods, and exercising regularly, so too breaking sinful habits requires replacing wrong actions with new patterns of thinking and behaving.

Let's say no-no to the yo-yo patterns in our lives and ask the Lord for help in developing lifelong solutions.
—K.D.

Through preaching, teaching, and the Bible, God is telling me . . . _____

_____

Through nature and the lives of other believers, God is showing me . . . _____

_____

I will respond by . . . _____

_____

A SOUND MIND

Run for the Boulder

A tostada, a taco, and an Orange Slice. When you're on the road, you tend to eat these things. Okay, I tend to eat these things.

Anyway, I was heading back to my hotel after talking with students on the campus of the University of Colorado. But there was one problem. I didn't know exactly how to get back to where I was staying. So I asked the drive-thru clerk for directions to South Boulder Road. Slight problem. She didn't understand English. She motioned for me to pull ahead and talk to the clerk at the next window. She did understand English, but she didn't have a clue as to where South Boulder Road was. I was beginning to wonder if I'd ever find my hotel again. I mean, maybe I had taken a one-way road into the Twilight Zone.

Nope. Turned out I was in Boulder, Colorado, after all. The second clerk summoned the manager, who told me exactly how to get back on the right road. All I had to do was find the right source.

There will be times in life when you'll feel as if you're in a strange city, when you'll have no idea which way to turn to get where you want to go. For example, you'll hear something in philosophy or science class that contradicts your religious beliefs. Should you accept it? Where should you go to find out if it's true? Or you'll be asked out for a date but you're not sure the person is a Christian. Should you go?

To get the right directions, you have to go to the right source.

"If any of you lacks wisdom, he should ask God, who gives generously to all" (James 1:5). There's the answer. Turn to God and follow His directions. He'll never steer you wrong.

—D.P.

Through preaching, teaching, and the Bible, God is telling me . . . _____

_____

_____

Through nature and the lives of other believers, God is showing me . . . _____

_____

_____

I will respond by . . . _____

_____

_____

Ya gotta have

OCTOBER 1

The ultimate test

READ
Colossians 3:15–25

MEDITATE
Colossians 3:23
Whatever you do, work at it with all your heart.

REFLECT
➡ Why does God want me to do my best? How does my performance affect those around me?
➡ If I'm stuck in a rut of mediocrity, how can I get out?
➡ What is keeping me from doing the best I can?

CONSIDER
Don't rest till you've given your best.

A young Jimmy Carter once faced Admiral Hyman Rickover, a stern and demanding Navy leader, in an all-important interview. Here is a condensed version of Carter's account from the book *Rickover: Controversy and Genius*.

"I had applied for the nuclear submarine program, and Admiral Rickover was interviewing me for the job. It was the first time I met him. We sat in a large room by ourselves for more than two hours, and he let me choose any subjects I wished to discuss. I chose those about which I knew most at the time. He began to ask me a series of questions of increasing difficulty. In each instance, he soon proved that I knew relatively little about the subject I had chosen.

"He always looked right into my eyes, and he never smiled. I was saturated with sweat.

"Finally, he asked a question and I thought I could redeem myself. He said, 'How did you stand in your class at the Naval Academy?' I swelled my chest with pride and answered, 'Sir, I stood fifty-ninth in a class of 820!' I sat back to wait for the congratulations—which never came. Instead, the question; 'Did you do your best?' I finally gulped and said, 'No sir, I didn't always do my best.'

"He looked at me for a long time, and then he turned his chair around to end the interview. He asked one final question, which I have never been able to forget—or answer. He said, 'Why not?' I sat there for a while, shaken, and then slowly left the room."

Someday God may ask you if you worked "with all your heart" for Him. What would your answer be?
—T.F.

Through preaching, teaching, and the Bible, God is telling me . . . _____

Through nature and the lives of other believers, God is showing me . . . _____

I will respond by . . . _____

What is your focus?

MEDITATE
Romans 12:1
Therefore, I urge you . . . to offer your bodies as living sacrifices.

REFLECT

➡ What do the words "Always be willing to die for Christ" mean to me?

➡ What do my activities and priorities over the past few months say about the focus of my life?

➡ How can I bring my life more in line with my Christian ideals?

CONSIDER
If you're not focused on Christ, you're out of focus.

Brad Newlin was a sophomore at Taylor University when he wrote these words:

My Focus

To live and fight over the edge.

To allow God to conform me to the image of His Son.

To always place God's will above my needs.

To deny myself; to become less so that God may become more.

To stand firm among 10,000 who are falling on either side.

To always be willing to die for Christ or the will of God.

To live my short-vapored life devoted fully to the will of God.

To make every thought, motive, and desire obedient to the will of Christ.

To never play games with my merciful Savior.

To live by faith and not by sight.

To never own anything.

To fear God in His mighty justice.

To let the heart of Christ beat in me.

Later that year, Brad learned that he had a rare form of cancer. He went through extensive chemotherapy. Many Christians prayed for him. His love for Christ and his concern for the lost remained strong, right up until his death two years later in the summer of 1990.

Brad Newlin is gone. But he left behind a challenge to live 100 percent for his Savior.

Read Brad's list again. Why not pick up where he left off and make his focus the focus of your life? —D.E.

Through preaching, teaching, and the Bible, God is telling me . . . _____

_____

Through nature and the lives of other believers, God is showing me . . . _____

_____

I will respond by . . . _____

_____

Student power

READ
2 Timothy 1:3–7

MEDITATE
2 Timothy 1:7
God did not give us a spirit of timidity, but a spirit of power.

REFLECT
➡ Am I afraid to speak out for what's right? To stand up for what I believe?

➡ Are my Christian friends the kind to take action? Are they willing to risk popularity for a just cause? Am I?

➡ What could I do to make an impact for God in my school or community? What is stopping me?

CONSIDER
Evil grows when good people do nothing about it.

Sometimes young people think their opinions don't count, and that the world is controlled by adults. But that is not always true.

Consider best friends Stacy Katz and Robin Holton. They were senior honor students and co-captains of the cheerleading team in their high school in Bastrop, Louisiana. They decided one day that it was wrong for their school to have two proms, one for white students and one for African-American students. They went first to the prom committee, then to the principal. Nothing happened. So they went to the superintendent. He told them all about the dangers and potential trouble, and he warned that it would never work. But they persisted, and finally it went before the school board. The board opted to let the students themselves decide with a vote. When the ballots were counted, in spite of strong pressure, the students voted in favor of an integrated prom. Unheard of in that part of Louisiana!

These two good friends (Stacy is white; Robin is black) saw a need and responded to it. In spite of opposition and discouragement, they persisted.

We who are God's people can do the same. We can change the world around us. We can speak out in the name of Christ against injustice or unfairness or evil. And we can be heard.

I'm not telling you to become a troublemaker. But I am saying this: If you see a wrong that needs to be made right, don't just sit there. If you display the right spirit and follow the proper channels, you can make a difference!

God did not give you a spirit of fear. He gave you a spirit of power. Perhaps it's time to use it for His glory!
—D.E.

Through preaching, teaching, and the Bible, God is telling me . . . _____

_____

_____

Through nature and the lives of other believers, God is showing me . . . _____

_____

_____

I will respond by . . . _____

_____

_____

Date rape

READ
2 Timothy 3:1–9

MEDITATE
2 Timothy 3:2
People will be lovers of
themselves, lovers of
money.

REFLECT

➡ What is more
important to me
when I get ready
for a date: having a
"Colgate" smile
and every hair in
place or having
desires and motives
that please God?

➡ When I feel my
sexual drive steer-
ing me in the
wrong direction,
what will I do to
regain control?

CONSIDER
*Purity is a gift
that can never
be returned.*

The words *date* and *rape* don't even go together. Date: When a couple goes out for food, entertainment, and conversation. A warm, friendly time. Rape: A violent act caused by one person forcing unwanted sexual contact with another. A brutal, damaging crime.

So why are these words linked so frequently? A recent survey shows a connection between substance abuse and rape on college campuses. The victims and those who commit the crime both tend to be more frequent abusers of drugs and alcohol than other students.

But the reason date rape occurs is not found in the survey results. The crime is committed by a selfish person who is concerned only with satisfying his own wants. Paul referred to this type of person in today's reading. "People will be lovers of themselves, . . . abusive, . . . without love, . . . lovers of pleasure rather than lovers of God" (2 Timothy 3:1–4). Rapists are obsessed with "me." They place God and others in the "you" category, which to them is less important. The result is sin that hurts and destroys.

So how can you avoid becoming a date rape statistic? Young women need to be selective about whom they go out with. Make sure your dates are spiritually alive young men who demonstrate Christlike characteristics. Young men should make sure their walk with the Lord is strong. Look at your date as someone God loves and treasures. She does not belong to you in any way.

Seek God's wisdom as you go out. Think of God and others instead of yourself.   —T.F.

Through preaching, teaching, and the Bible, God is telling me . . . _____
_____
_____

Through nature and the lives of other believers, God is showing me . . . _____
_____
_____

I will respond by . . . _____
_____
_____

The safest way to go

READ
2 Timothy 1:8–12

MEDITATE
2 Timothy 1:8
Join with me in suffering for the gospel.

REFLECT

➡ How does obedience to God frighten me? What am I actually afraid of?

➡ What do Numbers 23:19 and Psalm 119:50 tell me about the character of God?

➡ As I think about walking with God, do I see it as a perilous journey or a pleasant one?

CONSIDER
Walking with God is safer than running with the devil.

Let's say your best friend lives in Birmingham, Alabama. You're planning to go for a visit, but you live in Tacoma, Washington, or some other faraway place. It's too far to walk, and you don't feel like driving that far. So you decide to fly. But what about crashes? Would it be safer to gas up your 1978 Volkswagen and drive?

Actually, it wouldn't. Commercial airline travel is thirty times safer than going by car. It may not seem like that to the person who would rather fight rush hour traffic on the ground than cruise in solitude at 500 mph in a Boeing 747 at 33,000 feet. But of the five million scheduled flights in a recent year, only five resulted in fatal accidents. Being carried by tons of metal thrust through the air by huge jet engines is actually a lot safer than being propelled along the road by a four-cylinder machine.

Like flying, following the Lord Jesus may seem to be dangerous. It must have seemed so to Timothy, who apparently had more than his share of white-knuckle experiences along the path of discipleship. It also looked that way to the believers in Asia who turned away from Paul when he was thrown into prison.

In reality, however, Paul had chosen the safest way to travel through life. He wanted young Timothy to experience it too, so he explained to him why suffering for Christ was the safest and only way to get where he wanted to go.

Living for Jesus and following Him can seem scary—especially in a non-Christian school, work environment, or military setting. But because of the power, promises, and provision of God, it's the safest way to go.   —M.D.

Through preaching, teaching, and the Bible, God is telling me . . . _____

_____

Through nature and the lives of other believers, God is showing me . . . _____

_____

I will respond by . . . _____

_____

The secret life

READ
Ephesians 4:17–24

MEDITATE
1 Corinthians 4:5
He will bring to light what is hidden in darkness.

REFLECT
➡ What little things have I been trying to get away with?
➡ What makes me think I can stop being deceitful without help from the Holy Spirit?
➡ What does 1 Corinthians 4:2 mean? How should I apply it in my life?

CONSIDER
God is never in the dark.

You wonder why these guys think they can get away with things like this. First, it was some guy who calls himself a preacher being accused by more than twenty young men of seducing them into homosexual acts. Then, it was a pastor everybody loved and adored who got caught robbing banks. And what turned the man of the cloth into a man behind the gun? He needed money to support his habit of picking up prostitutes.

Before you jump to conclusions, this is not about pastors. The vast majority of them are honest, God-fearing people of high morals.

No, this is about people. People like you and me. Just like those two ministers, we are all capable of getting ourselves mixed up in things that would make a mother hang her head in shame. Scripture tells us that the heart is "deceitful above all things" (Jeremiah 17:9). We have a built-in tendency toward immorality. And sometimes we think we can get away with it by doing it secretly.

Our secret life may not take us to the bank for a withdrawal at gunpoint, but it does make us do stuff we know we shouldn't. Like renting a raunchy video and watching it when nobody's around. Or slipping a pair of earrings into a coat pocket and "accidentally" taking them home without paying for them. Or . . . well, I don't need to give you any more ideas.

Sure, we can fool parents, dorm advisors, friends, employers, and almost everybody else. But we sure aren't fooling God. And according to Paul, God "will bring to light what is hidden in darkness." So why do we still think we can get away with living a secret life?   —D.B.

Through preaching, teaching, and the Bible, God is telling me . . . _____
_____
_____

Through nature and the lives of other believers, God is showing me . . . _____
_____
_____

I will respond by . . . _____
_____
_____

Return of the Raiders

READ
Colossians 2:6–10

MEDITATE
Colossians 2:6
So then, just as you received Christ Jesus as Lord, continue to live in him.

REFLECT
➡ According to Colossians 2:6–7, what four qualities are best for my life?
➡ Am I doing pretty well right now? Or have I slipped? Do I need to return?
➡ What is the biggest threat to my spiritual life? How can I fight it?

CONSIDER
No self-control; no success.

It's one thing to win the Super Bowl. It's quite another to stay at that level. Consider the Los Angeles Raiders. They were a powerhouse football team in the seventies and early eighties. They were always in the playoffs; they even won the big prize in 1976, 1980, and 1983.

But then, according to reports, they began to "party hearty." Soon they couldn't even make the wild card selection. As former Raider Lester Hayes put it, "Can you imagine what it is like to spend every day of your life drunk? Every strip bar in LA knew us. It was like Nightmare on Elm Street. Our team had the highest divorce rate in the NFL."

Hayes concluded, "Our examples, the all-pro players, were leading it. The power of tequila and Satan will make even a good man sin. That was our downfall. We partied too much."

But the Raiders made a comeback under new coach Art Shell and reached the semi-finals before falling to the powerful Buffalo Bills. Why? Because Shell stopped the partying.

You don't have to be a Harvard Ph.D. to see what I'm saying. Where are you right now? Are you in championship form? Has your outlook on life soured, have your relationships fouled, and has your spirituality dropped off to zero? Why? Too much partying? Too much goofing off? Too much time spent on life's frivolities?

Come back to Christ. Let Him help you regain the self-control you once had, reestablish your priorities, and reassess your true needs. Only He can get you back into championship form.
—D.E.

Through preaching, teaching, and the Bible, God is telling me . . . _____

Through nature and the lives of other believers, God is showing me . . . _____

I will respond by . . . _____

Tomorrow's troubles

READ
Matthew 6:25–34

MEDITATE
Matthew 6:34
"Therefore do not worry about tomorrow."

REFLECT
➡ How does my schedule look for tomorrow, next week, next month?
➡ How does worry about what's ahead affect my actions and attitudes?
➡ What problem am I facing today?

CONSIDER
An army of anxiety is best defeated one worry at a time.

Was Jesus kidding when He said, "Do not worry about tomorrow"? Didn't He know about chemistry exams, blind dates, or making speeches? If we think about everything we have to do and all the problems we face, we don't even want to get out of bed.

The essence of what Jesus was saying is that taking life one day at a time will help us win the battle over worry. When we look at today's problems, and tomorrow's, and next week's—it's too much.

In 480 B.C. large forces from Persia (which is now Iran) were advancing toward Sparta (which was, and still is, in Greece). Sparta's King Leonidas directed his men to meet the Persians at a narrow mountain pass, where they could fight one soldier at a time. The Spartans were able to hold off the horde of invaders by picking them off as they came through the pass in single file.

Do all your tomorrows seem like an invading army? Follow Jesus' wisdom. Deal with problems as they come—one at a time.

But that's not the whole answer. Jesus said more. Another reason we can and should quit fretting about all the things that will or might happen is that we can give tomorrow over to God. We can trust our Father to meet our every need (Matthew 6:30–33).

Skeptical? Worried that this advice won't work? Try it. Plan ahead and don't worry. Everything you would worry about is in God's hands. So ask for His help. Trusting is much better than worrying.   —K.D.

Through preaching, teaching, and the Bible, God is telling me . . . _____
_____
_____

Through nature and the lives of other believers, God is showing me . . . _____
_____
_____

I will respond by . . . _____
_____
_____

What makes you happy?

READ
Ecclesiastes 11:7–10

MEDITATE
Ecclesiastes 11:9
Be happy, young man,
while you are young.

REFLECT
➡ Does God want me
to be happy? Is
something wrong
if I'm happy?

➡ If only I had _____
_____,
I'd be happy. Do I
ever say that? Is it
true?

➡ Do I think that
everyone's happy
but me? What
makes me think
that?

CONSIDER
*A thankful
person is a
happy person.*

What would it take to make you happy? Would winning $14 million do the trick? Would being able to buy anything you want put an end to all your troubles?

A psychologist named Denier did some research on happiness. He wanted to know if winning the lottery made people happier than other people. Or if a tragedy made them sadder.

His research came up with some surprising results. Denier studied two major changes and how they affected people's happiness. Half the people were big lottery winners. The other half had been badly hurt in car accidents.

Unbelievable as it sounds, a few weeks after the big event, both groups were equally happy! The lottery winners were not any happier than the people who had been injured.

Happiness does go deeper than having good things happen to you. It has its source in your thinking and your heart, and it works itself out in positive, healthy responses to life.

And here is where being a Christian helps a lot. If you have received the Lord Jesus as your Savior, you have the deep issues of sin and guilt taken care of. You have God's Word and the Holy Spirit to help you evaluate things correctly and give you the strength to respond properly to any situation. You have the power to be content with what you have and where you are in life.

Let me ask you again. Are you happy? Or do you spend a lot of time envying others or wishing for something you don't have? Here's my suggestion. Accept what God has given you, and thank Him for it. Then you'll know the secret of being happy "while you are young"! —D.E.

Through preaching, teaching, and the Bible, God is telling me . . . _____

_____

Through nature and the lives of other believers, God is showing me . . . _____

_____

I will respond by . . . _____

_____

Honking can hurt

READ
Ephesians 4:25–32

MEDITATE
Ephesians 4:29

Do not let any unwholesome talk come out of your mouths, but only what is helpful.

REFLECT

➡ How can I use more words like those described in Proverbs 16:24?

➡ What causes me to say mean things to another person? What will make me change?

CONSIDER
Sharp words are often pointless.

Let's consider one of life's most frustrating experiences. Yes, the much-hated "car stalled in heavy traffic" scenario. Here's the story of one woman's experience with her dead sled.

Beatrice (okay, I don't know her real name) buried the pedal one last time. She turned the key, only to hear a pathetic groan coming from under the hood. The old bomb was in a bad way, and she was stuck in bumper-to-bumper traffic. Then a steady, pulsating sound filled her ears. No, it wasn't the happy hum of her car's engine. (Wishful thinking.) It was the man in the Ford 4x4 behind her, laying on the horn.

Bea was not pleased. She left her car and headed back to the two-fisted tooter. Confronting the man, she said, "I'm having some difficulty getting my car started. If you'll go try to start it, I'll honk your horn for you!"

Honking at a person stuck in traffic is definitely rude (not to mention futile). But there's something we all do that's just as unkind. We use biting or sarcastic words. Like a honking horn, unkind words are annoying and useless. And they are also hurtful.

The Bible seems to indicate that God would rather we use kinder, gentler words. He wants us to say things that are "helpful for building others up" (Ephesians 4:29). He wants us to be "kind and compassionate to one another" (v. 32).

It's easy to sit back and verbally blast someone. But it never helps the situation. Instead, we need to use soft, building words. Who knows, it may be the way to jump-start a new friendship. —T.F.

Through preaching, teaching, and the Bible, God is telling me . . . _____
_____
_____

Through nature and the lives of other believers, God is showing me . . . _____
_____
_____

I will respond by . . . _____
_____

You can't explain it

READ
1 Thessalonians 1

MEDITATE
1 Thessalonians 1:5
Our gospel came to you . . . with power, with the Holy Spirit, and with deep conviction.

REFLECT
➡ Why do I need God's help when I witness?
➡ How am I going to use that power in sharing the Gospel?

CONSIDER
God's power works whether we understand it or not.

I don't know anything about electricity. Okay, I do know one thing: When I flick the switch, the light comes on. (When it doesn't, I know it's time to call the electrician!)

But as mysterious as electricity is, at least it can be explained. There's another kind of power, however, that can't be explained: the power of the Gospel. We waste our time when we try to reason through God's plan of salvation.

Paul reminded the Thessalonians that the Gospel was not just a matter of his words of explanation. Their conversion combined power, conviction, and the Holy Spirit.

We tend to go the words route. When we're telling our friends about Jesus Christ, we reduce the decision to intellectual agreement: Simply believe the historical facts about Jesus, and you're a Christian. Or we try to turn it into an emotional experience: If you feel different, then you're saved.

But salvation is more than that. It combines the intellect, the emotions, and the will. And it's the most important decision a person can make about life. Bringing people to such a turning point requires God's help. Jesus told His disciples, "No one can come to me unless the Father who sent me draws him" (John 6:44).

Books providing intellectual and historical support for the Gospel can be helpful. But what actually happens when a person makes the life-changing decision to trust Christ is something only God can fully understand. What's more important than understanding what happens, however, is believing His guarantee that it works.

—J.C.

Through preaching, teaching, and the Bible, God is telling me . . . _____

_____

Through nature and the lives of other believers, God is showing me . . . _____

_____

I will respond by . . . _____

_____

Man-made hail

READ
Ephesians 4:17–32

MEDITATE
Ephesians 4:31
Get rid of all bitterness, rage and anger.

REFLECT
➡ How have I been hurt by angry words?
➡ How do I deal with my anger?
➡ What can I do to help get my temper under control?

CONSIDER
Use anger's energy constructively.

Hail produced by a severe thunderstorm can devastate crops, injure people and animals, damage airplanes, and destroy a car's paint job. During my amateur meteorologist days, I learned that these ice balls range from pellet-size to grapefruit-size. Hailstones are formed when a cloud has a violent updraft, reaching up into the freezing zone of the atmosphere. At that point, moisture freezes and creates snow pellets. The higher and longer the thunderstorm tosses the particles around, the larger and more destructive the hailstones become.

Hail from a thundercloud has a lot in common with angry words. Under certain circumstances, violent winds of bitterness and hurt feelings will carry anger higher and higher, where it grows bigger and bigger. When it becomes too heavy to stay aloft, it pours out in verbal attacks on others.

Paul pointed out the damage anger can do (Ephesians 4). When we hold in anger and allow it to seethe in our hearts, we give the devil an opportunity (v. 27). What's worse, our bitterness, wrath, and anger grieve the Holy Spirit (vv. 30–31).

But don't despair. Paul told us how to control this powerful emotion before it turns into a damaging downpour: ". . . forgiving each other, just as in Christ God forgave you" (v. 32). Immediate forgiveness is the key to controlling anger.

If we harbor bitter feelings and nurture grudges, the result will be verbal storms that injure people we care about. And the damage can be long-lasting.

Are you angry with someone? Resolve it quickly—before it grows into a hailstorm of hurt.   —K.D.

Through preaching, teaching, and the Bible, God is telling me . . . _____

_____

_____

Through nature and the lives of other believers, God is showing me . . . _____

_____

_____

I will respond by . . . _____

_____

OCTOBER 13

"I'm depressed"

READ
I Kings 19:1–18

MEDITATE
I Kings 19:14

"I am the only one left, and now they are trying to kill me too."

REFLECT

➥ Do I have underlying feelings of sadness? Worthlessness? Failure? Aloneness? Am I depressed?

➥ If I have had these feelings for some time, isn't it about time I did something about them? Should I consider talking about them with a pastor or Christian counselor?

CONSIDER
With God, the helpless are never hopeless.

"I'm depressed!" Sometimes we say this flippantly, like when our team loses an important game or someone buys the car we've had our eye on. But it's when we don't say it and we really are feeling low for a long period of time that we have cause for concern.

Defined as a condition of prolonged sadness, depression is marked by feelings of hopelessness and an inability to think things through clearly. Depressed people say things like this to themselves: "I'm just a bad person. I'm a failure. I can't handle responsibility or stress. I'll never change. It's hopeless."

If I've been describing you, you're not alone. Some of the most godly men and women have felt this way. Elijah the prophet is an example. After being on the mountaintop, he suffered a great letdown. He had won a stunning victory over the prophets of Baal on Mount Carmel. In the strength of the Lord he had run seventeen miles. But when he learned that Jezebel had vowed to kill him, fear gripped his heart. He ran for his life. Finally, physically and emotionally exhausted, he gave in to despair.

The Lord was gentle with Elijah. He let him rest. He fed him, strengthening him for the next leg of the journey. But Elijah's sadness continued. So the Lord promised to stay with him, gave him a companion named Elisha, and challenged him with a new task.

Feeling hopeless? Feel as if God has let you down? The story of Elijah shows that feelings alone do not prove that God has turned His back on us. They simply block our awareness of His presence.

Those who wait helplessly on the Lord may feel hopeless. But because of God's presence, they never are.

—M.D.

Through preaching, teaching, and the Bible, God is telling me . . . _____

_____

Through nature and the lives of other believers, God is showing me . . . _____

_____

I will respond by . . . _____

_____

Three key words

READ
Psalm 116

MEDITATE
Psalm 116:1
I love the Lord.

REFLECT
➡ How do I feel when someone tells me he or she loves me?
➡ Why is it hard for me to express my love to God?
➡ What are five reasons I have for loving God?

CONSIDER
When did you last tell God, "I love you"?

Name the most powerful three-word phrase in the English language. Is it "The pizza's here"? Or what about "No class today!" Or maybe "Mom, I'm home!"

As good as these expressions are, I think the most powerful words in the world are "I love you." No other words can made us feel so good. No other words can melt our hearts so quickly. No other words can do as much to mend a broken relationship. No other words from a parent could ever mean more to a young person. No better words can parents hear from their children.

One evening when I was playing with my two-year-old daughter, she ran to me, put her arms around my neck, and said, "I love you, Daddy!" That moment will always be precious to me. Her words went straight to my heart because they were sincere, unrehearsed, and pure. She wasn't just saying words I wanted to hear to get me to give her something she wanted.

God desires the same kind of response from each of His children. As we think about what God does for us, we will love and appreciate Him more. He gives us new life through Jesus Christ. He equips us with spiritual gifts to serve Him. And He's building an eternal home for us.

When we recognize all the ways He shows His love to us, we will want to express our love for Him. We won't hesitate to say to Him, "I love you." Has the Lord heard those three powerful words from you recently?

—K.D.

Through preaching, teaching, and the Bible, God is telling me . . . _____
_____
_____

Through nature and the lives of other believers, God is showing me . . . _____
_____
_____

I will respond by . . . _____
_____
_____

"Mother still loves me!"

READ
1 John 4:7–12

MEDITATE
1 John 4:10
This is love: not that we loved God, but that he loved us.

REFLECT
➡ When I sin, do I feel that God doesn't love me anymore? Where do I get that feeling?

➡ Does the awareness of God's unending love for me give me an excuse to keep sinning? What does Romans 6:1–2 say about this?

CONSIDER
One thing God can't do is stop loving you.

Greg Louganis was a great Olympic competitor for the United States in the 1988 Games, and he has won numerous medals as a diver. His sport calls for perfection. Years of rigorous training and sacrifice, intense competition, and the hopes of his nation may ride on one dive. Someone asked him one time how he handles the pressure. He said, "As I walk out on the platform, I tell myself this: 'Even if I blow this dive, my mother will still love me.'" Then he does the best he can.

It's the same with a Christian and God.

When we mess up, we wonder how anyone could possibly love us—especially God. In spite of all we know about Him, we still feel unloved when we blow it.

We want to honor Him with our lives, but sometimes our emotional timing gets out of whack and we make a cutting remark before our brain has time to intercept it. Or our priorities get out of balance and we neglect an important commitment.

We're afraid to talk to God about it. Why would He even want to hear from us? We feel crummy about ourselves, and think God must feel the same way.

Not true! His love for us is not based on our performance, but on His grace through Christ. It's like the Energizer bunny—it keeps going and going and going. God's love doesn't stop because we made a bad decision or said some really stupid things.

Even when we blow it, God still loves us. This can give us great confidence. The Lord will never take back His unending love for us.

—D.E.

Through preaching, teaching, and the Bible, God is telling me . . . _____

Through nature and the lives of other believers, God is showing me . . . _____

I will respond by . . . _____

Time for evaluation

READ
Acts 14:21–28

MEDITATE
Acts 14:21–22
They returned . . . strengthening the disciples and encouraging them to remain true to the faith.

REFLECT
➡ Where would be a good place to find someone willing and qualified to disciple me?
➡ What frightens me the most about having my life open to scrutiny?

CONSIDER
How much you grow may depend on who you know.

Talk about candid camera. Three high school teachers in a Midwest city were recently caught off guard by a student with a hidden video camera, and the camera was not kind. It showed them failing in their own classrooms.

One teacher allowed students to play dice in the back of the room while he taught. Another read a magazine while pupils went totally out of control. And the third was shown being backed into a chair by some students.

All three were suspended.

We could all use a little zoom lens lesson in our lives. Those teachers were in need of some direction. They needed a principal who knew their weaknesses and could help them overcome them. Likewise, we Christians need someone who will point out our weak areas and give us biblical direction—someone who will encourage our strengths and motivate us to excellence.

Paul and Barnabas strengthened the disciples and encouraged them "to remain true to the faith" (Acts 14). Later the passage states that these two teachers spent a long time visiting—and discipling—another group of believers.

It's important for you as a young Christian to have a relationship like this with a Christian who is more spiritually mature—and often older. As he or she helps you grow in your knowledge of God and His Word and assists you in uncovering and working on your areas of weakness, your spiritual life will hit fast forward.

Ask God to bring into your life someone who can be a Paul or Barnabas to you. When we make ourselves accountable to an older, wiser Christian, our lives won't be filled with "bloopers."   —T.F.

Through preaching, teaching, and the Bible, God is telling me . . . _____
_____
_____

Through nature and the lives of other believers, God is showing me . . . _____
_____
_____

I will respond by . . . _____
_____
_____

Signs of infection

READ
Psalm 51:1–12

MEDITATE
1 Corinthians 5:6
A little yeast works through the whole batch of dough.

REFLECT
➡ What "little" sins have I been ignoring?

➡ What are the possible long-term effects of neglecting sin?

➡ What can I learn from David in Psalm 51 about the right attitude toward sin?

CONSIDER
Little sins can cause big damage.

Three against one. The odds were against me. But I had a huge pair of hedge trimmers—they had only thorns—so I was confident of victory. To maximize my advantage, I hit them without warning. Several hours later, those three thorny bushes were down.

I came out of the conflict with just a few scratches and only five thorns in my fingers. They caused only moderate discomfort, so I ignored them.

The next day, though, three of my fingers were showing signs of infection. Still, no big deal. They weren't bullets or anything—just small thorns. I'd take care of them later. But I couldn't shake the feeling that if I ignored them now I would have to pay later. So I decided to have my wife remove them. She did a little digging, and I did a little wincing, and the thorns were out.

Like a thorn in your finger, sin left untreated can cause serious damage later on. Think about the "little" sins you might easily ignore. That half truth. That unkind word. The "colorful" language you sometimes use. That occasional cheating. That envy you feel for a classmate. Those are just small things. Nothing major really. But the Bible warns us that "a little yeast works through the whole batch of dough." A little sin can go a long way. What might seem insignificant can eventually do a lot of damage.

So what about those "small problems" we neglect? If we want to be right with God, we have to take care of them. Not later. Right now.   —D.P.

Through preaching, teaching, and the Bible, God is telling me . . . _____

_____

_____

Through nature and the lives of other believers, God is showing me . . . _____

_____

_____

I will respond by . . . _____

_____

_____

How the Mercedes-Benz

READ
Romans 15:14–20

MEDITATE
Romans 15:19
I have fully proclaimed the gospel of Christ.

REFLECT
➡ What, besides hell, has Jesus saved me from?
➡ Am I excited about telling others about Christ? Am I as confident as Paul in Romans 15?
➡ I know _____
_____
is not a believer. When would be a good opportunity for me to tell him/her about Jesus?

CONSIDER
The Christian faith is not the secret service.

I admit it. I've always wanted a BMW. Head-quartered in Munich, BMW produces what I feel is the finest engineered automobile in the world. Their rivals, the folks at Mercedes-Benz, disagree. They firmly believe their car is the best. And I'll admit, their claims are pretty hard to dispute.

Carmakers like these try to keep their design break-throughs secret. It helps them keep an edge on the competition.

So I was surprised at a recent Mercedes ad. It showed one of their cars running into a cement wall during a safety test. A voice asks a company spokesperson why Mercedes-Benz does not keep secret their energy-absorbing body design. (It's a great sales advantage because it saves so many lives. Yet other companies know they are free to use it in their own designs.) The Mercedes official replies to the voice, "Because some things in life are too important not to share."

We who are followers of Jesus also have something too important not to share. It is the wonderful news of the free gift of salvation. God offers it to all who believe. Jesus died for our sins. He paid the penalty for every one of them on the cross. We can have forgiveness and eternal life if we will trust in Him.

It's such good news that we shouldn't keep it a secret. Christ saves people from much more than the consequences of a car wreck. He saves them from hell. It's a message too important not to share! —D.E.

Through preaching, teaching, and the Bible, God is telling me . . . _____
_____
_____

Through nature and the lives of other believers, God is showing me . . . _____
_____
_____

I will respond by . . . _____
_____
_____

Fly right

READ
Psalm 119:97–105

MEDITATE
Psalm 119:105
Your word is a lamp to my feet and a light for my path.

REFLECT
➡ Am I being influenced more by friends, instructors, or the media than I am by God? How can I tell who influences me more?
➡ How can I make sure God has the strongest influence on me?
➡ What do I learn from Psalm 119:9–10?

CONSIDER
God's Word never sends you in the wrong direction.

For passengers continuing on to Grand Rapids, Michigan, your departure gate will be B-18."

I wrote it down. I had just spent a week talking with college students about life, and I was eager to get home. I didn't want to miss my connecting flight. I missed one once and spent seven hours walking around the airport. Boring.

After landing in Chicago I rushed off the plane and headed for B-18. It was quite a distance, but I had about a half hour to get there, so I wasn't worried. But then Murphy's Law kicked in (I'd like to kick him!) and when I got to B-18, the billboard read COLUMBUS.

Columbus? Wait a minute, what happened? I followed instructions and look where it . . . the screen! I didn't read the Departures screen. That's the official word. As it turned out, I needed to be at G-1. And

wouldn't you know, it was on the other side of the airport. Ten minutes before boarding. I became a blur, and . . . I made it!

As I sat on the plane (headed to Grand Rapids, not Columbus), I thought about the importance of getting the official word when it comes to staying on course spiritually. A lot of people who claim to know about life are eager to give us instructions. But if we take their word for it we could end up a long way from where we should be. We need to make sure we get the official word on life. And we get it by reading the Word of God.

"All Scripture is God-breathed and is useful for teaching . . . and training in righteousness, so that the man of God may be thoroughly equipped for every good work" (2 Timothy 3:16). So get the official word, and you'll fly right.

—D.P.

Through preaching, teaching, and the Bible, God is telling me . . . _____
_____
_____

Through nature and the lives of other believers, God is showing me . . . _____
_____
_____

I will respond by . . . _____
_____
_____

Too much money

READ
1 Timothy 6:6–19

MEDITATE
1 Timothy 6:10
For the love of money is a root of all kinds of evil.

REFLECT
➡ Why is greed such a strong emotion? Why are the qualities listed in 1 Timothy 6:11 more valuable than material goods?
➡ What is my philosophy of money? How does it relate to my happiness and future goals.

CONSIDER
Money is not just something you make; it's something that makes you.

Believe it or not, there once was a church with too much money. The congregation had bought some property for expansion but soon learned that they had purchased more than just land. The property sat on top of a rich oil reserve!

At first, the windfall seemed to be the answer to their prayers. When the profits came in, the members paid off some debts and remodeled the church. So far so good. But the oil and the money kept flowing. It came in so fast that the members decided to divide the profits among themselves. (Imagine passing the plate so people could take money out!)

As you might guess, the church suddenly became a popular place. But wait! Was it fair for all these "new people" to get a piece of the action? Something had to be done. So the church voted not to take in any more members!

The love of money made them lose sight of their mission.

Would we handle money any better than the people of Gusher Community Church? We like to think we would, but we really don't know how wealth might change us. Paul knew that the love of money could do weird things to us, so he called it "a root of all kinds of evil." It can make us lose sight of goals like loving others, trusting God, and serving Christ.

Does this mean we have to stay poor to be good Christians? Of course not. But it does mean this: If you strike it rich financially yet strike out spiritually, you're nothing but a rich loser.

—D.B.

Through preaching, teaching, and the Bible, God is telling me . . . _____

_____

Through nature and the lives of other believers, God is showing me . . . _____

_____

I will respond by . . . _____

_____

How to get all A's

OC **21** **BER**

READ
**1 Corinthians
3:1–15**

MEDITATE
1 Corinthians 3:13
Fire will test the quality of each man's work.

REFLECT
➡ If I were to receive a progress report on my development as a Christian, what grades would I get?

➡ The disciples spent time learning from Jesus Christ and then applied to their lives what they had learned. What can I learn from their example?

CONSIDER
You can't cram for God's final exam.

How were your grades last semester? I assume you passed everything—but did you get good grades? Want some suggestions for how to do better? Okay. Three things. Study. Study. Study.

No need to thank me. The advice is free.

All right, so you knew that already. But have you put it into practice?

This is important not only in school, you know, but also in your Christian life. One good thing about "spiritual life study" is that there's only one textbook: The Bible. But wow, are there ever a lot of assignments!

Along the way there'll be pop quizzes and major tests. And when we stand before Christ, it's that crucial final exam. We'll find out how well we did. Our "work will be shown for what it is, because the Day will bring it to light. It will be revealed with fire, and the fire will test the quality of each man's work" (1 Corinthians 3:13). And with God Himself looking over your heavenly transcripts, you'll want to get more than just passing grades.

Give this "All A's" study plan a try. You need to be:

Active in the Word and in prayer.

Applying the principles of the Bible to your everyday life.

Accountable to another Christian who can test your progress.

If you work hard now, someday you can look into His face, see Him smile, and hear Him say, "Well done."

—D.P.

Through preaching, teaching, and the Bible, God is telling me . . . _____

_____

_____

Through nature and the lives of other believers, God is showing me . . . _____

_____

_____

I will respond by . . . _____

_____

_____

Best part of waking up

READ
Psalm 3

MEDITATE
Psalm 143:8
Let the morning bring me word of your unfailing love.

REFLECT
➡ How much of yesterday did I live without giving thought to God?
➡ What problem in my life is keeping me from having a positive outlook? What evidence do I have that I am trusting God to help me handle it?
➡ What guidelines for living do I find in Psalm 37:1–11?

CONSIDER
It's not just a new day. It's a new opportunity.

The alarm goes off. You silence its irritating beep, beep, beep with a palm slam. You force yourself into an upright position, try to remember what day it is, and attempt to get to the bathroom without causing yourself serious bodily harm. Another day is underway.

After showering and dressing, you flick on the tube to catch the morning news. In the background you hear, "The best part of waking up is . . ." Immediately you mumble, "There is no best part of waking up!"

Sound familiar? Maybe the problem is your routine. Something's missing. No, it's not that first cup of coffee and your bowl of Cheerios. It's something far more satisfying. Let's allow the psalmist to tell us about it.

David was facing a day that looked downright bleak (Psalm 3). We know this is true because he began it by saying, "O Lord, how many are my foes! How many rise up against me!" A less than pleasant situation to wake up to, wouldn't you say? And yet David did have reason for a positive outlook. He had discovered the best part of waking up. He wrote, "In the morning, O Lord, you hear my voice; in the morning I lay my requests before you and wait in expectation" (Psalm 5:3).

The secret to David's morning routine was prayer for guidance. It was also a prayer of trust—a prayer of expectation. David knew that God would be there for him. And that gave him a positive outlook.

So why not include David's secret in your morning routine? Along with coffee and cereal, include a time with God. You'll discover that talking to Him is the best part of waking up.

—D.P.

Through preaching, teaching, and the Bible, God is telling me . . . _____
_____
_____

Through nature and the lives of other believers, God is showing me . . . _____
_____
_____

I will respond by . . . _____

Ya gotta have

WHAT DO YOU MEAN YOU'RE HAVING AN IDENTITY
CRISIS? JUST WHO DO YOU
THINK YOU ARE?

A SOUND MIND

Basic physics

READ
Proverbs 22:1–8

MEDITATE
Proverbs 22:8
He who sows wickedness reaps trouble.

REFLECT
➡ How does the sowing and reaping principle apply in my life?
➡ What have my friends or classmates sowed and reaped?
➡ How have I reaped what I have sown? Both good and bad.

CONSIDER
What you do will always come due.

A basic law of physics says that every action has an equal and opposite reaction. Apparently a sixteen-year-old honor student in Florida didn't think the law applied to stabbing physics teachers.

According to a news report, the student had straight A's. When it came to physics, however, he must have been less than perfect, because he didn't like a grade he received. During an argument about it, he pulled out a large kitchen knife and stabbed his teacher in the neck. The student faces charges of attempted murder.

It doesn't make much sense, does it? Obviously he didn't think things through very well. For whatever reason, an A became more important to him than life itself. His brain must have been shortcircuited by rage. He didn't consider the consequences—or better options.

Proverbs offers words of wisdom that relate to the basic law that this young student forgot—that we reap what we sow (22:8). Solomon said that we either get out of the way of trouble or we suffer (v. 3). He reminded us that sex outside of marriage is asking for trouble (v. 14). He explained that when we oppress others we endanger ourselves (vv. 16, 22–23). And he warned that a hot temper will boomerang (vv. 24–25). The principle of sowing and reaping also has its positive side. For example, God cares for those who care about Him (v. 4). Generosity toward others reaps generosity toward ourselves (v. 9). And integrity, kindness, and skilled work are rewarded (vv. 11, 29).

So next time you're tempted to get even, remember a basic law of God's universe: Every action has a corresponding reaction. —K.D.

Through preaching, teaching, and the Bible, God is telling me . . . _____

Through nature and the lives of other believers, God is showing me . . . _____

I will respond by . . . _____

It's okay to doubt

READ
Luke 7:18–28

MEDITATE
Luke 7:28
"There is no one greater than John."

REFLECT
➡ What is the wisest way for me to handle my doubts?
➡ How can doubt help me to believe more strongly?

CONSIDER
Doubt is good when it insists on truth.

Madeline L'Engle, a popular religious author, was asked, "Do you totally believe in God, without any doubts at all?" She responded, "No, I totally believe in God, with all kinds of doubts!"

You may think doubts are wrong; that they are an indication of weak faith. But God knows they are a necessary contributor to your Christian maturity. Far from indicating weak faith, doubt can demonstrate a commitment to find the truth and hold on to it.

John the Baptist struggled with doubts. He had baptized Jesus and had seen the heavens open and had heard God speak, identifying Jesus as His beloved Son. But now, in prison, John felt abandoned. Burdened by doubts, he sent friends to ask Jesus, "Are you the one who was to come, or should we expect someone else?"

The Lord Jesus did not cut John down for doubting. Rather, He identified John as the greatest man born of women (v. 28).

Dietrich Bonhoeffer said, "To believe greatly, you must doubt greatly."

Doubt will keep you from falling for any cult or false religion that pops up. And it will help you cling more strongly to the truth! —J.C.

Through preaching, teaching, and the Bible, God is telling me . . . _____

Through nature and the lives of other believers, God is showing me . . . _____

I will respond by . . . _____

A plan for winners

MEDITATE
2 Corinthians 1:9
We [should] not rely on ourselves but on God.

REFLECT
➡ What causes me to question God's goodness?
➡ How does Christ's suffering on the cross help me to believe that God cares about my pain?

CONSIDER
Our pain can be for our gain.

A well-known and out-spoken media giant has publicly denounced Christianity as "a religion for losers." He hasn't always felt that way. As a young man he had Bible training, including a few years in a Christian prep school. Joking about his background, Ted Turner said, "I think I was saved seven or eight times." But then a painful situation changed his outlook. His sister became very ill, and he prayed for her healing. But after five years of suffering she died. He became disillusioned with God. He said, "I began to lose my faith, and the more I lost it the better I felt."

While still a teenager, Joni Eareckson Tada was paralyzed in a diving accident. In *Where Is God When It Hurts?* Philip Yancey described how Joni's attitude turned from bitterness to trust.

"A turning point came the evening that a close friend, Cindy, told her, 'Joni, you aren't the only one. Jesus knows how you feel—why He was paralyzed too.' Cindy described how Jesus was fastened to the cross, paralyzed by the nails. . . . The realization was profoundly comforting."

Yancey then writes, "Joni now calls her accident a 'glorious intruder,' and claims it was the best thing that ever happened to her. God used it to get her attention and direct her thoughts toward Him."

Have you had a tragedy interrupt your life? Are you questioning why? Are you angry with God?

Remember, problems can be God's way of encouraging us to trust Him. As we do, we'll be less interested in the why of our pain, and more interested in finding in God the strength and comfort we need to carry on.

That sounds to me like a plan for winners!　　—K.D.

Through preaching, teaching, and the Bible, God is telling me . . . _____

_____

_____

Through nature and the lives of other believers, God is showing me . . . _____

_____

_____

I will respond by . . . _____

_____

_____

Madonna speaks

READ
Philippians 3:17–21

MEDITATE
1 Corinthians 11:1
Follow my example, as
I follow the example
of Christ.

REFLECT
➡ What media per-
sonalities are get-
ting all the atten-
tion right now?
➡ Are they good
examples for me to
follow? Why?
➡ Who are some
Christians I could
benefit from by
being with them
and listening to
them?

CONSIDER
*Who we follow
affects who we
become.*

Madonna is no Sunday school teacher. She gains fame by exploiting the decadence of our culture. Because of that, she's not the kind of person you'd expect to find quoted in a Christian devotional book. But in an MTV interview, she made an observation that deserves our attention. She said, "The actors and singers and entertainers I know are emotional cripples. Really healthy people aren't in this business, let's face it."

That's quite a statement. Especially when you think of the people who practically worship today's media stars. Millions of dollars are offered by adoring fans to the gods of the entertainment industry; yet in the opinion of an insider, the gods must be crazy.

We need to think about the kind of people we admire. Who do you look to as an example of what you want to be like? Whose behavior influences the way you act? Is it your favorite musician or group? A superstar athlete? A big-screen hunk or hunkette? An instructor who really knows his or her subject? A person on campus who always seems to get everybody's attention?

Did you ever consider following the apostle Paul? He encouraged his readers to do just that, and he wasn't an egomaniac, nor was he getting royalties from selling books or videos. Paul wanted people to follow him because he wanted them to follow the example of Christ. He challenged them to examine his life and teaching carefully and follow what was consistent with his profession of faith and devotion to the Lord.

Who do you want to be like? The emotional cripples Madonna was talking about? Or someone like Paul, who patterned his life after the Lord Jesus? —K.D.

Through preaching, teaching, and the Bible, God is telling me . . . _____

_____

_____

Through nature and the lives of other believers, God is showing me . . . _____

_____

_____

I will respond by . . . _____

_____

_____

Get the wrinkles out!

OCTOBER 27

READ
James 1:1–8

MEDITATE
James 1:3
The testing of your faith develops perseverance.

REFLECT
→ What is happening to me when I endure the testing of my faith (James 1:4)?
→ What wrinkles in my life is God working to get rid of right now?
→ What should I be working on?
→ How do I respond when the heat and pressure come on? Do I complain? Or learn?

CONSIDER
God loves us too much to leave us the way we are.

You've got a big date. A real date—not jeans, T-shirt, and pizza, but something fancy.

So you go to the closet and grab your favorite outfit. You hold it up for inspection and what do you see? Wrinkles! They may be the result of an overcrowded closet, carelessness, or outright negligence. But they've got to go. You plug in the steam iron and apply a little heat and pressure. Soon the wrinkles are gone, and you're ready for a big night out.

In a sense, we are like that outfit. We get "wrinkles" in our Christian lives. They may result from over-scheduling ourselves, careless thinking, or neglecting time with God. We know they've got to go, but where do we find a spiritual steam iron?

No one likes trouble. We grumble when we have to go through tough times. We hate it when we lose a good job or get terminal writer's block while working on a term paper or have difficulty with a boyfriend or girlfriend or have to pay the consequences of some foolish choices we've made.

But guess what. Trials are God's steam irons. He uses them to get the wrinkles out of our lives. A little (or a lot) of heat and pressure applied at the right time in the right place makes us presentable for our date with Jesus in eternity.

God knows all about the wrinkles in our thinking and the creases in our character. And He loves us too much to leave us all wadded up on the floor.

When trouble comes, remember: God is getting the wrinkles out. —D.E.

Through preaching, teaching, and the Bible, God is telling me . . . _____

_____

Through nature and the lives of other believers, God is showing me . . . _____

_____

I will respond by . . . _____

_____

How will you get out?

READ
Ephesians 2:1–10

MEDITATE
Ephesians 2:6
God raised us up with Christ and sealed us with him in the heavenly realms.

REFLECT
→ What provisions have I made for my life?
→ Have I thought as much about how I will spend eternity?
→ What kind of death does Paul tell us about in Ephesians 2:1–10?
→ What does it mean to me that I have been made alive in Christ?

CONSIDER
The time to prepare for tomorrow is today.

Alaska. America's final frontier. The natural beauty and mysterious, unexplored tundra of the forty-ninth state drew one young man in the early 1980s who was looking for the adventure of a lifetime.

Equipped with 500 rolls of film to capture the majesty of Alaska, several firearms to protect himself, and 1,400 pounds of provisions to sustain him, the explorer was more than adequately prepared for his stay in the Alaskan wilderness. In the spring of 1981, he was flown into a remote area where he set up camp.

At first, he wrote excitedly about the wonder and fascination of observing the wildlife and the breathtaking marvels of creation. But after a while, the diary entries began to take on a pathetic tone. He began to realize that his preparation for life in Alaska was flawed. In August he wrote, "I think I should have used more foresight about arranging my departure. I'll soon find out."

He waited, but no one came. In November the entries in his diary stopped. He froze to death in a nameless valley, beside a nameless lake, 225 miles northeast of Fairbanks. An investigation revealed that he was more than prepared for his time in Alaska, but he had not made plans to be flown out.

Like this explorer, millions of people are failing to plan ahead. They are so busy stocking up on provisions for this life that they forget they won't be here forever.

If we want to get out of this life successfully, we must use God's plan. We must receive Jesus as Savior. When we do, we can be confident that when it is time for us to go God will usher us into heaven. Have you made plans to get out?   —D.B.

Through preaching, teaching, and the Bible, God is telling me . . . _____

_____

_____

Through nature and the lives of other believers, God is showing me . . . _____

_____

_____

I will respond by . . . _____

_____

_____

The only one standing

READ
Daniel 3

MEDITATE
Daniel 3:7

As soon as they heard the sound . . . , all the peoples . . . fell down and worshiped.

REFLECT

➡ What insights into my own allegiance to God do I get from Daniel 3?

➡ What are some key issues about which I am being called to take a stand for the Lord?

CONSIDER
When you stand up for your beliefs, you never stand alone.

I'm visiting this big church in LA. I'm excited to be there. The songleader announces the hymn. I find the page and jump up, ready to sing. The rest of the congregation remains seated. Huge embarrassment!

I'm sure you can relate. It's pretty uncomfortable being the one who is different. But as Christians, we have to get used to it. It happens all the time.

Look at Shadrach, Meshach, and Abednego. They bucked the system when it could have cost them their lives. Nebuchadnezzar made a ninety-foot statue and put it in the middle of town. Then he decreed that everyone was to bow down and worship it when the music sounded. The smelting furnace awaited any who refused.

Test run. The image gleams in the afternoon sun. The music sounds. There's a rustle as everyone bows down to the statue.

Everyone, that is, except three kids from Israel. Sure, there's fear in their eyes, but they don't bow. They're the only ones standing because they have resolved not to break the second commandment of Jehovah.

You know the story. The king is livid. He has his men fire up the furnace, and they toss the boys in. The king looks into the fire and there they are, still standing. But there's Someone else in there. God is with them. The king is so impressed that he begins to worship Jehovah.

There are times when you'll be the only one standing. When everyone goes to see an immoral movie. When they all make fun of some helpless person. When they laugh at God.

When everyone else is bowing to the will of Satan, you might feel as if you're standing alone. But you're not. Just remember the teenage Israelites.   —D.E.

Through preaching, teaching, and the Bible, God is telling me . . . _____
_____
_____

Through nature and the lives of other believers, God is showing me . . . _____
_____
_____

I will respond by . . . _____
_____

Loose lips

READ
Proverbs 11:9–13

MEDITATE
Proverbs 11:13
A gossip betrays a confidence.

REFLECT

➡ "The words of a gossip are like choice morsels; they go down to a man's inmost parts" (Proverbs 18:8). What does this verse mean to me?

➡ "Without wood a fire goes out; without gossip a quarrel dies down" (Proverbs 26:20). Am I a fire starter or a fire fighter?

CONSIDER
Loose lips sink ships—friendships.

LOOSE LIPS SINK SHIPS. This saying came along long before I did. It was used during World War II to remind sailors that when they talked too much in port about where their ships were headed, they could be overheard by enemy spies. Their ships would then be torpedoed.

But these words don't have to be reserved for war warnings. They are universally true. Few things are more destructive than an out-of-control mouth.

With loose lips a reputation can be destroyed. A heart can be broken. A confidence can be violated. All it takes is a well-placed rumor or a spilled secret.

As a young adult, you're not alone in your struggle to try to figure out what life is all about. You've got lots of friends in the same boat. At times you feel confused and vulnerable, and you confide in one another, seeking help

and protection. You need to be able to trust your friends. And they need to know that they can trust you.

How we use our tongues tells a lot about our character. What we say leaves a lasting impression on others. If people can trust you, it's because you've gained the reputation of being wise and discreet in what you say. That's what Solomon made so clear when he said, "The lips of the righteous know what is fitting" (Proverbs 10:32).

So when your roommate tells you something that is no one else's business, keep it to yourself. And don't spread rumors and dish out ugly gossip. You wouldn't want to be the kind of person the author of Proverbs had in mind when he said, "A perverse man stirs up dissension, and a gossip separates close friends" (16:28).

Don't let loose lips sink you.   —D.P.

Through preaching, teaching, and the Bible, God is telling me . . . _____

_____

Through nature and the lives of other believers, God is showing me . . . _____

_____

_____

I will respond by . . . _____

_____

_____

Deep-cleaning

READ
Leviticus 5:1–13

MEDITATE
Leviticus 19:2
"Be holy because I, the Lord your God, am holy."

REFLECT
➡ When was the last time I read Leviticus? How can I avoid getting bogged down in the little details?

➡ What kinds of things can make me unclean?

➡ How can I get clean? (See Acts 16:30–31.)

➡ How can I stay clean? (See 1 John 1:9.)

CONSIDER
Only Christ's blood removes all stains.

Have you read Leviticus lately? It wouldn't make a very good TV mini-series. Chapter after chapter contains tiny details about such things as skin diseases, forbidden sex, mildew treatment, bodily discharges, diet, bloody sacrifices, and elaborate cleansing rituals. Unless you have a tough stomach, you don't want to be eating while you're reading.

What's the point? I've wondered. Why all the blood and the extreme concern about cleanliness? Does somebody have some kind of obsession here? Then I came across Leviticus 11:44, where God said, "I am the Lord your God; consecrate yourselves and be holy, because I am holy."

Suddenly a light went on in my head (and I was beginning to think the bulb had burned out). I realized that the rituals were object lessons that point to God's holiness and our need to be holy.

But what does it mean to be holy? Theologians tell us it means to be different, to be set apart. God, in His awesome glory and majesty, is far different from us. Also, it means to be separate from sin—to be morally pure.

So now when I read Leviticus I think about how holy God is and how awful sin must seem to Him. The cleansings, the sacrifices—they call attention to His desire for us to be holy in action and attitude.

As we read Matthew, Mark, Luke, and John, we see the same emphasis. But Jesus' death and resurrection provide a once-for-all, deep-cleaning solution. Because of His sacrifice, we don't have to keep all those Leviticus laws.

How do you look to God?
—K.D.

Through preaching, teaching, and the Bible, God is telling me . . . _____
_____
_____

Through nature and the lives of other believers, God is showing me . . . _____
_____
_____

I will respond by . . . _____
_____
_____

Olivia's story, and mine

READ
Titus 3:1–8

MEDITATE
Ephesians 4:32
Be kind and compassionate to one another.

REFLECT
➡ To what extent am I un-Christlike in the way I treat people who don't look or dress or smell like me?
➡ What if I'm unpopular, rejected? What can I do to counteract the hurt?

CONSIDER
Be kind to those who are not your kind.

Olivia has been with me most of my life. That may not seem like a big problem, but it was for me. Olivia was, let's just say, unattractive. And slow. But here's the worse part: Olivia liked me. It started at summer camp in junior high. She told everyone that she wanted me to take her to the banquet on Friday night. "Dream on," I told her. Being neither unattractive nor slow (in my own eighth-grade opinion), I couldn't imagine anything worse than taking Olivia anywhere.

Then in high school she started coming to my church. Spare me! Now I had to face her every week. I handled the problem by ignoring her completely. I thought she would get the hint. But it got worse.

I attended a small Christian college. Olivia chose the same one. The school had a lot of rules, so I thought maybe it didn't allow girls to be unattractive or slow. I was wrong. Even in college Olivia wouldn't leave me alone. But by now I was a perfect gentleman. I even began to speak to her—politely—hoping no one would see us together.

Finally Olivia got married (to someone else, thankfully)—and I finally grew up. I started to wonder what I had been doing by rejecting her. I did the damage, but Olivia had to pick up the pieces.

Paul's advice about how to treat others didn't mean much to me when I was growing up and putting Olivia down (Titus 3:2). I was kind to those I thought deserved it. But it's not too late—for me nor for Olivia. Although I can't repair the past, I can ask for forgiveness and begin to treat her and others with the kindness and compassion that would please God—regardless of their I.Q. or appearance. —T.B.

Through preaching, teaching, and the Bible, God is telling me . . . _____
_____

Through nature and the lives of other believers, God is showing me . . . _____
_____

I will respond by . . . _____
_____
_____

Singing a different tune

READ
Titus 1:10–16

MEDITATE
Titus 1:16
They claim to know God, but by their actions they deny him.

REFLECT
➡ What is my philosophy of music? What do I expect to gain by listening to it?

➡ After listening to my favorite music for an hour, what has it done for me? Is my response pleasing to the Lord?

CONSIDER
It's not good enough to refer to God; we must defer to Him.

If Madonna sings one of her immoral songs in a church, does that make her religious? If Prince wears a cross, does that make him a Christian? Or if M.C. Hammer sings about prayer, does that mean we can overlook his lack of discretion in rapping about sex?

Mixed signals are confusing. It's easier to know what to do when musicians are blatantly anti-religion and anti-goodness. The trouble creeps in when a singer seems to accept some of the things we consider important: the cross, prayer, even the Lord. Those references attract some believers because they want so much for the artists to share their beliefs. Then, clinging to the "religious" aspects of the singer's repertoire, they soon find themselves justifying the immoral aspects.

If you find yourself thinking that way, be careful. The apostle Paul warned Titus about some people who were surprisingly similar to rock musicians who sing out of both sides of their mouths. Speaking of some "religious" people whose ideas were way off base, Paul said they were "ruining whole households by teaching things they ought not to teach—and that for the sake of dishonest gain" (Titus 1:11). They stood against God's standards—in the name of religion.

Notice something else. "They claim to know God, but by their actions they deny him" (v. 16). Apply that test to musicians you listen to. Are their views of sexuality biblical and godly? (Hebrews 13:4). Are their lifestyles free of materialism? (Hebrews 13:5). Is their language pure? (James 3:10).

Test the stars. Don't be fooled by musicians who sound religious but are singing a different tune.

—D.B.

Through preaching, teaching, and the Bible, God is telling me . . . _____
_____
_____

Through nature and the lives of other believers, God is showing me . . . _____
_____
_____

I will respond by . . . _____
_____
_____

MEDITATE
1 Corinthians 6:18
He who sins sexually sins against his own body.

REFLECT
→ Is anything or anyone pressuring me into sexual activity I think may be wrong?
→ What should I do to get rid of that influence?

CONSIDER
With God's help, you can control your "wait" problem.

My four-year-old son has more than 3,000 baseball cards. He doesn't look at them or touch them. He's never even seen most of them. They just sit there in his closet, accumulating. It's a little investment I'm making for him. Each year I buy him a complete set on his birthday. He opens the package, says thank you, and hands them over so we can store them away.

It's not easy to wait for long-range rewards when you're four years old. Stevie would much rather tear into those boxes of cards, fling them all over his room, draw on them, and wreak preschool havoc on them. But that would destroy the investment. If the cards are to be worth anything to him when he's fourteen, he has to protect them now.

Your body is an investment a lot more important than Stevie's baseball cards, but some young people treat it more lightly. God knows the rewards that will be yours if you refuse to use your body to fulfill sexual desires before marriage. But you keep thinking of all the fun everybody else seems to be having with sex. TV tells you about it. The movies are full of it. Some of your friends talk about it. The opportunity seems too good to pass up.

Yet the best thing is to be patient—to look at your sexuality as an investment that will be ruined if you cash it in early. Paul told the people that marriage is the accepted way to avoid sexual immorality (1 Corinthians 7). That's still true today.

You may think you'll die if you have to wait until you're married.

Let me assure you—you won't. These days, death is more likely if you don't wait. Trust God's guidelines. Don't wreck a perfectly good investment. —D.B.

Through preaching, teaching, and the Bible, God is telling me . . . _____

_____

Through nature and the lives of other believers, God is showing me . . . _____

_____

I will respond by . . . _____

_____

The pain of divorce

READ
Mark 10:2–12

MEDITATE
Mark 10:9
"What God has joined together, let man not separate."

REFLECT

➡ God compares marriage with His relationship to the church (Ephesians 5:22–33). How then does God view the marriage commitment?

➡ How does being faithful to God help me be faithful to my future husband/wife?

CONSIDER
Not only for better or for worse—but for "good."

The campfire circle was silent, except for the occasional sound of a teenager softly sobbing. During the evening share time, the subject had somehow gotten around to divorce. The pain was evident as young person after young person told about divorce in his or her family—a father's rejection, physical and emotional abuse, loneliness.

As we sat there in silence, our youth pastor spoke quietly: "Remember this night twenty years from now," he told us, "if you are considering divorce. Remember the pain it causes."

I still remember.

The statistics indicate that many are not aware of the pain. With half of all marriages ending in divorce, couples aren't thinking about the trouble it can cause; they're thinking only about getting out, and getting out quick!

But God does not take the commitment of marriage lightly. In Jesus Christ's day, men could divorce their wives for the smallest reason. But Jesus wanted to put an end to that—to remind His listeners of how God sought righteousness and purity in every area of life.

This is not to condemn families who have suffered through a divorce. Jesus came to bring forgiveness, not condemnation. And there are scriptural reasons for divorce—like unfaithfulness and desertion.

But as you contemplate your future mate, make a commitment at the same time. Promise yourself that you will do everything in your power to make your marriage work. Let the lingering memory of divorce's pain—whether you've experienced it or witnessed it—keep you from making the same mistake. —J.C

Through preaching, teaching, and the Bible, God is telling me . . . _____

_____

_____

Through nature and the lives of other believers, God is showing me . . . _____

_____

_____

I will respond by . . . _____

_____

Ya gotta have

That sinking feeling

READ
1 John 3:16–24

MEDITATE
1 John 3:21
If our hearts do not condemn us, we have confidence.

REFLECT
→ When was the last time I got "that sinking feeling?" Why?

→ How does my faith give me confidence before God?

CONSIDER
When God forgives, it's time for us to forget.

In a graduate-level class I was taking, the prof assigned a twenty-five-page paper. I had written sixteen pages, and when I double-spaced my bibliography it came out to twenty-three pages—close enough, I figured.

Then, as he collected the assignment, he mentioned that our papers were supposed to be twenty-five pages not including the bibliography. My heart sank. I was condemned by my own stupidity.

During a break, I went to the prof to confess my transgression and beg for a chance to make it right. He informed me that twenty-five pages was the upper limit; he just didn't want to have to read long papers. If sixteen pages was adequate to make my point, he could live with it. My heart rejoiced. I wouldn't have to suffer for my stupidity.

That feeling of relief was great, but it was nothing compared to the freedom my heart experienced when I accepted Jesus Christ. He freed me from the guilt of my sins so that I can't condemn myself. And when I sin, I can continue to experience freedom through confession and His forgiveness (1 John 1:9).

All of this gives believers confidence. We're not like Adam and Eve, who hid from God because they were so ashamed. We have the confidence to talk openly and boldly to God. Nothing is between us and Him to make us feel uncomfortable.

And when we appear before God at the final judgment, we won't have the sinking feeling that we missed the point of an important assignment. Instead, we'll have the freedom of heart that comes from doing it right. —J.C.

Through preaching, teaching, and the Bible, God is telling me . . . _____
_____
_____

Through nature and the lives of other believers, God is showing me . . . _____
_____
_____

I will respond by . . . _____
_____
_____

Burn off the clutter

READ
John 15:1–9

MEDITATE
John 15:2

"Every branch that does bear fruit he prunes so that it will be even more fruitful."

REFLECT

➡ How long since I've stepped back and taken a look at how I'm living? Is it time for honest self-analysis?

➡ Is it hard for me to admit I'm wrong? To be honest with myself? With God?

➡ What sins am I hiding?

CONSIDER
Don't let dead wood choke new growth.

Early one summer a bolt of lightning started a fire in King's Canyon National Park in California. A month later the fire was still burning. It had covered 3,000 acres of land, and no attempt had been made to put it out.

Why? The National Park Service has learned that low-intensity fires are essential to the successful maintenance of forest land. In the late 1800s, when the park service started putting out all forest fires immediately, our beautiful national forests began to clutter up. Dead trees and branches, thickets of shade trees, and underbrush became so thick that a small fire would quickly grow into a destructive holocaust.

Controlled, low-intensity burning keeps the forest clear of unhealthy debris. The result: fewer major fires, richer forest lands, and better prepared seedbeds.

Like a forest, our lives get cluttered with debris as well. We don't know how it happens, but it does. Nasty little habits and attitudes pile up and destroy our inner beauty. We snap at our friends. We turn things in late. We treat church like a duty rather than a privilege.

When this happens, we need to allow some low-intensity fires in our lives to purge our thoughts and attitudes. It will hurt some to burn the litter that has accumulated. Yet how much better to get rid of it before it becomes large enough to fule a raging inferno.

Allow the flames of confession and repentance to burn the clutter out of your life. It may not feel great now, but it will spare you a lot of anguish later.   —M.D.

Through preaching, teaching, and the Bible, God is telling me . . . _____
_____
_____

Through nature and the lives of other believers, God is showing me . . . _____
_____
_____

I will respond by . . . _____
_____
_____

Heart and pocket

READ
1 John 3:10–18

MEDITATE
1 John 3:18
Let us not love with words or tongue but with actions and in truth.

REFLECT
➡ If I received $1,000 unexpectedly, how much would I give away? What would I spend the rest on? Why?

➡ What does God have to say about my giving?

CONSIDER
When it comes to giving, some people stop at nothing.

Churches that are a little tight on cash might be tempted to try something called Tithe-o-Vision. Cameras are attached to the offering plates, and a large screen in front of the church reveals to the congregation how much each member gives.

If you measure with a ruler, the distance from the heart to the pocket is about eighteen inches (on my body at least). But where giving is concerned, the distance sometimes has to be measured in light-years!

Our natural response to God's love should be to give of ourselves—not only money but also time and talents. God loved us so much He gave His Son, but we seem a little reluctant to make sacrifices. What we do doesn't match what we say we believe.

Talk is cheap; actions are what demonstrate our love for God. If we have material possessions (a big if for a lot of us) yet don't help those around us, how can we say we love God?

A man raising money to help the homeless approached the richest man in town. Declining the request to give, the rich man said, "I really feel sorry for these people very deeply in my heart."

The fundraiser grumbled, "I wish you felt it in your pocket!"

You may not think you have much to give. (You have enough trouble finding quarters to do your laundry!) But chances are you have something—even if it is not financial—that will help someone else. Just cut down the distance between your words and your actions . . . and between your heart and your pocket!   —J.C.

Through preaching, teaching, and the Bible, God is telling me . . . _____

_____

Through nature and the lives of other believers, God is showing me . . . _____

_____

I will respond by . . . _____

_____

Dual workout plan

READ
1 Timothy 4:1–16

MEDITATE
1 Timothy 6:11
Pursue righteousness, godliness, faith, love, endurance and gentleness.

REFLECT
➡ Which sport do I enjoy the most? Why? How do the things I learn in that sport help in my Christian life?

CONSIDER
The best spiritual exercise is lifting your heart toward God.

Earlier this year, I took the plunge: I joined a health club.

Now, three days a week, I get together with fellow Southern Californians who are sitting at all sorts of machines and paying all sorts of money (don't ask how much) so we can sweat.

Aerobicising and lifting weights are fine, but Paul pointed Timothy toward a different kind of workout: spiritual training. Physical exercise yields many benefits, but none of them eternal. Spiritual workouts, on the other hand, promise everlasting benefits.

How do we get in shape spiritually? Here are three steps:

1. Read the Word of God (1 Timothy 4:13; 2 Timothy 2:15). There is no substitute for Bible study, both public and private. Some people who find it easy to exercise every day have a hard time getting up fifteen minutes early to spend time with God. The principle is the same: If you want to see results, you have to put in the work.

2. Set an example (1 Timothy 4:15). One difference with spiritual exercise is that you can't leave it in the gym. A spiritual workout results in changed behavior. People will see your progress.

3. Examine yourself (v. 16). The best athletes make sure their bodies stay in top condition. In the same way, Paul exhorted Timothy, "Watch your life and doctrine closely."

Are you looking forward to working out tomorrow? Don't stop with a "hard body." Set some time aside for a spiritual workout and firm up your faith.   —J.C.

Through preaching, teaching, and the Bible, God is telling me . . . _____
_____
_____

Through nature and the lives of other believers, God is showing me . . . _____
_____
_____

I will respond by . . . _____
_____
_____

Killin' time

READ
Mark 6:6–13, 30–32

MEDITATE
Mark 6:31
"Come with me by yourselves . . . and get some rest."

REFLECT
➠ Do I need to pull back a bit? Is my busyness taking away from my relationship with God?
➠ Do I recognize when enough is enough?
➠ What am I afraid of missing if I say no to some activity?

CONSIDER
Sometimes the best thing to do is nothing.

Did you ever pick out a rock and try to kick it all the way home? I did. Up one street and down the next. It would take a while, but that was the idea. Just killin' time. Relaxing. Takin' it easy.

Maybe your thing was skipping rocks across a pond. What did you work up to? Five? Six? Maybe seven skips?

Or maybe you liked to find a stick, open up your pocket knife, and see what you could whittle out of it. Whatever it took, we knew how to relax when we were kids. Today, though, relaxing seems to be a lost art. We're always busy. And when we're not, we feel guilty about it.

Think about your own schedule. Between studies, church activities, a part-time job, and your social life, you really don't have much time to just take it easy and recover, do you? Even when you do crawl your way to the weekend, you stay busy. And you hate it when you're not.

We live in a fast-paced, overactive society. We're like children who've eaten too much sugar. We get a little hyper. Can't slow down. Gotta burn it off.

You've heard the old saying, "If you don't come apart (get away), sooner or later you'll come apart." In other words, if you don't chill out, you'll stress out. Sure, the Bible teaches us that we should take full advantage of the time we have available to us (Ephesians 5:16). But it also reminds us of the importance of a little R & R. In fact, after a particularly hectic schedule, Jesus told His disciples that they needed to get away and relax for a while (Mark 6:31). That's good advice for you and me as well.

Think it's time to find a good rock?   —D.P.

Through preaching, teaching, and the Bible, God is telling me . . . _____

_____

_____

Through nature and the lives of other believers, God is showing me . . . _____

_____

_____

I will respond by . . . _____

_____

_____

Stinky socks

READ
Psalm 139

MEDITATE
Psalm 139:23
Search me, Oh God, and know my heart.

REFLECT
➡ What keeps me from dealing with the sin in my life?
➡ How can I remind myself of the truths of Psalm 139?
➡ What specific areas of my life do I need to clean up today?

CONSIDER
If God sees everything, why try to hide anything?

What's under your bed? Shoes? Rolls of dust? A banana peel? Coins? A dead animal? Bills? Yesterday's math assignment? Candy wrappers?

I had a roommate in college who used to throw his dirty socks (the partially decomposed kind) under his bed. One time the smell was so bad that I picked them up on the end of a long pencil, took them down the hall, and dumped them into a sink.

You've probably seen your Mom or Dad go nearly berserk after finding out what was under your bed. (Parents don't seem to appreciate the great storage space that is just crying to be filled under there.)

Unfortunately, what goes under the bed is forgotten in the head—at least until the smell gets too bad or you need to find that missing sock or shirt.

Many times we casually toss "under the bed" issues that need to be either "thrown away" or "put into the wash." Sins that we fail to deal with—bad attitudes, harmful habits, careless words—only clutter up our hearts. And even though we may keep things hidden from other people, God can see everything (Psalm 139).

So what's "under your bed"? A "minor" relationship problem? A "little" cheating? A "small" struggle with sexual desire? A "tiny" inability to deal with anger? Whatever the situation, don't "shove it under the bed." Take care of it.   —K.D.

Through preaching, teaching, and the Bible, God is telling me . . . _____

_____

_____

Through nature and the lives of other believers, God is showing me . . . _____

_____

_____

I will respond by . . . _____

_____

_____

Couch potato Christian

READ
Luke 10:25–37

MEDITATE
1 John 3:18
Let us not love with words or tongue but with actions.

REFLECT

➡ Do I have a "live and let live" philosophy? How does that keep me from helping those who really need it?

➡ Is someone close to me struggling and in need of my help?

➡ What am I going to do about it?

CONSIDER
A hurting friend needs a helping hand.

You know this guy. He's a spectator, not a doer. His main interest is entertainment. He is unaware of and unaffected by what goes on around him. He's Mr. Couch Potato.

You're probably not as physically inactive as he is. I mean, you do play tennis once in a while. But could you possibly be an emotional couch potato? Do you sit idly by, unaware of those around you who are struggling? Or do you show compassion by stepping in to help those who hurt?

A couple of years ago, my young son taught me the difference between the two. It was my wife's first day home after back surgery. Her discomfort was obvious, and we were all sympathetic. But my son took his sympathy a step further. While his mom was trying to rest, he came into the room and laid his teddy bear on the pillow beside her. Our normally rambunctious little boy showed a tender, compassionate heart. In leaving that well-worn but well-loved stuffed bear with his mother, my son was giving what was closest to his heart—and teaching me that we give most and best when we give of ourselves.

Jesus taught us about true compassion in His story of the Good Samaritan (Luke 10). Although a number of people saw the helpless man who had been beaten and robbed, only one person helped. He went beyond awareness. He demonstrated compassion by doing something to help.

Is one of your good friends hurting? Is your brother or sister in the pits? Mom or Dad having a rough time? Then do the loving thing with the help of God. Reach out to them now—while they need you. —D.P.

Through preaching, teaching, and the Bible, God is telling me . . . _____
_____
_____

Through nature and the lives of other believers, God is showing me . . . _____
_____
_____

I will respond by . . . _____
_____
_____

Cross communication

READ
1 Corinthians 2:1–5

MEDITATE
1 Corinthians 2:2
I resolved to know nothing . . . except Jesus Christ and him crucified.

REFLECT
➡ What does the cross mean to me?
➡ Am I ashamed of the cross? Or proud of it? How does that affect the way I talk to my friends?

CONSIDER
The cross sends a clear signal of love.

They're something we have taken for granted for years. In fact, most of us don't know of a time when they weren't all over the place. What are they?

Telephone poles.

In developing countries telephone poles have become important symbols of a new way of life. By supporting lines of communication, the poles allow people to "reach out and touch" other people in just about every place on the globe. Those same telephone poles also carry power lines to remote areas. People who have always done everything by hand can now use electric motors to run appliances and make their lives easier.

Think about those poles a minute. What do they look like? They consist of one high, straight pole and a crossbar. That's right; they look like a cross.

The old rugged cross of Christ symbolizes a new way of life a lot more important than the way of life represented by telephone poles. Think of the "lines" of communication and power the cross carries!

Because of that cross, heaven listens to the prayers of any believer here on earth, including you and me. And because Jesus shed His blood on that cross for lost humanity, godly men and women have a deep desire to "reach out and touch" others with the life-changing power of the Gospel.

For the apostle Paul, the cross was everything. It was the heart of his missionary communication and the basis of his spiritual power.

The next time you see a telephone pole, think of the cross. It was the means of Christ's sacrifice and it conveys the message of His power. As it did to Paul, that should mean everything to us! —M.D.

Through preaching, teaching, and the Bible, God is telling me . . . _____

_____

_____

Through nature and the lives of other believers, God is showing me . . . _____

_____

_____

I will respond by . . . _____

_____

_____

Ya gotta have

Unlikely Christian

READ
1 Samuel 17:20–50

MEDITATE
1 Samuel 17:47
"It is not by sword or spear . . . for the battle is the Lord's."

REFLECT
→ When have I felt small? What kinds of "Goliaths" have I faced at school, at home, on the job?
→ What happens when I focus too much on my own abilities or my inabilities?

CONSIDER
Undedicated talents are unused talents.

Dwight never earned a college degree—not even a high school diploma. In fact, he probably never got more than a sixth-grade education. He grew up in a family of nine children; his dad died when he was four; the family struggled financially; and he had little or no religious training. He left home at age seventeen and got a job at a shoe store in Boston. One day Dwight decided to go to church. When the Sunday school teacher asked the students to find the gospel of John, Dwight started looking in Genesis.

His teacher eventually led him to faith in Christ, and Dwight asked to become a member of the church. But the membership committee postponed his application for a year. Someone on that committee later mentioned that he had seldom seen a young person who knew so little about the Bible and who seemed so unlikely to be used by God.

That unlikely person was Dwight (D.L.) Moody, who became the most influential evangelist of his era. In Great Britain and America he spoke to millions of people about Christ. In the U.S. he founded several schools (including Moody Bible Institute).

How could someone with such a poor start in life do so well? According to Stanley Gundry, "In 1867 Moody heard Henry Varley say, 'The world has yet to see what God can do with and through and in and by the man who is fully and wholly consecrated to Him.' Moody determined to be that man."

The Lord can do great things through those who rely on Him. Natural talents and formal education are great, but they mean nothing unless we are dedicated to serving God. What can God do with, through, in, and by you?　　—K.D.

Through preaching, teaching, and the Bible, God is telling me . . . _____

Through nature and the lives of other believers, God is showing me . . . _____

I will respond by . . . _____

14

Against the wall

READ
Nehemiah 4:1–9

MEDITATE
Deuteronomy 3:22
The Lord your God himself will fight for you.

REFLECT

➡ Is "trust God" my first thought when I face problems or an afterthought? What can I learn from Nehemiah's experience that will help me think differently?

➡ How can I use prayer as a way to start giving God my problems every day?

CONSIDER
God can turn problems into praises.

Incredible things can happen to us when we give God our problems.

Just ask Nehemiah. Talk about being against the wall! He's the guy who headed up the project of rebuilding the walls of Jerusalem. And as is normally the case when you're trying to do something for God, there was plenty of opposition. Introducing . . . (minor key, please) Sanballat, his sidekick Tobia, and their posse, the Arabians, the Ammonites, and the Ashdodites. "They all plotted together to come and fight against Jerusalem and stir up trouble against it" (Nehemiah 4:7–8). To make matters worse for Nehemiah, the enemies seemed to be in the best position. They had Jerusalem surrounded on all sides.

But like I said, incredible things can happen when we give our problems to God. And that's exactly what Nehemiah did. Instead of trying to handle things on his own, he "prayed to our God" (Nehemiah 4:9). As he did so, Nehemiah's problem became God's problem.

So what happened? I thought you'd never ask. Let's fast-forward in the book of Nehemiah to find out. "When our enemies heard that we were aware of their plot and that God had frustrated it, we all returned to the wall" (Nehemiah 4:15). "So the wall was completed. . . . They realized that this work had been done with the help of our God" (Nehemiah 6:15–16).

Are you against the wall right now? Pressure from friends? Some private battle? An argument with Mom or Dad? How are you handling it? Have you given it to God, or are you struggling with it on your own? Take a lesson from Nehemiah. Give that problem to God. And watch incredible things start to happen.   —D.P.

Through preaching, teaching, and the Bible, God is telling me . . . _____

_____

_____

Through nature and the lives of other believers, God is showing me . . . _____

_____

_____

I will respond by . . . _____

_____

_____

A radical prayer

READ
John 14:1–14

MEDITATE
John 14:13
"I will do whatever you ask in my name."

REFLECT

→ Why is it easier to pray for material possessions than for spiritual riches?

→ What spiritual riches am I asking for in Jesus' name these days?

→ What material things?

CONSIDER
What's good for Jesus' name is good for you.

Some folks have tried to make Jesus into a kind of magic genie. Instead of rubbing a lamp, they quote John 14:13 and expect to have their wishes granted.

Is it really so simple? Look a little closer. Jesus said if we ask for anything in His name He would do it. That bothersome phrase "in my name" throws a wrench into the works.

To do something in Jesus' name means to do it as if He were doing it Himself. I have a hard time picturing Jesus standing in front of a Porsche or a stash of money praying for it to become His.

But I could picture Him praying for my non-Christian friends, or praying that I would be stronger in my faith, or praying that my personal Bible study would be more meaningful. I think that is what it means to ask for something in Jesus' name.

What will happen when we dare to trust Christ so radically? Jesus promised that "anyone who has faith in me will do what I have been doing. He will do even greater things than these, because I am going to the Father" (John 14:12).

When you think about it, things like cars and money pale in comparison to having your friends become Christians or having yourself grow closer to God. But Jesus obviously knew that. That's why He challenged you with radical results of radical prayer!

—J.C.

Through preaching, teaching, and the Bible, God is telling me . . . _____

_____

Through nature and the lives of other believers, God is showing me . . . _____

_____

I will respond by . . . _____

_____

What are they afraid of?

READ
Acts 4:8–12

MEDITATE
Philippians 2:9
God . . . gave him the name that is above every name.

REFLECT
➡ What do non-Christians say about the name "Jesus"? Why do so many people use it as profanity?
➡ In what ways does our society mock Jesus' name? Why do people do that?

CONSIDER
No name says more than "Jesus."

If you like the music of DeGarmo & Key, you're not alone. So do some of the top secular record producers in the land. In fact, some of them have approached Ed DeGarmo and Dana Key and asked them to produce some mainstream music. You know, the kind that gets played on Top 40 stations and maybe even MTV.

No thanks, say D & K.

In an article written by Terry DeBoer of the *Grand Rapids Press,* Key told why. "Every time, they've wanted to restrict what we say on a record and in concert. Basically what they wanted [us] to do is drop the J-word." Apparently, the music moguls have an aversion to the mention of Jesus. "It's weird," Key continues, "because they don't mind if you mention God. You can mention Satan and the devil all you like." However, he says, when you talk about Jesus, "man, you're really rufflin' feathers."

What is it about this Person we love and worship that makes people so nervous? In a society that claims to value freedom of expression, why is His name singled out as somehow taboo? What are they afraid of?

People who don't know Jesus as Savior consider His message to be foolish—and even dangerous. They've heard that Jesus is a really good person, but they aren't about to let Him influence their lives.

What happens when you mention the name "Jesus" to your friends? Why does His name make people uneasy?

It's too bad they don't all realize that there is "no other name under heaven . . . by which we must be saved" (Acts 4:12).   —D.B.

Through preaching, teaching, and the Bible, God is telling me . . . _____

Through nature and the lives of other believers, God is showing me . . . _____

I will respond by . . . _____

Characternotcalendars

READ
Luke 10:38–42

MEDITATE
Luke 10:41
"You are worried and upset about many things."

REFLECT
➡ I tend to be more (action-oriented/ relationship-oriented) in my Christian life. Do I need to make a change?

➡ What will I do to improve my relationship with Jesus Christ? When will I start?

CONSIDER
God wants our devotion before He wants our service.

Ask most young people how their Christian life is going, and their answer hits you like a calendar:

"Great! etreatwasablastan dchurchwasawesomepastorg avegreatmessageandIbought thisradnewtapebySteveCamp andIcan'twaituntilourgroupta kesthatshorttermmissionstrip toMexiconextsummer . . . "

Sounds great, but the question wasn't *what* are you doing; it was *how* are you doing. Many Christians get the two mixed up.

The Christian life was never meant to be a series of religious activities. It is a personal relationship with God through Jesus Christ. How well we are doing depends on that relationship.

Jesus' friend Martha was action-oriented. She was cooking, cleaning, hostessing—while her sister, Mary, preferred to sit at Jesus' feet and learn from Him. When Martha complained, Jesus rebuked her gently.

If you have nothing more than an action mode, your Christian walk is only as good as your last activity. But when you focus on a personal relationship with Jesus, you have something that will never let you down. Maybe that's what Jesus meant when He said, "Mary has chosen what is better, and it will not be taken away from her" (v. 42).

So if you want to improve your Christian life, don't just sign up for the next retreat or plan to spend more time at church. Make sure you spend time alone with your good friend and Savior, Jesus. You'll gain something that will never wear out on you!
—J.C.

Through preaching, teaching, and the Bible, God is telling me . . . _____
_____
_____

Through nature and the lives of other believers, God is showing me . . . _____
_____
_____

I will respond by . . . _____
_____
_____

Legend of the pelican

READ
Acts 20:17–24

MEDITATE
Acts 20:24
"I consider my life worth nothing to me."

REFLECT
➡ How often should I thank the Lord for the sacrificial death of Jesus?
➡ Is there someone I should make a sacrifice for right now? Am I going to do it?

CONSIDER
When Jesus gave Himself for us, He showed us how to give for others.

From a book on religious art I learned that the pelican has been a spiritual symbol of self-sacrifice for centuries. When I lived in Florida, I watched these strange birds while fishing in the gulf waters and had a somewhat different opinion of them. I saw pelicans as a lazy bunch of freeloaders, not self-denying saints. With pitiful stares that masked hearts full of envy, they would sit nearby and look hungrily at every fish I caught. Once in a while one would even dive down and try to get my fish before I could reel it in. (It's true! This is not a fish story.)

The reason pelicans are symbols of self-sacrifice is not because of what they do. The association is made because of their appearance. The tip of a pelican's huge beak appears to have been dipped in red dye.

According to the legend, when a mother pelican can-not find food for her young, she thrusts her beak into her breast and keeps her little ones alive with her own blood. The early church artists and teachers saw in this a beautiful picture of what Christ did for us, and what we in turn should do for one another.

The legend of the pelican, then, speaks of the sacrifice of Jesus Christ shedding His own blood to pay for our sins and bring us redemption.

It also pictures us. All too often we are known more for our greed than our self-sacrifice. We won't give up anything for anybody. But that can change. We are forgiven and transformed through Christ's death. He will give us the power to overcome our selfishness.

Because Christ sacrificed for us, let's learn to do the same for others.   —M.D.

Through preaching, teaching, and the Bible, God is telling me . . . _____

_____

Through nature and the lives of other believers, God is showing me . . . _____

_____

I will respond by . . . _____

_____

Scoots

READ
Mark 8:31–37

MEDITATE
Proverbs 11:28
Whoever trusts in his riches will fall.

REFLECT
➡ What is my real purpose for being in school or at work? What am I hoping to accomplish?
➡ What important values can I get from 1 Timothy 6:6–10?

CONSIDER
The most important things in life are not things.

The two of us were sitting on some steps across from the Lair, the student union at West Virginia University. We were talking about what life is like on the college campus. The student mentioned such things as drugs and alcohol on the weekends and studies during the week. As he spoke, his gaze kept switching between me and his feet and the seemingly endless stream of students that passed by.

When I asked him why he was in school, he smiled wryly and answered, "Scoots. That's the reason I'm here." (For the completely unenlightened, which included me, scoots means money.) He was in school to learn how to make the big buck. He's not alone. In our country, we worship at the shrine of the money god. Money means power and influence and independence.

But according to market researcher Florence Skelly, people are beginning to realize that money can't buy the most important things in life. The president of Telematics, Inc., says the things people are beginning to value are a marriage that doesn't end up in divorce court, developing relationships with family and friends, and time to relax.

If Florence Skelly is right, if we really are beginning to redefine personal fulfillment, then we're taking a step in the right direction. Our hearts yearn for something "scoots" can't buy. Inner peace. Significance and fulfillment in life. These things are possible only through a personal relationship with God. Jesus said it best: "What good is it for a man to gain the whole world, yet forfeit his soul?" (Mark 8:36).

Okay, so which are you going to trust? Scoots or God? Make the right choice. The rest of your life depends on it. —D.P.

Through preaching, teaching, and the Bible, God is telling me . . . _____

_____

Through nature and the lives of other believers, God is showing me . . . _____

_____

I will respond by . . . _____

_____

'Cause I said so!

READ
James 1:19–25

MEDITATE
2 Timothy 2:15
Present yourself to
God as one . . . who
correctly handles the
word of truth.

REFLECT
➠ What pet idea do I
like to spout off
about? Is it really
true, or do I just
like to think it is?
➠ What might God
think of my effort
to be His spokes-
person?

CONSIDER
*One truth from
the Bible is
worth all of the
world's wisdom.*

Does it bug you when people spout off about stuff they don't know much about? You hear a lot of this blustering on radio talk shows—especially sports shows. Some guy who couldn't hit .250 in Little League calls in and says, "I know what's wrong with Jose Canseco. He's not con-centratin' at the plate. All he's thinkin' about is his fat paycheck."

Right, fella. And the next caller will be the owner of the Oakland A's inviting you to be their batting coach.

As irritating as a sports know-it-all is, he's harmless enough. The real problem comes when people start spouting their opinions as if they are scriptural truths. It happened in sixteenth-century Europe when the church fathers declared that the earth was the center of the universe and that Coper-nicus should be excommuni-cated for saying otherwise.

In happened again in 1870 when a church bishop stuck his foot in his mouth. While visiting the president of a small college, he expressed his firm biblical conviction that nothing new would ever be invented. The educator disagreed. "Why, in fifty years," he argued, "I believe it may be possible for men to soar through the air like birds!" The good bishop was shocked. "Flight is strictly reserved for the angels," he insisted, "and I beg you not to repeat your suggestion lest you be guilty of blas-phemy!" The mistaken bish-op was Milton Wright. Thirty-three years later his sons Orville and Wilbur made history by flying the first airplane at Kitty Hawk, North Carolina.

We must not declare that our ideas are based on Scrip-ture when they are nothing more than our opinions. Let's make sure we interpret the Bible correctly. —D.B.

Through preaching, teaching, and the Bible, God is telling me . . . _____

_____

_____

Through nature and the lives of other believers, God is showing me . . . _____

_____

_____

I will respond by . . . _____

_____

_____

MY PASTOR SAYS I SHOULD BE CAREFUL TO APPLY
SCRIPTURE TO ALL OF MY PROBLEMS . . . BUT I'M
NOT SEEING MUCH PROGRESS WITH THESE ZITS.

A SOUND MIND

How embarrassing!

READ
Hebrews 4:12–16

MEDITATE
Hebrews 4:13
Everything is uncovered and laid bare before . . . him.

REFLECT
➡ What kinds of thoughts displease the Lord? Why?
➡ How can I deal with wrong thoughts in the right way?
➡ How do my reading and viewing habits affect my thoughts?
➡ How can I control what enters my brain?

CONSIDER
What you think, God knows.

Imagine this: You're out shopping for clothes. You find something you like, but you want to make sure it fits. So you take it into the store's dressing room to try it on. As you're trying on these great new clothes, you hear giggling. You look around—then up. You see faces.

A woman in Aurora, Illinois, doesn't have to imagine what it would be like. It happened to her. During some remodeling, a dressing room booth had been placed under a plexiglass panel which had been installed to help store employees keep an eye on cash registers.

Understandably upset, the woman complained, and the store attempted to compensate her for the embarrassment by giving her an apology and the sixty-dollar dress she was trying on.

Now imagine something worse. What if a mirror placed above our heads could reflect all our thoughts for others to see? Would you be embarrassed? Now think about a related truth: God knows every thought we have. He doesn't use mirrors. He just knows—everything.

Hebrews 4 tells us how much God knows. That's humbling. And it should make us more careful about what thoughts we allow into our heads. But along with that sobering reminder, Hebrews 4 also gives us help in our thought life. It tells us about our great high priest, Jesus Christ, who had to deal with the same temptations we do (v. 15). And chapter 4 concludes with the great invitation to approach God confidently, "so that we may receive mercy and find grace to help us in our time of need" (v. 16).

God not only knows what we are thinking, but He can also help us control our thoughts and change them.
—K.D.

Through preaching, teaching, and the Bible, God is telling me . . . _____
_____
_____

Through nature and the lives of other believers, God is showing me . . . _____
_____
_____

I will respond by . . . _____
_____
_____

Take out the garbage

READ
Matthew 7:15–23

MEDITATE
Matthew 7:20
"Thus, by their fruit you will recognize them."

REFLECT
➡ What criteria should I use in choosing someone to follow?
➡ What kind of example am I to others?

CONSIDER
A sin by any other name still smells as bad.

According to a ruling by the Seventh District Court of Appeals, when you take out the garbage your privacy goes too. A Milwaukee thief had been charged with stealing $3,000 in coins from several banks. The suspect's guilt was confirmed when investigators went through his trash and discovered coin wrappers and bank trays.

The defendant readily confessed his crime and was convicted. Later he appealed to a higher court, contending that his privacy had been violated. His lawyers argued that he had a reasonable expectation of privacy because "he assumed his garbage would be mixed up with that of others." The three-judge panel disagreed, however, and said that no warrant was needed to go through someone's rubbish. The conviction held.

Some prominent Christians whose lives are cluttered with trash also appeal to the "right of privacy." They say the garbage in their lives—moral indiscretions, unloving attitudes, money-hungry decisions—is no one's business but theirs. They insist that any harm done by their private deeds is incidental and has nothing to do with their relationship to God.

Nonsense! The rubbish in their lives clearly shows that they are not interested in personal holiness. According to the Bible, people who say they are believers but live blatantly for themselves are like wolves in sheep's clothing. Someday Jesus will say to people like that, "Away from me, you evildoers" (Matthew 7:23).

Don't follow any so-called Christian leader whose life is filled with trash. Don't mix with anyone who claims to be a believer but who will not take out the garbage.
—M.D.

Through preaching, teaching, and the Bible, God is telling me . . . _____

_____

Through nature and the lives of other believers, God is showing me . . . _____

_____

I will respond by . . . _____

_____

What Jesus learned

READ
Hebrews 5:1–10

MEDITATE
Hebrews 5:8

He learned obedience from what he suffered.

REFLECT
→ Do I learn better by reading or doing? Why?

→ Why is learning by doing so important to the Christian life?

CONSIDER
We never know enough to stop learning.

How do you teach someone who already knows everything? Some of your instructors probably ask that question about the students they have to put up with in class. Know-it-alls are basically unteachable. To learn we must first admit there's something we don't know.

I was a little surprised, therefore, to read that Jesus "learned obedience from what he suffered" (Hebrews 5:8). Hmm. Jesus was God; why did He have to learn anything, I wondered.

So I did a little research about the word *learn* and discovered that it doesn't refer to something not already known. It means to experience something for yourself that you only knew about before, thus gaining a deeper appreciation for it.

In that sense, Jesus did learn obedience by dying on the cross for our sins. The suffering He endured went so far beyond anything He had experienced that it helped Him understand the concept of obedience in a different way.

That's not all. Jesus was also modeling for us how we are to learn. Living for God doesn't mean simply knowing the definitions of obedience, discipleship, prayer, and evangelism. It means experiencing these concepts.

You may think you know all about the Christian life—and maybe you do know a lot. But don't become a know-it-all. Think about Jesus, and how He had to learn certain things only through experience. If even Jesus learned, imagine what that means to us.   —J.C.

Through preaching, teaching, and the Bible, God is telling me . . . _____

_____

_____

Through nature and the lives of other believers, God is showing me . . . _____

_____

_____

I will respond by . . . _____

_____

_____

Those nasty notes

READ
2 Timothy 3:14–17

MEDITATE
2 Timothy 3:16
All Scripture is . . . useful for . . . training in
righteousness.

REFLECT
➡ Which do I read for
devotions, the
Bible or a devo-
tional book? Which
is more important?
➡ What do I know
about the Bible
that indicates to
me that it is spe-
cial?

CONSIDER
*The only word
you can always
depend on is
God's Word.*

The label on the cigarette pack says, "Cigarette Smoke Contains Carbon Monoxide." The aspirin bottle says, "Keep this and all medicines out of children's reach." But my favorite warning is the one found in each edition of Cliff's Notes: "These notes are not a substitute for the text itself . . . Students who attempt to use them in that way are depriving themselves of the very education they are presumably giving their most vital years to achieve."

Cliff's publishes notes on the New Testament. Written by a professor who has his Ph.D. in philosophy, the notes use about 1,200 words to discuss the life of Christ, then 20,000 words to analyze the Gospels, Epistles, Acts, and Revelation. The very uninspired commentary wanders widely from the important issues and requires more familiarity with the Bible than most students have today. It provides a lot of information that takes us "farther from God and nearer to Dust," to quote T. S. Eliot, who was addressing a different matter.

Reading these disclaimers and the hype makes me wonder how students use this devotional book. We sincerely hope it "makes the Bible come alive," and "improves your performance in life." More than anything, we want to "prepare you well for the final exam—Judgment Day."

So today we offer a disclaimer similar to the one in Cliff's Notes: "We shouldn't have to remind you that this devotional book is not a substitute for the original."

—T.F.

Through preaching, teaching, and the Bible, God is telling me . . . _____

Through nature and the lives of other believers, God is showing me . . . _____

I will respond by . . . _____

A SOUND MIND

Pursuing excellence

READ
Proverbs 2:1–6

MEDITATE
Proverbs 2:2
Turning your ear to wisdom and applying your heart to understanding.

REFLECT
➡ What are my priorities in life and where does my education fit?
➡ Am I taking full advantage of my educational opportunities? If not, what can I do about it?

CONSIDER
Don't just get a degree, get an education.

"Pursue your education with intellectual rigor and freshness." These eight words express the passion of a midwestern college dean who spoke to a group of students about the status of academics in our society. As I sat and listened, I was gripped by the power of his convictions.

He spoke of a strong anti-academics current in our country, evidenced by the rise in derisive terms that throw academically gifted students into dishonor. Terms like *nerd* and *bookworm*. He also issued a warning to a society that has banished values from the educational process. To his thinking, we've become a society that is more interested in the way things are than in the way things ought to be. As a result, we've become "morally impoverished, a generation gone astray."

He makes a strong point. We pat the head of the academically gifted student while we lift the athletically gifted on our shoulders. Our priorities are all mixed up.

A good education is priceless—not to mention expensive. And we let our God, our family, and ourselves down when we fail to take education seriously.

If we want to get the most out of our years of formal learning, laziness just won't do. "One who is slack in his work is brother to one who destroys" (Proverbs 18:9). So, chill out after, not during, class.

Educational success doesn't come automatically. It's the by-product of commitment. Commitment to Christ. Commitment to excellence. So if you're in school, go for it 100 percent. That's the best way to get the wisdom and understanding that Solomon was writing about.   —D.P.

Through preaching, teaching, and the Bible, God is telling me . . . _____

_____

Through nature and the lives of other believers, God is showing me . . . _____

_____

I will respond by . . . _____

_____

One at a time

READ
James 2:14–26

MEDITATE
James 2:26
Faith without deeds is dead.

REFLECT

➡ One thing God has gifted me with is

_____
_____ .

➡ A place where I can use that talent or knowledge is _____
_____ .

➡ My plan for getting in touch with a ministry or organization that needs someone with my abilities and interests is _____
_____ .

CONSIDER
To change the world, start with one person.

Jeff Ostrander was director of the Pregnancy Resource Center, one of the largest crisis pregnancy centers in North America. Every year this agency provides counseling and material support to thousands of pregnant women.

Because of the enormous demand, Jeff always needed more volunteers. One of the biggest hindrances to would-be volunteers, he said, is that they just can't see how they could possibly make a difference. He told the following story to illustrate how shortsighted this viewpoint is.

One morning a retired resident of a New England coastal town noticed a youngster walking along the beach. From time to time the little girl would stoop down, pick something up off the sand, and throw it into the water. Curious, the old-timer followed her and discovered that she was picking up stranded starfish and

putting them back into the ocean. Shaking his head, he caught up to her and said, "Miss, there are thousands of starfish along this beach. What difference is it going to make if you throw a few back?" The little girl looked down at the starfish in her hand and said, "It will make a difference to this one."

The book of James makes it clear that what we believe about God must be lived out through acts of kindness. And we can't get out of it by suggesting that the job is too big. Whether we befriend one pregnant teenager or help one immigrant learn to read, we must do something. Ask God's Holy Spirit today to show you how you can demonstrate your faith by what you do. You'll make a difference—even if you help just one person at a time. —T.B.

Through preaching, teaching, and the Bible, God is telling me . . . _____
_____

Through nature and the lives of other believers, God is showing me . . . _____
_____

I will respond by . . . _____
_____

27

Giving blood; giving life

MEDITATE
Hebrews 9:22
Without the shedding of blood there is no forgiveness.

REFLECT
➡ What kinds of personal sacrifices have I made for other people? Why?
➡ Why would Jesus give His life for people who rebelled against Him?
➡ Are my sins forgiven? How do I express my thankfulness?

CONSIDER
Jesus died that we might live.

Somewhat reluctantly, I allowed the woman in white to stick a needle into my arm. As I lay on the padded table while my blood flowed out, I had a strange sensation that I was on an altar. And I thought, *Why am I doing this?*

The blood bank had phoned a few days before. They said they needed my type of blood: A-positive. Someone's life could depend on it.

The nurse jiggled the plastic bag, now full of the red fluid, and told me I was done. After pulling out the gigantic needle, she told me I could go—but first I should have something to drink and eat some of the cookies they provide.

I walked over to a table and sat down across from another man who had just given blood. I began a conversation, learning a little bit about him and using the occasion as an opportunity

to witness. As we talked, I tried to find out if he knew what Jesus had done for him.

Jesus had given His blood too. But the cross that He hung on wasn't softly padded. He wasn't lying down—He was hanging by nails hammered through His hands and feet. He didn't hear soft music in the background—He heard only the taunts of the crowd, a few sobs, and then silence.

Why did He do all that? Why did He subject Himself to such abuse, humiliation, and even death? He did it because "without the shedding of blood there is no forgiveness" (Hebrews 9:22). He died so that we might live.　　—K.D.

Through preaching, teaching, and the Bible, God is telling me . . . _____
_____
_____

Through nature and the lives of other believers, God is showing me . . . _____
_____
_____

I will respond by . . . _____
_____
_____

Green eyes obedience

READ
Acts 5:27–33

MEDITATE
Acts 5:29
Peter and the other apostles replied: "We must obey God rather than men!"

REFLECT
➡ In what ways have I let my guard down to the things of this world? What things am I struggling with?
➡ Why does God demand obedience from me?

CONSIDER
It's always right to resist wrong.

Keith Green was never at a loss for words. The late contemporary Christian musician was the kind of guy you would like to have on your school debate team. But he was also a person who could prick your conscience until you were really uncomfortable.

The theme of obedience to God often cried out from Keith's lyrics and writings. Here's an article he wrote in *The Last Days Newsletter* in 1984:

"A poll was taken in the U.S. and they asked men and women how much money it would take for them to agree to sleep with a stranger. The average amount for men was $10. The average amount for women was $10,000.

"But as the dollar amount got higher, almost everybody said, 'Yes, I'd sleep with a stranger for a million dollars.' And what I'd say to all of them is, 'You're willing to be a prostitute. All you're changing is the price. You're willing to set aside your convictions for money. If you can be bought at any price, then God doesn't care about the price. He only cares that you can be bought.'

"What's your price? At what point are you willing to disobey God? What is there that can buy you? Are you for sale? Is obedience for sale?"

Tough questions. And you alone can answer them. Here's one more to consider. In the face of worldly temptations, will you declare, "We must obey God rather than men!" (Acts 5:29), as Peter and John did? Or can you be bought? —T.F.

Through preaching, teaching, and the Bible, God is telling me . . . _____

_____

_____

Through nature and the lives of other believers, God is showing me . . . _____

_____

I will respond by . . . _____

_____

Like kissing your sister!

READ
1 Corinthians
13:1–13

MEDITATE
1 Timothy 5:1–2
Treat younger men as brothers . . . and younger women as sisters.

REFLECT
➡ Am I willing to live by the biblical model for relationships?
➡ What effect does my purity, or lack of it, have on my relationship to friends, to parents, to God?

CONSIDER
Love and respect go together.

If a couple are going together, how far should they go in expressing their physical love for each other?" That's the question David Wyrtzen, author of *Love Without Shame,* gets asked most often when he speaks to young people about dating.

Here's how he responds. "When the audience is a group of Christian kids, the basic premise behind this question remains the same. Almost anybody with morals and some knowledge of Scripture knows that sexual intercourse outside of marriage is sin. But whether or not it is wrong to engage in the physical actions of kissing, petting, and progressive exposure of their bodies to one another is negotiable. . . . The teenagers want an authority to tell them where to stop. . . . What they need is not a stop sign along the road but a totally different route.

"Instead of making sexual love the doorway and sustaining force of dating relationships, we must learn to relate to the opposite sex as brothers and sisters. Paul is clear: for a man to treat a woman in ways not appropriate for a brother to treat his sister is impure; for a woman to treat a man in ways not appropriate for a sister to treat her brother is impure. Young people are no exception to this principle. Even in a day when incest has raised its ugly head, I believe we understand the purity and tenderness of the true brother-sister relationship. This model needs to be our guide in dating."

Real love is so much more than physical involvement. When you're dating, try living up to the standard of 1 Corinthians 13. After you're married, add the legitimate privileges and delights that only marriage can bring.   —T.B.

Through preaching, teaching, and the Bible, God is telling me . . . _____

_____

_____

Through nature and the lives of other believers, God is showing me . . . _____

_____

_____

I will respond by . . . _____

_____

_____

Sneak attack

READ
Judges 14:1–7

MEDITATE
1 Peter 5:8
The devil prowls around like a roaring lion.

REFLECT
➡ When am I weakest against Satan's attack? How can I become stronger?
➡ What methods does Satan use to defeat me?
➡ When did I last have to defend myself against attack?

CONSIDER
The best defense against Satan is to stay close to God.

Scott Lancaster didn't see it coming. He was jogging near his high school in Idaho Springs, Colorado, when a three-year-old mountain lion attacked him from behind and killed him.

Many families like Scott's have moved to the foothills of the Rocky Mountains because of the natural beauty and abundant wildlife. A Colorado Springs wildlife officer remarked, "People who move here haven't the foggiest notion how to live with [mountain lions]. They find deer, they find raccoons, but they forget that there are mountain lions and, by the way, bears too."

Although few of us live where lions roam, we all are in danger of being attacked by one—an invisible one. When we least expect it, Satan can sneak up on us.

Samson was able to fight off a big cat attack because God gave him incredible strength. But tragically, even though he was able to fight off the lion, he fell victim to more subtle attacks. Lust crept up on him and got him (Judges 14:1–3; 16:1, 4–21).

What can we do to protect ourselves from attack? First, we can't be naive. Satan is roaming our streets and campuses, looking for a chance to sink his teeth into us (1 Peter 5:8). Second, we need to resist him (James 4:7). Third, we have to wear the lion-proof armor of God (Ephesians 6:11–18). Fourth, we should be strong in the Lord (Ephesians 6:10).

Where will you be walking today? Are you prepared to face a lion? Are you relying on God to help you fight off an attack?   —K.D.

Through preaching, teaching, and the Bible, God is telling me . . . _____
_____
_____

Through nature and the lives of other believers, God is showing me . . . _____
_____
_____

I will respond by . . . _____
_____
_____

Tattoo testimony

READ
Galatians 2:15–21

MEDITATE
Galatians 2:20
"I have been crucified with Christ."

REFLECT
➡ How can I show others that I have been crucified with Christ?

➡ What can I do to prepare my heart so that God can use me?

CONSIDER
If Christ is in our hearts, it should show in our lives.

They're not just for motorcycle gangs anymore. More and more young people are becoming walking billboards—they're getting tattooed. Why? It has a lot to do with self-image.

A study at the University of Washington revealed that tattooing can be a "form of self-abuse characteristic among suicidal and depressed adolescents." Tattooed teens are more likely than others to drop out of school, belong to gangs, and even pray to the devil. (These are not healthy things to do.)

Most of the skin scrawlings indicate an affinity for a favorite rock band. Others show affection for a particular girlfriend or boyfriend. (Yes, women get tattooed too.)

What is truly bizarre, however, is that 83 percent of these straight-pin pictures are self-inflicted. People engrave their own flesh with pins and then apply ink for a lasting effect.

Tattooees are sending a message. But you know what? It's only skin deep. What's going on inside them is what counts.

Christians too have been "tattooed," but in a much deeper way. We have given our lives to Christ, and we are identified with Him. When Paul said, "I have been crucified with Christ," he was proclaiming a wonderful fact. We are dead to the law. We have received the precious gift of salvation by the grace of Christ. We are free from sin, both its past guilt and its present power. We are His, and our lives are to reflect His image.

People who wear tattoos advertise what's important to them. What do people see when they look at you—the way of the world or the image of Christ?   —T.F.

Through preaching, teaching, and the Bible, God is telling me . . . _____

_____

_____

Through nature and the lives of other believers, God is showing me . . . _____

_____

_____

I will respond by . . . _____

_____

_____

The discomfort zone

READ
Philippians 2:12–15

MEDITATE
Colossians 1:10
Live a life worthy of the Lord and . . . please him in every way.

REFLECT

➡ What things in my life are out of line with my position as a Christian?

➡ What does my conscience bug me about the most?

➡ Why don't I do something about it?

CONSIDER
The best ability is compatibility.

Johns Hopkins University, one of the nation's most prestigious medical schools, held large amounts of stock in tobacco companies. What's wrong with that? INCOMPATIBILITY.

Johns Hopkins agreed. They decided to sell their millions in stock.

Lines up a little better with a school whose mission is to fight deadly diseases like cancer, doesn't it?

Johns Hopkins could use some company in its attempt to match actions with purpose. You and I should be concerned, too. I mean, let's be honest. Haven't you sometimes thought, "Maybe I shouldn't be watching this movie." Or, "What am I doing in this place?" INCOMPATIBILITY.

But instead of acting on these quiet promptings from the Holy Spirit, we slurp a little louder on our Pepsi to drown out His voice. It isn't long before the voice is

gone, and we start to feel comfortable enough to continue doing that incompatible something we're doing.

God knew this would be a problem, so He told us to "live a life worthy of the Lord and . . . please him in every way" (Colossians 1:10). He also said, "Live lives worthy of God, who calls you into His kingdom in glory" (1 Thessalonians 2:12). When we follow these instructions, what we do will line up with the One we represent.

Maybe God's been trying to tell you something. Could it be that you have some areas of inconsistency in your life? Then do what the folks at Johns Hopkins did. Act on what you know.   —D.P.

Through preaching, teaching, and the Bible, God is telling me . . . _____

_____

_____

Through nature and the lives of other believers, God is showing me . . . _____

_____

I will respond by . . . _____

_____

_____

One really bad day

READ
Psalm 30:1–5

MEDITATE
Psalm 30:2
I called to you for help and you healed me.

REFLECT
➡ What was my worst day this week? This month? Did God help me? Did I ask Him?
➡ When a crisis comes, do I call on God first or last?

CONSIDER
When everything goes wrong, go to God.

Lori was having a genuinely bad day. I mean *really* bad. Not just the kind when you can't find the pants you wanted to wear, you get to lunch just after they run out of pizza, your car is about to run out of gas and you've only got a buck, and you spill Coke on the front page of your research paper. Days like that are a pain, but you can survive them.

No, Lori's day was *unbelievably* bad. First, she got word from the academic office that due to a mixup about the requirements for her major she was going to have to stay an extra semester to get her degree. That afternoon a guy in a pickup truck went through a red light and smashed into the side of her little car. She was banged up, and the policeman told her he thought the car was totaled. And that night her mom called to tell her that Grandma had suffered a severe stroke and wasn't expected to live through the night.

It was too much. When Lori hung up the phone, she put her head down and sobbed. She had never felt so bad. She hurt so much on the inside. She was ready to give up.

After a while she picked up her Bible. Reading it was the only thing she could do that wouldn't turn out bad. In it she found one promise after another. She told God all about her hurt and frustration and anger and fear.

The Lord heard Lori. He gave her the strength she needed—the faith to keep going. The next few days were among the most difficult of Lori's life. But in His time and in His way, God brought her healing and peace. She had turned to the only One she could, the Lord, and He had helped her through her bad day. —D.E.

Through preaching, teaching, and the Bible, God is telling me . . . _____

_____

Through nature and the lives of other believers, God is showing me . . . _____

_____

I will respond by . . . _____

_____

"Get out of my car!"

READ
Psalm 9:1–10

MEDITATE
Psalm 9:8
He will judge the world
in righteousness.

REFLECT
➡ When was the last time someone misjudged me? How did I feel?

➡ Who has the wrong impression of me? What can I do to correct it?

➡ God's judgment is always right. Does that comfort me or scare me? Why?

CONSIDER
Jesus will never judge you unfairly.

Here you are, four normal teenage guys, sitting in your car in the mall parking lot. You're minding your own business, talking basketball and girls (not necessarily in that order) when suddenly a well-dressed woman walks up to your car with her arms full of packages. She sees you, gets all excited, and orders you out of the car. You snicker and wonder what's with her. She starts shouting, so you roll down the window to tell her to get a life. About that time she gets real serious. She sets down her bundles, opens her purse, and takes out a gun! "Get out or I'll start shooting!" she yells. Four doors fly open all at once. Being cool is the last thing on your mind as you pile out of the car and hightail it out of there.

When she tries her key in the ignition she realizes her mistake. Her car, which looks exactly like yours, is parked three slots away!

Why did this incident, reported by Paul Harvey, happen? The woman saw four teenagers and instantly misjudged them. It happens all the time. Normal kids are seen to be bad dudes just because they're kids. When this happens, you start to wonder if maybe people will be incorrectly judging you all through life. Count on it. They will!

There is one Person, however, who will never judge you wrongly. God, the righteous judge, knows what's really going on inside your heart. And He is always totally fair.

If you are fearful that you will always be judged unfairly because of your age, the color of your skin, your body structure, the way you talk, or some other superficial characteristic, be encouraged. The Lord looks on the inside, and His judgments are always just and right.

—D.E.

Through preaching, teaching, and the Bible, God is telling me . . . _____

_____

Through nature and the lives of other believers, God is showing me . . . _____

_____

I will respond by . . . _____

_____

Chopped liver

READ
1 Kings 12:1–19

MEDITATE
Proverbs 14:31
He who oppresses the poor shows contempt for their Maker.

REFLECT
➡ When have I felt mistreated? Why? How did it feel?
➡ When have I mistreated others? Why?
➡ How can I help others to be more people-conscious? How can I become more people-conscious myself?

CONSIDER
What we think of people reflects what we think of God.

Have you ever felt like a hunk of chopped liver? Ignored? Stepped on? Used? Treated as if you had no feelings? Bossed around? (Am I causing flashbacks of an encounter with an impossible teacher, a boss, or someone you once dated?)

If you've ever felt like that (and who hasn't!), you should be able to identify with the way the Russian people have felt for decades. For years the citizens have been slaves to the communist system that put programs ahead of people. A high-ranking Soviet official, Georgi Arbatov, described the system: "We developed a huge bureaucracy. We forgot human beings for a while."

Vitaly Korotich, legislator and journalist in the USSR, contends that even with the changes that have occurred, "the system is destroying the will to survive in our children. It comes down to how you treat people—that is what is important."

King Rehoboam could have used some classes on how to treat people with respect (1 Kings 12:1–19). Instead he followed the rotten advice of his friends. When the citizens asked for reforms, Rehoboam promised even harsher treatment. The people rebelled, and I can't say that I blame them.

How do you treat other people? Do you see them only as a means to an end— to get what you want? Are you ever so blinded by power or ego that you treat people like chopped liver, or give them a dose of Soviet bureaucracy?

Take it from the author of Proverbs: How we treat others is a reflection of what we think of the One who made them (14:31). We can honor Him by treating others as the God-image they really are.
—K.D.

Through preaching, teaching, and the Bible, God is telling me . . . _____

_____

_____

Through nature and the lives of other believers, God is showing me . . . _____

_____

_____

I will respond by . . . _____

_____

_____

WHAT DO YOU MEAN? I LOVE PEOPLE! I WOULDN'T
BE HERE TODAY IF IT WEREN'T FOR THE
SCORES OF WONDERFUL PEOPLE I'VE BEEN ABLE
TO USE ALONG THE WAY.

A LOVING HEART

When to call 911

READ
Ecclesiastes 5:1–7

MEDITATE
Ecclesiastes 5:2
Do not be hasty in your heart to utter anything before God.

REFLECT
➡ What have I been asking God for lately? How much thought did I put into those requests?
➡ How can I keep my praying from becoming routine?

CONSIDER
God thinks most of prayers that take thought.

Emergency operators in Los Angeles have received some rather bizarre cries for help. One person dialed 911 because he was out of breath after running from the police. A woman called to complain that she had blisters after working three days at Taco Bell. An eighteen-year-old wanted a ride to the hospital because he couldn't get any rest at home. A thirteen-year-old called to report that she had stubbed her toe. Another person punched 911 to complain that he had slept wrong on his neck.

Those are strange but true examples of ridiculous requests made to an important source of help. But if we could read transcripts of the things people pray about, I wonder if we'd find much difference.

I know, I know, I should be able to talk to God about everything. But could it be that my prayers sound a bit absurd at times?

Is it appropriate, for example, to ask God whether or not we should give in to temptation? Or to ask God to do something before we've thought through the consequences of what we are asking? Wouldn't it be absurd to make an emergency call to God to get us out of a mess that we got ourselves into while knowing full well that we were disobeying Him? Wouldn't it be wrong to promise to do something for God in exchange for His promise to do something for us?

What the author of Ecclesiastes told us about God should help us have the right attitude when we pray. We are talking to the God of the universe. Solomon said, "Stand in awe of God" (5:2, 7).

When we pray, whether in an emergency or when all is well, let's choose our words carefully. We are talking to God. —K.D.

Through preaching, teaching, and the Bible, God is telling me . . . _____

Through nature and the lives of other believers, God is showing me . . . _____

I will respond by . . . _____

Watching heaven open

READ
Revelation 7:9–17

MEDITATE
Revelation 19:1

I heard what sounded like the roar of a great multitude in heaven.

REFLECT

➡ What day this month can I spend locked in my room with my Bible and a notebook?

➡ Do I listen to music strictly for entertainment or to get closer to God?

CONSIDER
It's okay to get excited about the Lord.

Sometime during the Christmas season you will hear the familiar chords of the organ, the crowd will stand, and you too will rise and sing the word *hallelujah* ten times straight. And you'll probably enjoy it.

No, it's not DC Talk. Or Margaret Becker. Or Michael W. Smith. It's George Frideric Handel. And he has a story worth knowing.

By the time Handel was nine years old, he was writing cantatas. A few years later he was asked to play for the king of Prussia. But then his father died, his music no longer sold, his health broke, and he went bankrupt.

Almost in despair, he closed himself in his room. Alone with God for the next twenty-four days, he wrote his inspiring oratorio *The Messiah*. Describing that time he said, "I did see the heavens open and the great God Himself seated on His throne!" In writing *The Messiah*, he was most moved by passages from Revelation 7 and 19.

And now, each Christmas season, we relive his excitement when we stand and sing the "Hallelujah Chorus."

It may not be acceptable among your friends to get overly excited by church music. You might even feel uncool if you act as if you like it. But just this once, in celebration of what Jesus has done, go ahead, enjoy it. Feel the thrill of praising the Lord as you sing, "For the Lord God omnipotent reigneth! Forever. And ever. Hallelujah! Hallelujah!" And think about what it must have been like for Handel to be so wrapped up in the biblical theme that he saw the heavens open. —D.B.

Through preaching, teaching, and the Bible, God is telling me . . . _____

_____

_____

Through nature and the lives of other believers, God is showing me . . . _____

_____

_____

I will respond by . . . _____

_____

_____

On my honor

MEDITATE
Leviticus 19:11
"Do not steal. Do not lie. Do not deceive."

REFLECT
→ Am I ever tempted to cheat? How do I resist the temptation?
→ Have I ever cheated? Have I confessed it to God and determined not to do it again?
→ How can I improve my study habits so that cheating will not be an attractive option?

CONSIDER
Cheating hurts more than studying.

A Stanford University freshman who was suspended for cheating, said, "My advice if you get caught is to deny everything."

After his professor accused him of copying another student's answer on a class assignment, the student admitted what he had done. He expected leniency, but school officials suspended him. In response the student said, "I got punished for telling the truth."

I was puzzled by his conclusion that he was "punished for telling the truth." He had forgotten something very important. His punishment was for cheating, not for admitting it. Merely acknowledging guilt does not mean that we deserve a lighter sentence than the person who tries to cover it up.

If our goal is to escape responsibility and punishment for our actions, we might choose to follow his advice to "deny everything."

But that only compounds the problem. According to the Lord, that makes us guilty of two things: lying and stealing. He condemns both (Leviticus 19:11).

I don't know of anyone who wants the full punishment for doing something wrong. We all want leniency. Actually we would prefer to be able to say "I'm sorry" and have everything be forgiven. But justice doesn't work that way. Justice means that when you "do the crime" you'd better be prepared to "do the time."

How much better our lives would be if we were to take God seriously and agree with Him that stealing and lying are wrong. Then, instead of trying to avoid the consequences of our actions, we'd choose to do what is right in the first place.

After all, the ultimate judge of our situation is not a teacher or a school official. It's God Himself.　　—K.D.

Through preaching, teaching, and the Bible, God is telling me . . . _____

_____

Through nature and the lives of other believers, God is showing me . . . _____

_____

I will respond by . . . _____

_____

Ya gotta have

Southern hospitality

MEDITATE
Ephesians 4:32
Be kind and compassionate to one another.

REFLECT

➡ What words characterize the way I treat other people? Kindness, respect, courtesy? Or indifference, coldness, selfishness?

CONSIDER
If your actions are unkind, they're the wrong kind.

I left my hear-r-r-t, in Opelika. I know. That's not how the song goes. But if Tony Bennett, the guy who sang about San Francisco, had spent some time in Opelika, Alabama, I'll bet he would have changed his tune. I spent the night in that small southern town and I discovered that southern hospitality lives! From the college-age person who worked behind the counter to the waitress in the restaurant next door, I was treated as if I was doing them a favor by allowing them to serve me. They were kind, attentive, considerate, and oh, so polite.

And it didn't stop there. When I arrived at Auburn University many of the students were just as responsive. They weren't cold or indifferent to this visitor from the north. I asked some of the students how they developed this warm, friendly manner. And to a person

their answer was the same. From home. From Mama and Daddy, as they usually referred to them.

Their kindness reminded me of some spiritual characteristics that should be found in the life of every Christian.

"Be kind and compassionate to one another" (Ephesians 4:32).

"Make every effort to add to your faith . . . brotherly kindness; and to brotherly kindness, love" (2 Peter 1:5, 7).

"Be devoted to one another. . . . Honor one another. . . . Practice hospitality" (Romans 12:10, 13).

We don't automatically treat people this way. But it is certainly how we want others to treat us.

I left my hear-r-r-t in Opelika. Do people say something like that after they have talked with you?
—D.P.

Through preaching, teaching, and the Bible, God is telling me . . . _____

_____

_____

Through nature and the lives of other believers, God is showing me . . . _____

_____

_____

I will respond by . . . _____

_____

_____

Dead or alive?

READ
Revelation 3:1–6

MEDITATE
Revelation 3:1
"You have a reputation of being alive, but you are dead."

REFLECT
➡ What evidence do I have that I am spiritually alive?
➡ Have I done anything to help my church grow in the past few weeks? If it were up to me alone, what would be the outlook for the future of the church?

CONSIDER
If we don't evangelize, the church will fossilize.

Several years ago when I was helping my son, Ben, prepare for a science test, we came across this question: "What are four characteristics of living things?" Ben was ready with the answer: (1) Living things are made up of cells. (2) They need food. (3) They grow. (4) They reproduce.

If these four "tests of life" were applied to Christians, how would we fare? Would we be alive or dead?

Test 1: Cells. I am one of the "cells" that make up the church. Am I a contributing member or do I just go for what I can get out of it? Have I ceased to function as part of the body?

Test 2: Food. Do I eat a healthy diet of spiritual food? Do I listen carefully to Sunday school lessons? Sermons? Am I reading the Bible? Good Christian books? Good devotional material?

Test 3: Growth. Am I growing? Am I putting what I know about the Bible and Christian life into practice? Have I tested my faith by witnessing or serving? Or have I been content to stay immature?

Test 4: Reproduction. Have I been planting the seed of the Gospel through my life and witness? Do my classmates, roommates, and instructors know that I am a believer? How long since I have led someone to Christ?

Dead Christians don't witness. Jesus said that the church at Sardis looked alive but was dead. Don't let that be true of you!   —M.D.

Through preaching, teaching, and the Bible, God is telling me . . . _____
_____
_____

Through nature and the lives of other believers, God is showing me . . . _____
_____
_____

I will respond by . . . _____
_____

To tell the truth . . .

READ
John 8:42–47

MEDITATE
Colossians 3:9
Do not lie to each other.

REFLECT

➡ Is there someone I am so afraid of that I sometimes lie to protect myself? How can God help me overcome that fear?

➡ Do I lie to myself? What about?

➡ Do I lie to my instructors? Why?

CONSIDER
Sometimes the truth hurts . . . but a lie hurts worse.

I listened with interest as some college students argued about who was telling the truth: Supreme Court nominee Clarence Thomas or law professor Anita Hill. Some sided with her; others with him. Finally one girl said in frustration, "How can you decide who is telling the truth?" No one could answer that one.

This led me to think about an even deeper question. Why do people lie? Dr. Elissa Benedek, a professor at the University of Michigan, has some answers. "Motivations for lying are as diverse as humans themselves," she explains. "People lie to get out of trouble, to get someone into trouble, to manipulate, to receive or avoid punishment, and to protect themselves." A member of the American Polygraph Association commented, "The reason for lying is always the same: To avoid the consequences of telling the truth."

God expects us to tell the truth. It's the ninth commandment (Exodus 20:16). Also, Paul instructed the believers in the church at Colosse not to lie to each other. And Solomon, the wise writer of Proverbs, went so far as to say that it is "better to be poor than [to be] a liar" (19:22). Since most of us feel poor most of the time anyway, there's no use being both poor and a liar.

Most lies are born out of fear. Because we're afraid of the results of telling the truth, we lie. It may be that the truth is too painful to face. Or that the consequences of telling the truth seem too severe. But this is where God comes in. Sure, it may seem easier to avoid some pain and hassle by lying, but why take the coward's way out? God can give you the courage and faith to face reality—and to tell the truth.   —D.E.

Through preaching, teaching, and the Bible, God is telling me . . . _____

_____

_____

Through nature and the lives of other believers, God is showing me . . . _____

_____

_____

I will respond by . . . _____

_____

_____

How will I get in?

I was riding with retired Air Force officer Wally Hall. We were approaching the hut guarding the entrance to Wurtsmith Air Force Base in Oscoda, Michigan. Wally was going to take me on my first-ever tour of a U.S. military installation.

I was impressed with the high fences and barbed wire. They obviously did not want just anyone wandering around their B-52s. "How will I get in?" I wondered, since I had not applied for clearance. Would I be asked a lot of questions? Did they have a computer hook-up to Washington to check some files?

But when we got to the gate, we were waved right through. "How did we get in so easily?" I asked my host.

"That sticker in the corner of the window," he replied. "It gets me and any-one with me onto the base. I have clearance."

Because I was with Wally, I could enter the base un-challenged.

And that's exactly how I'm going to get into heav-en. If I were on my own, I wouldn't stand a chance of entering heaven's glory. I wouldn't deserve it, and I could never earn it. But when I trusted Jesus Christ as my personal Savior, I became identified with Him. I am now "in Christ." And because of Him, I have access into the grace of God. I know for sure that one day I will enjoy all the glories of heaven.

If you have put your faith in Christ, you too will have no problem "at the gate." Because you are "with Him," you will be waved right in.

—D.E.

Through preaching, teaching, and the Bible, God is telling me . . . _____

_____

_____

Through nature and the lives of other believers, God is showing me . . . _____

_____

I will respond by . . . _____

_____

_____

Standing up to Sarge

READ
Daniel 1:1–15

MEDITATE
Daniel 1:8
Daniel . . . asked the chief official for permission not to defile himself.

REFLECT
➡ The last time I had a chance to stand up for right, here's what I did: _____ _____ _____.

CONSIDER
Stand for God or you will fall for everything.

Matt didn't like what he was hearing from the drill sergeant. It was Army boot camp, and Matt was only a few months removed from his senior year of high school. He was doing his best to live for God as a soldier, but his sergeant wasn't making it easy.

"All right, you recruits," he bellowed. "Tomorrow we're going to do something different. We're going to start using obscene cadences." The whole unit would be forced to chant profanities, swear words, and obscenities as they marched. Continuing, the sergeant said, "And if anybody doesn't like it, he can come and see me."

This wasn't a friendly invitation to come and chat over coffee. But it was all the invitation Matt needed. Later he approached the sergeant and said, "Sir, I can't do the obscene cadences."

"Why not?" the non-com barked.

"Because I'm a Christian, sir," Matt explained. "And I know God would not be pleased if I used that kind of language."

What gives someone like Matt the boldness to stand up for what is right? And what can you do to prepare yourself for the next time you have to stand up against someone on an issue like sexual purity or honesty? Or when you have to go up against a whole dorm or an entire classroom or a professor on an issue that really matters?

Like Daniel in Babylon, Matt could stand up for what is right because he had already developed the courage to support his convictions. He had a background of trusting God and living for Him. And, like Daniel's, Matt's stand was honored. The sergeant canceled his orders.   —D.B.

Through preaching, teaching, and the Bible, God is telling me . . . _____

Through nature and the lives of other believers, God is showing me . . . _____

I will respond by . . . _____

The great turnabout

READ
Ezra 7:21–28

MEDITATE
Philippians 4:6
Do not be anxious about anything, but . . . present your requests to God.

REFLECT
➡ Why do I find it so hard to involve God, especially in those situations that need God's miraculous help?

CONSIDER
The impossible is easy for God

A professor at Azusa Pacific University had a favorite saying: "There is no limit to what we can do together when we don't care who gets the credit, as long as God gets the glory." Unfortunately, God can't get the glory in a lot of our situations because we don't involve Him to begin with!

Look at today's passage. It tells of the happy ending to the controversy that surrounded Israel's rebuilding of the temple. The high-level communiqués make great reading. Check out this scenario:

The Jews' opponents warn King Artaxerxes that temple-building today means revolution tomorrow (Ezra 4:8–16).

The king issues an order to stop (Ezra 4:17–22).

The opponents write to King Darius that the Jews won't stop; they claim that King Cyrus authorized it (Ezra 5:8–17).

King Darius writes back that, sure enough, they found the previous king's memo in their files. Not only is the building to continue, but the revenues for it will come out of the royal treasury! (Ezra 6:3–17).

Such turnabouts are not limited to the Old Testament. God can still work miraculous changes in circumstances. Are you dealing with a situation that requires divine intervention? There are no jobs available and you really want (make that *need*) to work. Certain doors need to open where school is concerned. What to do?

I suggest you get God involved. Bring your situation to God's attention, leave it in His hands, and see what He does about it. A group of fifth-century B.C. Jews did that, and look what happened to them! —J.C.

Through preaching, teaching, and the Bible, God is telling me . . . _____

_____

Through nature and the lives of other believers, God is showing me . . . _____

_____

I will respond by . . . _____

_____

One price fits all

READ
Ephesians 1:3–10

MEDITATE
1 Corinthians 7:23
You were bought at a price.

REFLECT
➡ What do I learn about God's love for me from Ephesians 1:3–10?

➡ If someone suggests to me that God is not fair because He allows people to go to hell, how can I respond?

CONSIDER
Consider salvation: You can't beat the price.

You have to be pretty hungry to want a cheeseburger, fries, and a Coke in Copenhagen, Denmark. Those three items will ring up a bill of $11.25. Other cities around the world will also lighten your wallet if you decide to go for the All-American lunch. In Paris, the tab will be $7.97. In Madrid, $6.19, and in Tokyo, $5.39.

According to this survey by Runzheimer International, the two low-priced cities were New York at $4.53 and Beijing, China, at $3.30. Of course, you can plug in your own town's price structure to see where you stand against the world when it comes to burgers. Here in Grand Rapids you could get by on less than $2.50 at the right fast-food emporium.

It doesn't seem quite fair, does it—a difference of close to $9 for a meal that would hardly keep a person alive?

There is one price, how-ever, that never changes, and it is as fair as they come. It is the price of salvation. It doesn't matter who you are, where you live, what you've done, who you know, when you were born, where you go to school, who your parents are, how much money you have, or what your grades are. Whether you live in Copenhagen; Madrid; Tokyo; New York; Bellevue, Nebraska; or Blacksburg, Virginia; the price is the same.

Free.

The cost to Jesus was terribly high. He suffered a humiliating death on the cross. But He did it to pay the penalty for our sins. As a result, one price fits all. Have you put your faith in Jesus Christ? It's the fairest offer you'll ever receive.   —D.B.

Through preaching, teaching, and the Bible, God is telling me . . . _____

Through nature and the lives of other believers, God is showing me . . . _____

I will respond by . . . _____

State of the Union

READ
1 Peter 2:9–12

MEDITATE
1 Peter 2:11
I urge you, as aliens and strangers in the world, to abstain from sinful desires.

REFLECT
➡ Where and how should I be taking a stand for Christ?
➡ What's more important to me—popularity or truth?

CONSIDER
It's your right to stand up for what's right.

Ah, yes. The wild, wild West. Full of glittering Hollywood stars and expensive cars. Originator of bizarre fads and foods. And (here comes the surprise) home of one of the most conservative newspapers in the world, the Sacramento *Union.* Say what?

Yup. Standing taller than a California redwood, the *Union* has a "decidedly pro-Christian, pro-family flavor and a strong pro-life stance." In fact, the editor has replaced the word *gay* with *homosexual* as part of the editorial policy. Women's health centers are called abortion clinics. Pro-choice activists have become abortion rights activists. And for the flick fans, the paper refuses to advertise any movies with a NC-17 rating.

What is the *Union* getting for its pure and moral stance? A lot of flack. The much larger media are ripping it from coast to coast.

And groups like the AIDS coalition and ACT UP have been ripping off its papers from the news racks.

Why is the paper getting so much grief? Because it's standing up for truth and morality. Will it fold? Not likely. Churches are rallying around the *Union,* and it is operating on a break-even basis for the first time in years.

Are we as brave? Do we stand up and stand out in this world? Or have we conformed so much to our culture that nobody can tell the difference?

How should you live? Peter said you should "live such good lives . . . that, though they accuse you of doing wrong, they may see your good deeds and glorify God on the day he visits us" (1 Peter 2:12).

Stand up for what God's Word says is right. No matter the cost. No matter how weird it makes you look.

—T.F.

Through preaching, teaching, and the Bible, God is telling me . . . _____

_____

_____

Through nature and the lives of other believers, God is showing me . . . _____

_____

_____

I will respond by . . . _____

_____

_____

Dare to be disciplined

READ
Psalm 119:9–16

MEDITATE
Psalm 119:9

How can a young man keep his way pure?

REFLECT
➡ I will start to do my best to memorize God's Word, beginning with Psalm 119:9–16.

➡ What strategy can I develop for reading, meditating, and memorizing portions of the Bible.

CONSIDER
Keep the Bible in mind.

The administrators and faculty of Aswan University in Egypt have a unique attitude toward higher education. They believe that the more you know before you enter, the better off you'll be after you graduate. That's why the school requires that each student memorize the entire Koran before being considered for admission.

Really! Each of the 20,000 students must recite from memory the complete holy book of the Islamic faith—whether the student's goal is business, law, or physical education. The recitation takes more than two days to complete and several years to prepare for.

The Koran is roughly the same length as the New Testament of the Bible. If we strung together all the verses we have memorized, most North Americans would be hard-pressed to quote even one chapter's worth of Scripture. We'd be going home early if we had to meet such a requirement as the one at Aswan U.

So why the huge difference in standards between the best Muslim students and the best Christian students? I doubt that the Muslims believe any stronger or care any more about their faith than you and I do. But they do take very seriously a habit David practiced and enjoyed with his copy of God's Word: "I have hidden your word in my heart. . . . *With my lips I recount all the laws that come from your mouth. . . . I delight in your decrees; I will not neglect your word*" (Psalm 119:11, 13, 16, italics added).

Perhaps we can be challenged by the Egyptian students to develop a regular habit of hiding God's Word in our hearts. It is the best way for a young person to "keep his way pure."   —T.B.

Through preaching, teaching, and the Bible, God is telling me . . . _____

_____

_____

Through nature and the lives of other believers, God is showing me . . . _____

_____

_____

I will respond by . . . _____

_____

_____

No better book

READ
Psalm 119:105–112

MEDITATE
Hebrews 4:12
The word of God is living and active.

REFLECT
➡ Do I know enough about the Bible to convince someone that it is unique among books because it is God's Word?
➡ What will I do today to increase my Bible knowledge?

CONSIDER
Do you have a read Bible?

While doing graduate studies in English at Western Michigan University, I learned something surprising about my professors: they were very familiar with the Bible. They had to be to understand the many biblical allusions made by great British and American writers.

The sad thing, though, was that most of them didn't understand the special nature of the Bible. To them, it was nothing more than a book of good stories and quotable lines. Beyond that, they found no value.

How unfortunate for them. They're missing the best part.

What makes the words of Paul and Moses and David more important than those of Dickens, Twain, and Brontë?

It is God's word to us— His message. God could have just thought these words or just spoken these words, but He did more—He made sure someone wrote them so we could read them.

It is absolute truth. Nowhere else in literature— British, American, or any other—can you find truth that is eternal.

Sure Chaucer's writings are still around after 600 years, and Shakespeare's plays continue to fill up theaters 400 years after he wrote them. But neither writer wrote anything that will last into eternity as God's words will.

His Book is perfect. Others may be inspired in the sense that the authors felt something driving them to write, but the Bible is inspired in a special way—by God. He directed the biblical authors to write His words.

It's important to read widely and to know the classics. But until you understand the special place of the Bible among books, you aren't well-read.   —D.B.

Through preaching, teaching, and the Bible, God is telling me . . . _____
_____
_____

Through nature and the lives of other believers, God is showing me . . . _____
_____
_____

I will respond by . . . _____
_____
_____

Looking pretty poor

READ
Nehemiah 5

MEDITATE
Nehemiah 5:15

Their assistants also lorded it over the people. But out of reverence for God I did not act like that.

REFLECT

➡ Do I treat people differently because of the way they look or what they own?

➡ God sees the heart and not the exterior facade. Am I preoccupied with what's skin-deep?

CONSIDER
It takes real class to treat all classes alike.

You've heard of the $64,000 question. Call this the $1 million blunder.

John Barrier looked pretty ordinary in his baseball cap and jeans when he tooled into the bank parking lot to cash a $25 check. He got his two tens and a five and headed for his pickup. As he tried to exit the lot, however, a young man at the parking booth told him he'd have to pay 60 cents or get his ticket validated.

Barrier grumbled but headed back into the bank. Unfortunately he couldn't find the teller who had cashed his check. Another teller "just said no" when he asked for help. She thought he was a low life. Oops!

At that point, John Barrier, a multimillionaire real-estate developer, demanded all his money from his account. He then took the $1,000,000.60 and deposited it at the new bank on the block. It was a classic case of acting poorly to a man who looked poor.

In contrast, notice what Nehemiah did. He acted kindly to the poor. He was angry with his fellow countrymen for the way they were treating the less fortunate. He said, "What you are doing is not right. Shouldn't you walk in the fear of our God?" (Nehemiah 5:9). Later, he was able to pray, "Remember me with favor, O my God, for all I have done for these people" (5:19). Nehemiah had a clear conscience and a clear standing before God because he had helped people who were hurting.

Are you more like the teller at John Barrier's former bank, or like Nehemiah? We should treat people with love and compassion—regardless of their social class. It's a sure way to avoid embarrassment and please God at the same time.   —T.F.

Through preaching, teaching, and the Bible, God is telling me . . . _____
_____
_____

Through nature and the lives of other believers, God is showing me . . . _____
_____
_____

I will respond by . . . _____
_____
_____

Arm your conscience

MEDITATE
Psalm 119:11
I have hidden your word in my heart.

REFLECT

→ Do I welcome the voice of my conscience? Or do I ignore it?

→ Am I arming my conscience with the world's view of morality or with God's?

→ Is my conscience overactive? Do I feel guilty about something I shouldn't? What can I do about that?

CONSIDER
Arm your conscience with truth.

Man, do I feel guilty! I knew it was wrong when I did it, but I never thought I would feel like this. Now I wish I could take it all back." These are the words of a guilty conscience.

I heard a Christian college student joke, "Conscience? I don't have one anymore."

Sad words!

Conscience is a gift from God. The Lord gave it to us to send us signals about right and wrong. It helps us make right choices, or make wrong ones right. When we do something wrong, we should have a guilty conscience.

But how does a conscience know what to make us feel guilty about? Where does it get its information? It comes from our homes. And from society. And from the information we feed it.

That's why it's so important for us to know the Bible. As we read it, hear it preached, and meditate on it, the Bible gives our conscience God's view of right and wrong. It arms our conscience with truth, strengthening us to resist the rationalizations and excuses of a morally weak society.

A young man who had been a Christian only a few months was sent to Asia for a military assignment. He was surrounded by temptation and open invitations to sin. If he were to do something wrong, no one back home would ever know. When he got back to the States, he said, "I'm so glad I studied the Bible before I left. When you're 10,000 miles from home, you think you're 10,000 miles away from God. But the Scriptures and my conscience were my source of strength in resisting temptation."

Thank God for your conscience. Arm it with the truth of God by reading the Bible. You'll be glad you did— wherever you are.   —D.E.

Through preaching, teaching, and the Bible, God is telling me . . . _____
_____
_____

Through nature and the lives of other believers, God is showing me . . . _____
_____
_____

I will respond by . . . _____
_____

Chewing and choosing

READ
Psalm 119:97–104

MEDITATE
Psalm 119:103
How sweet are your
words to my taste.

REFLECT
→ How has the Word
of God helped me
in a specific situa-
tion to do what is
right this past
week?
→ How would I have
acted if I had not
known what God
said I should do?
→ How can I make
more time to read
or think about the
Word of God?

CONSIDER
*What you do
depends on what
you "chew."*

Based on the findings of researchers at two Japanese universities, you might be hearing a commercial that goes something like this: "Double your grade-point, double your A's with double-good, double-good, Doublemint Gum."

Experiments conducted jointly by groups at Kurme and Kyushu Universities reveal the benefits of chewing gum while driving. They found that seven out of eight drivers responded more quickly while chewing gum. Scientists think that chewing stimulates blood flow to the brain and also that the muscles transmit signals that activate brain functions. If that's true, then chewing a wad of gum might improve test scores.

The benefits of gum-chewing are still inconclusive, but we can be sure of the benefits of another kind of "chewing"—mentally "chewing" on the Word of God. Psalm 119 is full of statements about the proven value of reflecting on what God has said.

The psalmist mentioned these benefits of "chewing" on the Word: He gains more insight than his enemies, his teachers, and the elders (vv. 98–100) and he makes better decisions—he doesn't follow evil paths (vv. 100–104).

So if you want to be more alert as a driver—or maybe even as a student—try chewing gum. (The least it could do is keep you awake during a less-than-scintillating lecture on the French Revolution.) And if you want to be spiritually alert and make wise decisions, try "chewing" on the Word of God.

As you do, you will discover all you need to know to make right choices. As you meditate on truth, you will be prepared to act on what you know. So keep chewing!   —K.D.

Through preaching, teaching, and the Bible, God is telling me . . . _____

_____

Through nature and the lives of other believers, God is showing me . . . _____

_____

I will respond by . . . _____

_____

What's in a name?

READ
Isaiah 9:1–7

MEDITATE
Isaiah 9:6
He will be called Wonderful Counselor, Mighty God, Everlasting Father, Prince of Peace.

REFLECT
➡ How many of the names of Jesus can I recall from memory?
➡ Would it help me to look them up in a concordance and list them?
➡ What name of Jesus do I like best?

CONSIDER
*Jesus:
A name to live up to.*

I hate the forms you have to fill out that ask for your whole name because I have to reveal that the name I go by—Dave—is not my first name. It's John David. If you go by your middle name, you know the grief it causes.

But that's nothing compared to what a young girl in England has to put up with. Her parents saddled her with 139 names! She answers to the name Tracy, but her official name is Tracy Mariclare Lisa Tammy Samantha Christine Alexandra . . . (ad infinitum, almost). Tracy's going to have big-time trouble when she's old enough to fill out those forms.

Why did Mom and Dad dump out the baby name book on Tracy? "We just wanted to give her something for when she grows up," her Dad explains. (Someone should have told him about savings bonds.)

Whether we like our names or not, we'll all admit that they're pretty important. But the person who has the most important name of all is Jesus. The Bible is filled with different names for Jesus, and each name or title is significant, for it tells of His character.

Jesus is called Wonderful Counselor, Mighty God, Everlasting Father, and Prince of Peace in Isaiah 9:6. What do these names mean?

Wonderful Counselor: He has a royal program that one day will be carried out.

Mighty God: He has divine power as a warrior.

Everlasting Father: His protection will never cease.

Prince of Peace: When Jesus reigns, goodness will prevail.

At Christmas, we think about many names—names of people we still have to get gifts for, names of classmates we need to call, names of relatives. But most of all, let's think about this name: Jesus.
—D.B.

Through preaching, teaching, and the Bible, God is telling me . . . _____
_____
_____

Through nature and the lives of other believers, God is showing me . . . _____
_____
_____

I will respond by . . . _____
_____
_____

ABC's of right and wrong

READ
Galatians 5:16–26

MEDITATE
Galatians 5:19
The acts of the sinful nature are obvious.

REFLECT
➡ What are some circumstances that I need to run through the grid of God's standards before making a decision?
➡ On what occasions have I ignored the obvious right answer because I really wanted to do what was wrong? What happened?

CONSIDER
Don't decide till with God you confide.

Let's say you're working as a third-shift stock person at a small local grocery store. Just a couple of nights a week to help knock off a few school bills. You and your co-worker hit it off pretty well and become friends.

One night there isn't much to do, so your friend suggests that you spend a couple of hours watching a video on the TV that's set up in the produce aisle to show customers how to fix kiwi fruit. Both of you are sports nuts, and he has a couple of football follies and baseball blunders tapes you've wanted to see. The boss doesn't come in until about 6 A.M. and it's only 1:30, so there's plenty of time.

When you tell him you can't do that, he can't believe you'd pass up such a great opportunity. All he sees are (a) the circumstance (slow night and no boss around) and (c) the opportunity to get two hours of pay without working. What he doesn't know is that you add a third element to the mix of every decision: (b) God. So instead of looking only at the circumstances, you look at the circumstances through the filter of God's Word. That's what makes your response different. It is obvious to you that taking two hours' pay without earning it is wrong, and you won't do it.

Ever wonder why so many people seem blind to right and wrong? It's as easy as ABC. They forget part B. The acts of the sinful nature are not obvious to them because they don't see them through the filter of God's standards.   —D.B.

Through preaching, teaching, and the Bible, God is telling me . . . _____
_____
_____

Through nature and the lives of other believers, God is showing me . . . _____
_____
_____

I will respond by . . . _____
_____
_____

How to be a doormat

A fun-loving fellow named J. Upton Dickson founded a group for submissive people and called it DOORMATS (Dependent Organization Of Really Meek And Timid Souls), according to writer Bill Farmer. Their motto is, "The meek shall inherit the earth—if that's okay with everybody." Their symbol is the yellow traffic light. And Mr. Dickson is writing a manual for the group called *Cower Power.*

J. Upton Dickson sounds like an all-right kind of guy, but something disturbs me about all of this: Too many people think the ridiculous ideas behind DOORMATS and *Cower Power* represent the quality of meekness Jesus described in Matthew 5:5. Many, even in the church, are convinced that to be meek is to be weak.

Actually, it's just the opposite. Jesus was talking about a powerful virtue. The slogan "Strong enough to be gentle" comes close to defining it.

True meekness is best seen in Jesus. He was submissive, never resisting nor disputing the will of God. His absolute trust in the Father enabled Him to show compassion, courage, and self-sacrifice in even the most hostile situations. And remember—as the omnipotent God, Jesus could have wiped out His enemies in a second! He was the epitome of power under control.

When we are meek, we will take insults without lashing back. We will thank God in every circumstance. We will see every situation, good or bad, as an opportunity to submit to Him. We will—as Joni Tada sings in one of her songs—let God be God.

Meekness comes from goodness and godliness, and it is a great strength! —M.D.

Through preaching, teaching, and the Bible, God is telling me . . . _____
_____
_____

Through nature and the lives of other believers, God is showing me . . . _____
_____
_____

I will respond by . . . _____
_____
_____

Get them to try it!

READ
Psalm 34:1–8

MEDITATE
Psalm 34:8
Taste and see that the Lord is good.

REFLECT
➡ Are there people I know who have rejected Christ without even "tasting"? Why?

➡ What kind of "taste" do I leave with my classmates and friends? My family?

CONSIDER
Have you given out samples of God's love lately?

An unbeliever was ripping Christianity. He told his audience, "If any of you can prove I'm wrong, step up to the platform." An elderly gentleman accepted his challenge. The speaker demanded, "Present your proof!" Without saying a word, the man showed everyone an orange, peeled it, and began to eat it. The speaker impatiently asked, "So where is the proof?" "Well," the old man said, "what did this orange taste like?" "How should I know?" the speaker replied, "I didn't taste it!" "Exactly!" the old man said. "But I have. And I have tasted Christianity too. Like the orange, it is good. But you'll never know, because you refuse to even try it!"

For our friends and classmates who are non-Christians, we are an important link to the Gospel of Christ. Because we have tasted and seen that the Lord is good, we can give our friends a good reason to get in touch with God.

David was willing to tell people how God helped him. He said, "This poor man called, and the Lord heard him; he saved him out of all his troubles" (34:6). God had pulled David through some bad times, and David wanted everyone to know about it!

We tend to think of evangelism only as presenting the plan of salvation to our friends—right Bible verses included—every chance we get. We forget that when we tell our friends about how God has helped us through situations, that is a powerful means of sharing the Gospel too.

How has God helped you recently? If you tell your friends about it, that may just be the "taste" that will make them want to learn more.
—J.C.

Through preaching, teaching, and the Bible, God is telling me . . . _____

Through nature and the lives of other believers, God is showing me . . . _____

I will respond by . . . _____

Hanging out

READ
Hebrews 10:19–25

MEDITATE
Hebrews 10:25
Let us not give up meeting together.

REFLECT

→ Who are the people I like to be with most? Do they like to do the spiritual things mentioned in Hebrews 10?

→ Why is it so important to get together with other Christians?

→ What can I learn from being with them?

→ When I'm with non-Christians, what things can I do to help them?

CONSIDER
Christians grow best in bunches.

Who you hang around with tells a lot about who you are. Athletes tend to hang around with athletes. Music majors like to do things with music majors. Skateboard riders with skateboard riders.

And writers like to get together with writers. That's what author Philip Yancey said at a writers' conference I attended. Yancey was there to talk about the Chrysostom Society—a group of Christian writers that gets together to talk about writing.

But it's more than talk. The people of the Chrysostom Society meet to carry on a tradition of excellence "by encouraging one another to pursue the highest quality of writing possible." These people hang around together to make themselves better writers.

There's another group that should have good reason to get together, and it's a group that normally hangs around together at least once a week. I'm talking, of course, about the church, a bunch of people who like to be with each other because of a common love for Jesus Christ.

Hebrews 10 (which contains the famous passage about church attendance: "Let us not give up meeting together," v. 25) begins by giving some good reasons to get together. Because of the "new and living way" (v. 20) we have of entering God's presence and the great high priest we have, he told us to draw near to God, hold unswervingly to our hope, meet together, and encourage one another.

Do you have some people with whom you can do those things? Are there some Christians in your dorm, on your team, or at your church you can meet with? Don't stop hanging out with other believers. —D.B.

Through preaching, teaching, and the Bible, God is telling me . . . _____

_____

Through nature and the lives of other believers, God is showing me . . . _____

_____

I will respond by . . . _____

_____

A trip to prison

READ
Matthew 25:31–46

MEDITATE
Matthew 25:36
"I was in prison and you came to visit me."

REFLECT

➡ Why does Jesus identify Himself with the kind of people described in Matthew 25:35–36?

➡ To whom does Jesus want me to reach out? How will I do that?

CONSIDER
Obedience leads to action.

Let me tell you about my new friend, Jim. He is 19 years old and likes baseball, heavy metal, and movies. He is also serving a prison term at a medium-security institution in southern California.

Jim (not his real name) is more than just an inmate I visit every other week. For me, he is part of a journey of obedience. He lives a reality I try to ignore. And maybe he is a way for me to reach out to Jesus Christ Himself.

First, the journey part. When I read Matthew 25 a couple of years ago I made a mental note: "Prison visits. Jesus' command. Future reference."

Then M-2 (which stands for "Match-2"), a one-on-one Christian prison visitation ministry, did a program at my church. Reluctantly, I let God pull that thought out of my reference file. (My lazy, selfish side grumbled something about avoiding such verses in the future.)

So I applied, was accepted, and was matched up with Jim. Yes, it's a jolt to walk through prison doors, even though you know that you can walk back out. And it certainly is depressing to think that Jim has to live there every day for two more years.

But something feels right about my being there; about Jim knowing that a friend is coming especially to talk to him; about not feeling like I'm hiding from the unpleasant aspects of life.

So I would encourage you: Don't run from reality. The sick, the needy, the imprisoned—that's where we have a chance to minister directly to Jesus.   —J.C.

Through preaching, teaching, and the Bible, God is telling me . . . _____
_____
_____

Through nature and the lives of other believers, God is showing me . . . _____
_____

I will respond by . . . _____
_____
_____

How to lose friends

READ
Proverbs 18

MEDITATE
Proverbs 18:1
An unfriendly man pursues selfish ends.

REFLECT
➡ Who are my friends?
➡ How do I treat them? How do they treat me?
➡ What is good and bad about my friendships?
➡ How can I be more friendly?

CONSIDER
To have friends, you have to be friendly.

Want to get rid of a few friends? Here are some ways to do it: Never wash your hair. Wear a T-shirt that says, "I have the flu." Hang a skunk-on-a-rope around your neck. Or try one of the following actions, which wise old Solomon says make for pretty poor interpersonal relationships (Proverbs 18).

1. Think only about yourself (v. 1).
2. Act like a know-it-all (v. 2).
3. Pick on defenseless people (v. 5).
4. Mouth off at everyone (v. 7).
5. Be the campus gossip (v. 8).
6. Refuse to pull your own weight (v. 9).
7. Don't listen to others (v. 13).
8. Take off when someone has trouble (v. 24).

We all want to be liked. It's strange, though, that we often do exactly the opposite of what we should do to make and keep friends. Can you think of a few times when you've participated in any of the self-defeating actions mentioned above? More than a few times?

People who think only about themselves are foolish (v. 1). No one wants to be around a know-it-all (v. 2). Who would want a wicked person for a friend? (v. 5). Why would anyone want to hang around someone who has an out-of-control tongue? (v. 7). How could you trust a gossip not to spread stories about you? (v. 8). No one likes a leech (v. 9). How can you carry on a meaningful conversation with someone who won't listen? (v. 13). And what kind of friend takes off when trouble comes? (v. 24).

To get along with others, live by the teachings of Proverbs 18. You and your friends will be glad you did.

—K.D.

Through preaching, teaching, and the Bible, God is telling me . . . _____

_____

Through nature and the lives of other believers, God is showing me . . . _____

_____

I will respond by . . . _____

_____

A stand-by friend

READ
Proverbs 18:12–24

MEDITATE
Proverbs 18:24
There is a friend who sticks closer than a brother.

REFLECT
➡ What experience has taught me what a help it can be to have someone stand by me in a tough time?
➡ Do I have a friend who needs me to stand by him or her right now? Am I willing to reach out and help?

CONSIDER
A good friend doubles your joy and divides your grief.

Suppose you have to go through a really tough time. A family member dies. A major disappointment hits. A cherished dream goes up in smoke. Who, besides the Lord, can help you survive a tragic experience like that?

A good friend.

That's right. Many people will testify that the faithful encouragement and support of a good friend is what carried them through when tough times hit. Our best chance of keeping our hope strong is having a trusted friend who will stand with us.

Sixteen-year-old Michelle King can attest to that. Michelle has cancer, and she's had to go through months of chemotherapy. Without this powerful treatment, she had no chance of survival. But chemo can be devastating to a lovely teenage girl.

Michelle was apprehensive and afraid. But each time she went to get an injection, her best high school friend went in with her. "I would lie on my back after those treatments and be emotionally and physically exhausted," she said. "But my friend would hold my hand and softly repeat these words: 'You're going to make it, Michelle. I know you're going to make it.' It gave me the hope and courage to go on."

Do you have a friend who is going through a crisis? Struggling through a major loss or a big disappointment? That person needs someone to say, "You're not alone in this fight. Let me hold your hand. You can make it. I know you can."

Why not let that friend be you? Then you'll be like Christ, the One "who sticks closer than a brother."

—D.E.

Through preaching, teaching, and the Bible, God is telling me . . . _____

_____

_____

Through nature and the lives of other believers, God is showing me . . . _____

_____

_____

I will respond by . . . _____

_____

_____

It's up to you

READ
Romans 14:1–19

MEDITATE
Romans 14:13
Let us stop passing judgment on one another.

REFLECT
➡ What kind of criticism do I hear among Christians?
➡ What have I complained about in the past week? Was I violating Scripture (see Romans 14)?
➡ What would happen if I went an entire week without criticizing anyone? How might it change me? How might it change others?

CONSIDER
It's easier to complain than to help.

If you're a literature buff who understands all those marvelous terms like personification, metaphor, denouement, and genre, you'll know what I mean when I say that this article is dripping with irony. You see, I want to talk about criticism. But to do so, I need to be a little, well, critical. (If you don't get the irony in that, perhaps you need to schedule a visit with your English instructor.)

From what I observe, Christian criticism is nearing national pastime status. We hear griping about pastors who don't preach what people want to hear. We hear criticism about school choices—whether Christian, public, or home. We hear griping about people, griping about programs, griping, griping, griping.

The other day after our family came home from church, one of our kids started to complain about something. My wife cut in and said, "Please, I can't stand one more criticism about anyone or anything."

Paul seemed to have a similar attitude. He said, "Let us stop passing judgment on one another." That's pretty clear, don't you think?

Christians are good at keeping tabs on certain taboos that we feel are wrong because they will damage the body or contaminate the mind. Yet we ignore a clear, no-question-about-it teaching like "stop passing judgment."

It's up to you to change the reputation of the believers in your community. If young Christians would stop passing judgment, we could make criticism extinct in the church. Now there's a denouement that makes for a very happy ending. —D.B.

Through preaching, teaching, and the Bible, God is telling me . . . _____

_____

_____

Through nature and the lives of other believers, God is showing me . . . _____

_____

_____

I will respond by . . . _____

_____

_____

That's radical!

READ
Matthew 9:9–13

MEDITATE
Matthew 9:12
"It is not the healthy who need a doctor, but the sick."

REFLECT
➡ What risks do I take by reaching out to people on the fringe? Am I willing to take those risks today?
➡ How can Jesus' example affect the way I behave toward people with serious problems?

CONSIDER
Have you done anything extraordinary for God today?

Picture this: You live in one of the most violent and depressed neighborhoods in one of America's most troubled cities—Newark, New Jersey. You believe that God has called you to penetrate the darkness of the inner city and make a difference. You are surrounded by the sight of whole blocks burned to their foundations. The sound of sirens continually fills the air, and the stench is inescapable.

But your problems are more basic than that. How do you get the drug dealers to leave the front steps of your ministry's teen center without getting shot? This is what World Impact missionary Al Warren faced. So he decided to do something radical. He started by asking them, politely, to move down the street. Chill out, they said, business is good here. Then he tried calling the police. The police won't go near that neighborhood, he was told. So Al got creative. "What would Jesus do?" he asked himself. After a lot of prayer he got an idea.

Al understood that beneath the violent, self-destructive behavior of these drug dealers was a common human need: love. So Al baked a cake. That's right! He knew that one of the pushers used to attend the evangelistic outreaches at the teen center, so he looked up his birthday. Although disappointed by the dealer's life choices, Al set out to love him into the kingdom by throwing him a birthday party. Oddly enough, it worked. The dealer hasn't stopped pushing, but he respected Al enough to move his business to a vacant lot across the street.

Al took that tough first step. Are you willing to be as bold? Why not ask Jesus to help you follow His example and do something radical for the kingdom.　　—T.B.

Through preaching, teaching, and the Bible, God is telling me . . . _____
_____
_____

Through nature and the lives of other believers, God is showing me . . . _____
_____

I will respond by . . . _____
_____
_____

NOTE TO THE READER

The publisher invites you to share your response to the message of this book by writing Discovery House Publishers, P.O. Box 3566, Grand Rapids, MI 49501 U.S.A. or by calling 1-800-653-8333.

For information about other Discovery House publications, contact us at the same address and phone number.